FORTUNE GUIDE TO THE
500 LARGEST
U.S. CORPORATIONS

By the editors of

FORTUNE

and

HOOVER'S HANDBOOKS

COPYRIGHT

10 9 8 7 6 5 4 3 2 1

Publisher Cataloging-In-Publication Data

FORTUNE Guide To The 500 Largest U.S. Corporations

1. Business enterprises — Directories. 2. Corporations — Directories.

HF3010 338.7

Company information and profiles from the **Hoover's** series of handbooks, guides, and directories published by The Reference Press, Inc. are also available on America Online, Bloomberg Financial Network, CompuServe, LEXIS/NEXIS, Microsoft Network, Reuters NewMedia, Wall Street Journal Interactive, and on the Internet at Hoover's Online (http://www.hoovers.com), Pathfinder (http://pathfinder.com), Europe Online (http://www.europeonline.com), Farcast (http://www.farcast.com), IBM infoMarket (http://infomkt.ibm.com), InfoSeek (http://www.infoseek.com), and PAWWS (http://pawws.com).

A catalog of Reference Press products is available on the World Wide Web (http://www.hoovers.com).

ISBN 1-878753-94-0

This book was produced by The Reference Press using Claris Corporation's FileMaker Pro 3.0, Quark, Inc.'s Quark XPress 3.32, and EM Software, Inc.'s Xdata 2.5. Typefaces are Adobe Systems Incorporated's Minion and Myriad and Daniel Pelavin's Fatline. Cover design is by George Sutton. Cover illustration is by Anthony Russo. Electronic prepress and printing were done by Quebecor Printing (USA) Corp. in New Canton, Tennessee.

US AND WORLD DIRECT SALES

The Reference Press, Inc.
1033 La Posada Drive, Suite 250
Austin, Texas 78752
Phone: 512-374-4500
Fax: 512-454-9401

US WHOLESALER ORDERS

Warner Publisher Services, Book Division
9210 King Palm Drive
Tampa, Florida 33619
Phone: 800-873-BOOK
Fax: 813-664-8193

US BOOKSELLERS AND JOBBERS

Little, Brown and Co.
200 West Street
Waltham, Massachusetts 02154
Phone: 800-759-0190
Fax: 617-890-0875

EUROPE

William Snyder Publishing
5, Five Mile Drive
Oxford OX2 8HT
England
Phone & fax: +44-(01)86-551-3186

The term FORTUNE 500 long ago secured its place in the language.

Top of the heap. The pinnacle of success. The mightiest of the mighty. The FORTUNE 500. In the corporate world, at least, they all mean the same.

Now, for the 41st year, the editors of FORTUNE magazine have compiled their list of the largest corporations in the United States — a newsmaking event in itself.

Because the list is in such widespread use as a benchmark for corporate America, we at The Reference Press — publishers of a wide range of business reference materials in both print and electronic formats — concluded that there is a varied audience of business executives, financial analysts, investors, salespersons, and students who would find useful an expanded version of the FORTUNE 500 list as printed in FORTUNE magazine.

In **FORTUNE Guide To The 500 Largest U.S. Corporations** you will find the list of the 500 largest service and industrial corporations. You will also find the magazine's extensive lists of companies ranked by performance, by state, and by industry.

From the extensive database of company information maintained by The Reference Press, we have added an overview of company operations, headquarters addresses, phone and fax numbers, stock symbol and exchange, and the names of key executives. In recognition of the growing importance of the World Wide Web, we also include Web addresses for those companies that have established Web sites.

FORTUNE Guide To The 500 Largest U.S. Corporations is the latest in a long line of business reference products brought to you by The Reference Press. We recommend to you *Hoover's Handbook of American Companies, Hoover's Handbook of World Business, Hoover's Guide to Private Companies, Hoover's Guide to Computer Companies,* and *Hoover's Top 2,500 Employers,* as well as our series of regional business guides and our MasterLists of U.S., Latin American, and European businesses. Slated for publication for the first time this year are *Hoover's Guide to Media Companies, Hoover's 500: Profiles of American's Largest Business Enterprises, Hoover's Hot 250: The Stories Behind America's Fastest Growing Companies,* and *Cyberstocks: An Investor's Guide to Internet Companies.* Our company profiles and other information are also available electronically on diskette and CD-ROM and on online services (e.g., America Online and CompuServe) and the Internet (e.g., Hoover's Online at http://www.hoovers.com).

The FORTUNE 500 list appearing in this book has been updated because of corrections made since the list was first published in the magazine of April 29, 1996. These corrections caused some rankings to change. The tables beginning on Page 5 have been footnoted to show which companies were affected.

As always, we hope you find our books useful and informative. We invite your comments via phone (512-374-4500), fax (512-454-9401), mail (1033 La Posada Drive, Suite 250, Austin, Texas 78752), or e-mail (comments@hoovers.com).

THE EDITORS
Austin, Texas
May 1996

MISSION
STATEMENT ········► THE REFERENCE PRESS

1   To produce business information products and services of the highest quality, accuracy, and readability.

2   To make that information available whenever, wherever, and however our customers want it through mass distribution at affordable prices.

3   To continually expand our range of products and services and our markets for those products and services.

4   To reward our employees, suppliers, and shareholders based on their contributions to the success of our enterprise.

5   To hold to the highest ethical business standards, erring on the side of generosity when in doubt.

M ost of the figures in the FORTUNE 500 Directory were prepared by **Henry Goldblatt** and **Richard Tucksmith**, who are responsible for the columns reporting on companies' revenues, profits, assets, and stockholders' equity as well as for the industry table numbers. They were assisted by **Lynne Ferguson, Gregory McCarthy, Patricia McCarthy,** and **Kathleen Smyth**. List editor **Gopal Khar** and statistics editor **Catherine Haight** oversaw the project. Earnings per share, total return to investors, and market value were compiled from information found in company annual reports and data supplied by **Deloitte & Touche's PeerScape.**

CONTENTS

PROFITS

THE

FLOWED

Like Old Man River, corporate America's profits seem a force of nature by now — rolling along mightily from one year to the next. Earnings of companies in the FORTUNE 500 rose 13.4% in 1995, the fourth straight year of double-digit increases (excluding 1992–93 write-offs for retiree health benefits). The latest results are especially impressive because the US economy grew only 2% and inflation was just 2.8%. Also noteworthy: the broad swath of industries where profits surged, from heavy manufacturing to high tech to financial services. GM, No. 1 on the FORTUNE 500, saw earnings rise 40%, on top of a gangbuster 99% increase the year before.

This year's 500 ranking, which begins on page 5, also shows that not all news was good news. One of the big exceptions to the strong showing is the general merchandise industry, where companies threw up too many new stores, resulting in more competition and lower profits (down 19%). Retailing also nabbed the distinction of including the worst investment among the 500: Caldor, which had a negative 85% return to investors. (Total-return and market-value calculations used data provided by PeerScape, a service of Deloitte & Touche.)

Another big exception to the boom in profits: telephone companies, which prepared for decreased regulation by slashing their workforces and taking huge write-offs. AT&T alone took a $6 billion hit, causing a 97% decline in profits.

But it wasn't just the headline grabbers that squeezed employee rolls. Read no further than the industry comparisons (beginning on page 203) — the aerospace group saw revenues rise just 5%

REVENUES $4,690 BILLION Change 1994–95 up 9.9%

PROFITS $244 BILLION up 13.4 %

ASSETS $10,491 BILLION up 9.7 %

TOTALS

last year, but profits took off by 22% as employment dipped 1%. Even electric and gas utilities, hardly the most dynamic and competitive sector of the US economy, reduced the number of jobs by 3% while increasing profits.

Indeed, the driving force of this five-year-old business expansion has been corporate restructuring Will it continue? Most economists and stock market strategists think corporate managers have about run out of ways to make their organizations more efficient. Even so, NatWest Securities chief  strategist Peter Canelo believes earnings will again grow at double-digit rates this year because the economy is picking up briskly, the consensus "worry-warts" notwithstanding. Rising domestic and foreign demand will benefit a broad array of industries, including cyclical groups such as metals and machinery producers, he says. As support for his view, Canelo points to the recent rise in oil prices. FORTUNE 500 petroleum companies turned in one of the worst profit performances of any group in 1995 — median profits fell 4% — as crude prices remained subdued. But with oil lately fetching the highest prices since the Gulf War, industry profits should gush.

More certain than the outlook for profits is the way the economy is evolving toward services and high-tech industries. Consider the employment gains and losses on this year's list. The number of people working for FORTUNE 500 companies rose a barely perceptible 0.2% in 1995, skimpy gains given the robust 9.9% rise in revenues. But check out the right industries and there was hiring aplenty: computer hardware employees, up 11%; computer services and software, up 14%; health care, up 25%; entertainment, up 13%. Oh, yes, and the number of workers on temp-agency payrolls jumped 13%. That, too, looks fundamental to the evolutionary process.

Joe Spiers

THE WINNERS	500 RANK	
BIGGEST MONEYMAKER General Motors	1	$6.9 billion
BIGGEST REVENUES INCREASE First Chicago NBD Corp.	118	$208.6 %
BEST INVESTMENT 1-year return* Continental Airlines	226	353.3%

THE LOSERS	500 RANK	
BIGGEST MONEY-LOSER Pacific Telesis Group	144	($2.3)billion
BIGGEST REVENUES DECREASE ITT Industries	151	(62.6%)
WORST INVESTMENT 1-year return* Caldor	455	(85.4%)

* Including capital gains or losses plus reinvested dividends.

Rank 1995	1994	Company	Revenues $ MILLIONS	% CHANGE FROM '94	Profits $ MILLIONS	RANK	% CHANGE FROM '94	Assets $ MILLIONS	RANK	Stockholders' Equity $ MILLIONS	RANK
1	1	GENERAL MOTORS	168,828.6	9.0	6,880.7	1	40.4	217,123.4	7	23,345.5	5
2	2	FORD MOTOR	137,137.0	6.8	4,139.0	6	(22.0)	243,283.0	3	24,547.0	4
3	3	EXXON	110,009.0E	8.4	6,470.0	3	26.9	91,296.0	26	40,436.0	1
4	4	WAL-MART STORES[1]	93,627.0	12.2	2,740.0	12	2.2	37,871.0	67	14,762.0	14
5	5	AT&T	79,609.0	6.0	139.0	345	(97.0)	88,884.0	28	17,274.0	11
6	7	INTL. BUSINESS MACHINES[2]	71,940.0	12.3	4,178.0	5	38.3	80,292.0	33	22,423.0	6
7	6	GENERAL ELECTRIC	70,028.0	8.3	6,573.0	2	39.1	228,035.0	5	29,609.0	2
8	8	MOBIL	66,724.0E	11.9	2,376.0	18	120.2	42,138.0	62	17,951.0	10
9	11	CHRYSLER	53,195.0	1.9	2,025.0	22	(45.5)	53,756.0	50	10,959.0	28
10	10	PHILIP MORRIS	53,139.0E	(1.2)	5,450.0	4	15.3	53,811.0	49	13,985.0	16
11	13	PRUDENTIAL INS. CO. OF AMERICA	41,330.0	9.8	579.0	130	–	219,380.0	6	11,410.0	26
12	12	STATE FARM GROUP	40,809.9	5.0	1,271.2	49	–	85,293.4	29	25,143.0	3
13	14	E.I. DU PONT DE NEMOURS	37,607.0E	7.5	3,293.0	10	20.8	37,312.0	68	8,436.0	42
14	16	TEXACO	36,787.0	8.9	607.0	125	(33.3)	24,937.0	98	9,519.0	35
15	9	SEARS ROEBUCK[3]	35,181.0⁴	(35.8)	1,801.0	31	23.9	33,130.0	78	4,385.0	119
16	15	KMART[1]	34,654.0	1.0	(571.0)	487	(292.9)	15,397.0	146	5,280.0	88
17	19	PROCTER & GAMBLE[5]	33,434.0	10.4	2,645.0	14	19.6	28,125.0	88	10,589.0	30
18	18	CHEVRON	32,094.0E	3.3	930.0	69	(45.1)	34,330.0	75	14,355.0	15
19	17	CITICORP	31,690.0	0.1	3,464.0	8	2.9	256,853.0	2	19,581.0	9
20	22	HEWLETT-PACKARD[6]	31,519.0	26.1	2,433.0	16	52.2	24,427.0	99	11,839.0	22
21	20	PEPSICO	30,421.0	6.8	1,606.0	36	(8.3)	25,432.0	94	7,313.0	50
22	27	METROPOLITAN LIFE INSURANCE	27,977.0	1.4	(559.4)	486	(666.8)	158,800.0	13	6,600.0	60
23	21	AMOCO	27,665.0E	2.6	1,862.0	26	4.1	29,845.0	84	14,848.0	13
24	28	MOTOROLA	27,037.0	21.5	1,781.0	32	14.2	22,801.0	109	11,048.0	27
25	26	AMERICAN INTL. GROUP	25,874.0	15.6	2,510.4	15	15.4	134,136.4	16	19,827.1	8
26	24	CONAGRA[7]	24,108.9	2.5	495.6	151	13.4	10,801.0	190	2,495.4	206
27	25	KROGER	23,937.8	4.3	302.8	225	25.0	5,044.7	288	(1,603.0)	493
28	30	DAYTON HUDSON[1]	23,516.0	10.3	311.0	221	(28.3)	12,570.0	174	3,403.0	160
29	70	LOCKHEED MARTIN[8]	22,853.0	74.1	682.0	114	53.3	17,648.0	131	6,433.0	63
30	31	UNITED TECHNOLOGIES	22,802.0	7.6	750.0	93	28.2	15,958.0	140	4,021.0	136
31	•	ALLSTATE	22,793.0	–	1,904.0	25	–	70,029.0	39	12,680.0	18
32	36	FED. NATL. MORTGAGE ASSN.	22,246.0	19.8	2,372.0	19	11.3	316,550.0	1	10,959.0	28
33	40	MERRILL LYNCH	21,513.0	18.0	1,114.0	57	9.6	176,857.0	12	6,141.0	69
34	32	J.C. PENNEY[1]	21,419.0	1.6	838.0	78	(20.7)	17,102.0	135	5,884.0	72
35	35	UNITED PARCEL SERVICE	21,045.0	7.5	1,043.0	61	10.6	12,645.0	173	5,151.0	94
36	33	DOW CHEMICAL	20,957.0	4.7	2,078.0	21	121.5	23,582.0	105	7,361.0	49
37	46	BANKAMERICA CORP.	20,386.0	23.3	2,664.0	13	22.4	232,446.0	4	20,222.0	7
38	34	GTE	19,957.0	0.1	(2,144.0)*	493	(187.5)	37,019.0	69	6,871.0	56
39	60	INTERNATIONAL PAPER[9]	19,797.0	32.3	1,153.0	53	223.0	23,977.0	102	7,797.0	48
40	29	BOEING	19,515.0	(11.0)	393.0	188	(54.1)	22,098.0	114	9,898.0	33
41	41	XEROX	18,963.0¶	6.3	(472.0)	484	(159.4)	25,969.0	92	4,641.0	109
42	38	CIGNA	18,955.0	3.1	211.0	299	(61.9)	95,903.0	24	7,157.0	52
43	52	JOHNSON & JOHNSON	18,842.0	19.8	2,403.0	17	19.8	17,873.0	128	9,045.0	37
44	64	LOEWS[10]	18,770.0	38.9	1,765.7	33	559.3	65,058.0	41	8,240.0	43
45	39	AMERICAN STORES[1]	18,308.9	(0.3)	316.8	220	(8.2)	7,363.0	236	2,354.5	214
46	47	PRICECOSTCO[11]	18,247.3	10.7	133.9	349	–	4,437.4	305	1,530.7	298
47	45	USX	18,214.0E	8.4	214.0	296	(57.3)	16,743.0	138	4,328.0	122
48	48	COCA-COLA	18,018.0	11.4	2,986.0	11	16.9	15,041.0	148	5,392.0	85
49	44	BELLSOUTH	17,886.0	6.2	(1,232.0)*	491	(157.0)	31,880.0	79	11,825.0	23
50	56	SARA LEE[5]	17,719.0	14.1	804.0	82	304.0	12,431.0	179	4,273.0	126

MARKET VALUE 3/15/96		PROFITS AS % OF...						EARNINGS PER SHARE				TOTAL RETURN TO INVESTORS				RANK 1995
		REVENUES		ASSETS		STOCK-HOLDERS EQUITY		1995 $		1985-95 ANNUAL GROWTH RATE		1995		1985-1995 ANNUAL RATE		
$ MILLIONS	RANK	%	RANK	%	RANK	%	RANK		% CHANGE FROM '94	%	RANK	%	RANK	%	RANK	
39,308.8	23	4.1	280	3.2	271	29.5	42	7.21	40.0	1.6	233	28.5	255	9.2	299	1
34,907.9	27	3.0	327	1.7	343	16.9	167	3.58	(28.0)	4.7	201	8.1	370	16.9	103	2
98,092.6	4	5.9	206	7.1	122	16.0	187	5.18	27.3	4.8	199	38.1	192	16.7	107	3
54,495.4	11	2.9	332	7.2	119	18.6	133	1.19	1.7	23.4	25	5.3	380	19.3	64	4
98,121.7	3	0.2	442	0.2	439	0.8	431	0.09	(97.0)	(23.8)	316	32.1	231	13.8	192	5
68,256.8	7	5.8	212	5.2	193	18.6	130	7.23	44.0	(3.8)	285	25.7	278	(1.8)	367	6
126,523.3	1	9.4	114	2.9	285	22.2	86	3.90	40.8	11.8	111	45.3	142	18.2	80	7
44,191.5	17	3.6	303	5.6	175	13.2	270	5.87	128.4	8.7	149	37.5	200	19.6	62	8
23,313.6	45	3.8	295	3.8	249	18.5	135	5.30	(47.6)	(1.6)	271	16.5	326	14.5	168	9
79,612.9	5	10.3	96	10.1	54	39.0	23	6.48	18.9	17.3	57	64.8	58	28.2	15	10
N.A.		1.4	402	0.3	432	5.1	403	N.A.	–	–		–		–		11
N.A.		3.1	320	1.5	354	5.1	404	N.A.	–	–		–		–		12
45,120.0	16	8.8	130	8.8	79	39.0	22	5.61	40.3	13.8	86	28.4	257	16.1	125	13
21,888.1	48	1.7	394	2.4	308	6.4	390	2.10	(33.8)	(8.5)	301	37.3	204	17.7	86	14
19,571.2	56	5.1	236	5.4	182	41.1	17	4.50	23.0	2.5	227	30.7	241	11.3	261	15
4,708.5	237	(1.6)	464	(3.7)	468	(10.8)	456	(1.25)	(298.4)	–		(42.3)	444	(0.8)	365	16
57,058.2	10	7.9	152	9.4	72	25.0	70	3.71	20.1	14.6	79	36.7	208	20.0	54	17
35,791.3	25	2.9	334	2.7	291	6.5	389	1.43	(45.0)	(4.5)	289	22.0	299	15.9	131	18
33,221.7	31	10.9	81	1.3	361	17.7	152	7.21	2.6	7.3	168	66.1	53	15.1	150	19
50,931.8	12	7.7	156	10.0	57	20.6	101	4.63	50.8	17.1	62	69.4	44	17.4	95	20
49,146.8	13	5.3	227	6.3	151	22.0	87	2.00	(8.3)	12.0	108	56.9	81	23.5	31	21
N.A.		(2.0)	468	(0.4)	445	(8.5)	451	N.A.	–	–		–		–		22
34,898.0	28	6.7	178	6.2	155	12.5	286	3.76	4.4	0.1	258	25.4	283	13.5	204	23
32,872.3	32	6.6	183	7.8	99	16.1	184	2.93	10.6	34.4	16	(1.1)	405	20.7	49	24
43,684.2	19	9.7	108	1.9	334	12.7	282	5.30	15.7	18.4	46	42.2	162	17.8	84	25
10,417.3	110	2.1	368	4.6	220	18.9	120	2.06	13.8	13.3	92	35.2	217	18.4	77	26
4,515.5	246	1.3	407	6.0	162	–		2.52	18.3	2.1	230	54.9	89	26.5	21	27
6,048.7	193	1.3	405	2.5	307	9.1	353	4.03	(30.2)	3.3	217	8.6	366	7.4	320	28
15,135.6	73	3.0	330	3.9	245	10.6	332	3.28	(23.6)	(1.3)	269	81.4	23	14.1	184	29
13,542.9	84	3.3	313	4.7	209	18.7	127	5.70	29.5	10.4	130	54.8	91	11.7	250	30
18,515.3	58	8.4	136	2.7	289	15.0	210	4.24	–	–		77.3	29	–		31
34,261.5	29	10.7	91	0.7	406	21.6	90	2.15	10.7	28.6	21	75.0	35	33.1	9	32
9,769.1	122	5.2	234	0.6	414	18.1	142	5.44	14.5	17.0	63	45.6	139	14.6	165	33
11,211.6	103	3.9	289	4.9	202	14.2	233	3.48	(18.9)	10.1	132	11.3	353	17.6	89	34
N.A.		5.0	242	8.2	89	20.2	106	1.83	12.3	8.1	292	–		–		35
23,233.3	46	9.9	102	8.8	80	28.2	49	7.72	129.1	43.6	8	8.8	363	14.3	177	36
27,148.6	38	13.1	48	1.1	376	13.2	272	6.49	21.1	–		69.4	45	17.8	82	37
40,465.0	21	(10.7)	489	(5.8)	477	(31.1)	468	(2.21)	(186.7)	–		52.6	100	17.5	93	38
10,244.3	111	5.8	210	4.8	207	14.8	216	4.50	214.7	23.6	24	2.9	391	14.7	162	39
27,817.2	37	2.0	372	1.8	338	4.0	413	1.15	(54.2)	(3.6)	282	69.6	43	15.6	137	40
14,357.8	81	(2.5)	473	(1.8)	460	(10.2)	453	(4.69)	(169.7)	–		42.0	164	13.7	197	41
8,941.8	135	1.1	413	0.2	434	2.9	421	2.86	(62.7)	–		68.8	47	10.5	276	42
62,629.5	8	12.8	50	13.4	24	26.6	63	3.72	19.2	16.0	70	59.1	71	23.1	34	43
9,279.3	129	9.4	113	2.7	290	21.4	92	14.98	573.3	15.3	76	81.9	22	12.4	231	44
4,317.9	258	1.7	388	4.3	230	13.5	260	2.16	(10.7)	15.4	74	1.5	397	14.6	166	45
3,686.3	285	0.7	427	3.0	281	8.7	360	0.69	–	(3.8)	283	18.4	317	(7.6)	377	46
N.A.		1.2	410	1.3	368	4.9	406	N.A.	–	–		–		–		47
101,279.7	2	16.6	16	19.9	6	55.4	9	2.37	19.7	17.8	49	46.1	133	29.3	12	48
36,029.0	24	(6.9)	485	(3.9)	469	(10.4)	455	(1.24)	(157.0)	–		67.7	50	16.1	126	49
15,973.6	68	4.5	261	6.5	144	18.8	123	1.62	337.8	13.6	88	29.9	250	20.6	50	50

			REVENUES		PROFITS			ASSETS		STOCK-HOLDERS' EQUITY	
			$ MILLIONS		$ MILLIONS			$ MILLIONS		$ MILLIONS	
RANK 1995	1994	COMPANY		% CHANGE FROM '94		RANK	% CHANGE FROM '94		RANK		RANK
51	97	COLUMBIA/HCA HEALTHCARE[12]	17,695.0	59.0	961.1*	66	52.6	19,892.0	119	7,129.0	53
52	51	FLEMING	17,501.6	11.1	42.0	422	(25.2)	4,296.7	316	1,083.3	356
53	55	AMERICAN EXPRESS†	16,942.0	2.6	1,564.0	38	10.7	107,405.0	22	8,220.0	44
54	49	AMR†	16,910.0	4.8	167.0*	323	(26.8)	19,556.0	122	3,720.0	146
55	53	ATLANTIC RICHFIELD†	16,739.0E	6.7	1,376.0	43	49.7	23,999.0	101	6,758.0	57
56	59	MERCK†	16,681.1	11.4	3,335.2	9	11.3	23,831.8	104	11,735.7	24
57	37	TRAVELERS GROUP†	16,583.0	(10.2)	1,834.0	28	38.3	114,500.0	21	11,700.0	25
58	50	SUPERVALU[13],†	16,563.8	3.9	43.3	421	(76.6)	4,305.1	314	1,193.2	342
59	54	SAFEWAY†	16,397.5	4.9	326.3*	215	36.1	5,194.3	282	795.4	386
60	71	NATIONSBANK CORP.†	16,298.0	24.2	1,950.0	24	15.4	187,298.0	9	12,801.0	17
61	90	INTEL†	16,202.0	40.6	3,566.0	7	55.9	17,504.0	132	12,159.0	19
62	84	NEW YORK LIFE INSURANCE†	16,201.7	13.0	625.2	119	54.7	74,280.6	36	3,756.4	143
63	58	MINNESOTA MINING & MFG.†	16,105.0	6.8	976.0	64	(26.2)	14,183.0	158	6,884.0	55
64	61	CATERPILLAR†	16,072.0	12.2	1,136.0	55	19.0	16,830.0	136	3,388.0	161
65	57	RJR NABISCO HOLDINGS†	16,008.0	4.2	611.0	121	17.7	31,518.0	81	10,329.0	32
66	77	HOME DEPOT[1]	15,470.4	24.0	731.5	102	21.0	7,354.0	237	4,987.8	100
67	43	EASTMAN KODAK	15,269.0	(9.4)	1,252.0	50	124.8	14,477.0	154	5,121.0	95
68	66	MCI COMMUNICATIONS	15,265.0	14.4	548.0	137	(31.1)	19,301.0	124	9,602.0	34
69	141	FEDERATED DEPT. STORES[1],[14]	15,048.5	81.0	74.6	398	(60.3)	14,295.1	156	4,273.7	125
70	62	UAL	14,943.0	7.1	349.0	206	584.3	11,641.0	185	(239.0)	486
71	74	CHEMICAL BANKING CORP.[15]	14,884.0	17.3	1,805.0	30	39.5	182,926.0	11	11,912.0	21
72	100	COMPAQ COMPUTER	14,755.0	35.8	789.0	88	(9.0)	7,818.0	228	4,614.0	111
73	72	ALLIEDSIGNAL	14,346.0	11.9	875.0	75	15.3	12,465.0	177	3,592.0	153
74	69	MCDONNELL DOUGLAS	14,332.0	8.8	(416.0)	482	(169.6)	10,466.0	198	3,041.0	174
75	73	GEORGIA-PACIFIC	14,292.0	12.2	1,018.0	63	228.4	12,335.0	180	3,519.0	155
76	87	J.P. MORGAN & CO.	13,838.0	16.1	1,296.0	47	6.7	184,879.0	10	10,451.0	31
77	65	DIGITAL EQUIPMENT[5]	13,813.1	2.7	121.8	361	–	9,947.2	201	3,528.3	154
78	160	KIMBERLY-CLARK[16]	13,788.6	87.2	33.2	427	(93.8)	11,439.2	187	3,650.4	151
79	86	BRISTOL-MYERS SQUIBB	13,767.0	14.9	1,812.0	29	(1.6)	13,929.0	161	5,822.0	75
80	75	SPRINT	13,599.5	7.4	395.3*	186	(55.6)	15,195.9	147	4,642.6	108
81	79	PHILLIPS PETROLEUM	13,521.0E	9.3	469.0	157	(3.1)	11,978.0	183	3,188.0	166
82	122	LEHMAN BROTHERS HOLDINGS[17]	13,476.0	46.6	242.0	270	114.2	115,303.0	20	3,698.0	149
83	63	BELL ATLANTIC	13,429.5	(2.6)	1,858.3	27	–	24,156.8	100	6,683.6	58
84	76	AMERITECH	13,427.8	6.8	2,007.6	23	–	22,011.2	115	7,014.5	54
85	67	NYNEX	13,406.9	0.8	(1,849.9)*	492	(333.4)	26,220.0	91	6,079.2	70
86	130	AMERICAN HOME PRODUCTS	13,376.1	49.2	1,680.4	35	10.0	21,362.9	118	5,543.0	80
87	78	MCKESSON[18]	13,325.5	7.2	404.5	180	197.0	3,479.2	336	1,013.5	365
88	81	GOODYEAR TIRE & RUBBER	13,165.9	7.1	611.0	121	7.8	9,789.6	204	3,281.7	162
89	106	TEXAS INSTRUMENTS	13,128.0	27.3	1,088.0	60	57.5	9,215.0	214	4,095.0	133
90	94	ROCKWELL INTERNATIONAL[19]	13,009.0	16.1	742.0	95	17.0	12,505.0	175	3,782.0	141
91	42	AETNA LIFE & CASUALTY	12,978.0	(25.9)	251.7	260	(46.2)	84,323.7	31	7,272.8	51
92	92	ARCHER DANIELS MIDLAND[5]	12,671.9	11.4	795.9	85	64.4	9,756.9	205	5,854.2	74
93	89	SBC COMMUNICATIONS	12,669.7	9.0	(930.0)*	490	(156.4)	22,002.5	116	6,255.8	68
94	83	IBP	12,667.6	4.9	257.9	254	41.5	2,027.6	422	1,022.9	364
95	104	ALCOA	12,654.9	21.8	790.5	87	110.7	13,643.4	165	4,444.7	115
96	88	ALBERTSON'S[1]	12,585.0	5.8	465.0	159	16.1	4,135.9	319	1,952.5	249
97	85	ANHEUSER-BUSCH	12,325.5E¶	2.3	642.3	117	(37.8)	10,590.9	195	4,433.9	116
98	80	DELTA AIR LINES[5]	12,194.0	(1.3)	408.0**	178	–	12,143.0	182	1,827.0	258
99	82	MAY DEPARTMENT STORES[1]	12,187.0E¶	(0.3)	752.0	91	(3.8)	10,122.0	199	4,585.0	112
100	•	ITT HARTFORD GROUP[20]	12,150.0	–	559.0	133	–	93,855.0	25	4,702.0	106

MARKET VALUE 3/15/96		PROFITS AS % OF...						EARNINGS PER SHARE				TOTAL RETURN TO INVESTORS				RANK 1995
		REVENUES		ASSETS		STOCK-HOLDERS EQUITY		1995 $		1985-95 ANNUAL GROWTH RATE		1995		1985-1995 ANNUAL RATE		
$ MILLIONS	RANK	%	RANK	%	RANK	%	RANK		% CHANGE FROM '94	%	RANK	%	RANK	%	RANK	
23,982.8	42	5.4	223	4.8	206	13.5	259	2.90	61.1	–		39.4	185	–		51
635.5	443	0.2	438	1.0	387	3.9	414	1.12	(25.8)	(9.0)	302	(6.9)	413	(2.8)	369	52
23,433.1	44	9.9	104	1.5	356	19.0	117	3.11	13.1	5.8	189	43.7	153	9.2	300	53
6,938.5	171	1.0	418	0.9	398	4.5	409	2.11	(53.2)	(9.8)	305	39.4	184	6.0	330	54
18,093.5	59	8.2	143	5.7	172	20.4	104	8.42	49.6	–		14.3	343	11.1	264	55
76,495.6	6	20.0	8	14.0	21	28.4	47	2.70	13.4	20.4	38	76.8	31	27.1	19	56
19,692.2	55	11.1	78	1.6	348	15.7	197	5.51	42.7	10.7	128	97.6	11	–		57
2,135.8	362	0.3	436	1.0	384	3.6	415	0.61	(76.4)	(8.3)	300	33.6	225	6.0	331	58
5,862.6	196	2.0	374	6.3	153	41.0	18	1.34	36.7	–		61.6	62	–		59
20,295.9	54	12.0	61	1.0	380	15.2	205	7.13	16.5	12.0	106	59.7	70	16.0	127	60
48,348.2	14	22.0	7	20.4	4	29.3	43	4.03	53.8	117.9	1	78.2	28	28.0	16	61
N.A.		3.9	291	0.8	399	16.6	170	N.A.	–	–		–		–		62
26,587.6	40	6.1	201	6.9	129	14.2	235	2.32	(25.9)	4.9	197	28.3	258	15.2	149	63
13,969.1	82	7.1	169	6.7	133	33.5	30	5.72	21.7	18.9	44	8.8	364	12.5	226	64
9,105.0	133	3.8	294	1.9	332	5.9	391	1.53	22.4	–		16.1	332	–		65
23,602.5	43	4.7	251	9.9	60	14.7	222	1.54	16.7	47.0	5	4.3	384	44.5	1	66
25,293.1	41	8.2	144	8.6	82	24.4	72	3.67	121.1	14.2	82	44.4	149	13.6	201	67
19,160.9	57	3.6	302	2.8	287	5.7	394	0.80	(39.4)	12.8	99	42.5	158	16.8	105	68
6,660.3	180	0.5	434	0.5	420	1.7	425	0.39	(72.3)	–		41.6	166	–		69
2,494.8	340	2.3	358	3.0	282	–		20.01	–	–		104.3	9	13.9	189	70
16,971.3	64	12.1	58	1.0	385	15.2	207	6.73	45.0	(0.9)	265	70.5	41	9.3	296	71
10,613.3	108	5.3	225	10.1	55	17.1	160	2.88	(10.8)	33.4	17	21.5	300	36.1	7	72
15,905.8	69	6.1	198	7.0	126	24.4	73	3.09	15.3	–		42.3	161	12.5	227	73
10,180.2	113	(2.9)	475	(4.0)	470	(13.7)	458	(3.66)	(172.5)	–		96.3	12	17.5	92	74
6,484.6	185	7.1	168	8.3	88	28.9	44	11.29	224.4	21.3	31	(1.7)	407	13.1	209	75
15,003.5	74	9.4	115	0.7	410	12.4	289	6.42	6.6	5.1	193	49.4	117	14.0	187	76
9,858.7	121	0.9	422	1.2	372	3.5	418	0.59	–	(16.8)	310	92.9	13	(0.3)	363	77
21,270.6	50	0.2	437	0.3	431	0.9	430	0.12	(96.4)	(22.1)	315	73.7	36	21.4	41	78
42,635.9	20	13.2	47	13.0	27	31.1	37	3.58	(1.1)	6.4	184	55.0	88	14.3	176	79
12,396.6	92	2.9	333	2.6	301	8.5	363	1.12	(56.1)	28.7	20	47.6	125	17.5	91	80
10,220.7	112	3.5	306	3.9	243	14.7	221	1.79	(3.2)	2.2	229	7.9	372	15.6	139	81
2,482.4	342	1.8	386	0.2	435	6.5	387	1.76	–	–		45.5	141	–		82
26,894.3	39	13.8	38	7.7	104	27.8	57	4.24	–	4.5	205	41.1	169	15.6	138	83
30,117.1	36	15.0	28	9.1	78	28.6	45	3.63	–	7.1	174	52.1	102	18.8	71	84
21,080.4	52	(13.8)	492	(7.1)	480	(30.4)	467	(4.34)	(329.6)	–		55.4	86	14.8	160	85
30,841.1	35	12.6	54	7.9	98	30.3	39	5.42	9.1	8.7	148	60.7	66	16.6	112	86
2,450.2	343	3.0	325	11.6	42	39.9	20	N.A.	–	–		59.0	72	–		87
7,868.1	154	4.6	257	6.2	154	18.6	131	4.02	7.2	7.7	161	38.1	191	14.5	170	88
9,942.9	118	8.3	139	11.8	41	26.6	62	5.63	54.9	–		39.0	188	13.2	208	89
12,410.2	91	5.7	216	5.9	166	19.6	114	3.42	19.2	5.5	191	51.5	106	14.8	158	90
8,658.3	139	1.9	378	0.3	430	3.5	417	2.21	(46.6)	(4.0)	288	53.7	97	8.3	311	91
9,695.8	123	6.3	193	8.2	90	13.6	255	1.47	65.4	17.4	55	(7.7)	415	14.8	159	92
31,153.5	34	(7.3)	486	(4.2)	471	(14.9)	460	(1.53)	(155.8)	–		46.8	130	20.7	46	93
2,286.4	351	2.0	370	12.7	29	25.2	69	2.67	40.9	–		67.8	49	–		94
10,754.3	107	6.2	194	5.8	168	17.8	150	4.43	111.0	–		24.0	290	13.8	193	95
9,576.9	125	3.7	298	11.2	44	23.8	76	1.84	16.5	19.1	42	15.2	341	25.2	26	96
17,167.1	63	5.2	233	6.1	159	14.5	228	2.49	(36.3)	5.8	188	35.2	216	14.8	161	97
4,332.9	255	3.3	311	3.4	264	22.3	84	6.32	–	(0.3)	260	46.2	131	8.3	309	98
12,541.9	88	6.2	195	7.4	112	16.4	177	2.73	(10.8)	7.3	167	28.3	260	14.0	188	99
5,518.3	214	4.6	259	0.6	416	11.9	309	N.A.	–	–		–		–		100

RANK 1995	1994	COMPANY	REVENUES $ MILLIONS	% CHANGE FROM '94	PROFITS $ MILLIONS	RANK	% CHANGE FROM '94	ASSETS $ MILLIONS	RANK	STOCK-HOLDERS' EQUITY $ MILLIONS	RANK
101	99	SYSCO[5]	12,118.0	10.7	251.8	259	16.2	3,094.7	357	1,403.6	317
102	108	WALT DISNEY[19,21]	12,112.1	20.5	1,380.1	42	24.3	14,605.8	153	6,650.8	59
103	98	WINN-DIXIE STORES[5]	11,787.8	6.4	232.2	278	7.4	2,482.8	391	1,241.2	332
104	103	WEYERHAEUSER	11,787.7	13.4	798.9	84	35.6	13,253.0	168	4,486.0	114
105	153	VIACOM	11,780.2	54.3	222.5	287	148.3	29,026.0	87	12,091.6	20
106	91	US WEST	11,746.0	2.1	1,317.0	46	(7.6)	25,071.0	97	7,948.0	46
107	109	RAYTHEON[22]	11,716.0	17.0	792.5	86	32.8	9,740.1	206	4,292.0	124
108	96	NATIONWIDE INS. ENTERPRISE	11,702.4	4.6	182.7	312	(59.0)	60,664.0	44	5,109.9	96
109	101	TEACHERS INSURANCE & ANNUITY	11,646.2	10.4	752.0	92	62.3	79,794.6	34	4,056.2	134
110	93	MELVILLE	11,516.4¶	2.0	(657.1)	489	(313.7)	3,961.6	322	1,547.8	295
111	114	NORTHWESTERN MUTUAL LIFE INS.	11,483.3	19.9	458.5	160	15.1	54,875.5	47	2,786.0	187
112	95	CHASE MANHATTAN CORP.[23]	11,336.0	1.3	1,165.0	52	(3.3)	121,173.0	19	9,134.0	36
113	115	ASHLAND	11,251.1ᴱ	18.4	23.9	433	(87.9)	6,991.6	241	1,655.4	281
114	123	APPLE COMPUTER[19]	11,062.0	20.4	424.0	172	36.7	6,231.0	252	2,901.0	184
115	107	WMX TECHNOLOGIES	10,979.3	8.7	603.9	126	(23.0)	18,695.3	126	4,942.3	101
116	118	MORGAN STANLEY GROUP[24]	10,949.0	–	720.0	106	–	143,753.0	14	5,174.0	92
117	332	FIRST CHICAGO NBD CORP.[25,†]	10,681.0	208.6	1,150.0	54	116.3	122,002.0	18	8,450.0	41
118	187	FIRST UNION CORP.[26,†]	10,582.9	69.2	1,430.2	40	54.6	131,879.9	17	9,043.1	38
119	148	PRINCIPAL MUTUAL LIFE INS.[†]	10,561.0	32.7	554.0	135	264.2	56,947.0	46	4,018.0	137
120	113	CSX[†]	10,504.0	9.3	618.0	120	(5.2)	14,282.0	157	4,242.0	128
121	117	OCCIDENTAL PETROLEUM[†]	10,423.0ᴱ	10.7	511.0	148	–	17,815.0	129	4,630.0	110
122	120	WALGREEN[11,†]	10,395.1	12.6	320.8	218	13.8	3,252.6	347	1,792.6	261
123	127	DEERE[6,†]	10,290.5	14.0	706.1	110	17.0	13,847.4	164	3,085.4	171
124	110	COASTAL[†]	10,223.4ᴱ	2.1	270.4	246	16.3	10,658.8	192	2,678.8	193
125	126	TRW[†]	10,172.4	11.9	446.2	166	34.0	5,890.0	262	2,172.0	226
126	144	PFIZER[†]	10,021.4	21.0	1,572.9	37	21.1	12,729.3	172	5,506.6	81
127	133	EMERSON ELECTRIC[19,†]	10,012.9	16.3	907.7	72	15.1	9,399.0	213	4,870.8	102
128	124	ABBOTT LABORATORIES[†]	10,012.2	9.4	1,688.7	34	11.3	9,412.6	212	4,396.8	117
129	112	TEXTRON[†]	9,973.0	3.0	479.0	154	10.6	23,172.0	107	3,412.0	159
130	149	ALCO STANDARD[19,†]	9,891.8	23.7	202.2	303	187.1	4,737.6	296	1,868.5	254
131	140	MCDONALD'S[†]	9,794.5	17.7	1,427.3	41	16.6	15,414.6	145	7,861.3	47
132	119	BAXTER INTERNATIONAL[†]	9,730.0¶	4.4	649.0	116	8.9	9,437.0	211	3,704.0	148
133	102	PACIFIC GAS & ELECTRIC[†]	9,621.8	(7.9)	1,338.9	44	32.9	26,850.3	89	9,001.2	39
134	121	WESTINGHOUSE ELECTRIC[27,†]	9,605.0	4.3	15.0	441	(80.5)	16,752.0	137	1,508.0	303
135	168	FEDERAL HOME LOAN MORTGAGE[†]	9,519.0	37.5	1,091.0	59	11.0	137,181.0	15	5,863.0	73
136	132	PUBLIX SUPER MARKETS	9,470.7	8.3	242.1	269	1.5	2,559.0	388	1,614.7	286
137	131	TOYS "R" US[1]	9,426.9	7.8	148.1	336	(72.1)	6,735.4	243	3,433.3	158
138	136	FEDERAL EXPRESS[7]	9,392.1	10.8	297.6	228	45.6	6,433.4	246	2,245.6	222
139	128	LIBERTY MUTUAL INS. GROUP	9,308.0	3.6	410.0	176	0.7	36,587.0	70	4,660.0	107
140	134	FLUOR	9,301.4	8.7	231.8	279	20.5	3,228.9	349	1,430.8	312
141	129	ENRON	9,189.0	2.3	519.7	145	14.6	13,238.9	169	3,165.2	168
142	142	SOUTHERN	9,180.0	10.6	1,103.0	58	11.5	30,554.0	82	8,772.0	40
143	125	NORTHWEST AIRLINES	9,084.9	(0.6)	392.0**	189	66.0	8,412.3	219	(818.0)	489
144	116	PACIFIC TELESIS GROUP	9,042.0	(4.8)	(2,312.0)*	494	(299.5)	15,841.0	142	2,190.0	224
145	150	BANC ONE CORP.	8,970.9	14.2	1,277.9	48	27.1	90,454.0	27	8,197.5	45
146	145	MONSANTO	8,962.0	8.3	739.0	98	18.8	10,611.0	194	3,732.0	145
147	138	MARRIOTT INTERNATIONAL	8,960.7	6.5	246.9	266	23.5	4,018.0	321	1,053.6	360
148	146	UNION PACIFIC[28]	8,942.0¶	9.9	946.0	68	73.3	19,446.0	123	6,364.0	66
149	184	SALOMON	8,933.0	42.3	457.0	161	–	188,000.0	8	4,143.0	130
150	68	TENNECO	8,899.0	(32.7)	735.0	100	80.1	13,451.0	166	3,148.0	169

MARKET VALUE 3/15/96 $ MILLIONS	RANK	PROFITS AS % OF... REVENUES %	RANK	ASSETS %	RANK	STOCK-HOLDERS EQUITY %	RANK	EARNINGS PER SHARE 1995 $	% CHANGE FROM '94	1985-95 ANNUAL GROWTH RATE %	RANK	TOTAL RETURN TO INVESTORS 1995 %	RANK	1985-1995 ANNUAL RATE %	RANK	RANK 1995
6,052.4	192	2.1	366	8.1	91	17.9	145	1.38	16.9	16.7	65	28.2	264	20.4	51	101
47,107.1	15	11.4	70	9.4	71	20.8	100	2.60	27.5	23.2	27	28.8	252	24.4	29	102
5,324.4	221	2.0	376	9.4	74	18.7	126	3.11	7.2	8.9	146	48.0	123	18.2	78	103
9,093.7	134	6.8	175	6.0	161	17.8	148	3.93	37.4	16.1	69	19.3	314	11.9	244	104
14,603.2	78	1.9	380	0.8	403	1.8	423	0.43	514.3	–		16.3	330	–		105
14,418.6	80	11.2	74	5.3	190	16.5	173	N.A.	–	–		–		–		106
12,512.5	89	6.8	176	8.1	92	18.5	136	3.25	44.1	10.9	123	50.9	109	16.6	113	107
N.A.		1.6	398	0.3	429	3.6	416	N.A.	–	–		–		–		108
N.A.		6.5	185	0.9	394	18.5	134	N.A.	–	–		–		–		109
3,625.5	286	(5.7)	482	(16.6)	487	(42.5)	473	(6.41)	(333.1)	–		4.2	385	5.4	338	110
N.A.		4.0	286	0.8	400	16.5	174	N.A.	–	–		–		–		111
12,616.4	86	10.3	95	1.0	389	12.8	280	5.76	(1.9)	(1.0)	267	82.4	21	11.9	243	112
2,424.7	345	0.2	441	0.3	427	1.4	426	0.08	(97.3)	(27.7)	317	5.1	381	9.8	287	113
3,199.6	304	3.8	293	6.8	132	14.6	223	3.45	32.2	21.4	30	(17.3)	429	12.3	233	114
14,901.1	75	5.5	221	3.2	269	12.2	294	1.24	(23.5)	11.2	119	16.4	328	14.4	173	115
7,527.4	160	6.6	184	0.5	422	13.9	244	N.A.	–	–		38.3	190	–		116
12,351.1	94	10.8	85	0.9	393	13.6	254	3.45	3.0	9.3	139	50.0	114	17.0	100	117
16,815.0	66	13.5	42	1.1	379	15.8	194	5.04	1.2	8.8	147	39.9	181	14.4	172	118
N.A.		5.2	230	1.0	388	13.8	247	N.A.	–	–		–		–		119
9,498.6	127	5.9	205	4.3	229	14.6	226	2.94	(5.6)	–		34.1	223	15.3	144	120
8,120.4	144	4.9	246	2.9	286	11.0	326	1.31	–	(11.7)	308	16.3	329	3.5	347	121
7,968.8	147	3.1	322	9.9	62	17.9	147	1.30	14.0	13.0	96	39.1	186	17.4	94	122
11,025.0	105	6.9	172	5.1	196	22.9	82	2.71	(61.3)	19.7	41	64.0	60	17.1	98	123
4,121.8	264	2.6	344	2.5	303	10.1	340	2.40	17.1	4.1	208	45.7	138	9.3	298	124
5,770.3	203	4.4	268	7.6	106	20.5	102	6.69	32.5	–		20.7	307	9.5	294	125
39,998.2	22	15.7	22	12.4	35	28.6	46	2.50	19.3	11.3	117	66.6	52	20.7	47	126
17,895.0	60	9.1	122	9.7	65	18.6	129	4.06	15.3	8.4	151	34.5	220	15.1	151	127
32,279.6	33	16.9	15	17.9	10	38.4	24	2.12	13.4	15.9	72	30.4	244	19.7	59	128
6,700.9	179	4.8	249	2.1	325	14.0	237	5.51	14.8	5.0	194	37.5	199	–		129
5,715.2	207	2.0	369	4.3	231	10.8	330	1.67	203.6	11.2	120	47.4	126	19.8	58	130
35,684.3	26	14.6	32	9.3	77	18.2	141	1.97	17.3	13.5	90	55.3	87	18.7	73	131
12,352.9	93	6.7	179	6.9	130	17.5	156	2.35	10.3	10.7	126	53.0	98	14.4	175	132
9,988.4	117	13.9	37	5.0	200	14.8	217	2.99	35.3	1.2	237	25.0	284	11.4	257	133
7,890.0	152	0.2	443	0.1	440	1.0	429	(0.05)	(171.4)	–		35.5	214	0.2	361	134
14,732.1	77	10.0	101	0.8	401	18.6	132	5.69	12.0	17.3	58	68.2	48	–		135
N.A.		2.6	348	9.5	69	15.0	211	1.07	3.9	(3.1)	279	–		–		136
7,441.6	162	1.6	397	2.2	318	4.3	410	0.53	(71.4)	2.6	225	(29.0)	438	7.6	316	137
3,968.2	272	3.2	318	4.6	214	13.3	266	5.27	44.4	12.6	101	22.6	297	2.0	353	138
N.A.		4.4	267	1.1	378	8.8	359	N.A.	–	–		–		–		139
5,862.2	197	2.5	354	7.2	120	16.2	183	2.78	19.8	–		54.8	92	16.7	110	140
8,775.4	137	5.7	220	3.9	242	16.4	176	2.07	15.0	–		27.9	267	17.8	83	141
15,404.9	72	12.0	60	3.6	255	12.6	284	1.66	9.2	0.4	251	30.2	248	16.8	106	142
4,656.7	239	4.3	270	4.7	212	–		4.17	42.8	–		223.8	2	–		143
11,300.0	102	(25.6)	494	(14.6)	486	(105.6)	474	(5.43)	(298.9)	–		26.4	276	14.5	171	144
14,807.4	76	14.2	35	1.4	359	15.6	199	2.91	32.3	11.3	116	54.9	90	15.2	148	145
17,703.3	61	8.2	142	7.0	128	19.8	113	6.36	19.5	–		78.7	27	21.9	39	146
6,212.4	187	2.8	340	6.1	158	23.4	79	1.87	23.8	–		37.1	206	–		147
14,442.1	79	10.6	92	4.9	204	14.9	213	4.60	72.9	8.2	153	50.0	113	12.7	219	148
3,856.5	277	5.1	238	0.2	433	9.8	345	3.64	–	(0.4)	261	(4.0)	412	(0.1)	362	149
9,557.7	126	8.3	141	5.5	180	23.0	81	4.16	89.1	18.7	45	20.7	306	7.7	315	150

RANK 1995	1994	COMPANY	REVENUES $ MILLIONS	% CHANGE FROM '94	PROFITS $ MILLIONS	RANK	% CHANGE FROM '94	ASSETS $ MILLIONS	RANK	STOCK-HOLDERS' EQUITY $ MILLIONS	RANK
151	23	ITT INDUSTRIES[20]	8,884.0[29]	(62.6)	708.0*	109	(30.7)	5,879.0	263	627.0	415
152	155	BANKERS TRUST NEW YORK CORP.	8,600.0	14.6	215.0	295	(65.0)	104,000.0	23	5,000.0	99
153	156	BERGEN BRUNSWIG[19]	8,447.6	12.9	63.9	408	13.9	2,405.5	396	519.3	434
154	157	CPC INTERNATIONAL	8,431.5	13.5	512.1	147	48.4	7,501.6	234	1,987.3	243
155	139	EDISON INTERNATIONAL[30]	8,405.0	0.7	739.0	97	2.4	23,946.0	103	6,360.0	67
156	135	GENERAL MILLS[7]	8,393.6¶	(1.4)	367.4	197	(21.8)	3,358.2	342	141.0	476
157	151	SUN	8,370.0ᴱ	7.4	140.0	343	55.6	5,184.0	283	1,699.0	269
158	154	COLGATE-PALMOLIVE	8,358.2	10.2	172.0	317	(70.4)	7,642.3	232	1,679.8	272
159	147	WHIRLPOOL	8,347.0	3.0	209.0	301	32.3	7,800.0	229	1,877.0	253
160	169	JOHNSON CONTROLS[19]	8,330.3	21.2	195.8	307	18.5	4,320.9	312	1,340.2	323
161	143	WOOLWORTH[1]	8,224.0	(0.8)	(164.0)	473	(448.9)	3,506.0	335	1,229.0	337
162	164	H.J. HEINZ[31]	8,086.8	14.8	591.0	128	(2.0)	8,247.2	221	2,472.9	208
163	159	TIME WARNER	8,067.0	9.1	(166.0)*	474	–	22,132.0	113	3,667.0	150
164	•	COLLEGE RETIREMENT EQ. FUND	7,950.6	4.3	N.A.		–	80,789.7	32	N.A.	
165	175	DEAN WITTER DISCOVER	7,934.4	20.2	856.4	76	15.6	38,208.0	66	4,833.7	103
166	267	FLEET FINANCIAL GROUP[32]	7,919.4	78.2	610.0	123	(0.5)	84,432.2	30	6,364.8	65
167	161	LIMITED[1]	7,881.4	7.7	961.5	65	114.5	5,266.6	281	3,201.0	164
168	203	CARDINAL HEALTH[5]	7,806.1	34.8	85.0	387	141.8	1,841.8	437	548.2	429
169	170	DANA	7,794.5	15.6	288.1	234	26.2	5,694.1	268	1,164.6	348
170	197	NORWEST CORP.	7,582.3	25.7	956.0	67	19.4	72,134.4	38	5,312.1	87
171	165	ELI LILLY	7,535.4¶	7.6	2,290.9	20	78.1	14,412.5	155	5,432.6	84
172	163	UNOCAL	7,527.0ᴱ	6.4	260.3	252	–	9,891.0	202	2,930.0	181
173	172	AMERADA HESS	7,524.8	12.3	(394.4)	481	(635.1)	7,756.4	230	2,660.4	196
174	166	USAIR GROUP	7,474.3	6.8	119.3	364	–	6,955.0	242	(835.8)	491
175	204	STONE CONTAINER	7,351.2	27.9	255.5*	256	–	6,398.9	247	1,005.3	368
176	182	TOSCO	7,284.1	14.4	77.1	394	(8.1)	2,003.2	424	627.1	414
177	173	CAMPBELL SOUP[33]	7,278.0	8.8	698.0	111	10.7	6,315.0	249	2,468.0	209
178	174	FARMLAND INDUSTRIES[11,34]	7,256.9	8.7	N.A.		–	2,185.9	410	687.3	404
179	198	REYNOLDS METALS	7,252.0	20.6	389.0	190	219.6	7,740.0	231	2,617.0	199
180	152	RALSTON PURINA[19]	7,210.3	(6.4)	296.4	229	41.9	4,567.2	302	494.2	438
181	298	GENERAL RE	7,210.2	87.9	824.9	80	24.0	35,946.0	72	6,587.0	61
182	191	AFLAC	7,190.6	17.7	349.1	205	19.2	25,338.0	95	2,134.1	229
183	319	PHARMACIA & UPJOHN[35]	7,094.6	99.0	738.7	99	50.5	11,460.6	186	6,388.9	64
184	192	LOWE'S[1]	7,075.4	15.8	226.0	283	1.1	3,556.4	332	1,656.7	278
185	183	PPG INDUSTRIES	7,057.7	11.5	767.6	90	49.2	6,194.3	256	2,569.2	201
186	179	WARNER-LAMBERT	7,039.8	9.7	739.5	96	6.6	6,101.0	257	2,246.0	221
187	176	KELLOGG	7,003.7	6.7	490.3	152	(30.5)	4,414.6	306	1,590.9	289
188	220	CHAMPION INTERNATIONAL	6,972.0	31.1	771.8	89	1,119.2	9,543.3	208	3,646.7	152
189	185	UNICOM	6,910.0	10.1	639.5	118	80.2	23,247.0	106	5,770.0	77
190	233	TELE-COMMUNICATIONS	6,851.0	38.8	(171.0)	475	(410.9)	25,130.0	96	4,550.0	113
191	196	EATON	6,821.7	12.7	398.8	185	19.8	5,052.6	286	1,975.3	246
192	171	NORTHROP GRUMMAN	6,818.0	1.6	252.0	258	620.0	5,455.0	274	1,459.0	309
193	218	MASS. MUTUAL LIFE INS.[36]	6,804.1	29.1	229.4	281	146.4	39,339.4	65	2,073.0	238
194	213	JAMES RIVER CORP. OF VIRGINIA	6,799.5	25.5	126.4	354	–	7,258.9	238	2,254.2	220
195	194	GILLETTE	6,794.7	11.9	823.5	81	17.9	6,340.3	248	2,513.3	205
196	199	COCA-COLA ENTERPRISES	6,773.0	12.7	82.0	389	18.8	9,064.0	215	1,435.0	311
197	195	HONEYWELL	6,731.3	11.1	333.6	213	19.6	5,060.2	285	2,040.1	242
198	193	LEVI STRAUSS ASSOCIATES[17]	6,707.6	10.4	734.7	101	128.9	4,709.2	297	2,115.3	232
199	167	LINCOLN NATIONAL	6,633.3	(5.0)	482.2	153	37.8	63,257.7	42	4,378.1	120
200	189	UNITED SVCS. AUTOMOBILE ASSN.	6,610.9	6.9	730.3	103	29.4	22,244.1	111	5,215.0	91

DEFINITIONS, EXPLANATIONS, AND FOOTNOTES ARE FOUND ON PAGE 2[...]

| MARKET VALUE 3/15/96 | | PROFITS AS % OF... | | | | | | EARNINGS PER SHARE | | | | TOTAL RETURN TO INVESTORS | | | | RANK 1995 |
$ MILLIONS	RANK	REVENUES %	RANK	ASSETS %	RANK	STOCK-HOLDERS EQUITY %	RANK	1995 $	% CHANGE FROM '94	1985-95 ANNUAL GROWTH RATE %	RANK	1995 %	RANK	1985-1995 ANNUAL RATE %	RANK	
2,971.4	316	8.0[29]	150	12.0	39	112.9	3	N.A.	–	–		–		–		151
5,252.4	224	2.5	352	0.2	436	4.3	411	2.03	(71.7)	(9.3)	304	28.3	259	11.5	256	152
979.1	428	0.8	426	2.7	297	12.3	292	1.61	11.2	7.6	163	27.7	270	8.1	313	153
10,075.0	116	6.1	200	6.8	131	25.8	65	3.43	52.4	16.7	64	32.0	232	21.7	40	154
7,402.9	163	8.8	127	3.1	277	11.6	316	1.66	9.2	0.2	256	27.9	268	10.1	284	155
9,188.4	131	4.4	269	10.9	48	260.6	1	2.33	(21.0)	–		23.7	291	19.7	60	156
2,155.5	361	1.7	391	2.7	293	8.2	367	1.29	53.6	(12.2)	309	(0.1)	403	5.5	335	157
11,519.3	99	2.1	367	2.3	315	10.2	336	1.04	(72.8)	4.1	207	13.7	346	19.0	67	158
4,320.2	257	2.5	351	2.7	294	11.1	322	2.80	33.3	1.2	240	8.6	365	11.4	258	159
2,910.4	321	2.4	357	4.5	222	14.6	224	4.53	19.2	6.6	182	44.4	150	14.7	163	160
2,112.1	365	(2.0)	467	(4.7)	472	(13.3)	457	(1.23)	(441.7)	–		(12.5)	423	1.8	355	161
12,614.7	87	7.3	165	7.2	121	23.9	75	2.38	1.3	9.4	137	40.0	178	15.2	147	162
16,854.8	65	(2.1)	469	(0.8)	452	(4.5)	447	(0.57)	–	–		8.8	362	10.8	268	163
N.A.		–		–		–		N.A.	–	–		–		–		164
9,120.4	132	10.8	84	2.2	316	17.7	151	4.88	12.2	–		40.7	173	–		165
10,428.7	109	7.7	159	0.7	408	9.6	350	1.57	(58.1)	(3.9)	286	31.8	236	11.8	246	166
6,929.6	172	12.2	57	18.3	8	30.0	40	2.68	114.4	21.0	34	(3.5)	411	6.4	326	167
2,900.9	323	1.1	414	4.6	217	15.5	201	2.01	–	20.5	36	18.4	319	25.2	25	168
3,378.0	292	3.7	296	5.1	197	24.7	71	2.84	22.9	6.8	180	28.5	254	12.3	232	169
12,268.6	95	12.6	52	1.3	363	18.0	144	2.76	12.7	17.9	48	45.5	140	24.7	28	170
33,574.4	30	30.4	3	15.9	13	42.2	14	4.03	81.1	15.9	73	77.1	30	18.5	75	171
7,877.6	153	3.5	307	2.6	299	8.9	356	0.91	–	(2.6)	277	10.0	358	11.2	262	172
4,952.7	232	(5.2)	480	(5.1)	475	(14.8)	459	(4.24)	(636.7)	–		17.6	322	8.3	308	173
1,108.9	421	1.6	396	1.7	341	–		0.55	–	(18.1)	312	211.8	3	(8.9)	378	174
1,425.1	398	3.5	305	4.0	240	25.4	68	2.63	–	42.1	10	(15.8)	424	3.3	349	175
1,705.0	388	1.1	416	3.8	247	12.3	293	2.06	(9.3)	3.6	215	32.8	227	8.7	305	176
15,571.1	71	9.6	110	11.1	47	28.3	48	2.80	11.6	13.9	85	39.9	179	19.9	55	177
N.A.		–		–		–		N.A.	–	–		–		–		178
3,712.5	283	5.4	224	5.0	198	14.9	214	5.35	276.8	–		18.5	316	14.4	174	179
7,125.5	168	4.1	278	6.5	143	56.2	8	2.72	33.3	–		42.9	156	–		180
11,678.7	98	11.4	67	2.3	314	12.5	287	9.92	24.5	21.2	32	27.2	271	13.9	191	181
4,342.0	253	4.9	247	1.4	360	16.4	179	2.33	23.1	20.5	37	37.6	196	19.9	57	182
20,967.5	53	10.4	94	6.4	145	11.6	318	1.43	(48.2)	2.7	223	31.0	240	9.1	302	183
5,668.5	211	3.2	317	6.4	147	13.6	251	1.41	(2.1)	13.1	94	(3.0)	410	19.6	63	184
9,236.6	130	10.9	82	12.4	34	29.9	41	3.80	56.4	12.8	98	26.7	274	17.2	97	185
13,927.8	83	10.5	93	12.1	37	32.9	32	5.48	6.0	–		30.0	249	18.5	76	186
16,687.5	67	7.0	170	11.1	46	30.8	38	2.24	(28.9)	7.0	177	35.8	213	18.9	69	187
4,584.3	243	11.1	77	8.1	93	20.8	98	8.01	2,007.9	17.6	54	15.6	336	7.3	323	188
6,713.2	178	9.3	119	2.8	288	11.1	324	2.98	79.5	(3.9)	287	44.5	147	9.6	292	189
12,892.9	85	(2.5)	474	(0.7)	450	(3.8)	445	(0.11)	(222.2)	–		13.6	348	23.0	35	190
4,626.9	241	5.8	208	7.9	96	20.2	108	5.13	16.6	8.2	154	11.3	352	12.9	215	191
3,004.6	315	3.7	297	4.6	215	17.3	158	5.11	609.7	1.0	242	56.8	82	8.3	310	192
N.A.		3.4	309	0.6	418	11.1	325	N.A.	–	–		–		–		193
2,385.2	347	1.9	382	1.7	339	5.6	396	0.81	–	(9.2)	303	22.1	298	1.4	357	194
23,075.4	47	12.1	59	13.0	28	32.8	33	1.85	17.8	19.0	43	41.1	171	31.2	10	195
3,728.0	282	1.2	409	0.9	395	5.7	393	0.62	19.2	–		49.6	116	–		196
6,793.3	174	5.0	242	6.6	141	16.4	180	2.62	21.9	5.5	192	58.2	76	13.6	200	197
N.A.		11.0	80	15.6	14	34.7	29	N.A.	–	–		–		–		198
5,274.4	223	7.3	166	0.8	404	11.0	327	4.60	36.5	6.5	183	60.2	69	13.0	213	199
N.A.		11.0	79	3.3	267	14.0	240	N.A.	–	–		–		–		200

RANK 1995	1994	COMPANY	REVENUES $ MILLIONS	% CHANGE FROM '94	PROFITS $ MILLIONS	RANK	% CHANGE FROM '94	ASSETS $ MILLIONS	RANK	STOCKHOLDERS' EQUITY $ MILLIONS	RANK
201	235	R.R. DONNELLEY & SONS	6,511.8	33.2	298.8	227	11.2	5,384.8	277	2,173.2	225
202	238	AMERICAN GENERAL	6,495.0	34.2	545.0	138	6.3	61,153.0	43	5,801.0	76
203	158	UNISYS	6,460.4	(12.7)	(624.6)	488	(721.5)	7,113.2	240	1,860.2	256
204	188	CONSOL. EDISON OF NEW YORK	6,401.5E	2.6	723.9	105	(1.4)	13,949.9	160	6,062.7	71
205	246	PNC BANK CORP.37	6,389.5	36.4	408.1	177	(33.1)	73,404.0	37	5,768.0	78
206	201	QUAKER OATS5	6,365.2	6.9	802.0	83	246.4	4,826.9	291	1,147.6	350
207	•	ITT20	6,346.0	–	147.0	338	–	8,692.0	217	2,936.0	180
208	217	NAVISTAR INTERNATIONAL6	6,342.0	18.8	164.0	329	100.0	5,566.0	269	870.0	381
209	200	ENTERGY	6,274.4	5.2	520.0	144	52.1	22,265.9	110	6,471.7	62
210	229	BURLINGTON NORTHERN SANTA FE38	6,183.0	23.8	92.0	381	(77.9)	18,269.0	127	5,037.0	97
211	190	GUARDIAN LIFE INS. CO. OF AMERICA	6,172.3	3.7	125.0	356	(13.0)	15,811.0	143	1,115.0	353
212	202	PUBLIC SVC. ENTERPRISE GROUP	6,164.2	4.2	662.3	115	(2.5)	17,171.4	134	5,444.9	83
213	216	TRANSAMERICA	6,101.1	13.9	470.5	156	16.9	47,944.5	55	4,299.9	123
214	206	DILLARD DEPARTMENT STORES1	6,097.1	6.4	167.2	322	(33.6)	4,778.5	294	2,478.3	207
215	207	CHUBB	6,089.2	6.6	696.6	112	31.8	22,996.5	108	5,262.7	89
216	215	KEYCORP	6,054.0	12.7	825.0	79	(3.3)	66,339.1	40	5,152.5	93
217	326	ASSOCIATED INSURANCE	6,037.5	71.9	(98.0)	469	(586.9)	5,345.7	280	1,314.9	325
218	205	HALLIBURTON	5,951.3	3.7	168.3	320	(5.3)	3,646.6	329	1,749.8	265
219	250	MICROSOFT5	5,937.0	27.7	1,453.0	39	26.8	7,210.0	239	5,333.0	86
220	249	ARROW ELECTRONICS	5,919.4	27.3	202.5	304	81.0	2,701.0	379	1,195.9	341
221	137	AMERICAN BRANDS	5,904.9E	(30.0)	540.4	140	(26.4)	8,021.2	225	3,863.1	140
222	244	SUN MICROSYSTEMS5	5,901.9	25.8	335.8	212	71.5	3,544.6	333	2,122.6	230
223	236	UNION CARBIDE	5,888.0	21.0	925.0	70	137.8	6,256.0	251	2,045.0	241
224	209	JOHN HANCOCK MUTUAL LIFE INS.	5,845.5	6.0	340.8	209	86.6	54,505.1	48	2,533.5	203
225	232	TANDY	5,839.1	18.1	212.0	298	(5.5)	2,722.1	378	1,601.3	288
226	208	CONTINENTAL AIRLINES	5,825.0	2.7	224.0	286	–	4,821.0	292	305.0	457
227	227	MERISEL39	5,801.8	27.7	(9.2)	449	(135.2)	1,468.8	458	231.3	466
228	180	W.R. GRACE	5,784.2¶	12.6	(325.9)	479	(491.2)	6,297.6	250	1,231.8	336
229	271	BROWNING-FERRIS INDUSTRIES19	5,779.4	34.0	384.6	193	38.0	7,460.4	235	2,741.8	190
230	259	INGERSOLL-RAND40	5,729.0	27.1	270.3	247	28.0	5,563.3	270	1,795.5	260
231	211	AMERICAN ELECTRIC POWER	5,670.3	3.0	529.9	142	6.0	15,902.3	141	4,339.8	121
232	303	UNITED HEALTHCARE	5,670.0	50.4	286.0*	235	(82.8)	6,200.0	254	3,200.0	165
233	210	TEXAS UTILITIES	5,638.7	(0.4)	(138.6)	472	(125.5)	21,535.9	117	5,731.8	79
234	219	DRESSER INDUSTRIES6	5,628.7	5.6	197.1	306	(45.5)	4,707.4	298	1,656.8	277
235	223	ARAMARK19	5,600.6	8.5	93.5	377	8.6	2,599.7	386	252.3	464
236	212	FPL GROUP	5,592.5	3.1	553.3	136	6.7	12,459.2	178	4,392.5	118
237	280	CIRCUIT CITY STORES13	5,582.9	35.2	167.9	321	26.8	2,004.1	423	877.5	380
238	221	BLACK & DECKER	5,566.2¶	6.1	224.0*	284	75.8	5,545.4	271	1,423.2	314
239	225	TYSON FOODS19	5,511.2	7.8	219.2	291	–	4,444.3	304	1,467.7	307
240	286	LORAL18	5,484.4	36.8	288.4	233	26.3	4,810.3	293	1,687.5	271
241	273	MANPOWER	5,484.2	27.6	128.0	352	52.6	1,517.8	454	455.0	442
242	234	DUN & BRADSTREET	5,415.1	10.6	320.8	217	(49.0)	5,515.8	272	1,182.5	345
243	256	BANK OF BOSTON CORP.	5,410.6	19.0	541.0	139	24.4	47,397.0	56	3,751.0	144
244	243	ST. PAUL COS.	5,409.6	15.1	521.2	143	17.7	19,656.5	121	3,719.2	147
245	231	WELLS FARGO & CO.41	5,409.0	8.9	1,032.0	62	22.7	50,316.0	53	4,055.0	135
246	240	CORNING	5,346.1	11.4	(50.8)	462	(118.2)	5,987.1	260	2,103.0	233
247	275	BANK OF NEW YORK CO.	5,327.0	25.3	914.0	71	22.0	53,685.0	51	5,223.0	90
248	289	PAINE WEBBER GROUP	5,320.1	34.2	80.8	391	163.4	45,671.3	58	1,552.3	294
249	274	OFFICE DEPOT	5,313.2	24.5	132.4	351	26.1	2,531.2	389	1,003.0	369
250	330	DELL COMPUTER1	5,296.0	52.4	272.0	245	82.3	2,148.0	413	973.0	371

14

MARKET VALUE 3/15/96 $ MILLIONS	RANK	PROFITS AS % OF... REVENUES %	RANK	ASSETS %	RANK	STOCK-HOLDERS EQUITY %	RANK	EARNINGS PER SHARE 1995 $	% CHANGE FROM '94	1985-95 ANNUAL GROWTH RATE %	RANK	TOTAL RETURN TO INVESTORS 1995 %	RANK	1985-1995 ANNUAL RATE %	RANK	RANK 1995
5,677.0	210	4.6	260	5.5	177	13.7	248	1.95	11.4	7.2	169	35.9	211	11.7	247	201
7,295.7	166	8.4	135	0.9	396	9.4	351	2.64	7.8	4.1	209	28.1	265	11.9	241	202
1,114.3	420	(9.7)	488	(8.8)	482	(33.6)	469	(4.35)	–	–		(36.2)	442	(10.9)	379	203
7,312.8	165	11.3	72	5.2	194	11.8	310	2.93	(1.7)	3.2	218	32.2	230	12.2	235	204
9,938.2	119	6.4	189	0.6	419	7.1	381	1.19	(53.7)	(4.8)	290	61.4	63	11.5	255	205
4,616.9	242	12.6	53	16.6	11	69.9	6	5.97	255.4	20.3	39	16.0	333	12.9	216	206
7,099.2	169	2.3	360	1.7	344	5.0	405	N.A.	–	–		–		–		207
802.3	438	2.6	345	2.9	284	18.9	121	1.83	154.2	–		(29.8)	439	(18.8)	381	208
6,184.5	189	8.3	140	2.3	313	8.0	372	2.28	53.0	1.3	236	43.8	152	15.1	152	209
12,435.9	90	1.5	400	0.5	421	1.8	424	0.67	(84.7)	(22.0)	314	65.4	55	18.5	74	210
N.A.		2.0	371	0.8	402	11.2	321	N.A.	–	–		–		–		211
6,331.6	186	10.7	86	3.9	246	12.2	299	2.71	(2.5)	0.3	253	24.5	287	12.0	238	212
5,204.7	226	7.7	157	1.0	386	10.9	328	6.58	20.7	11.8	110	51.5	107	13.7	195	213
4,140.3	263	2.7	341	3.5	261	6.7	385	1.48	(33.6)	6.8	179	7.0	375	8.9	303	214
8,263.2	142	11.4	68	3.0	280	13.2	269	7.85	31.9	23.4	26	28.0	266	16.4	117	215
8,671.2	138	13.6	41	1.2	370	16.0	186	3.45	0.0	8.7	150	51.6	105	15.0	154	216
N.A.		(1.6)	463	(1.8)	461	(7.5)	450	N.A.	–	–		–		–		217
6,610.9	181	2.8	338	4.6	216	9.6	348	1.47	(5.8)	–		56.6	83	9.7	291	218
60,811.2	9	24.5	6	20.2	5	27.2	60	2.32	23.4	–		43.6	154	–		219
2,353.0	348	3.4	308	7.5	109	16.9	165	4.21	75.4	–		19.9	311	10.8	269	220
7,940.2	148	9.2	120	6.7	134	14.0	241	2.89	(20.4)	4.6	202	24.6	286	15.6	134	221
8,409.2	140	5.7	218	9.5	68	15.8	193	3.61	78.7	–		157.0	4	–		222
6,537.1	183	15.7	21	14.8	20	45.2	12	6.44	163.9	–		30.6	242	18.7	72	223
N.A.		5.8	209	0.6	415	13.5	261	N.A.	–	–		–		–		224
2,969.4	317	3.6	300	7.8	101	13.2	268	3.12	7.2	4.0	211	(15.8)	425	1.9	354	225
1,130.3	417	3.8	292	4.6	213	70.5	5	7.20	–	–		353.3	1	–		226
80.3	460	(0.2)	447	(0.6)	448	(4.0)	446	N.A.	–	–		(45.3)	446	–		227
7,808.2	156	(5.6)	481	(5.2)	476	(26.5)	465	(3.40)	(486.4)	–		56.1	84	14.1	186	228
6,725.6	176	6.7	180	5.2	195	14.0	238	1.93	29.5	9.2	141	5.7	378	8.6	306	229
4,492.4	247	4.7	254	4.9	205	15.1	209	2.55	27.5	12.9	97	13.8	345	15.7	133	230
7,544.5	159	9.3	116	3.3	265	12.2	295	2.85	5.2	2.7	224	32.0	233	14.1	185	231
11,106.6	104	5.0	240	4.6	218	8.9	355	1.57	(83.5)	38.6	13	45.0	145	38.3	4	232
8,836.0	136	(2.5)	472	(0.6)	449	(2.4)	438	(0.61)	(125.4)	–		40.4	175	12.5	228	233
5,198.2	227	3.5	304	4.2	234	11.9	307	1.08	(45.5)	–		33.0	226	14.2	181	234
N.A.		1.7	392	3.6	257	37.1	25	1.88	11.2	–		–		–		235
7,980.2	146	9.9	103	4.4	227	12.6	283	3.16	8.6	0.2	257	38.1	193	12.2	234	236
2,944.2	319	3.0	328	8.4	86	19.1	116	1.72	26.5	21.6	29	24.6	285	24.9	27	237
3,230.3	300	4.0	283	4.0	239	15.7	196	2.42	76.6	–		50.3	111	7.4	321	238
3,261.2	297	4.0	287	4.9	201	14.9	212	1.51	–	17.8	50	23.4	293	19.3	65	239
8,090.0	145	5.3	229	6.0	163	17.1	161	3.38	24.3	14.2	81	89.1	14	16.7	108	240
2,698.3	332	2.3	359	8.4	84	28.1	51	1.65	47.3	–		0.5	402	–		241
10,118.5	114	5.9	204	5.8	167	27.1	61	1.89	(48.9)	(0.3)	259	23.3	294	8.5	307	242
5,310.1	222	10.0	100	1.1	377	14.4	229	4.55	22.0	4.9	195	84.7	19	12.6	225	243
4,564.7	244	9.6	109	2.7	298	14.0	239	5.99	17.0	17.7	51	28.2	262	15.0	153	244
11,342.5	101	19.1	9	2.1	328	25.5	67	20.37	37.8	17.2	60	52.8	99	25.7	23	245
7,928.1	149	(1.0)	456	(0.8)	453	(2.4)	437	(0.23)	(117.4)	–		9.5	359	10.1	282	246
10,101.5	115	17.2	13	1.7	342	17.5	157	4.57	16.6	7.9	157	69.9	42	16.4	116	247
2,058.4	368	1.5	399	0.2	437	5.2	401	0.54	31.7	(1.1)	268	37.1	207	7.5	318	248
3,163.3	306	2.5	353	5.2	192	13.2	271	0.85	23.2	–		(16.6)	427	–		249
3,106.6	309	5.1	235	12.7	31	28.0	53	2.67	58.0	–		68.9	46	–		250

RANK 1995	1994	COMPANY	REVENUES $ MILLIONS	% CHANGE FROM '94	PROFITS $ MILLIONS	RANK	% CHANGE FROM '94	ASSETS $ MILLIONS	RANK	STOCK-HOLDERS' EQUITY $ MILLIONS	RANK
251	247	CONSOLIDATED FREIGHTWAYS	5,281.1	12.8	57.4	414	4.7	2,750.1	375	722.4	401
252	237	GENUINE PARTS	5,261.9	8.3	309.2	222	7.1	2,274.1	406	1,650.9	283
253	241	CUMMINS ENGINE	5,245.0	10.7	224.0	284	(11.4)	3,056.0	359	1,183.0	344
254	285	AMP	5,227.2	29.8	427.3	170	15.7	4,518.0	303	2,768.0	189
255	265	AMERICAN STANDARD	5,221.5	17.1	111.7*	368	–	3,519.6	334	(390.1)	487
256	224	MEAD	5,179.4	1.1	350.0	204	(49.7)	4,372.8	309	2,160.2	227
257	214	FOXMEYER HEALTH[18]	5,177.1	(4.3)	41.6	423	41.0	1,777.0	440	304.2	458
258	245	RYDER SYSTEM	5,167.4	10.3	147.7	337	(3.8)	5,893.8	261	1,240.0	333
259	248	SCHERING-PLOUGH	5,150.6	10.6	886.6	73	(3.8)	4,664.6	299	1,662.9	276
260	251	HOUSEHOLD INTERNATIONAL	5,144.4	11.8	453.2	163	23.3	29,218.8	86	2,895.9	185
261	•	CASE	5,105.0	15.9	337.0	211	157.3	5,469.0	273	1,520.0	301
262	373	BEST BUY[13]	5,079.6	69.0	57.7	412	39.6	1,507.1	455	376.1	452
263	228	VONS	5,070.7	1.5	68.1	405	156.0	2,186.5	409	623.3	419
264	230	VF	5,062.3	1.8	157.3	332	(42.7)	3,447.1	338	1,771.5	264
265	279	BOISE CASCADE	5,057.7	22.1	351.9	202	–	4,656.2	300	1,694.4	270
266	266	CROWN CORK & SEAL	5,053.8	13.5	74.9	396	(42.8)	5,051.7	287	1,461.2	308
267	269	EASTMAN CHEMICAL	5,040.0	16.4	559.0	134	66.4	4,854.0	289	1,528.0	299
268	255	ECKERD[1]	4,997.1	9.8	93.4	378	95.5	N.A.		N.A.	
269	252	PANENERGY[42]	4,967.5	8.3	303.6	223	34.8	7,627.3	233	2,227.3	223
270	293	LYONDELL PETROCHEMICAL	4,936.0	28.0	389.0	190	74.4	2,606.0	385	380.0	451
271	186	COOPER INDUSTRIES	4,885.9	(21.9)	94.0	376	–	6,063.9	258	1,716.4	266
272	239	BETHLEHEM STEEL	4,867.5	1.0	179.6	315	123.1	5,700.3	267	1,238.3	335
273	260	PACCAR	4,848.2	7.8	252.8	257	23.6	4,390.5	308	1,251.2	330
274	276	FIRST INTERSTATE BANCORP[43]	4,827.5	13.7	885.1	74	20.7	58,071.0	45	4,154.0	129
275	261	INLAND STEEL INDUSTRIES	4,781.5	6.3	146.8	339	36.7	3,558.3	331	748.6	393
276	264	MASCO	4,779.0	7.0	(441.7)	483	(328.0)	3,778.6	327	1,655.4	280
277	301	NIKE[7]	4,760.8	25.6	399.7	183	33.8	3,142.7	353	1,964.7	248
278	355	LEAR SEATING	4,714.4	49.8	91.6	382	53.2	3,061.3	358	580.0	424
279	308	HUMANA	4,702.0	28.7	190.0	309	8.0	2,878.0	366	1,287.0	327
280	263	DUKE POWER	4,676.7	4.2	714.5	107	11.8	13,358.5	167	5,469.2	82
281	284	BINDLEY WESTERN	4,672.5	15.7	16.4	440	11.2	844.1	482	200.8	469
282	272	AMERISOURCE HEALTH[44]	4,668.9	8.5	10.2*	442	–	838.7	483	(135.7)	484
283	253	NORFOLK SOUTHERN	4,668.0	1.9	712.7	108	6.7	10,904.8	189	4,829.0	104
284	343	THRIFTY PAYLESS HOLDINGS[19]	4,658.8	39.2	(34.7)*	459	(396.6)	2,094.0	418	161.4	475
285	262	DOMINION RESOURCES	4,651.7	3.6	425.0	171	(11.1)	13,903.3	162	4,742.0	105
286	277	AON[†]	4,610.7	10.9	403.0	181	11.9	19,736.0	120	2,674.0	195
287	281	FMC[†]	4,566.6	12.7	215.6	294	24.3	4,301.1	315	653.4	408
288	328	SEAGATE TECHNOLOGY[5,45,†]	4,539.6	29.7	260.1	253	15.5	3,361.3	341	1,541.8	296
289	349	TYCO INTERNATIONAL[5,†]	4,534.7	39.0	214.0	297	71.8	3,381.5	340	1,634.7	285
290	268	RITE AID[13,†]	4,533.9	4.7	141.3	341	1,421.2	2,472.6	393	1,011.8	366
291	291	MELLON BANK CORP.[†]	4,514.0	14.1	691.0	113	59.6	40,129.0	64	4,106.0	132
292	270	AVON PRODUCTS[†]	4,492.1	3.9	256.5	255	31.0	2,052.8	420	192.7	470
293	295	BERKSHIRE HATHAWAY[46,†]	4,487.7	16.6	725.2	104	46.6	29,928.8	83	17,217.1	12
294	296	TJX[1,†]	4,447.5	15.7	26.3*	431	(68.2)	2,745.6	376	764.6	389
295	449	REVCO D.S.[7,†]	4,431.9	77.0	58.3	411	50.6	2,157.0	411	773.1	388
296	339	H.F. AHMANSON[†]	4,397.5	30.1	216.2	293	(8.9)	50,529.6	52	3,056.9	173
297	305	GAP[1,†]	4,395.3	18.1	354.0	200	10.6	2,343.1	399	1,640.5	284
298	287	HOUSTON INDUSTRIES[†]	4,388.4	9.7	1,124.0	56	181.5	11,819.6	184	4,123.6	131
299	320	AVNET[5,†]	4,300.0	21.0	140.3	342	64.4	2,125.6	415	1,239.4	334
300	258	LTV[†]	4,283.2	(5.4)	184.8	311	45.4	5,380.1	278	1,375.2	322

MARKET VALUE 3/15/96 $ MILLIONS		PROFITS AS % OF... REVENUES		ASSETS		STOCK-HOLDERS EQUITY		EARNINGS PER SHARE 1995 $		1985-95 ANNUAL GROWTH RATE		TOTAL RETURN TO INVESTORS 1995		1985-1995 ANNUAL RATE		RANK 1995
1,170.0	413	1.1	415	2.1	321	7.9	373	1.10	14.6	(6.1)	295	20.5	309	1.7	356	251
5,450.8	216	5.9	207	13.6	22	18.7	125	2.52	8.2	9.3	140	17.6	323	12.7	220	252
1,663.3	389	4.3	272	7.3	115	18.9	119	5.52	(9.7)	7.7	160	(16.2)	426	2.9	351	253
9,348.2	128	8.2	145	9.5	70	15.4	202	1.96	11.4	14.6	78	7.6	373	10.5	277	254
2,192.7	354	2.1	365	3.2	270	–		1.50	–	–		–		–		255
2,823.7	324	6.8	177	8.0	94	16.2	182	6.33	(43.5)	15.4	75	9.5	360	11.5	253	256
267.9	451	0.8	424	2.3	312	7.4	378	1.52	38.2	–		85.0	18	0.5	358	257
2,168.4	358	2.9	336	2.5	305	11.9	306	1.86	(4.6)	0.7	244	15.4	338	4.8	341	258
21,126.7	51	17.2	12	19.0	7	53.3	10	2.40	(0.4)	17.7	52	51.8	104	25.5	24	259
6,536.9	184	8.8	126	1.6	349	15.6	198	4.31	22.4	9.0	145	64.4	59	17.6	88	260
3,795.0	279	6.6	182	6.2	156	21.7	89	4.60	–	–		114.3	5	–		261
779.1	440	1.1	412	3.8	248	15.3	204	1.33	166.0	35.4	15	(48.0)	448	17.6	90	262
1,355.9	402	1.3	403	3.1	275	10.9	329	1.55	154.1	–		56.9	80	–		263
3,594.2	288	3.1	321	4.6	221	8.6	361	2.41	(42.6)	0.7	245	11.5	351	10.4	278	264
2,027.6	371	7.0	171	7.6	108	20.8	99	5.93	–	11.1	121	31.2	239	5.5	336	265
6,091.8	190	1.5	401	1.5	355	5.1	402	0.83	(43.5)	1.4	235	10.6	355	15.4	143	266
5,743.3	206	11.1	76	11.5	43	36.6	26	6.78	67.4	–		27.1	273	–		267
1,634.1	390	1.9	381	–		–		2.73	85.7	–		49.4	118	–		268
4,391.2	252	6.1	197	4.0	241	13.6	252	2.03	34.4	(3.3)	280	46.2	132	9.4	295	269
2,520.0	339	7.9	153	14.9	19	102.4	4	4.86	74.8	–		(8.3)	416	–		270
4,018.3	268	1.9	379	1.6	350	5.5	397	0.84	–	(4.9)	291	12.0	350	9.1	301	271
1,548.0	396	3.7	299	3.2	272	14.5	227	1.24	254.3	–		(22.9)	432	(0.5)	364	272
1,913.9	376	5.2	232	5.8	169	20.2	107	6.50	23.6	14.0	84	1.5	398	12.1	236	273
12,138.0	96	18.3	10	1.5	352	21.3	93	11.02	26.5	4.9	196	108.5	7	15.6	135	274
1,255.9	409	3.1	323	4.1	235	18.4	137	2.69	48.6	–		(28.1)	437	2.2	352	275
4,777.6	236	(9.2)	487	(11.7)	485	(26.7)	466	(2.77)	(327.0)	–		42.4	159	6.9	325	276
11,405.5	100	8.4	134	12.7	30	20.3	105	5.44	37.4	44.7	7	88.8	15	36.8	6	277
1,827.7	382	1.9	377	3.0	283	15.8	195	1.74	–	–		46.8	129	–		278
3,885.3	274	4.0	282	6.6	139	14.8	219	1.17	6.4	(2.2)	275	21.0	301	10.8	270	279
9,884.4	120	15.3	24	5.3	187	13.1	275	3.25	12.8	5.7	190	30.3	245	16.3	120	280
187.9	454	0.4	435	1.9	331	8.2	368	1.42	6.0	6.0	186	10.2	357	6.3	328	281
698.4	442	0.2	440	1.2	374	–		0.56	–	–		–		–		282
11,014.1	106	15.3	25	6.5	142	14.8	220	5.44	11.0	7.5	165	34.8	219	15.3	145	283
N.A.		(0.7)	455	(1.7)	458	(21.5)	462	N.A.	–	–		–		–		284
6,717.3	177	9.1	121	3.1	278	9.0	354	2.45	(12.8)	0.2	255	22.6	296	13.1	210	285
5,617.5	212	11.6	63	2.0	329	15.1	208	3.48	10.8	6.7	181	61.4	64	15.8	132	286
2,706.3	330	4.7	252	5.0	199	33.0	31	5.72	22.7	(2.7)	278	17.1	324	18.2	79	287
5,888.1	195	5.7	214	7.7	103	16.9	166	3.52	14.3	67.7	3	97.9	10	20.7	48	288
5,452.1	215	4.7	253	6.3	150	13.1	274	2.83	4.8	11.7	112	51.1	108	20.7	45	289
2,722.1	328	3.1	319	5.7	173	14.0	242	1.67	1,418.2	7.0	175	50.4	110	13.0	214	290
7,476.7	161	15.3	23	1.7	340	16.8	168	4.50	86.0	(1.0)	266	83.8	20	9.6	293	291
5,895.9	194	5.7	215	12.5	33	133.1	2	3.76	35.7	–		30.2	247	16.0	130	292
43,879.5	18	16.2	18	2.4	310	4.2	412	611.00	45.5	4.9	198	57.4	78	29.4	11	293
1,892.2	378	0.6	431	1.0	391	3.4	419	0.23	(77.7)	(17.7)	311	25.9	277	3.4	348	294
1,867.2	380	1.3	406	2.7	292	7.5	376	0.91	18.2	–		19.6	313	–		295
2,702.1	331	4.9	245	0.4	423	7.1	382	1.40	(11.9)	(6.1)	294	70.9	40	9.9	286	296
7,912.2	151	8.1	149	15.1	17	21.6	91	2.46	11.8	28.4	22	39.6	182	28.4	13	297
5,746.0	205	25.6	5	9.5	66	27.3	59	4.54	179.4	7.5	164	46.1	134	14.6	167	298
2,067.9	367	3.3	316	6.6	140	11.3	320	3.32	58.9	9.1	143	22.6	295	4.7	342	299
1,380.0	401	4.3	271	3.4	262	13.4	262	1.71	32.6	–		(16.7)	428	–		300

Rank 1995	1994	COMPANY	REVENUES $ MILLIONS	% CHANGE FROM '94	PROFITS $ MILLIONS	RANK	% CHANGE FROM '94	ASSETS $ MILLIONS	RANK	STOCK-HOLDERS' EQUITY $ MILLIONS	RANK
301	338	UNION CAMP†	4,211.7	24.0	451.1	165	297.4	4,838.3	290	2,121.7	231
302	283	PECO ENERGY†	4,186.2	3.6	609.7	124	42.9	14,960.6	149	5,032.7	98
303	346	PHELPS DODGE†	4,185.4	27.2	746.6	94	175.5	4,645.9	301	2,677.7	194
304	162	SUPERMARKETS GENL. HOLDINGS[1,†]	4,182.1	(6.6)	75.5	395	1,613.2	N.A.		N.A.	
305	297	DOLE FOOD†	4,152.8	8.1	23.3	434	(65.6)	2,442.2	394	508.4	437
306	331	ILLINOIS TOOL WORKS†	4,152.2	20.0	387.6	192	39.5	3,613.1	330	1,924.2	251
307	288	MUTUAL OF OMAHA INSURANCE†	4,134.3	3.8	70.7	401	(12.6)	10,663.4	191	1,326.8	324
308	314	UNUM†	4,122.9	13.8	281.1	238	81.7	14,787.8	151	2,302.9	216
309	302	STOP & SHOP[1,†]	4,116.1	8.6	67.9*	406	(6.7)	N.A.		N.A.	
310	292	NORDSTROM[1,†]	4,113.5	5.6	165.1	325	(18.6)	2,733.0	377	1,423.0	315
311	351	JEFFERSON SMURFIT†	4,093.0	26.6	243.1	268	–	2,783.3	371	(487.2)	488
312	499	FIRST DATA[47,†]	4,081.2	84.9	(84.2)	466	(152.6)	12,217.8	181	3,145.1	170
313	290	CHIQUITA BRANDS INTERNATIONAL†	4,026.6	1.6	9.2*	443	–	2,623.5	383	672.2	406
314	282	SERVICE MERCHANDISE†	4,018.5	(0.8)	50.3	416	(10.4)	1,940.6	431	386.7	450
315	299	GANNETT†	4,006.7	4.8	477.3	155	2.5	6,503.8	244	2,145.6	228
316	310	WABAN[1,†]	3,978.4	9.0	73.0	400	12.3	1,332.5	467	555.1	427
317	278	NIAGARA MOHAWK POWER†	3,917.3	(5.7)	248.0	263	40.1	9,477.9	210	2,954.0	179
318	365	STUDENT LOAN MARKETING ASSN.†	3,916.6	28.1	496.4	150	23.2	48,920.5	54	1,081.2	358
319	455	FHP INTERNATIONAL[5,†]	3,909.4	58.1	37.3	424	(37.1)	2,315.8	401	1,140.1	351
320	329	AIR PRODUCTS & CHEMICALS[19,†]	3,891.0	11.7	368.2	196	48.6	5,816.0	264	2,398.0	211
321	316	CMS ENERGY†	3,890.0	7.5	204.0	302	14.0	8,143.0	224	1,469.0	306
322	323	ROHM & HAAS†	3,884.0	9.9	292.0	231	10.6	3,916.0	323	1,781.0	263
323	372	WILLAMETTE INDUSTRIES†	3,873.6	28.8	514.8	146	189.8	3,413.6	339	1,846.9	257
324	300	PITNEY BOWES†	3,861.2	1.0	583.1	129	112.8	7,844.6	227	2,071.1	239
325	311	GENERAL PUBLIC UTILITIES†	3,804.7	4.3	440.1	168	168.9	9,869.7	203	2,974.6	177
326	336	MARSH & MCLENNAN†	3,770.3	9.8	402.9	182	8.5	4,329.5	310	1,665.5	274
327	309	OWENS-ILLINOIS†	3,763.2	3.0	169.1	319	116.0	5,439.2	275	531.9	431
328	382	WACHOVIA CORP.†	3,755.4	26.4	602.5	127	11.8	44,981.3	59	3,773.8	142
329	335	BEAR STEARNS[5,†]	3,753.6	9.1	240.6	271	(37.8)	74,597.2	35	2,352.5	215
330	312	NORTHEAST UTILITIES†	3,749.0	2.9	282.4	236	(1.5)	10,545.0	196	2,423.6	210
331	361	DOVER†	3,745.9	21.4	278.3	241	37.5	2,666.7	382	1,227.7	338
332	350	SUNTRUST BANKS†	3,740.3	15.0	565.5	132	8.2	46,471.5	57	4,269.6	127
333	315	CENTRAL & SOUTH WEST†	3,735.0	3.1	420.8	173	2.0	13,869.0	163	3,470.0	156
334	390	PACIFICARE HEALTH SYSTEMS[19,†]	3,731.0	29.0	108.1	370	19.8	1,385.4	464	732.0	399
335	321	SAFECO†	3,722.7	4.8	399.0	184	26.9	18,767.8	125	3,982.6	138
336	318	GIANT FOOD[13,†]	3,695.6	3.6	94.2	375	(1.1)	1,416.7	461	755.5	392
337	317	HERSHEY FOODS†	3,690.7	2.3	281.9	237	53.0	2,830.6	369	1,083.0	357
338	304	CONRAIL†	3,686.0	(1.3)	264.0	248	(18.5)	8,424.0	218	2,977.0	176
339	360	BARNETT BANKS†	3,680.0	18.8	533.3	141	9.3	41,553.5	63	3,272.2	163
340	421	GATEWAY 2000†	3,676.3	36.1	173.0	316	80.2	1,124.0	471	555.5	426
341	•	NGC†	3,665.9	14.7	92.7	379	120.2	1,902.5	433	552.4	428
342	498	WORLDCOM[48,†]	3,640.0	63.9	234.5	277	–	N.A.		N.A.	
343	354	MATTEL†	3,638.8	13.5	357.8	198	39.9	2,695.5	380	1,275.2	328
344	325	DTE ENERGY[49,†]	3,635.5	3.3	405.9	179	(3.3)	11,130.6	188	3,436.3	157
345	•	AMERICAN FINANCIAL GROUP[50,†]	3,629.6	105.4	191.2	308	–	14,953.9	150	1,440.1	310
346	342	OWENS-CORNING†	3,612.0	7.8	231.0	280	45.3	3,261.0	345	(212.0)	485
347	322	DIAL†	3,575.1	0.8	(16.6)	451	(111.8)	4,225.2	318	548.2	430
348	333	PREMARK INTERNATIONAL[1,†]	3,573.6	3.6	237.6	274	5.4	1,961.3	428	1,008.8	367
349	•	CIRCLE K[31,†]	3,565.6	7.4	18.7*	438	(10.9)	1,019.0	474	262.8	463
350	374	GREAT WESTERN FINANCIAL CORP.†	3,556.4	18.6	261.0	251	3.9	44,586.8	60	2,822.5	186

DEFINITIONS, EXPLANATIONS, AND FOOTNOTES ARE FOUND ON PAGE 26

MARKET VALUE 3/15/96 $ MILLIONS	Rank	PROFITS AS % OF... REVENUES	Rank	ASSETS	Rank	STOCKHOLDERS EQUITY	Rank	EPS 1995 $	% Chg.	1985-95 ANNUAL GROWTH RATE	Rank	TOTAL RETURN TO INVESTORS 1995	Rank	1985-1995 ANNUAL RATE	Rank	RANK 1995
3,607.4	287	10.7	89	9.3	75	21.3	95	6.45	298.1	17.4	56	4.3	383	9.7	289	301
5,859.8	198	14.6	33	4.1	237	12.0	304	2.64	50.0	0.3	252	30.4	243	14.2	180	302
4,643.8	240	17.8	11	16.1	12	27.9	55	10.65	179.5	42.7	9	3.7	388	23.5	32	303
N.A.		1.8	385	–		–		N.A.	–	–		–		–		304
2,557.9	337	0.6	432	1.0	392	4.6	407	0.39	(65.8)	–		76.6	32	12.7	223	305
7,861.4	155	9.3	117	10.7	49	20.1	110	3.29	34.3	26.5	23	36.5	210	22.6	37	306
N.A.		1.7	389	0.7	412	5.3	398	N.A.	–	–		–		–		307
4,266.7	259	6.8	173	1.9	333	12.2	296	3.87	85.2	–		49.0	119	–		308
1,329.8	404	1.7	393	–		–		1.30	(7.1)	–		(9.3)	419	–		309
4,007.9	269	4.0	284	6.0	160	11.6	317	2.02	(18.2)	12.0	107	(2.4)	408	14.1	183	310
1,262.5	408	5.9	203	8.7	81	–		2.19	–	–		(44.1)	445	–		311
15,742.7	70	(2.1)	470	(0.7)	451	(2.7)	439	(0.39)	(115.2)	–		63.3	61	27.5	18	312
833.5	436	0.2	439	0.4	426	1.4	427	0.02	–	(28.2)	318	2.4	393	5.8	334	313
560.7	446	1.3	408	2.6	302	13.0	276	0.50	(9.1)	16.0	71	2.6	392	7.5	317	314
9,604.1	124	11.9	62	7.3	114	22.2	85	3.41	5.6	8.0	156	18.2	320	10.1	283	315
857.5	435	1.8	383	5.5	179	13.1	273	2.20	12.8	–		4.9	382	–		316
974.2	429	6.3	191	2.6	300	8.1	369	1.44	44.0	(6.7)	297	(27.2)	435	(1.7)	366	317
5,252.2	225	12.7	51	1.0	383	45.9	11	7.20	46.6	11.4	115	109.5	6	7.7	314	318
1,315.5	405	1.0	419	1.6	347	3.3	420	0.29	(83.0)	–		10.7	354	–		319
6,988.8	170	9.5	112	6.3	149	15.4	203	3.29	50.9	10.7	125	20.6	308	15.2	146	320
2,597.2	334	5.2	231	2.5	306	13.9	245	2.27	8.6	–		35.4	215	16.7	111	321
4,676.9	238	7.5	162	7.5	110	16.4	178	4.22	11.3	7.7	159	15.7	335	12.8	218	322
3,258.2	298	13.3	44	15.1	18	27.9	56	9.34	189.2	22.9	28	20.8	303	16.7	109	323
7,390.3	164	15.1	27	7.4	111	28.2	50	3.83	120.1	15.0	77	52.5	101	17.2	96	324
3,799.5	278	11.6	64	4.5	226	14.8	215	3.79	166.9	17.3	59	37.7	195	20.3	52	325
6,822.1	173	10.7	90	9.3	76	24.2	74	5.53	9.5	9.5	136	16.2	331	11.9	240	326
1,882.9	379	4.5	264	3.1	276	31.8	34	1.40	118.8	–		31.8	234	–		327
7,623.6	157	16.0	19	1.3	362	16.0	188	3.50	11.8	9.1	142	46.9	128	16.4	119	328
2,781.9	326	6.4	187	0.3	428	10.2	337	1.70	(38.2)	–		39.9	180	13.1	211	329
2,626.5	333	7.5	161	2.7	295	11.7	313	2.24	(2.6)	(1.9)	274	21.0	302	12.1	237	330
5,395.0	218	7.4	163	10.4	51	22.7	83	2.45	38.4	13.2	93	45.2	144	16.4	118	331
7,922.5	150	15.1	26	1.2	373	13.2	267	4.94	13.0	11.5	113	46.9	127	17.0	101	332
5,553.2	213	11.3	73	3.0	279	12.1	302	2.10	1.0	1.5	234	31.8	237	14.7	164	333
3,038.0	313	2.9	335	7.8	100	14.8	218	3.62	12.4	21.2	33	31.8	234	26.0	22	334
4,408.9	251	10.7	88	2.1	319	10.0	342	3.17	27.1	10.3	131	37.5	201	15.4	141	335
1,893.7	377	2.5	349	6.6	137	12.5	288	1.59	(0.6)	7.6	162	48.6	122	11.7	249	336
5,699.6	208	7.6	160	10.0	58	26.0	64	3.40	60.4	11.0	122	37.6	198	17.0	99	337
6,072.4	191	7.2	167	3.1	274	8.9	357	3.19	(18.2)	–		42.3	160	–		338
5,774.9	201	14.5	34	1.3	366	16.3	181	5.30	10.6	7.2	171	59.0	73	10.8	267	339
2,033.7	370	4.7	255	15.4	15	31.1	36	2.19	79.5	–		13.3	349	–		340
1,205.9	410	2.5	350	4.9	203	16.8	169	0.82	–	–		–		–		341
8,159.7	143	6.4	186	–		–		1.30	–	–		81.4	24	–		342
7,557.2	158	9.8	106	13.3	25	28.1	52	1.26	40.6	12.5	102	54.4	93	22.6	38	343
4,843.4	235	11.2	75	3.6	254	11.8	311	2.80	4.9	1.9	232	41.7	165	17.0	102	344
1,789.1	383	5.3	228	1.3	367	13.3	264	3.87	–	10.9	124	20.8	304	6.0	329	345
2,184.1	355	6.4	188	7.1	123	–		4.64	28.5	0.5	248	40.8	172	23.5	33	346
2,775.0	327	(0.5)	451	(0.4)	446	(3.2)	443	(0.20)	(112.4)	–		43.0	155	12.4	229	347
3,206.0	303	6.6	181	12.1	38	23.6	77	3.72	9.7	–		15.4	339	–		348
725.9	441	0.5	433	1.8	335	7.1	380	0.97	–	–		–		–		349
3,091.8	310	7.3	164	0.6	417	9.2	352	1.72	1.8	(1.5)	270	65.3	57	11.3	260	350

RANK 1995	1994	COMPANY	REVENUES $ MILLIONS	% CHANGE FROM '94	PROFITS $ MILLIONS	RANK	% CHANGE FROM '94	ASSETS $ MILLIONS	RANK	STOCK-HOLDERS' EQUITY $ MILLIONS	RANK
351	307	GENERAL DYNAMICS†	3,544.0¶	(4.3)	321.0	216	34.9	3,164.0	352	1,567.0	293
352	344	PENN TRAFFIC[1,†]	3,536.6	6.1	(79.6)	465	(702.8)	N.A.		N.A.	
353	381	U.S. HEALTHCARE†	3,517.8	18.3	380.7	194	(2.7)	1,667.1	445	964.1	372
354	435	FOOD 4 LESS HOLDINGS[39,†]	3,494.0	–	(216.0)	476	–	3,107.0	355	(73.1)	482
355	294	TIMES MIRROR†	3,491.0	(9.5)	1,226.8	51	608.6	3,817.2	326	1,806.2	259
356	347	REEBOK INTERNATIONAL†	3,481.5	5.9	164.8	327	(35.2)	1,656.2	448	895.3	379
357	345	HARRIS[5,†]	3,480.9	3.3	154.5	334	38.2	2,836.0	368	1,248.8	331
358	358	INTELLIGENT ELECTRONICS[52,53,†]	3,474.6	11.1	(19.0)	453	(181.8)	894.2	478	183.3	471
359	379	NUCOR†	3,462.0	16.3	274.5	244	21.1	2,296.1	404	1,382.1	320
360	387	TEMPLE-INLAND†	3,460.0	17.8	281.0	239	114.5	12,764.0	171	1,975.0	247
361	352	USF&G†	3,458.8	7.4	209.4	300	12.6	14,650.9	152	1,716.1	267
362	389	NATIONAL CITY CORP.†	3,449.9	18.7	465.1	158	8.3	36,199.0	71	2,921.0	183
363	402	TURNER BROADCASTING†	3,437.0	22.4	103.0	373	386.8	4,395.4	307	437.7	443
364	357	FRED MEYER[1,†]	3,428.7	9.6	30.3	429	322.5	1,671.6	443	571.2	425
365	327	PACIFICORP†	3,400.9	(3.0)	505.0	149	7.9	14,015.2	159	3,944.6	139
366	385	PROVIDIAN†	3,388.0	14.5	345.0	208	16.1	26,839.0	90	2,961.0	178
367	436	COMPUTER SCIENCES[18,†]	3,372.5	30.6	110.7	369	15.6	2,333.7	400	1,148.6	349
368	•	QUANTUM[18]	3,368.0	58.0	81.6	390	2,951.3	1,481.0	457	509.5	436
369	•	COMCAST[54,†]	3,362.9	144.5	(43.9)*	461	–	9,580.3	207	(827.7)	490
370	394	MORTON INTERNATIONAL[5]	3,354.9	17.7	294.1	230	29.8	2,756.0	374	1,663.5	275
371	470	FIRST BANK SYSTEM	3,328.3	40.1	568.1	131	35.3	33,874.0	76	2,725.0	191
372	257	LITTON INDUSTRIES[33]	3,319.7	(26.8)	135.0	347	–	2,559.6	387	758.1	390
373	334	TENET HEALTHCARE[7,55]	3,318.0	(3.6)	165.0	326	–	7,918.0	226	1,986.0	244
374	337	TRANS WORLD AIRLINES	3,316.8	(2.7)	(227.5)**	477	–	N.A.		N.A.	
375	364	MAPCO	3,310.0	8.2	74.7	397	(5.6)	2,293.3	405	642.3	409
376	368	CONSOLIDATED NATURAL GAS	3,307.3	8.9	21.3	437	(88.3)	5,418.3	276	2,045.8	240
377	431	WESTVACO[6]	3,302.7	26.4	280.8	240	171.1	4,252.7	317	2,080.6	236
378	428	TURNER CORP.	3,281.5	24.4	1.3	444	(65.1)	792.9	487	61.3	480
379	380	UNIVERSAL[5]	3,280.9	10.3	25.6	432	180.0	1,808.0	438	390.0	449
380	353	CENTEX[18]	3,277.5	2.0	92.2	380	8.3	2,049.7	421	668.2	407
381	369	W.W. GRAINGER	3,276.9	8.4	186.7	310	46.0	1,662.7	447	1,179.1	347
382	359	SHERWIN-WILLIAMS	3,273.8	5.6	200.7	305	7.5	2,141.1	414	1,212.1	339
383	313	HARCOURT GENERAL[6]	3,241.9	(10.9)	165.9	324	(6.6)	2,884.3	365	941.1	375
384	348	ALLMERICA FINANCIAL	3,238.9	(1.1)	133.9	348	229.3	17,757.7	130	1,574.2	292
385	377	BEVERLY ENTERPRISES	3,228.6	8.2	(8.1)	448	(110.9)	2,506.5	390	820.3	384
386	437	PARKER HANNIFIN[5]	3,214.4	24.8	218.2	292	358.0	2,302.2	402	1,191.5	343
387	407	CYPRUS AMAX MINERALS	3,207.0	15.0	124.0	357	(29.1)	6,196.0	255	2,365.0	213
388	376	SERVICEMASTER	3,202.5	7.3	105.9[56]	371	24.5	1,649.9	449	746.7	394
389	•	ASARCO	3,197.8	57.4	169.2	318	164.2	4,326.7	311	1,707.5	268
390	•	PACIFIC MUTUAL LIFE INS.	3,160.5	12.6	85.1	386	5.1	22,221.6	112	723.3	400
391	356	SOUTHERN PACIFIC RAIL	3,151.3	0.3	(3.4)	446	(101.4)	4,749.4	295	1,060.9	359
392	426	OLIN	3,149.5	18.5	139.9	344	53.7	2,272.0	407	841.0	382
393	419	PRAXAIR[57]	3,146.0	16.0	262.0	250	29.1	4,134.0	320	1,121.0	352
394	393	AVERY DENNISON	3,113.9	9.0	143.7	340	31.4	1,963.6	427	815.8	385
395	443	COMERICA	3,112.6	21.7	413.4	175	6.7	35,469.9	73	2,607.7	200
396	384	ALLTEL	3,109.7	5.0	354.6	199	30.5	5,073.1	284	1,935.6	250
397	•	WELLPOINT HEALTH NETWORKS	3,107.1	11.3	180.0	314	(15.6)	2,679.3	381	1,670.2	273
398	464	TECH DATA	3,086.6	27.6	21.5	436	(38.3)	1,043.9	472	285.7	461
399	378	SMITH'S FOOD & DRUG CENTERS	3,083.7¶	3.4	(40.5)	460	(183.0)	1,686.2	442	416.7	446
400	488	FOSTER WHEELER	3,081.9	35.7	28.5	430	(56.4)	2,775.8	372	625.9	416

MARKET VALUE 3/15/96 $ MILLIONS		PROFITS AS % OF... REVENUES		ASSETS		STOCK-HOLDERS EQUITY		EARNINGS PER SHARE 1995 $	(1994–95 change)	1985-95 ANNUAL GROWTH RATE		TOTAL RETURN TO INVESTORS 1995		1985-1995 ANNUAL RATE		RANK 1995
3,731.6	281	9.1	123	10.1	52	20.5	103	5.10	36.0	1.2	239	40.1	177	13.4	206	351
169.4	456	(2.3)	471	–		–		(7.32)	(720.3)	–		(60.5)	451	–		352
7,177.6	167	10.8	83	22.8	3	39.5	21	2.42	0.0	32.0	19	15.8	334	28.3	14	353
N.A.		(6.2)	483	(7.0)	479	–		N.A.	–			–		–		354
4,003.3	270	35.1	2	32.1	1	67.9	7	10.02	–			–		–		355
2,182.3	356	4.7	250	10.0	59	18.4	138	2.07	(31.5)	16.4	67	(27.9)	436	21.2	42	356
2,578.0	336	4.4	266	5.4	181	12.4	291	3.95	40.1	7.0	176	31.7	238	10.6	273	357
215.9	453	(0.5)	452	(2.1)	465	(10.4)	454	N.A.	–			(21.6)	430	–		358
5,390.5	219	7.9	151	12.0	40	19.9	111	3.14	20.8	16.4	66	3.7	386	21.1	43	359
2,545.4	338	8.1	146	2.2	317	14.2	234	5.01	113.2	13.6	89	(0.4)	404	11.8	245	360
1,741.5	386	6.1	202	1.4	357	12.2	297	1.63	(23.8)	–		25.4	282	(3.1)	371	361
4,912.2	233	13.5	43	1.3	365	15.9	189	3.03	12.2	7.2	172	33.9	224	16.9	104	362
5,828.3	199	3.0	329	2.3	311	23.5	78	0.36	350.0	36.0	14	58.5	75	23.6	30	363
794.4	439	0.9	421	1.8	336	5.3	399	1.07	328.0	–		(26.8)	434	–		364
5,756.6	204	14.8	30	3.6	256	12.4	290	1.64	8.6	(0.5)	263	23.4	292	10.2	281	365
4,141.7	262	10.2	97	1.3	364	11.7	314	3.60	19.2	10.6	129	35.1	218	13.5	203	366
3,976.5	271	3.3	314	4.7	208	9.6	347	2.09	12.4	12.0	105	37.7	194	20.2	53	367
1,027.0	427	2.4	355	5.5	178	16.0	185	1.72	2,766.7	13.5	91	6.6	376	10.5	275	368
4,340.1	254	(1.3)	460	(0.5)	447	–		(0.18)	–			16.5	325	–		369
5,680.2	209	8.8	128	10.7	50	17.7	153	1.96	289.4	–		27.8	269	–		370
8,304.0	141	17.1	14	1.7	345	20.8	97	4.19	17.4	4.0	213	54.3	94	14.3	179	371
2,260.1	352	4.1	281	5.3	189	17.8	149	2.84	–	(2.4)	276	20.3	310	5.3	339	372
4,260.1	260	5.0	241	2.1	322	8.3	365	0.93	–	(0.6)	264	46.0	135	9.3	297	373
N.A.		(6.9)	484	–		–		(1.05)	–			–		–		374
1,629.8	391	2.3	362	3.3	268	11.6	315	2.41	(8.7)	3.0	220	8.5	367	13.3	207	375
4,026.8	267	0.6	429	0.4	424	1.0	428	0.23	(88.3)	(21.5)	313	34.4	221	10.7	272	376
3,144.2	308	8.5	132	6.6	138	13.5	258	2.78	169.0	9.9	134	9.0	361	11.6	252	377
47.6	463	0.0	444	0.2	438	2.1	422	(0.11)	(131.4)	–		1.5	396	(7.3)	376	378
950.5	430	0.8	425	1.4	358	6.6	386	0.73	180.8	(5.9)	293	28.4	256	12.0	239	379
817.1	437	2.8	339	4.5	224	13.8	246	3.04	16.9	10.7	127	53.9	95	11.6	251	380
3,496.4	289	5.7	217	11.2	45	15.8	192	3.64	45.6	11.4	114	16.4	327	14.8	157	381
3,709.6	284	6.1	196	9.4	73	16.6	172	2.34	8.8	11.3	118	24.2	289	16.0	128	382
3,351.2	293	5.1	237	5.8	170	17.6	154	2.16	(2.7)	6.4	185	20.8	305	10.9	266	383
1,272.2	406	4.1	277	0.8	405	8.5	362	N.A.	–			–		–		384
1,119.9	419	(0.3)	449	(0.3)	444	(1.0)	434	(0.16)	(121.1)	–		(26.1)	433	(4.9)	372	385
2,790.4	325	6.8	174	9.5	67	18.3	140	2.96	353.1	8.1	155	15.4	337	10.2	280	386
2,590.9	335	3.9	290	2.0	330	5.2	400	1.13	(33.1)	–		3.0	390	11.5	254	387
3,017.2	314	3.3	312	6.4	146	14.2	236	2.17	19.9	17.2	61	28.8	253	18.1	81	388
1,423.6	399	5.3	226	3.9	244	9.9	343	4.00	161.4	–		14.8	342	8.9	304	389
N.A.		2.7	343	0.4	425	11.8	312	N.A.	–			–		–		390
3,864.4	276	(0.1)	446	(0.1)	442	(0.3)	433	(0.02)	(101.3)	–		32.4	229	–		391
2,158.9	360	4.4	265	6.2	157	16.6	171	5.50	50.7	–		50.1	112	11.7	248	392
5,420.0	217	8.3	137	6.3	148	23.4	80	1.82	25.5	–		66.1	54	–		393
2,925.3	320	4.6	258	7.3	116	17.6	155	2.70	37.1	8.3	152	45.0	146	13.6	202	394
4,537.0	245	13.3	45	1.2	375	15.9	191	3.54	7.9	12.6	100	71.7	39	19.9	56	395
5,774.9	202	11.4	69	7.0	127	18.3	139	1.86	30.1	9.8	135	1.3	399	21.0	44	396
3,345.7	295	5.8	213	6.7	135	10.8	331	1.81	(15.4)	–		10.3	356	–		397
573.3	445	0.7	428	2.1	326	7.5	377	0.56	(38.5)	–		(11.8)	422	–		398
608.0	444	(1.3)	462	(2.4)	466	(9.7)	452	(1.62)	(193.6)	–		3.3	389	–		399
1,838.1	381	0.9	420	1.0	382	4.6	408	0.79	(56.8)	0.4	249	45.9	136	15.5	140	400

Rank 1995	1994	COMPANY	REVENUES $ MILLIONS	% CHANGE FROM '94	PROFITS $ MILLIONS	RANK	% CHANGE FROM '94	ASSETS $ MILLIONS	RANK	STOCK-HOLDERS' EQUITY $ MILLIONS	RANK
401	395	BRUNSWICK	3,076.5	8.5	127.2	353	(1.4)	2,360.5	398	1,043.1	361
402	362	LONG ISLAND LIGHTING	3,075.1	0.3	303.3	224	0.5	12,484.4	176	2,516.9	204
403	403	READER'S DIGEST ASSOCIATION[5]	3,068.5	9.3	264.0	249	7.2	1,958.7	430	640.8	410
404	•	STAPLES[1]	3,068.1	53.4	73.7	399	84.5	1,406.2	462	611.4	420
405	•	APPLIED MATERIALS[6]	3,061.9	84.5	454.1	162	105.7	2,965.4	363	1,783.5	262
406	392	YELLOW	3,056.6	6.6	(30.1)	456	–	1,434.9	459	422.7	445
407	409	FLORIDA PROGRESS	3,055.6	10.3	238.9	273	12.7	5,791.1	266	2,078.1	237
408	418	GEICO[58]	3,054.0	12.4	247.6	264	19.2	5,795.5	265	1,868.4	255
409	363	HORMEL FOODS[6]	3,046.2	(0.6)	120.4	363	2.1	1,223.9	468	732.0	398
410	340	MAYTAG	3,039.5	(9.9)	(20.5)*	454	(113.8)	2,125.1	416	637.4	411
411	388	CINERGY	3,031.4	3.7	347.2	207	81.6	8,220.1	223	2,548.8	202
412	•	VALERO ENERGY	3,019.8	64.3	59.8	409	122.6	2,876.7	367	1,033.8	363
413	465	PROGRESSIVE	3,011.9	24.7	250.5	262	(8.7)	5,352.5	279	1,475.8	305
414	391	CAROLINA POWER & LIGHT	3,006.6	4.5	372.6	195	19.0	8,227.2	222	2,718.5	192
415	485	BOATMEN'S BANCSHARES	2,996.1	30.6	418.8	174	17.9	33,703.8	77	2,928.1	182
416	466	OWENS & MINOR	2,976.5	24.2	(11.3)	450	(242.8)	857.8	480	235.3	465
417	•	ORACLE[7]	2,966.9	48.3	441.5	167	55.6	2,424.5	395	1,211.4	340
418	430	DIAMOND SHAMROCK	2,956.7	12.8	47.3	418	(37.6)	2,245.4	408	624.7	418
419	•	MICRON TECHNOLOGY[11]	2,952.7	81.3	844.1	77	110.8	2,774.9	373	1,896.2	252
420	425	WHITMAN	2,946.5	10.8	133.5	350	29.4	2,363.3	397	627.8	413
421	400	MERCANTILE STORES[1]	2,944.3	4.4	123.2	360	19.2	2,075.0	419	1,485.0	304
422	497	MICROAGE[6]	2,941.1	32.4	0.2	445	(98.5)	572.6	491	168.4	474
423	411	MCGRAW-HILL	2,935.3	6.3	227.1	282	11.8	3,104.4	356	1,035.1	362
424	408	BALTIMORE GAS & ELECTRIC	2,934.8	5.5	338.0	210	4.4	8,316.7	220	3,081.9	172
425	462	YORK INTERNATIONAL	2,929.9	21.0	(96.1)	468	(207.0)	1,927.0	432	624.8	417
426	341	KERR-MCGEE	2,928.0	(12.7)	(31.2)	457	(134.7)	3,232.0	348	1,416.0	316
427	412	ALUMAX	2,926.1	6.2	237.4	275	408.4	3,135.0	354	1,399.3	318
428	424	PITTSTON	2,926.1	9.7	98.0	374	264.2	1,807.0	439	522.0	433
429	•	U.S. INDUSTRIES[19]	2,908.4¶	–	(89.3)	467	–	1,900.0	434	412.1	447
430	366	RELIANCE GROUP HOLDINGS	2,906.0	(4.6)	88.1	385	100.9	9,988.2	200	678.3	405
431	375	PETER KIEWIT SONS'	2,902.0	(3.0)	244.0	267	121.8	3,463.0	337	1,607.0	287
432	•	ESTÉE LAUDER[5]	2,899.1	12.5	121.2	362	30.3	1,721.7	441	335.1	454
433	•	U.S. BANCORP	2,897.3	49.6	329.0	214	117.1	31,794.3	80	2,617.0	198
434	405	AMERICAN PRESIDENT	2,896.0	3.7	30.3	428	(59.2)	1,878.8	436	469.2	441
435	324	FLAGSTAR	2,893.8¶	(17.9)	(55.2)	464	(115.2)	1,500.9	456	(1,131.0)	492
436	456	AUTOMATIC DATA PROCESSING[5]	2,893.7	17.2	394.8	187	19.9	3,201.1	350	2,096.6	235
437	398	NASH FINCH	2,888.8	2.0	17.4	439	12.5	514.3	492	215.3	468
438	434	SOUTHWEST AIRLINES	2,872.8	10.8	182.6	313	1.8	3,256.1	346	1,427.3	313
439	406	SHAW INDUSTRIES	2,869.8	2.9	52.3	415	(58.8)	1,665.2	446	710.2	402
440	396	BRUNO'S[5]	2,869.6	1.2	33.3	426	(10.6)	895.6	477	429.8	444
441	451	CORESTATES FINANCIAL CORP.	2,868.0	14.9	452.2	164	84.3	29,620.6	85	2,379.4	212
442	•	TRIBUNE	2,863.6	32.9	278.2	242	14.9	3,288.3	343	1,379.9	321
443	404	NORAM ENERGY	2,862.1ᴱ	2.2	65.5	407	36.2	3,666.0	328	637.3	412
444	•	CONSECO	2,860.7	53.6	220.4	290	46.5	17,297.5	133	1,111.7	354
445	441	REPUBLIC NEW YORK CORP.	2,859.6	11.7	288.6	232	(15.1)	43,881.6	61	3,007.8	175
446	423	HASBRO	2,858.2	7.0	155.6	333	(11.1)	2,616.4	384	1,525.6	300
447	422	WILLIAMS[59]	2,855.7	6.8	1,318.2	45	434.3	10,494.8	197	3,187.1	167
448	471	FLEETWOOD ENTERPRISES	2,855.7	20.5	84.6	388	28.4	1,345.1	465	608.1	421
449	367	LOUISIANA-PACIFIC	2,843.2	(6.5)	(51.7)	463	(114.9)	2,805.4	370	1,656.0	279
450	468	ENGELHARD	2,840.1	19.0	137.5	346	16.6	1,645.6	450	737.7	395

Values are shown as **value (rank)**. Market value as of 3/15/96. EPS "1995 $" and the middle EPS percentage column are unranked; the EPS growth-rate column carries a rank.

MARKET VALUE $ MILLIONS	PROFITS AS % OF REVENUES	PROFITS AS % OF ASSETS	PROFITS AS % OF STOCKHOLDERS EQUITY	EPS 1995 $	EPS % chg	EPS 1985-95 ANNUAL GROWTH RATE	TOTAL RETURN TO INVESTORS 1995	TOTAL RETURN 1985-1995 ANNUAL RATE	RANK 1995
2,206.8 (353)	4.1 (276)	5.4 (185)	12.2 (298)	1.32	(2.2)	1.2 (238)	30.3 (246)	11.0 (265)	401
2,039.0 (369)	9.9 (105)	2.4 (309)	10.1 (341)	2.10	(2.3)	(6.2) (296)	19.2 (315)	12.6 (224)	402
4,976.6 (231)	8.6 (131)	13.5 (23)	41.2 (16)	2.35	11.4	–	8.1 (369)	–	403
3,043.0 (312)	2.4 (356)	5.2 (191)	12.1 (303)	0.70	64.1	–	47.7 (124)	–	404
6,207.5 (188)	14.8 (31)	15.3 (16)	25.5 (66)	2.56	96.9	40.1 (11)	86.4 (17)	40.7 (3)	405
316.2 (450)	(1.0) (457)	(2.1) (464)	(7.1) (449)	(1.07)	–	–	(46.9) (447)	(5.5) (373)	406
3,172.9 (305)	7.8 (154)	4.1 (236)	11.5 (319)	2.50	9.6	0.6 (247)	25.6 (279)	12.8 (217)	407
N.A.	8.1 (148)	4.3 (232)	13.3 (265)	3.66	23.2	7.1 (173)	45.2 (143)	16.5 (115)	408
1,956.3 (375)	4.0 (288)	9.8 (63)	16.5 (175)	1.57	1.9	12.1 (104)	1.8 (394)	16.5 (114)	409
2,160.8 (359)	(0.7) (453)	(1.0) (454)	(3.2) (442)	(0.19)	(113.7)	–	39.0 (189)	4.3 (345)	410
4,480.5 (248)	11.5 (66)	4.2 (233)	13.6 (253)	2.22	70.8	60.2 (4)	39.1 (187)	16.0 (129)	411
1,082.7 (423)	2.0 (375)	2.1 (323)	5.7 (395)	1.10	175.0	0.4 (250)	48.8 (121)	7.3 (322)	412
3,215.9 (302)	8.3 (138)	4.7 (211)	17.0 (163)	3.26	(9.2)	20.1 (40)	40.4 (176)	22.7 (36)	413
5,118.1 (229)	12.4 (55)	4.5 (223)	13.7 (249)	2.48	22.2	2.5 (226)	37.4 (202)	16.2 (123)	414
4,997.0 (230)	14.0 (36)	1.2 (371)	14.3 (232)	3.25	(4.4)	4.0 (212)	57.3 (79)	13.9 (190)	415
350.6 (449)	(0.4) (450)	(1.3) (457)	(4.8) (448)	(0.53)	(453.3)	–	(9.3) (418)	15.4 (142)	416
21,275.5 (49)	14.9 (29)	18.2 (9)	36.4 (27)	1.00	56.3	–	44.1 (151)	–	417
903.6 (434)	1.6 (395)	2.1 (320)	7.6 (375)	1.48	(39.6)	–	1.6 (395)	–	418
6,753.5 (175)	28.6 (4)	30.4 (2)	44.5 (13)	3.95	106.3	113.6 (2)	80.3 (25)	37.2 (5)	419
2,418.5 (346)	4.5 (262)	5.6 (174)	21.3 (94)	1.26	29.9	(1.9) (273)	37.3 (203)	14.5 (169)	420
2,127.7 (364)	4.2 (274)	5.9 (165)	8.3 (366)	3.35	19.2	(7.0) (298)	19.8 (312)	(2.9) (370)	421
134.6 (459)	0.0 (445)	0.0 (441)	0.1 (432)	0.02	(98.4)	–	(30.9) (440)	–	422
4,433.5 (250)	7.7 (155)	7.3 (117)	21.9 (88)	2.28	11.2	4.6 (203)	34.3 (222)	9.7 (290)	423
3,909.5 (273)	11.5 (65)	4.1 (238)	10.2 (339)	2.02	4.7	0.8 (243)	37.2 (205)	12.4 (230)	424
2,017.4 (372)	(3.3) (477)	(5.0) (474)	(15.4) (461)	(2.36)	(198.3)	–	28.2 (263)	–	425
3,244.4 (299)	(1.1) (458)	(1.0) (455)	(2.2) (436)	(0.60)	(134.5)	–	41.4 (167)	9.9 (285)	426
1,561.7 (395)	8.1 (147)	7.6 (107)	17.0 (164)	5.05	501.2	–	7.9 (371)	–	427
N.A.	3.3 (310)	5.4 (183)	18.8 (124)	N.A.	–	–	–	–	428
1,107.0 (422)	(3.1) (476)	(4.7) (473)	(21.7) (463)	N.A.	–	–	–	–	429
920.6 (432)	3.0 (326)	0.9 (397)	13.0 (277)	0.73	92.1	–	75.3 (34)	–	430
N.A.	8.4 (133)	7.0 (124)	15.2 (206)	N.A.	–	–	–	–	431
4,090.8 (266)	4.2 (275)	7.0 (125)	36.2 (28)	N.A.	–	–	–	–	432
4,865.1 (234)	11.4 (71)	1.0 (381)	12.6 (285)	2.09	49.3	7.4 (166)	66.8 (51)	17.7 (87)	433
548.6 (447)	1.0 (417)	1.6 (346)	5.7 (392)	0.95	(60.1)	0.2 (254)	(7.5) (414)	11.3 (259)	434
143.2 (458)	(1.9) (466)	(3.7) (467)	–	(1.64)	(122.9)	–	(55.4) (450)	–	435
11,691.3 (97)	13.6 (40)	12.3 (36)	18.8 (122)	2.77	18.4	16.2 (68)	28.2 (261)	18.8 (70)	436
176.7 (455)	0.6 (430)	3.4 (263)	8.1 (370)	1.60	12.7	3.1 (219)	15.3 (340)	5.1 (340)	437
4,479.9 (249)	6.4 (190)	5.6 (176)	12.8 (279)	1.23	0.8	13.6 (87)	37.6 (197)	14.9 (156)	438
1,579.8 (393)	1.8 (384)	3.1 (273)	7.4 (379)	0.38	(57.3)	7.2 (170)	1.1 (400)	26.9 (20)	439
N.A.	1.2 (411)	3.7 (251)	7.8 (374)	0.43	(10.4)	2.2 (228)	42.0 (163)	4.5 (344)	440
5,788.0 (200)	15.8 (20)	1.5 (351)	19.0 (118)	3.22	86.1	0.6 (246)	52.0 (103)	13.7 (198)	441
4,206.7 (261)	9.7 (107)	8.5 (83)	20.2 (109)	4.00	20.5	10.1 (133)	13.7 (347)	10.4 (279)	442
1,120.8 (418)	2.3 (361)	1.8 (337)	10.3 (335)	0.47	42.4	(10.2) (306)	71.9 (38)	(1.9) (368)	443
1,401.4 (400)	7.7 (158)	1.3 (369)	19.8 (112)	9.39	87.8	46.8 (6)	45.8 (137)	42.6 (2)	444
3,218.0 (301)	10.1 (99)	0.7 (413)	9.6 (349)	4.66	(19.5)	5.8 (187)	41.1 (170)	13.5 (205)	445
3,090.5 (311)	5.4 (222)	5.9 (164)	10.2 (338)	1.76	(10.2)	4.0 (210)	7.5 (374)	11.2 (263)	446
5,136.4 (228)	46.2 (1)	12.6 (32)	41.4 (15)	12.77	450.4	39.4 (12)	79.9 (26)	16.2 (124)	447
1,145.7 (415)	3.0 (331)	6.3 (152)	13.9 (243)	1.82	27.3	4.7 (200)	41.2 (168)	10.6 (274)	448
2,710.7 (329)	(1.8) (465)	(1.8) (462)	(3.1) (440)	(0.48)	(115.2)	–	(9.1) (417)	16.3 (122)	449
2,953.0 (318)	4.8 (248)	8.4 (87)	18.6 (128)	0.96	17.1	11.9 (109)	49.7 (115)	19.0 (66)	450

RANK 1995	1994	COMPANY	REVENUES $ MILLIONS	% CHANGE FROM '94	PROFITS $ MILLIONS	RANK	% CHANGE FROM '94	ASSETS $ MILLIONS	RANK	STOCK-HOLDERS' EQUITY $ MILLIONS	RANK
451	·	COMPUSA[5]	2,813.1	31.1	23.0	435	–	610.5	490	171.0	473
452	·	UTILICORP UNITED	2,798.5	84.8	79.8	393	(15.5)	3,885.9	324	946.3	373
453	415	AID ASSOCIATION FOR LUTHERANS	2,795.8	2.3	114.5	367	(24.3)	15,442.5	144	942.7	374
454	475	GRAYBAR ELECTRIC	2,774.4	17.3	36.7	425	96.3	823.3	484	174.2	472
455	414	CALDOR[53]	2,764.5	3.6	(4.6)*	447	(111.6)	1,417.9	460	294.3	459
456	427	KNIGHT-RIDDER	2,751.8	3.9	160.1	331	(6.3)	3,005.7	361	1,111.0	355
457	440	MANVILLE[60]	2,733.8¶	6.8	116.0	365	213.5	2,474.1	392	1,180.5	346
458	481	HEALTH SYSTEMS INTL.	2,732.1	18.5	89.6	384	1.7	1,213.6	469	285.9	460
459	494	ECHLIN[11]	2,717.9	21.9	154.4	335	24.9	1,961.0	429	909.3	378
460	454	ULTRAMAR	2,714.4	9.7	69.6	403	14.2	1,971.3	425	703.4	403
461	442	BECTON DICKINSON[19]	2,712.5	6.0	251.7	261	10.8	2,999.5	362	1,398.4	319
462	482	SONOCO PRODUCTS	2,706.2	17.7	164.5	328	26.7	2,115.4	417	918.7	376
463	476	KELLY SERVICES	2,689.8	13.9	69.5	404	13.8	718.7	489	476.1	439
464	416	PAYLESS CASHWAYS[17]	2,685.7	(1.7)	(128.5)	471	(386.4)	1,344.4	466	308.2	455
465	·	SCI SYSTEMS[5]	2,673.8	40.6	45.2	420	113.8	981.3	475	349.8	453
466	417	PP&L RESOURCES[61]	2,650.0ᴱ	(2.8)	350.4	203	43.4	9,491.7	209	2,768.5	188
467	459	ALLEGHENY POWER SYSTEM	2,647.8	8.0	239.7	272	(8.9)	6,447.3	245	2,300.0	217
468	444	LONGS DRUG STORES[1]	2,644.4	3.4	46.2	419	(5.1)	853.6	481	522.8	432
469	448	BAKER HUGHES[19]	2,637.5	5.3	105.4	372	147.1	3,166.6	351	1,513.6	302
470	397	COLUMBIA GAS SYSTEM	2,635.2	(7.0)	(360.7)**	480	(249.9)	6,057.0	259	1,539.9	297
471	413	ARMSTRONG WORLD INDUSTRIES	2,635.1	(4.3)	123.3	359	(41.4)	2,149.8	412	775.0	387
472	460	DEAN FOODS[7]	2,630.2	8.2	80.1	392	11.3	1,202.4	470	584.5	422
473	447	STANLEY WORKS	2,624.3	4.5	59.1	410	(52.8)	1,670.0	444	734.6	397
474	·	COMPUTER ASSOCIATES INTL.[18]	2,623.0	22.1	431.9	169	7.6	3,269.4	344	1,578.1	291
475	433	BALL	2,591.7	(0.1)	(18.6)	452	(125.5)	1,612.5	451	582.7	423
476	452	NORTHERN STATES POWER	2,568.6	3.3	275.8	243	13.3	6,228.6	253	2,267.9	219
477	486	HANNAFORD BROS.	2,568.1	12.1	70.2	402	12.7	961.8	476	518.7	435
478	467	TELEDYNE	2,567.8	7.4	162.0	330	–	1,606.2	452	395.6	448
479	·	MBNA	2,565.4	38.4	353.1	201	32.4	13,228.9	170	1,265.1	329
480	·	MAXXAM	2,565.2	21.2	57.5	413	–	3,832.3	325	(83.8)	483
481	410	PROVIDENT COS.[62]	2,555.3	(7.5)	115.6	366	(14.6)	16,301.3	139	1,652.3	282
482	254	CALIBER SYSTEMS[63]	2,547.6[64]	(44.3)	(27.2)	455	(239.1)	1,389.4	463	736.3	396
483	·	OFFICEMAX[1]	2,542.5	38.1	125.8	355	314.3	1,587.9	453	990.9	370
484	450	MORRISON KNUDSEN[39]	2,530.9	(4.2)	(484.0)	485	–	808.3	486	99.8	479
485	489	OLSTEN	2,518.9	11.4	90.5	383	29.0	891.9	479	472.0	440
486	463	CENTERIOR ENERGY	2,515.5	3.9	220.5	289	8.1	10,643.1	193	1,983.6	245
487	·	SPARTAN STORES[18,34]	2,512.4	14.7	N.A.		–	386.1	494	125.8	477
488	·	NEWELL	2,498.4	20.4	222.5	288	13.8	2,931.2	364	1,300.1	326
489	439	PENNZOIL	2,490.0	(2.8)	(305.1)	478	–	4,307.8	313	836.2	383
490	457	ROUNDY'S[34]	2,488.2	0.9	N.A.		–	407.3	493	100.0	478
491	·	GOLDEN WEST FINANCIAL CORP.	2,470.0	29.1	234.5	276	1.8	35,118.2	74	2,278.4	218
492	473	AST RESEARCH	2,467.8	4.2	(99.3)	470	(417.2)	1,021.5	473	263.2	462
493	472	OHIO EDISON	2,465.8	4.1	317.2	219	4.5	8,823.9	216	2,619.7	197
494	·	FOUNDATION HEALTH[5]	2,459.9	43.2	49.4	417	(39.8)	1,964.2	426	756.9	391
495	·	STATE STREET BOSTON CORP.	2,445.7	29.7	247.1	265	19.1	25,785.2	93	1,587.5	290
496	487	USG	2,444.0	6.7	(32.0)	458	–	1,890.0	435	(37.0)	481
497	438	COTTER[34]	2,437.0	(5.3)	N.A.		–	819.6	485	306.5	456
498	478	ACE HARDWARE[34]	2,436.0	4.7	N.A.		–	759.1	488	217.2	467
499	·	GENERAL INSTRUMENT	2,432.0	19.4	123.8	358	(49.8)	2,300.8	403	915.3	377
500	·	ADVANCED MICRO DEVICES	2,429.7	13.8	300.5	226	(1.6)	3,031.3	360	2,100.1	234

DEFINITIONS, EXPLANATIONS, AND FOOTNOTES ARE FOUND ON PAGE 26

MARKET VALUE 3/15/96 $ MILLIONS	PROFITS AS % OF... REVENUES	ASSETS	STOCK-HOLDERS EQUITY	EARNINGS PER SHARE 1995 $	1985-95 ANNUAL GROWTH RATE	TOTAL RETURN TO INVESTORS 1995	1985-1995 ANNUAL RATE	RANK 1995
1,034.1 426	0.8 423	3.8 250	13.4 263	1.21 –	–	107.5 8	–	451
1,333.0 403	2.9 337	2.1 327	8.4 364	1.72 (17.3)	(0.4) 262	17.8 321	15.0 155	452
N.A.	4.1 279	0.7 407	12.1 301	N.A. –	–	–	–	453
N.A.	1.3 404	4.5 225	21.1 96	8.11 101.2	–	–	–	454
72.1 461	(0.2) 448	(0.3) 443	(1.6) 435	N.A. –	–	(85.4) 453	–	455
3,347.5 294	5.8 211	5.3 188	14.4 230	3.19 1.3	3.8 214	27.1 272	7.2 324	456
1,568.3 394	4.2 273	4.7 210	9.8 346	0.73 630.0	–	44.4 148	10.7 271	457
1,786.8 384	3.3 315	7.4 113	31.3 35	1.83 3.4	–	5.8 377	–	458
2,179.2 357	5.7 219	7.9 97	17.0 162	2.60 23.8	9.0 144	24.4 288	13.8 194	459
1,265.2 407	2.6 347	3.5 260	9.9 344	1.73 10.9	–	5.4 379	–	460
5,328.4 220	9.3 118	8.4 85	18.0 143	3.59 17.7	13.1 95	58.6 74	19.0 68	461
2,493.8 341	6.1 199	7.8 102	17.9 146	1.72 29.0	12.3 103	28.9 251	16.3 121	462
1,140.4 416	2.6 346	9.7 64	14.6 225	1.83 13.7	7.9 158	3.7 387	5.4 337	463
159.7 457	(4.8) 479	(9.6) 483	(41.7) 472	(3.36) (439.4)	–	(54.1) 449	–	464
1,047.4 424	1.7 390	4.6 219	12.9 278	1.63 114.5	9.4 138	72.2 37	11.9 242	465
3,757.8 280	13.2 46	3.7 253	12.0 305	2.05 45.4	4.3 206	42.8 157	13.7 196	466
3,424.9 290	9.1 124	3.7 252	10.4 333	2.00 (10.3)	1.1 241	40.6 174	13.6 199	467
929.5 431	1.7 387	5.4 184	8.8 358	2.29 (2.6)	2.8 222	55.6 85	7.5 319	468
4,116.2 265	4.0 285	3.3 266	7.0 384	0.57 159.1	(7.6) 299	36.5 209	5.8 333	469
2,134.4 363	(13.7) 491	(6.0) 478	(23.4) 464	(7.15) (250.2)	–	86.7 16	4.5 343	470
2,325.5 349	4.7 256	5.7 171	15.9 190	2.90 (44.4)	3.3 216	65.3 56	14.2 182	471
1,038.5 425	3.0 324	6.7 136	13.7 250	2.01 11.0	6.9 178	(2.8) 409	6.0 332	472
2,438.3 344	2.3 363	3.5 259	8.0 371	1.33 (52.5)	(3.5) 281	48.9 120	12.7 221	473
17,570.2 62	16.5 17	13.2 26	27.4 58	2.57 9.8	32.7 18	76.5 33	35.1 8	474
914.0 433	(0.7) 454	(1.2) 456	(3.2) 441	(0.72) (130.6)	–	(10.2) 420	3.2 350	475
3,268.8 296	10.7 87	4.4 228	12.2 300	3.91 13.0	2.8 221	18.4 318	13.1 212	476
1,151.6 414	2.7 342	7.3 118	13.5 256	1.67 11.3	14.4 80	(1.4) 406	15.6 136	477
1,618.4 392	6.3 192	10.1 56	40.5 19	2.88 –	(11.1) 307	32.8 228	0.4 359	478
6,543.3 182	13.8 39	2.7 296	27.9 54	1.54 30.5	–	60.7 65	–	479
381.0 448	2.2 364	1.5 353	–	6.08 30.5	17.6 53	14.2 344	9.8 288	480
1,497.9 397	4.5 263	0.7 409	7.0 383	2.27 (16.2)	(3.8) 284	60.2 68	8.2 312	481
1,713.4 387	(1.1) 459	(2.0) 463	(3.7) 444	(0.69) (238.0)	–	(11.3) 421	6.4 327	482
2,006.1 373	4.9 244	7.9 95	12.7 281	1.56 –	–	26.7 275	–	483
49.6 462	(19.1) 493	(59.9) 488	(485.0) 475	N.A. –	–	(64.2) 452	(12.5) 380	484
1,994.4 374	3.6 301	10.1 53	19.2 115	1.39 24.9	20.6 35	25.6 280	19.6 61	485
1,184.3 411	8.8 129	2.1 324	11.1 323	1.49 8.0	–	8.5 368	–	486
N.A.	–	–	–	N.A. –	–	–	–	487
4,320.6 256	8.9 125	7.6 105	17.1 159	1.41 13.7	18.4 47	25.5 281	27.6 17	488
1,750.9 385	(12.3) 490	(7.1) 481	(36.5) 470	(6.60) –	–	1.0 401	0.3 360	489
N.A.	–	–	–	N.A. –	–	–	–	490
2,902.7 322	9.5 111	0.7 411	10.3 334	4.00 7.8	4.5 204	57.9 77	14.3 178	491
262.5 452	(4.0) 478	(9.7) 484	(37.7) 471	(3.07) (419.8)	–	(41.9) 443	(5.8) 375	492
3,394.7 291	12.9 49	3.6 258	11.9 308	2.05 4.1	(1.8) 272	35.9 212	12.7 222	493
2,094.0 366	2.0 373	2.5 304	6.5 388	0.90 (68.3)	–	39.5 183	–	494
3,879.4 275	10.1 98	1.0 390	15.6 200	2.98 10.4	14.1 83	60.2 67	17.8 85	495
1,180.1 412	(1.3) 461	(1.7) 459	–	(0.71) –	–	53.8 96	–	496
N.A.	–	–	–	N.A. –	–	–	–	497
N.A.	–	–	–	N.A. –	–	–	–	498
3,161.5 307	5.1 239	5.4 186	13.5 257	1.00 (50.0)	–	(22.1) 431	–	499
2,322.9 350	12.4 56	9.9 61	14.3 231	2.85 (5.6)	2.1 231	(33.6) 441	(5.5) 374	500

REVENUES

All companies on the list must publish financial data and must report part or all of their figures to a government agency. Private companies and cooperatives that produce a 10-K are, therefore, included; subsidiaries of foreign companies incorporated in the U.S. are excluded. Revenues are as reported, including revenues from discontinued operations when they are published. The revenues for commercial banks and savings institutions are interest and noninterest revenues. Such figures for insurance companies include premium and annuity income, investment income, and capital gains or losses, but exclude deposits. Revenues figures for all companies include consolidated subsidiaries and exclude excise taxes. Data shown are for the fiscal year ended on or before January 31, 1996. All figures are for the year ended December 31, 1995, unless otherwise noted.

PROFITS

Profits are shown after taxes, after extraordinary credits or charges if any appear on the income statement, and after cumulative effects of accounting changes. Figures in parentheses indicate a loss. Profit declines over 100% reflect swings from 1994 profits to 1995 losses. Cooperatives provide only net margin figures, which are not comparable with the profit figures in these listings, and therefore N.A. is shown in that column. Profits for mutual insurance companies are based on statutory accounting.

ASSETS

Assets shown are the company's year-end total.

STOCKHOLDERS' EQUITY

Stockholders' equity is the sum of all capital stock, paid-in capital, and retained earnings at the company's year-end. Preferred stock that is technically construed to be debt has been

excluded. Redeemable preferred stock whose redemption is either mandatory or outside the control of the company is excluded. Dividends paid on such stock have been subtracted from the profit figures used in calculating the return on equity.

MARKET VALUE

The figure shown was arrived at by multiplying the number of common shares outstanding by the price per common share as of March 15, 1996. Shares traded on a when-issued basis are excluded.

EARNINGS PER SHARE

The figures shown for each company are the primary earnings per share that appear on the income statement. Per share earnings for 1994 and 1985 are adjusted for stock splits and stock dividends. They are not restated for mergers, acquisitions, or accounting changes. Though earnings per share numbers are not marked by any footnotes, if a company's profits are footnoted to indicate an extraordinary charge or credit, it can be assumed that earnings per share are affected as well. Results are listed as not available (N.A.) if the companies are cooperatives, if the figures were not published, or if the stock traded on a limited basis or was not widely held. The 1985—95 growth rate is the annual rate, compounded.

TOTAL RETURN TO INVESTORS

Total return to investors includes both price appreciation and dividend yield to an investor in the company's stock. The figures shown assume sales at the end of 1995 of stock owned at the end of 1985 and 1994. It has been assumed that any proceeds from cash dividends, the sale of rights and warrant offerings, and stock received in spinoffs were reinvested when they were paid. Returns are adjusted for stock splits, stock dividends, recapitalizations, and corporate reorganizations as they occur; however, no effort has been made to reflect the cost of bro-

kerage commissions or of taxes. Results are listed as not available (N.A.) if shares are not publicly traded or are traded on a limited basis. If companies have more than one class of shares outstanding, only the more widely held and actively traded has been considered. Total return percentages shown are the returns received by the hypothetical investor described above. The 1985—95 return is the annual rate, compounded.

MEDIANS

The median figures in the tables refer only to results of companies in the 500, and no attempt has been made to calculate them in groups of fewer than four companies. The medians for profit changes from 1994 do not include companies that lost money in both 1994 and 1995, because no meaningful percentage changes can be calculated in such cases.

FOOTNOTES

N.A. Not available.

ᴱExcise taxes have been deducted.

*Reflects an extraordinary charge of at least 10%.

**Reflects an extraordinary credit of at least 10%.

¶ Includes revenues from discontinued operations of at least 10%.

†Ranking revised since publication of original Fortune 500 list in April 1996.

1–9

¹Figures are for fiscal year ended Jan. 31, 1996.

²Acquired Lotus Development (1994 rank: 879), July 5, 1995.

³Figures do not include spinoff of Allstate (1995 rank: 31), June 30, 1995.

⁴Figure does not include discontinued operations of Allstate (1995 rank: 31).

⁵Figures are for fiscal year ended June 30, 1995.

⁶Figures are for fiscal year ended Oct. 31, 1995.

⁷Figures are for fiscal year ended May 31, 1995.

⁸Company formed by the combination of Lockheed (1994 rank: 70) and Martin Marietta (1994 rank: 111), March 15, 1995.

⁹Figures do not reflect acquisition of Federal Paper Board (1995 rank: 595), March 12, 1996.

10–19

¹⁰Acquired Continental (1994 rank: 222), May 10, 1995.

¹¹Figures are for fiscal year ended August 31, 1995.

¹²Acquired HealthTrust (1994 rank: 383), April 24, 1995.

¹³Figures are for fiscal year ended Feb. 28, 1995.

¹⁴Acquired Broadway Stores (1994 rank: 524), July 29, 1995.

¹⁵Figures do not include acquisition of Chase Manhattan Corp. (1995 rank: 112), March 31, 1996.

¹⁶Acquired Scott Paper (1994 rank: 242), Dec. 12, 1995.

¹⁷Figures are for fiscal year ended Nov. 30, 1995.

¹⁸Figures are for fiscal year ended March 31, 1995.

¹⁹Figures are for fiscal year ended Sept. 30, 1995.

20–29

²⁰One of three companies resulting from the breakup of ITT (1994 rank: 23), Dec. 19, 1995.

²¹Figures do not include acquisition of Capital Cities/ABC (1994 rank: 181), Feb. 9, 1996.

²²Acquired E-Systems (1994 rank: 529), May 8, 1995.

²³Acquired by Chemical Banking Corp. (1995 rank: 71), March 31, 1996.

²⁴Fiscal year-end changed from Jan. 31 to Nov. 30, 1995. Figures are for ten months.

²⁵NBD Bancorp acquired First Chicago Corp. (1994 rank: 226), Dec. 1, 1995, and changed its name.

²⁶Acquired First Fidelity Bancorp (1994 rank: 445), Jan. 1, 1996.

²⁷Acquired CBS (1994 rank: 306), Nov. 24, 1995.

²⁸Acquired Chicago & Northwestern Transportation (1994 rank: 786), April 25, 1995.

²⁹Revenues from discontinued operations are not included.

30–39

³⁰Name changed from SCEcorp, Jan. 26, 1996.

³¹Figures are for fiscal year ended April 30, 1995.

³²Acquired Shawmut National Corp. (1994 rank: 479), Nov. 30, 1995.

³³Figures are for fiscal year ended July 31, 1995.

³⁴Cooperatives provide only net margin figures, which are not comparable with the profit figures on the list.

³⁵Company formed by the merger of Pharmacia and Upjohn (1994 rank: 319), Nov. 2, 1995.

³⁶Figures do not reflect acquisition of Connecticut Mutual Life Insurance (1995 rank: 567), March 1, 1996.

³⁷Acquired Midlantic Corp. (1994 rank: 811), Dec. 31, 1995.

³⁸Acquired Santa Fe Pacific (1994 rank: 386), Sept. 22, 1995.

³⁹Figures are for four quarters ended Sept. 30, 1995.

40–49

⁴⁰Acquired Clark Equipment (1994 rank: 880), May 31, 1995.

⁴¹Figures do not reflect acquisition of First Interstate Bancorp (1995 rank: 274), April 1, 1996.

⁴²Name changed from Panhandle Eastern, Jan. 2, 1996.

⁴³Acquired by Wells Fargo & Co. (1995 rank: 245), April 1, 1996.

⁴⁴Name changed from AmeriSource Distribution, March 30, 1995.

⁴⁵Figures do not reflect acquisition of Conner Peripherals (1994 rank: 474), Feb. 2, 1996.

⁴⁶Acquired Geico (1995 rank: 408), Jan. 2, 1996.

⁴⁷Name changed from First Financial Management (1994 rank: 499). Acquired First Data (1994 rank: 609), Oct. 27, 1995.

⁴⁸Name changed from LDDS Communications, May 25, 1995.

⁴⁹Name changed from Detroit Edison, Jan. 1, 1996.

50–59

⁵⁰American Premier Underwriters (1994 rank: 587) formed a holding company, April 3, 1995, and changed its name.

⁵¹Estimate.

⁵²Acquired Future Now (1994 rank: 986), August 17, 1995.

⁵³Figures are for four quarters ended Oct. 31, 1995.

⁵⁴Acquired QVC (1994 rank: 687), Feb. 15, 1995.

⁵⁵Name changed from National Medical Enterprises; acquired American Medical Holdings (1994 rank: 469), March 1, 1995.

⁵⁶Limited partnership; profits after tax estimated at corporate rate.

⁵⁷Figures do not reflect acquisition of CBI Industries (1995 rank: 607), March 13, 1996.

⁵⁸Acquired by Berkshire Hathaway (1995 rank: 293), Jan. 2, 1996.

⁵⁹Acquired Transco Energy (1994 rank: 401), May 1, 1995.

60–64

⁶⁰Name changed to Schuller, April 1, 1996.

⁶¹Name changed from Pennsylvania Power & Light (1994 rank: 417), April 27, 1995.

⁶²Name changed from Provident Life & Accident Insurance, Dec. 27, 1995.

⁶³Name changed from Roadway Services. Figures do not include spin-off of Roadway Express (1995 rank: 521), Jan. 2, 1996.

⁶⁴Figure does not include discontinued operations of Roadway Express (1995 rank: 521).

KEY TO ICONS

Energy
Crude Oil Products
Mining
Petroleum Refining
Pipelines

Financial Services
Banks
Brokerage
Diversified Financials
Insurance
Savings Institutions

High Tech
Computer & Data Services
Computers & Office Equipment
Electronics & Electrical Equipment
Scientific, Photographic & Control
  Equipment
Telecommunications

Manufacturing
Aerospace
Apparel
Beverages
Building Materials & Glass
Chemicals
Engineering & Construction
Food
Forest & Paper Products
Furniture
Industrial & Farm Equipment
Metal products
Metals
Pharmaceuticals
Rubber & Plastic Products
Soaps & Cosmetics

Textiles
Tobacco
Toys & Sporting Goods
Utilities

Retailing
Food & Drug Stores
General Merchandising
Specialty Retailing

Services
Entertainment
Food Services
Health Care
Hotels, Casinos & Resorts
Mail, Package & Freight Delivery
Publishing & Printing
Temporary Services
Waste Management

Transportation
Airlines
Marine Services
Motor Vehicles
Railroads
Transportation Equipment
Trucking
Truck Leasing

Miscellaneous
Wholesaling

CHANGES IN REVENUES

% CHANGE FROM 1994

		% Change				% Change
1	BROKERAGE	34.2	20	SOAPS, COSMETICS		10.2
2	HEALTH CARE	28.7	21	INSURANCE: P&C (STOCK)		9.4
3	COMPUTERS, OFFICE EQUIPMENT	26.1	22	PETROLEUM REFINING		8.4
4	COMPUTER AND DATA SERVICES	24.9	23	FOOD SERVICES		7.7
5	FOREST AND PAPER PRODUCTS	23.1	24	FOOD		6.9
6	ENTERTAINMENT	21.4	25	PIPELINES		6.8
7	COMMERCIAL BANKS	19.0	26	BUILDING MATERIALS, GLASS		6.8
8	DIVERSIFIED FINANCIALS	18.2	27	PUBLISHING, PRINTING		6.3
9	METALS	16.3	28	TELECOMMUNICATIONS		6.2
10	ELECTRONICS, ELECTRICAL EQUIP.	16.2	29	SCIENTIFIC, PHOTO, CONTROL EQUIP.		6.1
11	SPECIALIST RETAILERS	15.8	30	FOOD AND DRUG STORES		6.0
12	INDUSTRIAL AND FARM EQUIPMENT	14.9	31	RAILROADS		5.6
13	INSURANCE: LIFE, HEALTH (STOCK)	13.8	32	AEROSPACE		5.3
14	PHARMACEUTICALS	13.2	33	GENERAL MERCHANDISERS		4.4
15	METAL PRODUCTS	12.7	34	AIRLINES		3.8
16	CHEMICALS	12.6	35	ENGINEERING, CONSTRUCTION		3.7
17	MOTOR VEHICLES AND PARTS	11.9	36	ELECTRIC AND GAS UTILITIES		3.6
18	WHOLESALERS	11.1				
19	BEVERAGES	11.1		**THE 500 MEDIAN**		**9.9**

REVENUES PER EMPLOYEE

1995 $

		1995 $				1995 $
1	PIPELINES	993,500	20	TELECOMMUNICATIONS		205,491
2	PETROLEUM REFINING	741,230	21	ENTERTAINMENT		197,964
3	WHOLESALERS	621,908	22	METAL PRODUCTS		195,857
4	INSURANCE: LIFE, HEALTH (STOCK)	586,644	23	SCIENTIFIC, PHOTO, CONTROL EQUIP.		190,317
5	BROKERAGE	501,747	24	ELECTRONICS, ELECTRICAL EQUIP.		183,436
6	INSURANCE: P&C (STOCK)	487,464	25	AIRLINES		178,977
7	ELECTRIC AND GAS UTILITIES	430,969	26	RAILROADS		169,340
8	DIVERSIFIED FINANCIALS	424,510	27	AEROSPACE		168,533
9	COMPUTERS, OFFICE EQUIPMENT	374,190	28	INDUSTRIAL AND FARM EQUIPMENT		168,136
10	CHEMICALS	284,601	29	BUILDING MATERIALS, GLASS		163,745
11	HEALTH CARE	279,881	30	PUBLISHING, PRINTING		159,572
12	METALS	249,615	31	SPECIALIST RETAILERS		158,092
13	FOREST AND PAPER PRODUCTS	249,340	32	MOTOR VEHICLES AND PARTS		153,172
14	BEVERAGES	247,528	33	FOOD AND DRUG STORES		145,111
15	ENGINEERING, CONSTRUCTION	243,631	34	COMPUTER AND DATA SERVICES		144,244
16	COMMERCIAL BANKS	234,769	35	GENERAL MERCHANDISERS		126,988
17	PHARMACEUTICALS	228,871	36	FOOD SERVICES		43,103
18	FOOD	226,475				
19	SOAPS, COSMETICS	224,080		**THE 500 MEDIAN**		**248,392**

REVENUES PER DOLLAR OF EQUITY

		1995 %				1995 $
1	WHOLESALERS	13.28	20	METAL PRODUCTS		2.89
2	FOOD AND DRUG STORES	6.68	21	CHEMICALS		2.85
3	SOAPS, COSMETICS	6.52	22	METALS		2.81
4	SPECIALIST RETAILERS	6.09	23	SCIENTIFIC, PHOTO, CONTROL EQUIP.		2.80
5	AIRLINES	5.61	24	ELECTRONICS, ELECTRICAL EQUIP.		2.76
6	MOTOR VEHICLES AND PARTS	5.59	25	FOREST AND PAPER PRODUCTS		2.63
7	ENGINEERING, CONSTRUCTION	4.92	26	PUBLISHING, PRINTING		2.48
8	FOOD	4.40	27	PHARMACEUTICALS		2.18
9	FOOD SERVICES	4.16	28	COMPUTER AND DATA SERVICES		2.06
10	BEVERAGES	4.02	29	ENTERTAINMENT		2.01
11	COMPUTERS, OFFICE EQUIPMENT	3.81	30	TELECOMMUNICATIONS		2.01
12	AEROSPACE	3.77	31	DIVERSIFIED FINANCIALS		1.90
13	PETROLEUM REFINING	3.77	32	INSURANCE: LIFE, HEALTH (STOCK)		1.78
14	GENERAL MERCHANDISERS	3.64	33	INSURANCE: P&C (STOCK)		1.72
15	HEALTH CARE	3.43	34	RAILROADS		1.32
16	BROKERAGE	3.43	35	COMMERCIAL BANKS		1.19
17	INDUSTRIAL AND FARM EQUIPMENT	3.36	36	ELECTRIC AND GAS UTILITIES		1.13
18	BUILDING MATERIALS, GLASS	2.97				
19	PIPELINES	2.90		THE 500 MEDIAN		2.93

CHANGES IN PROFITS

		1995 %				1995 %
1	ENTERTAINMENT	148.3	20	WHOLESALERS		13.2
2	METALS	116.9	21	COMPUTER AND DATA SERVICES		11.6
3	FOREST AND PAPER PRODUCTS	75.1	22	PHARMACEUTICALS		11.3
4	BROKERAGE	61.9	23	DIVERSIFIED FINANCIALS		11.3
5	COMPUTERS, OFFICE EQUIPMENT	61.8	24	PUBLISHING, PRINTING		11.2
6	BUILDING MATERIALS, GLASS	45.3	25	SPECIALIST RETAILERS		10.6
7	PIPELINES	36.2	26	SCIENTIFIC, PHOTO, CONTROL EQUIP.		9.8
8	AIRLINES	33.9	27	FOOD AND DRUG STORES		7.4
9	CHEMICALS	29.5	28	ELECTRIC AND GAS UTILITIES		7.3
10	INDUSTRIAL AND FARM EQUIPMENT	28.0	29	ENGINEERING, CONSTRUCTION		1.5
11	ELECTRONICS, ELECTRICAL EQUIP.	26.3	30	FOOD SERVICES		0.1
12	INSURANCE: P&C (STOCK)	25.5	31	PETROLEUM REFINING		(4.3)
13	MOTOR VEHICLES AND PARTS	24.9	32	HEALTH CARE		(9.1)
14	AEROSPACE	21.7	33	RAILROADS		(11.9)
15	SOAPS, COSMETICS	19.6	34	METAL PRODUCTS		(14.5)
16	COMMERCIAL BANKS	19.1	35	GENERAL MERCHANDISERS		(18.6)
17	BEVERAGES	17.9	36	TELECOMMUNICATIONS		(156.4)
18	INSURANCE: LIFE, HEALTH (STOCK)	16.1				
19	FOOD	15.6		THE 500 MEDIAN		15.0

TOTAL RETURN TO INVESTORS*: 1 YEAR

		1995 %			1995 %
1	AIRLINES	104.3	20	RAILROADS	38.6
2	PIPELINES	59.0	21	ELECTRONICS, ELECTRICAL EQUIP.	35.0
3	COMMERCIAL BANKS	57.3	22	SOAPS, COSMETICS	33.4
4	PHARMACEUTICALS	57.0	23	INDUSTRIAL AND FARM EQUIPMENT	33.0
5	AEROSPACE	55.8	24	ELECTRIC AND GAS UTILITIES	32.1
6	FOOD SERVICES	55.3	25	FOOD	31.0
7	INSURANCE: LIFE, HEALTH (STOCK)	52.6	26	CHEMICALS	27.1
8	COMPUTERS, OFFICE EQUIPMENT	52.5	27	PUBLISHING, PRINTING	22.7
9	DIVERSIFIED FINANCIALS	50.5	28	ENTERTAINMENT	22.5
10	ENGINEERING, CONSTRUCTION	49.9	29	HEALTH CARE	21.0
11	SCIENTIFIC, PHOTO, CONTROL EQUIP.	48.7	30	MOTOR VEHICLES AND PARTS	20.7
12	TELECOMMUNICATIONS	44.6	31	PETROLEUM REFINING	17.6
13	BUILDING MATERIALS, GLASS	42.6	32	WHOLESALERS	17.6
14	FOOD AND DRUG STORES	42.0	33	FOREST AND PAPER PRODUCTS	12.5
15	BEVERAGES	41.7	34	GENERAL MERCHANDISERS	8.6
16	COMPUTER AND DATA SERVICES	40.7	35	SPECIALIST RETAILERS	4.2
17	INSURANCE: P&C (STOCK)	40.4	36	METALS	3.7
18	BROKERAGE	39.9			
19	METAL PRODUCTS	38.8		**THE 500 MEDIAN**	**32.8**

TOTAL RETURN TO INVESTORS*: 10 YEARS

		1985-95 ANNUAL RATE %			1985-95 ANNUAL RATE %
1	ENTERTAINMENT	23.6	20	ELECTRONICS, ELECTRICAL EQUIP.	13.2
2	FOOD SERVICES	21.1	21	ELECTRIC AND GAS UTILITIES	13.1
3	COMPUTER AND DATA SERVICES	19.5	22	PIPELINES	12.8
4	PHARMACEUTICALS	19.1	23	INDUSTRIAL AND FARM EQUIPMENT	12.5
5	HEALTH CARE	18.4	24	BUILDING MATERIALS, GLASS	12.5
6	METAL PRODUCTS	18.1	25	MOTOR VEHICLES AND PARTS	12.3
7	SOAPS, COSMETICS	17.5	26	COMPUTERS, OFFICE EQUIPMENT	12.1
8	TELECOMMUNICATIONS	17.1	27	DIVERSIFIED FINANCIALS	11.9
9	FOOD	17.0	28	FOREST AND PAPER PRODUCTS	11.8
10	CHEMICALS	16.0	29	WHOLESALERS	11.7
11	RAILROADS	15.3	30	PETROLEUM REFINING	11.1
12	INSURANCE: P&C (STOCK)	15.2	31	GENERAL MERCHANDISERS	11.1
13	FOOD AND DRUG STORES	15.1	32	ENGINEERING, CONSTRUCTION	10.6
14	COMMERCIAL BANKS	15.0	33	BROKERAGE	10.3
15	BEVERAGES	14.8	34	PUBLISHING, PRINTING	10.1
16	SCIENTIFIC, PHOTO, CONTROL EQUIP.	14.0	35	AIRLINES	8.3
17	METALS	13.8	36	SPECIALIST RETAILERS	7.5
18	INSURANCE: LIFE, HEALTH (STOCK)	13.5			
19	AEROSPACE	13.4		**THE 500 MEDIAN**	**13.9**

* INCLUDING CAPITAL GAINS OR LOSSES PLUS REINVESTED DIVIDENDS.

RETURN ON REVENUES

#		1995 %	#		1995 %
1	PHARMACEUTICALS	14.4	20	BUILDING MATERIALS, GLASS	4.4
2	COMMERCIAL BANKS	13.3	21	FOOD	4.2
3	DIVERSIFIED FINANCIALS	10.7	22	SOAPS, COSMETICS	4.2
4	ELECTRIC AND GAS UTILITIES	10.3	23	MOTOR VEHICLES AND PARTS	4.1
5	COMPUTER AND DATA SERVICES	9.8	24	HEALTH CARE	4.0
6	INSURANCE: P&C (STOCK)	8.9	25	AEROSPACE	3.5
7	PUBLISHING, PRINTING	8.6	26	FOOD SERVICES	3.5
8	CHEMICALS	8.2	27	GENERAL MERCHANDISERS	2.9
9	INSURANCE: LIFE, HEALTH (STOCK)	6.8	28	AIRLINES	2.8
10	RAILROADS	6.5	29	ENGINEERING, CONSTRUCTION	2.5
11	ELECTRONICS, ELECTRICAL EQUIP.	6.4	30	ENTERTAINMENT	2.4
12	FOREST AND PAPER PRODUCTS	6.4	31	METAL PRODUCTS	2.3
13	SCIENTIFIC, PHOTO, CONTROL EQUIP.	6.4	32	PETROLEUM REFINING	2.1
14	PIPELINES	5.7	33	SPECIALIST RETAILERS	1.8
15	METALS	5.4	34	FOOD AND DRUG STORES	1.7
16	COMPUTERS, OFFICE EQUIPMENT	5.1	35	WHOLESALERS	0.8
17	BROKERAGE	5.1	36	TELECOMMUNICATIONS	0.2
18	BEVERAGES	4.9			
19	INDUSTRIAL AND FARM EQUIPMENT	4.5		THE 500 MEDIAN	4.8

RETURN ON ASSETS

#		1995 %	#		1995 %
1	PHARMACEUTICALS	13.2	20	ENGINEERING, CONSTRUCTION	4.5
2	COMPUTER AND DATA SERVICES	9.1	21	AEROSPACE	4.2
3	CHEMICALS	8.4	22	PIPELINES	4.0
4	COMPUTERS, OFFICE EQUIPMENT	7.4	23	BUILDING MATERIALS, GLASS	3.9
5	PUBLISHING, PRINTING	7.3	24	RAILROADS	3.7
6	SOAPS, COSMETICS	7.0	25	ELECTRIC AND GAS UTILITIES	3.6
7	FOOD	7.0	26	METAL PRODUCTS	3.5
8	FOREST AND PAPER PRODUCTS	7.0	27	WHOLESALERS	3.4
9	ELECTRONICS, ELECTRICAL EQUIP.	6.9	28	AIRLINES	3.4
10	SCIENTIFIC, PHOTO, CONTROL EQUIP.	6.9	29	PETROLEUM REFINING	2.7
11	BEVERAGES	5.9	30	INSURANCE: P&C (STOCK)	2.2
12	FOOD AND DRUG STORES	5.6	31	ENTERTAINMENT	1.6
13	SPECIALIST RETAILERS	5.2	32	DIVERSIFIED FINANCIALS	1.2
14	MOTOR VEHICLES AND PARTS	5.1	33	COMMERCIAL BANKS	1.2
15	METALS	5.0	34	INSURANCE: LIFE, HEALTH (STOCK)	1.0
16	INDUSTRIAL AND FARM EQUIPMENT	5.0	35	BROKERAGE	0.2
17	FOOD SERVICES	5.0	36	TELECOMMUNICATIONS	(0.2)
18	GENERAL MERCHANDISERS	4.9			
19	HEALTH CARE	4.8		THE 500 MEDIAN	3.9

		1995 %			1995 %
1	PHARMACEUTICALS	30.7	20	COMMERCIAL BANKS	15.6
2	SOAPS, COSMETICS	25.0	21	INSURANCE: P&C (STOCK)	13.2
3	COMPUTER AND DATA SERVICES	23.0	22	SPECIALIST RETAILERS	13.1
4	FOOD SERVICES	22.0	23	FOOD AND DRUG STORES	13.0
5	PUBLISHING, PRINTING	21.9	24	BUILDING MATERIALS, GLASS	12.9
6	FOOD	21.4	25	ELECTRIC AND GAS UTILITIES	11.9
7	MOTOR VEHICLES AND PARTS	20.2	26	RAILROADS	11.7
8	CHEMICALS	19.8	27	ENTERTAINMENT	11.3
9	INDUSTRIAL AND FARM EQUIPMENT	18.3	28	WHOLESALERS	11.1
10	DIVERSIFIED FINANCIALS	18.2	29	INSURANCE: LIFE, HEALTH (STOCK)	11.0
11	BEVERAGES	17.9	30	HEALTH CARE	10.8
12	FOREST AND PAPER PRODUCTS	17.6	31	BROKERAGE	9.8
13	AIRLINES	17.6	32	ENGINEERING, CONSTRUCTION	9.6
14	ELECTRONICS, ELECTRICAL EQUIP.	17.4	33	GENERAL MERCHANDISERS	9.1
15	METALS	17.4	34	PETROLEUM REFINING	8.6
16	SCIENTIFIC, PHOTO, CONTROL EQUIP.	16.9	35	METAL PRODUCTS	8.0
17	COMPUTERS, OFFICE EQUIPMENT	16.9	36	TELECOMMUNICATIONS	0.8
18	PIPELINES	16.4			
19	AEROSPACE	15.7		**THE 500 MEDIAN**	**14.0**

Headed for the dustbin of corporate history just a couple of years ago, a reinvigorated GM and IBM have bounded back, earning among the highest profits. GM, with $6.9 billion, is now No. 1, up from third place last year. IBM jumped to fifth from ninth. Airlines, getting a handle on costs after a financially disastrous 1994, occupied the top three seats for highest one-year total return, while high tech stole the show on ten-year earnings growth.

BIGGEST INCREASES IN REVENUES

		500 REVENUES RANK	REVENUES % CHANGE FROM '94	1995 REVENUES $ MILLIONS
1	FIRST CHICAGO NBD CORP.	117	208.6	10,681.0
2	COMCAST	369	144.5	3,362.9
3	AMERICAN FINANCIAL GROUP	345	105.4	3,629.6
4	PHARMACIA & UPJOHN	183	99.0	7,094.6
5	GENERAL RE	181	87.9	7,210.2
6	KIMBERLY-CLARK	78	87.2	13,788.6
7	FIRST DATA	312	84.9	4,081.2
8	UTILICORP UNITED	452	84.8	2,798.5
9	APPLIED MATERIALS	405	84.5	3,061.9
10	MICRON TECHNOLOGY	419	81.3	2,952.7
11	FEDERATED DEPARTMENT STORES	69	81.0	15,048.5
12	FLEET FINANCIAL GROUP	166	78.2	7,919.4
13	REVCO D.S.	295	77.0	4,431.9
14	LOCKHEED MARTIN	29	74.1	22,853.0
15	ASSOCIATED INSURANCE	217	71.9	6,037.5
16	FIRST UNION CORP.	118	69.2	10,582.9
17	BEST BUY	262	69.0	5,079.6
18	VALERO ENERGY	412	64.3	3,019.8
19	WORLDCOM	342	63.9	3,640.0
20	COLUMBIA/HCA HEALTHCARE	51	59.0	17,695.0
21	FHP INTERNATIONAL	319	58.1	3,909.4
22	QUANTUM	368	58.0	3,368.0
23	ASARCO	389	57.4	3,197.8
24	VIACOM	105	54.3	11,780.2
25	CONSECO	444	53.6	2,860.7
26	STAPLES	404	53.4	3,068.1
27	DELL COMPUTER	250	52.4	5,296.0
28	UNITED HEALTHCARE	232	50.4	5,670.0
29	LEAR SEATING	278	49.8	4,714.4
30	U.S. BANCORP	433	49.6	2,897.3
31	AMERICAN HOME PRODUCTS	86	49.2	13,376.1
32	ORACLE	417	48.3	2,966.9
33	LEHMAN BROTHERS HOLDINGS	82	46.6	13,476.0
34	FOUNDATION HEALTH	494	43.2	2,459.9
35	SALOMON	149	42.3	8,933.0
36	INTEL	61	40.6	16,202.0
37	SCI SYSTEMS	465	40.6	2,673.8
38	FIRST BANK SYSTEM	371	40.1	3,328.3
39	THRIFTY PAYLESS HOLDINGS	284	39.2	4,658.8
40	TYCO INTERNATIONAL	289	39.0	4,534.7
41	LOEWS	44	38.9	18,770.0
42	TELE-COMMUNICATIONS	190	38.8	6,851.0
43	MBNA	479	38.4	2,565.4
44	OFFICEMAX	483	38.1	2,542.5
45	FEDERAL HOME LOAN MORTGAGE	135	37.5	9,519.0
46	LORAL	240	36.8	5,484.4
47	PNC BANK CORP.	205	36.4	6,389.5
48	GATEWAY 2000	340	36.1	3,676.3
49	COMPAQ COMPUTER	72	35.8	14,755.0
50	FOSTER WHEELER	400	35.7	3,081.9
	THE 500 MEDIAN		9.9	5,288.5

HIGHEST PROFITS

		500 REVENUES RANK	1995 PROFITS $ MILLIONS	PROFITS % CHANGE FROM 1994
1	GENERAL MOTORS	1	6,880.7	40.4
2	GENERAL ELECTRIC	7	6,573.0	39.1
3	EXXON	3	6,470.0	26.9
4	PHILIP MORRIS	10	5,450.0	15.3
5	INTL. BUSINESS MACHINES	6	4,178.0	38.3
6	FORD MOTOR	2	4,139.0	(22.0)
7	INTEL	61	3,566.0	55.9
8	CITICORP	19	3,464.0	2.9
9	MERCK	56	3,335.2	11.3
10	E.I. DU PONT DE NEMOURS	13	3,293.0	20.8
11	COCA-COLA	48	2,986.0	16.9
12	WAL-MART STORES	4	2,740.0	2.2
13	BANKAMERICA CORP.	37	2,664.0	22.4
14	PROCTER & GAMBLE	17	2,645.0	19.6
15	AMERICAN INTERNATIONAL GROUP	25	2,510.4	15.4
16	HEWLETT-PACKARD	20	2,433.0	52.2
17	JOHNSON & JOHNSON	43	2,403.0	19.8
18	MOBIL	8	2,376.0	120.2
19	FED. NATL. MORTGAGE ASSN.	32	2,372.0	11.3
20	ELI LILLY	171	2,290.9	78.1
21	DOW CHEMICAL	36	2,078.0	121.5
22	CHRYSLER	9	2,025.0	(45.5)
23	AMERITECH	84	2,007.6	—
24	NATIONSBANK CORP.	60	1,950.0	15.4
25	ALLSTATE	31	1,904.0	N.A.
26	AMOCO	23	1,862.0	4.1
27	BELL ATLANTIC	83	1,858.3	—
28	TRAVELERS GROUP	57	1,834.0	38.3
29	BRISTOL-MYERS SQUIBB	79	1,812.0	(1.6)
30	CHEMICAL BANKING CORP.	71	1,805.0	39.5
31	SEARS ROEBUCK	15	1,801.0	23.9
32	MOTOROLA	24	1,781.0	14.2
33	LOEWS	44	1,765.7	559.3
34	ABBOTT LABORATORIES	128	1,688.7	11.3
35	AMERICAN HOME PRODUCTS	86	1,680.4	10.0
36	PEPSICO	21	1,606.0	(8.3)
37	PFIZER	126	1,572.9	21.1
38	AMERICAN EXPRESS	53	1,564.0	10.7
39	MICROSOFT	219	1,453.0	26.8
40	FIRST UNION CORP.	118	1,430.2	54.6
41	MCDONALD'S	131	1,427.3	16.6
42	WALT DISNEY	102	1,380.1	24.3
43	ATLANTIC RICHFIELD	55	1,376.0	49.7
44	PACIFIC GAS & ELECTRIC	133	1,338.9	32.9
45	WILLIAMS	447	1,318.2	434.3
46	US WEST	106	1,317.0	(7.6)
47	J.P. MORGAN & CO.	76	1,296.0	6.7
48	BANC ONE CORP.	145	1,277.9	27.1
49	STATE FARM GROUP	12	1,271.2	—
50	EASTMAN KODAK	67	1,252.0	124.8
	THE 500 MEDIAN		267.2	

BIGGEST INCREASES IN PROFITS*	500 REVENUES RANK	PROFITS % CHANGE FROM '94	1995 PROFITS $ MILLIONS
1	QUANTUM	368	2,951.3	81.6
2	SUPERMARKETS GENL. HOLDINGS	304	1,613.2	75.5
3	RITE AID	290	1,421.2	141.3
4	CHAMPION INTERNATIONAL	188	1,119.2	771.8
5	NORTHROP GRUMMAN	192	620.0	252.0
6	TIMES MIRROR	355	608.6	1,226.8
7	UAL	70	584.3	349.0
8	LOEWS	44	559.3	1,765.7
9	WILLIAMS	447	434.3	1,318.2
10	ALUMAX	427	408.4	237.4
11	TURNER BROADCASTING	363	386.8	103.0
12	PARKER HANNIFIN	386	358.0	218.2
13	FRED MEYER	364	322.5	30.3
14	OFFICEMAX	483	314.3	125.8
15	SARA LEE	50	304.0	804.0
16	UNION CAMP	301	297.4	451.1
17	PITTSTON	428	264.2	98.0
18	PRINCIPAL MUTUAL LIFE INS.	119	264.2	554.0
19	QUAKER OATS	206	246.4	802.0
20	ALLMERICA FINANCIAL	384	229.3	133.9
21	GEORGIA-PACIFIC	75	228.4	1,018.0
22	INTERNATIONAL PAPER	39	223.0	1,153.0
23	REYNOLDS METALS	179	219.6	389.0
24	MANVILLE	457	213.5	116.0
25	MCKESSON	87	197.0	404.5
26	WILLAMETTE INDUSTRIES	323	189.8	514.8
27	ALCO STANDARD	130	187.1	202.7
28	HOUSTON INDUSTRIES	298	181.5	1,124.0
29	UNIVERSAL	379	180.0	25.6
30	PHELPS DODGE	303	175.5	746.6
31	WESTVACO	377	171.1	280.8
32	GENERAL PUBLIC UTILITIES	325	168.9	440.1
33	ASARCO	389	164.2	169.2
34	PAINE WEBBER GROUP	248	163.4	80.8
35	CASE	261	157.3	337.0
36	VONS	263	156.0	68.1
37	VIACOM	105	148.3	222.5
38	BAKER HUGHES	469	147.1	105.4
39	MASS. MUTUAL LIFE INSURANCE	193	146.4	229.4
40	CARDINAL HEALTH	168	141.8	85.0
41	UNION CARBIDE	223	137.8	925.0
42	LEVI STRAUSS ASSOCIATES	198	128.9	734.7
43	EASTMAN KODAK	67	124.8	1,252.0
44	BETHLEHEM STEEL	272	123.1	179.6
45	VALERO ENERGY	412	122.6	59.8
46	PETER KIEWIT SONS'	431	121.8	244.0
47	DOW CHEMICAL	36	121.5	2,078.0
48	MOBIL	8	120.2	2,376.0
49	NGC	341	120.2	92.7
50	U.S. BANCORP	433	117.1	329.0
	THE 500 MEDIAN		15.0	

* EXCLUDES COMPANIES THAT LOST MONEY IN 1994.

HIGHEST RETURNS ON REVENUES

		500 REVENUES RANK	1995 PROFITS AS % OF REVENUES			500 REVENUES RANK	1995 PROFITS AS % OF REVENUES
1	WILLIAMS	447	46.2	26	SUNTRUST BANKS	332	15.1
2	TIMES MIRROR	355	35.1	27	PITNEY BOWES	324	15.1
3	ELI LILLY	171	30.4	28	AMERITECH	84	15.0
4	MICRON TECHNOLOGY	419	28.6	29	ORACLE	417	14.9
5	HOUSTON INDUSTRIES	298	25.6	30	PACIFICORP	365	14.8
6	MICROSOFT	219	24.5	31	APPLIED MATERIALS	405	14.8
7	INTEL	61	22.0	32	MCDONALD'S	131	14.6
8	MERCK	56	20.0	33	PECO ENERGY	302	14.6
9	WELLS FARGO & CO.	245	19.1	34	BARNETT BANKS	339	14.5
10	FIRST INTERSTATE BANCORP	274	18.3	35	BANC ONE CORP.	145	14.2
11	PHELPS DODGE	303	17.8	36	BOATMEN'S BANCSHARES	415	14.0
12	SCHERING-PLOUGH	259	17.2	37	PACIFIC GAS & ELECTRIC	133	13.9
13	BANK OF NEW YORK CO.	247	17.2	38	BELL ATLANTIC	83	13.8
14	FIRST BANK SYSTEM	371	17.1	39	MBNA	479	13.8
15	ABBOTT LABORATORIES	128	16.9	40	AUTOMATIC DATA PROC.	436	13.6
16	COCA-COLA	48	16.6	41	KEYCORP	216	13.6
17	COMPUTER ASSOCIATES INTL.	474	16.5	42	FIRST UNION CORP.	118	13.5
18	BERKSHIRE HATHAWAY	293	16.2	43	NATIONAL CITY CORP.	362	13.5
19	WACHOVIA CORP.	328	16.0	44	WILLAMETTE INDUSTRIES	323	13.3
20	CORESTATES FINAN. CORP.	441	15.8	45	COMERICA	395	13.3
21	UNION CARBIDE	223	15.7	46	PP&L RESOURCES	466	13.2
22	PFIZER	126	15.7	47	BRISTOL-MYERS SQUIBB	79	13.2
23	MELLON BANK CORP.	291	15.3	48	BANKAMERICA CORP.	37	13.1
24	DUKE POWER	280	15.3	49	OHIO EDISON	493	12.9
25	NORFOLK SOUTHERN	283	15.3	50	JOHNSON & JOHNSON	43	12.8
	THE 500 MEDIAN						**4.8**

HIGHEST RETURNS ON ASSETS

		500 REVENUES RANK	1995 PROFITS AS % OF ASSETS			500 REVENUES RANK	1995 PROFITS AS % OF ASSETS
1	TIMES MIRROR	355	32.1	26	COMPUTER ASSOCIATES INTL.	474	13.2
2	MICRON TECHNOLOGY	419	30.4	27	BRISTOL-MYERS SQUIBB	79	13.0
3	U.S. HEALTHCARE	353	22.8	28	GILLETTE	195	13.0
4	INTEL	61	20.4	29	IBP	94	12.7
5	MICROSOFT	219	20.2	30	NIKE	277	12.7
6	COCA-COLA	48	19.9	31	DELL COMPUTER	250	12.7
7	SCHERING-PLOUGH	259	19.0	32	WILLIAMS	447	12.6
8	LIMITED	167	18.3	33	AVON PRODUCTS	292	12.5
9	ORACLE	417	18.2	34	PPG INDUSTRIES	185	12.4
10	ABBOTT LABORATORIES	128	17.9	35	PFIZER	126	12.4
11	QUAKER OATS	206	16.6	36	AUTOMATIC DATA PROC.	436	12.3
12	PHELPS DODGE	303	16.1	37	WARNER-LAMBERT	186	12.1
13	ELI LILLY	171	15.9	38	PREMARK INTERNATIONAL	348	12.1
14	LEVI STRAUSS ASSOCIATES	198	15.6	39	ITT INDUSTRIES	151	12.0
15	GATEWAY 2000	340	15.4	40	NUCOR	359	12.0
16	APPLIED MATERIALS	405	15.3	41	TEXAS INSTRUMENTS	89	11.8
17	GAP	297	15.1	42	MCKESSON	87	11.6
18	WILLAMETTE INDUSTRIES	323	15.1	43	EASTMAN CHEMICAL	267	11.5
19	LYONDELL PETROCHEMICAL	270	14.9	44	ALBERTSON'S	96	11.2
20	UNION CARBIDE	223	14.8	45	W.W. GRAINGER	381	11.2
21	MERCK	56	14.0	46	KELLOGG	187	11.1
22	GENUINE PARTS	252	13.6	47	CAMPBELL SOUP	177	11.1
23	READER'S DIGEST ASSN.	403	13.5	48	GENERAL MILLS	156	10.9
24	JOHNSON & JOHNSON	43	13.4	49	ILLINOIS TOOL WORKS	306	10.7
25	MATTEL	343	13.3	50	MORTON INTERNATIONAL	370	10.7
	THE 500 MEDIAN						**3.9**

HIGHEST RETURNS ON STOCKHOLDERS' EQUITY

		500 REVENUES RANK	1995 PROFITS AS % OF EQUITY			500 REVENUES RANK	1995 PROFITS AS % OF EQUITY
1	GENERAL MILLS	156	260.6	26	EASTMAN CHEMICAL	267	36.6
2	AVON PRODUCTS	292	133.1	27	ORACLE	417	36.4
3	ITT INDUSTRIES	151	112.9	28	ESTÉE LAUDER	432	36.2
4	LYONDELL PETROCHEMICAL	270	102.4	29	LEVI STRAUSS ASSOCIATES	198	34.7
5	CONTINENTAL AIRLINES	226	70.5	30	CATERPILLAR	64	33.5
6	QUAKER OATS	206	69.9	31	FMC	287	33.0
7	TIMES MIRROR	355	67.9	32	WARNER-LAMBERT	186	32.9
8	RALSTON PURINA	180	56.2	33	GILLETTE	195	32.8
9	COCA-COLA	48	55.4	34	OWENS-ILLINOIS	327	31.8
10	SCHERING-PLOUGH	259	53.3	35	HEALTH SYSTEMS INTL.	458	31.3
11	STUDENT LOAN MKTG. ASSN.	318	45.9	36	GATEWAY 2000	340	31.1
12	UNION CARBIDE	223	45.2	37	BRISTOL-MYERS SQUIBB	79	31.1
13	MICRON TECHNOLOGY	419	44.5	38	KELLOGG	187	30.8
14	ELI LILLY	171	42.2	39	AMERICAN HOME PRODUCTS	86	30.3
15	WILLIAMS	447	41.4	40	LIMITED	167	30.0
16	READER'S DIGEST ASSN.	403	41.2	41	PPG INDUSTRIES	185	29.9
17	SEARS ROEBUCK	15	41.1	42	GENERAL MOTORS	1	29.5
18	SAFEWAY	59	41.0	43	INTEL	61	29.3
19	TELEDYNE	478	40.5	44	GEORGIA-PACIFIC	75	28.9
20	MCKESSON	87	39.9	45	AMERITECH	84	28.6
21	U.S. HEALTHCARE	353	39.5	46	PFIZER	126	28.6
22	E.I. DU PONT DE NEMOURS	13	39.0	47	MERCK	56	28.4
23	PHILIP MORRIS	10	39.0	48	CAMPBELL SOUP	177	28.3
24	ABBOTT LABORATORIES	128	38.4	49	DOW CHEMICAL	36	28.2
25	ARAMARK	235	37.1	50	PITNEY BOWES	324	28.2
	THE 500 MEDIAN						14.0

HIGHEST TOTAL RETURN TO INVESTORS': 1 YEAR

		500 REVENUES RANK	1995 %			500 REVENUES RANK	1995 %
1	CONTINENTAL AIRLINES	226	353.3	26	WILLIAMS	447	79.9
2	NORTHWEST AIRLINES	143	223.8	27	MONSANTO	146	78.7
3	USAIR GROUP	174	211.8	28	INTEL	61	78.2
4	SUN MICROSYSTEMS	222	157.0	29	ALLSTATE	31	77.3
5	CASE	261	114.3	30	ELI LILLY	171	77.1
6	STUDENT LOAN MKTG. ASSN.	318	109.5	31	MERCK	56	76.8
7	FIRST INTERSTATE BANCORP	274	108.5	32	DOLE FOOD	305	76.6
8	COMPUSA	451	107.5	33	COMPUTER ASSOCIATES INTL.	474	76.5
9	UAL	70	104.3	34	RELIANCE GROUP HOLDINGS	430	75.3
10	SEAGATE TECHNOLOGY	288	97.9	35	FED. NATL. MORTGAGE ASSN.	32	75.0
11	TRAVELERS GROUP	57	97.6	36	KIMBERLY-CLARK	78	73.7
12	MCDONNELL DOUGLAS	74	96.3	37	SCI SYSTEMS	465	72.2
13	DIGITAL EQUIPMENT	77	92.9	38	NORAM ENERGY	443	71.9
14	LORAL	240	89.1	39	COMERICA	395	71.7
15	NIKE	277	88.8	40	H.F. AHMANSON	296	70.9
16	COLUMBIA GAS SYSTEM	470	86.7	41	CHEMICAL BANKING CORP.	71	70.5
17	APPLIED MATERIALS	405	86.4	42	BANK OF NEW YORK CO.	247	69.9
18	FOXMEYER HEALTH	257	85.0	43	BOEING	40	69.6
19	BANK OF BOSTON CORP.	243	84.7	44	HEWLETT-PACKARD	20	69.4
20	MELLON BANK CORP.	291	83.8	45	BANKAMERICA CORP.	37	69.4
21	CHASE MANHATTAN CORP.	112	82.4	46	DELL COMPUTER	250	68.9
22	LOEWS	44	81.9	47	CIGNA	42	68.8
23	LOCKHEED MARTIN	29	81.4	48	FEDERAL HOME LOAN MTG.	135	68.2
24	WORLDCOM	342	81.4	49	IBP	94	67.8
25	MICRON TECHNOLOGY	419	80.3	50	BELLSOUTH	49	67.7
	THE 500 MEDIAN						32.8

* INCLUDING CAPITAL GAINS OR LOSSES PLUS REINVESTED DIVIDENDS.

HIGHEST TOTAL RETURN TO INVESTORS*: 10 YEARS

		500 REVENUES RANK	1985-95 ANNUAL RATE %			500 REVENUES RANK	1985-95 ANNUAL RATE %
1	HOME DEPOT	66	44.5	26	ALBERTSON'S	96	25.2
2	CONSECO	444	42.6	27	CIRCUIT CITY STORES	237	24.9
3	APPLIED MATERIALS	405	40.7	28	NORWEST CORP.	170	24.7
4	UNITED HEALTHCARE	232	38.3	29	WALT DISNEY	102	24.4
5	MICRON TECHNOLOGY	419	37.2	30	TURNER BROADCASTING	363	23.6
6	NIKE	277	36.8	31	PEPSICO	21	23.5
7	COMPAQ COMPUTER	72	36.1	32	PHELPS DODGE	303	23.5
8	COMPUTER ASSOCIATES INTL.	474	35.1	33	OWENS-CORNING	346	23.5
9	FED. NATL. MORTGAGE ASSN.	32	33.1	34	JOHNSON & JOHNSON	43	23.1
10	GILLETTE	195	31.2	35	TELE-COMMUNICATIONS	190	23.0
11	BERKSHIRE HATHAWAY	293	29.4	36	PROGRESSIVE	413	22.7
12	COCA-COLA	48	29.3	37	ILLINOIS TOOL WORKS	306	22.6
13	GAP	297	28.4	38	MATTEL	343	22.6
14	U.S. HEALTHCARE	353	28.3	39	MONSANTO	146	21.9
15	PHILIP MORRIS	10	28.2	40	CPC INTERNATIONAL	154	21.7
16	INTEL	61	28.0	41	KIMBERLY-CLARK	78	21.4
17	NEWELL	488	27.6	42	REEBOK INTERNATIONAL	356	21.2
18	FIRST DATA	312	27.5	43	NUCOR	359	21.1
19	MERCK	56	27.1	44	ALLTEL	396	21.0
20	SHAW INDUSTRIES	439	26.9	45	TYCO INTERNATIONAL	289	20.7
21	KROGER	27	26.5	46	SBC COMMUNICATIONS	93	20.7
22	PACIFICARE HEALTH SYSTEMS	334	26.0	47	PFIZER	126	20.7
23	WELLS FARGO & CO.	245	25.7	48	SEAGATE TECHNOLOGY	288	20.7
24	SCHERING-PLOUGH	259	25.5	49	MOTOROLA	24	20.7
25	CARDINAL HEALTH	168	25.2	50	SARA LEE	50	20.6
	THE 500 MEDIAN						**13.9**

GREATEST GROWTH IN EARNINGS PER SHARE: 10 YEARS

		500 REVENUES RANK	1985-95 ANNUAL RATE %			500 REVENUES RANK	1985-95 ANNUAL RATE %
1	INTEL	61	117.9	26	CHUBB	215	23.4
2	MICRON TECHNOLOGY	419	113.6	27	WALT DISNEY	102	23.2
3	SEAGATE TECHNOLOGY	288	67.7	28	WILLAMETTE INDUSTRIES	323	22.9
4	CINERGY	411	60.2	29	CIRCUIT CITY STORES	237	21.6
5	HOME DEPOT	66	47.0	30	APPLE COMPUTER	114	21.4
6	CONSECO	444	46.8	31	GEORGIA-PACIFIC	75	21.3
7	NIKE	277	44.7	32	GENERAL RE	181	21.2
8	DOW CHEMICAL	36	43.6	33	PACIFICARE HEALTH SYSTEMS	334	21.2
9	PHELPS DODGE	303	42.7	34	LIMITED	167	21.0
10	STONE CONTAINER	175	42.1	35	OLSTEN	485	20.6
11	APPLIED MATERIALS	405	40.1	36	CARDINAL HEALTH	168	20.5
12	WILLIAMS	447	39.4	37	AFLAC	182	20.5
13	UNITED HEALTHCARE	232	38.6	38	MERCK	56	20.4
14	TURNER BROADCASTING	363	36.0	39	QUAKER OATS	206	20.3
15	BEST BUY	262	35.4	40	PROGRESSIVE	413	20.1
16	MOTOROLA	24	34.4	41	DEERE	123	19.7
17	COMPAQ COMPUTER	72	33.4	42	ALBERTSON'S	96	19.1
18	COMPUTER ASSOCIATES INTL.	474	32.7	43	GILLETTE	195	19.0
19	U.S. HEALTHCARE	353	32.0	44	CATERPILLAR	64	18.9
20	SPRINT	80	28.7	45	TENNECO	150	18.7
21	FED. NATL. MORTGAGE ASSN.	32	28.6	46	AMERICAN INTL. GROUP	25	18.4
22	GAP	297	28.4	47	NEWELL	488	18.4
23	ILLINOIS TOOL WORKS	306	26.5	48	NORWEST CORP.	170	17.9
24	INTERNATIONAL PAPER	39	23.6	49	COCA-COLA	48	17.8
25	WAL-MART STORES	4	23.4	50	TYSON FOODS	239	17.8
	THE 500 MEDIAN						**7.8**

* INCLUDING CAPITAL GAINS OR LOSSES PLUS REINVESTED DIVIDENDS.

HIGHEST MARKET VALUE

		500 REVENUES RANK	3/15/96 $ MILLIONS			500 REVENUES RANK	3/15/96 $ MILLIONS
1	GENERAL ELECTRIC	7	126,523	26	MCDONALD'S	131	35,684
2	COCA-COLA	48	101,280	27	FORD MOTOR	2	34,908
3	AT&T	5	98,122	28	AMOCO	23	34,898
4	EXXON	3	98,093	29	FED. NATL. MORTGAGE ASSN.	32	34,262
5	PHILIP MORRIS	10	79,613	30	ELI LILLY	171	33,574
6	MERCK	56	76,496	31	CITICORP	19	33,222
7	INTL. BUSINESS MACHINES	6	68,257	32	MOTOROLA	24	32,872
8	JOHNSON & JOHNSON	43	62,629	33	ABBOTT LABORATORIES	128	32,280
9	MICROSOFT	219	60,811	34	SBC COMMUNICATIONS	93	31,154
10	PROCTER & GAMBLE	17	57,058	35	AMERICAN HOME PRODUCTS	86	30,841
11	WAL-MART STORES	4	54,495	36	AMERITECH	84	30,117
12	HEWLETT-PACKARD	20	50,932	37	BOEING	40	27,817
13	PEPSICO	21	49,147	38	BANKAMERICA CORP.	37	27,149
14	INTEL	61	48,348	39	BELL ATLANTIC	83	26,894
15	WALT DISNEY	102	47,107	40	MINNESOTA MINING & MFG.	63	26,588
16	E.I. DU PONT DE NEMOURS	13	45,120	41	EASTMAN KODAK	67	25,293
17	MOBIL	8	44,192	42	COLUMBIA/HCA HEALTHCARE	51	23,983
18	BERKSHIRE HATHAWAY	293	43,880	43	HOME DEPOT	66	23,602
19	AMERICAN INTL. GROUP	25	43,684	44	AMERICAN EXPRESS	53	23,433
20	BRISTOL-MYERS SQUIBB	79	42,636	45	CHRYSLER	9	23,314
21	GTE	38	40,465	46	DOW CHEMICAL	36	23,233
22	PFIZER	126	39,998	47	GILLETTE	195	23,075
23	GENERAL MOTORS	1	39,309	48	TEXACO	14	21,888
24	BELLSOUTH	49	36,029	49	ORACLE	417	21,275
25	CHEVRON	18	35,791	50	KIMBERLY-CLARK	78	21,271
	THE 500 MEDIAN						**4,953**

MOST ASSETS

		500 REVENUES RANK	1995 $ MILLIONS			500 REVENUES RANK	1995 $ MILLIONS
1	FED. NATL. MORTGAGE ASSN.	32	316,550	26	EXXON	3	91,296
2	CITICORP	19	256,853	27	BANC ONE CORP.	145	90,454
3	FORD MOTOR	2	243,283	28	AT&T	5	88,884
4	BANKAMERICA CORP.	37	232,446	29	STATE FARM GROUP	12	85,262
5	GENERAL ELECTRIC	7	228,035	30	FLEET FINANCIAL GROUP	166	84,432
6	PRUDENTIAL INS. OF AMERICA	11	219,380	31	AETNA LIFE & CASUALTY	91	84,324
7	GENERAL MOTORS	1	217,123	32	COLLEGE RET. EQUITIES FUND	164	80,790
8	SALOMON	149	188,000	33	INTL. BUSINESS MACHINES	6	80,292
9	NATIONSBANK CORP.	60	187,298	34	TEACHERS INS. & ANNUITY	109	79,795
10	J.P. MORGAN & CO.	76	184,879	35	BEAR STEARNS	329	74,597
11	CHEMICAL BANKING CORP.	71	182,926	36	NEW YORK LIFE INSURANCE	62	74,281
12	MERRILL LYNCH	33	176,857	37	PNC BANK CORP.	205	73,404
13	METROPOLITAN LIFE INS.	22	158,800	38	NORWEST CORP.	170	72,134
14	MORGAN STANLEY GROUP	116	143,753	39	ALLSTATE	31	70,029
15	FEDERAL HOME LOAN MTG.	135	137,181	40	KEYCORP	216	66,339
16	AMERICAN INTL. GROUP	25	134,136	41	LOEWS	44	65,058
17	FIRST UNION CORP.	118	131,880	42	LINCOLN NATIONAL	199	63,258
18	FIRST CHICAGO NBD CORP.	117	122,002	43	AMERICAN GENERAL	202	61,153
19	CHASE MANHATTAN CORP.	112	121,173	44	NATIONWIDE INS. ENTERPRISE	108	60,664
20	LEHMAN BROTHERS HOLDINGS	82	115,303	45	FIRST INTERSTATE BANCORP	274	58,071
21	TRAVELERS GROUP	57	114,500	46	PRINCIPAL MUT. LIFE INS.	119	56,947
22	AMERICAN EXPRESS	53	107,405	47	NORTHWESTERN MUT. LIFE INS.	111	54,876
23	BANKERS TRUST N.Y. CORP.	152	104,000	48	JOHN HANCOCK MUTUAL LIFE	224	54,505
24	CIGNA	42	95,903	49	PHILIP MORRIS	10	53,811
25	ITT HARTFORD GROUP	100	93,855	50	CHRYSLER	9	53,756
	THE 500 MEDIAN						**6,370**

BIGGEST EMPLOYERS

		500 REVENUES RANK	1995 NUMBER OF EMPLOYEES			500 REVENUES RANK	1995 NUMBER OF EMPLOYEES
1	GENERAL MOTORS	1	709,000	26	AMERICAN STORES	45	121,000
2	WAL-MART STORES	4	675,000	27	FEDERATED DEPT. STORES	69	119,000
3	PEPSICO	21	480,000	28	WOOLWORTH	161	119,000
4	FORD MOTOR	2	346,990	29	SAFEWAY	59	113,000
5	UNITED PARCEL SERVICE	35	337,000	30	AMR	54	110,000
6	AT&T	5	299,300	31	GTE	38	106,000
7	SEARS ROEBUCK	15	275,000	32	BOEING	40	105,000
8	INTL. BUSINESS MACHINES	6	252,215	33	E.I. DU PONT DE NEMOURS	13	105,000
9	KMART	16	250,000	34	LIMITED	167	104,000
10	COLUMBIA/HCA HEALTHCARE	51	240,000	35	HEWLETT-PACKARD	20	102,300
11	GENERAL ELECTRIC	7	222,000	36	PROCTER & GAMBLE	17	99,200
12	DAYTON HUDSON	28	214,000	37	MELVILLE	110	96,832
13	MCDONALD'S	131	212,000	38	EASTMAN KODAK	67	96,600
14	J.C. PENNEY	34	205,000	39	BANKAMERICA CORP.	37	95,288
15	KROGER	27	200,000	40	PUBLIX SUPER MARKETS	136	95,000
16	MARRIOTT INTERNATIONAL	147	179,400	41	FEDERAL EXPRESS	138	94,201
17	UNITED TECHNOLOGIES	30	170,600	42	PRUDENTIAL INS. OF AMER.	11	92,966
18	LOCKHEED MARTIN	29	160,000	43	CONAGRA	26	90,871
19	PHILIP MORRIS	10	151,000	44	ALLIEDSIGNAL	73	88,500
20	SARA LEE	50	149,100	45	FLAGSTAR	435	88,000
21	MOTOROLA	24	142,000	46	BELLSOUTH	49	87,571
22	ARAMARK	235	140,000	47	GOODYEAR TIRE & RUBBER	88	87,390
23	MAY DEPARTMENT STORES	99	130,000	48	CITICORP	19	85,300
24	CHRYSLER	9	126,000	49	XEROX	41	85,200
25	WINN-DIXIE STORES	103	123,000	50	BEVERLY ENTERPRISES	385	83,000
	THE 500 MEDIAN						21,553

ABBOTT LABORATORIES

100 Abbott Park Rd.	CEO: Duane L. Burnham	1995 Sales: $10,012 million
Abbott Park, IL 60064	CFO: Gary P. Coughlan	1995 Profits: $1,689 million
Phone: 847-937-6100	Symbol: ABT	Mkt. Value: $32,280 million
Fax: 847-937-1511	Exchange: NYSE	Employees: 50,241

Abbott Laboratories is a diversified health care company. The company has 2 divisions: pharmaceutical and nutritional products (antibiotics, anticonvulsants, and nutritional drinks) and hospital and laboratory products (anesthetics, drug delivery systems, and diagnostic systems). It is the world leader in the production of the antibiotic erythromycin, and its baby formula Similac is #1 in the US market. The company also produces chemical and agricultural products for crops and livestock. Abbott sells its products in 130 countries, with almost 40% of sales made outside the US.

ACE HARDWARE CORPORATION

2200 Kensington Court	CEO: David Hodnik	1995 Sales: $2,436 million
Oak Brook, IL 60521	CFO: Rita D. Kahle	Employees: 3,917
Phone: 708-990-6600	Ownership: Cooperative	
Fax: 708-573-4894		

Web site: http://www.acehardware.com

The #2 hardware wholesaler (after Cotter), Ace has more than 5,300 dealers under its aegis. The cooperative, which is owned by its dealer-members, distributes products from 14 centers. Dealers receive dividends from Ace's net profits as well as from its paint sales (Ace manufactures its own). The company also provides a number of services to its members, including advertising, fixtures and in-store displays, insurance, store planning and development, and training.

ADVANCED MICRO DEVICES, INC.

1 AMD Place	CEO: W. J. Sanders III	1995 Sales: $2,430 million
Sunnyvale, CA 94088	CFO: Marvin Burkett	1995 Profits: $301 million
Phone: 408-732-2400	Symbol: AMD	Mkt. Value: $2,323 million
Fax: 408-982-6164	Exchange: NYSE	Employees: 12,797

Web site: http://www.amd.com

Advanced Micro Devices (AMD) makes midpriced clones of Intel microprocessors and other types of integrated circuits for budget-minded markets (such as education). Its main product is the AM486 microprocessor chip used in personal computers. AMD also makes other CPU and microprocessor chips, computer networking and communications products like Ethernet devices, and read-only memory (ROM) devices. The acquisition of NexGen gives the company an Intel Pentium clone, something it was unable to develop on its own. Around 1/4 of AMD's sales come from the US, while Europe and Asia account for the rest. By focusing on R&D and continuing its strategy of cloning Intel technology, AMD aims to increase its market share.

AETNA LIFE AND CASUALTY COMPANY

151 Farmington Ave.	CEO: Ronald E. Compton	1995 Sales: $12,978 million
Hartford, CT 06156	CFO: Robert E. Broatch	1995 Profits: $252 million
Phone: 860-273-0123	Symbol: AET	Mkt. Value: $8,658 million
Fax: 203-275-2677	Exchange: NYSE	Employees: 40,212

Web site: http://www.aetna.com

Back in the black after years of falling earnings, Aetna wants to ensure its continued success as a lean, mean insurance machine. The company sells life, group health, and financial services to corporations, organizations, and individuals. Cutting back on less-profitable types of insurance such as auto coverage, Aetna is branching out in other areas, especially health care, and has begun acquiring medical practices in a drive to form a health maintenance organization. To this end the company has acquired U.S. Healthcare, an HMO whose deal was partly financed by the sale of its property/casualty lines to insurance rival Travelers.

AFLAC INCORPORATED

1932 Wynnton Rd.
Columbus, GA 31999
Phone: 706-323-3431
Fax: 706-324-6330

CEO: Daniel P. Amos
CFO: Kriss Cloninger III
Symbol: AFL
Exchange: NYSE

1995 Sales: $7,191 million
1995 Profits: $349 million
Mkt. Value: $4,342 million
Employees: 4,070

Web site: http://www.aflac.com

Holding company AFLAC Incorporated sells supplemental medical insurance policies that cover conditions (such as cancer) that fall through the cracks of regular insurance. It operates primarily through its main subsidiary, American Family Life Assurance Company of Columbus (Georgia). Though based in the US, AFLAC sells most of its insurance in Japan through an agency system--a company forms a subsidiary to sell coverage to its employees. In the US, AFLAC uses cluster selling, where individuals buy coverage through their employer and can deduct premiums from their pay. The company also owns 7 TV stations, all network affiliates.

AID ASSOCIATION FOR LUTHERANS, INC.

4321 N. Ballard Rd.
Appleton, WI 54919
Phone: 414-734-5721
Fax: 414-730-4757

CEO: Richard L. Gunderson
CFO: Roger J. Johnson
Ownership: Nonprofit
     Organization

1995 Sales: $2,796 million
1995 Profits: $115 million
Employees: 1,580

Web site: http://www.aal.org

Aid Association for Lutherans (AAL) is the largest fraternal benefits society in the US, selling insurance and retirement products to nearly 1.7 million Lutheran families in the US. The nonprofit organization's benefit plans include employee retirement plans, employee savings plans, employee group term life insurance, employee disability benefits, group health insurance, agents' retirement plans, and long-term disability benefit plans. The company's investment arm, AAL Capital Management, provides mutual fund and brokerage services. AAL's business is also charity; the organization donates millions of dollars each year to various causes.

AIR PRODUCTS AND CHEMICALS, INC.

7201 Hamilton Blvd.
Allentown, PA 18195
Phone: 610-481-4911
Fax: 610-481-5900

CEO: Harold A. Wagner
CFO: Arnold H. Kaplan
Symbol: APD
Exchange: NYSE

1995 Sales: $3,891 million
1995 Profits: $368 million
Mkt. Value: $6,989 million
Employees: 14,800

Web site: http://www.airproducts.com

Air Products and Chemicals produces industrial gases and chemicals. The company provides argon, carbon dioxide, carbon monoxide, helium, hydrogen, nitrogen, and oxygen for use in industrial applications. It supplies industrial gases through 2 methods. For large-volume customers Air Products builds plants adjacent to customer facilities for "on-site" delivery. For smaller customers Air Products ships gas via tanker truck and tube trailers. It also operates a chemical business unit, a desulferization unit, and a waste-to-energy cogeneration unit.

Eliphalet Bulkeley, founder of **Aetna Life Insurance** in 1853, joined the Republican Party before it was either grand or old: he helped set up its state-level organization in Connecticut. His son Morgan, also a Republican, served as governor and US senator while running the company and lent the state $300,000 in Aetna funds during a financial pinch.

— Hoover's Handbook of American Business 1996

ALBERTSON'S, INC.

250 Parkcenter Blvd.	CEO: Gary G. Michael	1995 Sales: $12,585 million
Boise, ID 83706	CFO: A. Craig Olson	1995 Profits: $465 million
Phone: 208-385-6200	Symbol: ABS	Mkt. Value: $9,577 million
Fax: 208-385-6349	Exchange: NYSE	Employees: 80,000

Albertson's is the nation's 4th largest grocery-drug chain, with over 750 stores (all but 78 of them combination food and drug stores) in 19 western, midwestern, and southern states, operated primarily under the Albertson's name. The company intends to pony up several billion dollars for new stores, remodeling, upgraded distribution and information systems, and better store equipment in the next several years, when it hopes to have over 1,000 stores. The company's 40 warehouse stores operate under the name Max Food and Drug. J. B. Scott and Kathryn Albertson, founder Joe Albertson's grandson and widow, own over 10% of the company's stock, as does German investor Markus Stiftung.

ALCO STANDARD CORPORATION

825 Duportail Rd.	CEO: John E. Stuart	1995 Sales: $9,892 million
Wayne, PA 19087	CFO: O. Gordon Brewer Jr.	1995 Profits: $203 million
Phone: 610-296-8000	Symbol: ASN	Mkt. Value: $5,715 million
Fax: 610-296-8419	Exchange: NYSE	Employees: 36,500

Web site: http://www.alcolink.com

Alco Standard distributes office equipment, paper, and imaging products. Unisource Worldwide, which accounts for more than 2/3 of revenues, markets copier paper, food service papers, packaging materials, and printing and writing papers. The office products and services division, Alco, sells and leases fax machines, office equipment, and photocopiers. Alco Standard supplies customers in the printing and publishing, corporate imaging, manufacturing, food processing, and retail grocery industries. By buying over 2 dozen smaller businesses in recent years, Alco has become the corporate giant of selling and servicing office equipment.

ALLEGHENY POWER SYSTEM, INC.

12 E. 49th St.	CEO: Klaus Bergman	1995 Sales: $2,648 million
New York, NY 10017	CFO: Allan Noia	1995 Profits: $240 million
Phone: 212-752-2121	Symbol: AYP	Mkt. Value: $3,425 million
Fax: 212-836-4340	Exchange: NYSE	Employees: 5,905

Web site: http://www.alleghenypower.com

Allegheny Power System is a utility holding company for 3 operating electric companies. Subsidiary Monongahela Power provides electricity to about 345,000 customers in West Virginia, Ohio, and Pennsylvania; Potomac Edison serves about 360,000 in Maryland, Virginia, and West Virginia; and West Penn serves 653,000 in Pennsylvania and West Virginia. The company's combined total capacity is about 8,070 MW, of which 88% is coal-fired, 10% is pumped-storage, 1% is oil-fired, and 1% is hydroelectric. Allegheny Power's electricity is generated at 54 units throughout the service area.

ALLIEDSIGNAL INC.

101 Columbia Rd.
Morristown, NJ 07962
Phone: 201-455-2000
Fax: 201-455-4807

CEO: Lawrence A. Bossidy
CFO: Richard F. Wallman
Symbol: ALD
Exchange: NYSE

1995 Sales: $14,346 million
1995 Profits: $875 million
Mkt. Value: $15,906 million
Employees: 88,500

Web site: http://www.alliedsignal.com

73 AlliedSignal is a diversified industrial powerhouse. Its 3 segments -- Aerospace, Automotive, and Engineered Materials -- produce advanced technology products and services for military, commercial and general aviation, and space markets. Principal products include airplane engines, environmental control systems, airborne weather avoidance, wind shear detection systems, wing ice detection systems, and collision avoidance radar systems. Allied also makes products for missiles and spacecraft. Cutting much of its stake in the automotive market, the company decided in 1996 to sell its brake unit to Bosch for $1.5 billion.

ALLMERICA PROPERTY & CASUALTY COMPANIES, INC.

440 Lincoln St.
Worcester, MA 01653
Phone: 508-855-1000
Fax: 508-856-9092

CEO: John F. O'Brien
CFO: Eric A. Simonsen
Symbol: APY
Exchange: NYSE

1995 Sales: $3,239 million
1995 Profits: $134 million
Mkt. Value: $1,272 million
Employees: 6,800

384 Allmerica Property & Casualty is a major US property and casualty insuror. Primary subsidiaries Hanover Insurance and Citizens Insurance Company of America sell personal and commercial property and casualty insurance lines, including personal auto, homeowners, commercial auto, workers' compensation, and commercial multiple peril. The company also sells inland marine, fire, and fidelity and surety insurance. In addition, it provides administration services to self-insurers. Its 2,400 independent agencies sell the company's products primarily in the Northeast and Michigan. State Mutual Assurance Company of America indirectly owns 57.4% of Allmerica.

THE ALLSTATE CORPORATION

2775 Sanders Rd.
Northbrook, IL 60062
Phone: 847-402-5000
Fax: 847-402-0045

CEO: Jerry Choate
CFO: Thomas J. Wilson
Symbol: ALL
Exchange: NYSE

1995 Sales: $22,793 million
1995 Profits: $1,904 million
Mkt. Value: $18,515 million
Employees: 44,349

31 Allstate is the nation's 5th largest insurance company, selling life and property/casualty insurance in the US, Puerto Rico, and Canada through a network of 14,500 company agents and 2,000 independent agents. Allstate also operates in Korea and Japan and sells reinsurance worldwide. The company was spun off by Sears when the retailer shed many of its noncore businesses to cut costs. Since its independence, Allstate is attempting to strengthen nonproperty lines, especially its life, annuity, and pension plans and also is concentrating on areas less vulnerable to natural disasters.

ALLTEL CORPORATION

1 Allied Dr.
Little Rock, AR 72202
Phone: 501-661-8000
Fax: 501-661-8487

CEO: Joe T. Ford
CFO: Tom T. Orsini
Symbol: AT
Exchange: NYSE

1995 Sales: $3,110 million
1995 Profits: $355 million
Mkt. Value: $5,775 million
Employees: 15,698

Web site: http://www.alltel.com

396 ALLTEL is a diversified telephone, publishing, and product distribution company. It provides telephone service to 1.6 million customers in 19 states and cellular and paging services to nearly 470,000 customers, primarily in Sunbelt states. The company also delivers cable TV programming in the Southwest. Other operations include ALLTEL Supply, which distributes more than 35,000 telecommunications products; HWC Distribution Corp., which stocks 44,000 reels of specialty wire and cable; and ALLTEL Publishing, which produces telephone directories in 39 states. The purchase of Vertex Business Systems of New York gives the company added clients in Austria, Brazil, Hungary, and Luxembourg.

ALUMAX INC.

5655 Peachtree Parkway	CEO: Allen Born	1995 Sales: $2,926 million
Norcross, GA 30092	CFO: Lawrence B. Frost	1995 Profits: $237 million
Phone: 770-246-6600	Symbol: AMX	Mkt. Value: $1,562 million
Fax: 770-246-6756	Exchange: NYSE	Employees: 14,196

Alumax is the #3 aluminum company in the US after Alcoa and Reynolds. Subsidiaries include Alumax Engineered Metal Processes, the world leader in semisolid metal forging technology for the automotive industry; Alumax Extrusions, the largest US maker of soft-alloy aluminum shapes; Alumax Fabricated Products, a leading maker of fabricated aluminum and steel products for the building and transportation industries; and Alumax Foils, a maker of light- and heavy-gauge aluminum foil. Other subsidiaries include Alumax Mill Products, Alumax Primary Aluminum Corp., Alumax Technical Center (R&D), and Kawneer, the largest architectural aluminum producer in North America.

ALUMINUM COMPANY OF AMERICA

425 Sixth Ave.	CEO: Paul H. O'Neill	1995 Sales: $12,655 million
Pittsburgh, PA 15219	CFO: Jan H. M. Hommen	1995 Profits: $791 million
Phone: 412-553-4545	Symbol: AA	Mkt. Value: $10,754 million
Fax: 412-553-4498	Exchange: NYSE	Employees: 72,000

Web site: http://www.alcoa.com

The world's #1 aluminum producer, Aluminum Company of America (Alcoa) is a fully integrated aluminum company. Its operations in 26 countries include bauxite mining, alumina refining, and aluminum smelting. Primary products include alumina and its chemicals, automotive components, and beverage cans. The company also supplies aluminum in various forms to the packaging, automotive, shipping, construction, and aerospace industries. Alcoa materials go into the Audi A8, the first all-aluminum production car. To take advantage of emerging markets, Alcoa has investments in Eastern Europe and Latin America.

AMERADA HESS CORPORATION

1185 Sixth Ave.	CEO: John B. Hess	1995 Sales: $7,525 million
New York, NY 10036	CFO: John Y. Schreyer	1995 Loss: ($394) million
Phone: 212-997-8500	Symbol: AHC	Mkt. Value: $4,953 million
Fax: 212-536-8390	Exchange: NYSE	Employees: 9,574

Amerada Hess is an integrated oil and gas company. It has exploration operations in the US, Canada, the African nation of Gabon, and in the North Sea, where half of its proven reserves are located. The company refines more than 380,000 barrels a day and sells gasoline in more than 500 HESS stations (most of them company owned) clustered in New York, New Jersey, and Florida. Although it operates worldwide, over 80% of the company's sales come from within the US. Amerada Hess also owns 18% of the Central Area Transmission System pipeline, which carries natural gas from the North Sea to the UK.

AMERICAN BRANDS, INC.

1700 E. Putnam Ave.	CEO: Thomas C. Hays	1995 Sales: $5,905 million
Old Greenwich, CT 06870	CFO: Dudley L. Bauerlein Jr.	1995 Profits: $540 million
Phone: 203-698-5000	Symbol: AMB	Mkt. Value: $7,940 million
Fax: 203-637-2580	Exchange: NYSE	Employees: 27,700

Web site: http://www.americanbrands.com

American Brands is a multibillion dollar conglomerate that sells tobacco products, hardware and home improvement items, distilled spirits, office products, and sporting goods. The company's biggest profits come from cigarettes; its Gallaher unit (Benson & Hedges) produces the top 2 cigarette brands in the UK. Operations include ACCO office supply, Jim Beam distillers, Moen faucets, Titleist golf supplies, and Master Lock hardware. In 1996 American Brands agreed to buy Cobra Golf, a leading maker of golf clubs.

AMERICAN ELECTRIC POWER COMPANY, INC.

1 Riverside Plaza
Columbus, OH 43215
Phone: 614-223-1000
Fax: 614-223-1823

CEO: E. Linn Draper Jr.
CFO: Gerald P. Maloney
Symbol: AEP
Exchange: NYSE

1995 Sales: $5,670 million
1995 Profits: $530 million
Mkt. Value: $7,545 million
Employees: 18,502

Web site: http://www.aep.com

 231

One of the nation's largest investor-owned utilities, American Electric Power (AEP) is the holding company for 7 operating utilities. Its operating units (Appalachian Power, Indiana Michigan Power, Kentucky Power, Kingsport Power, Columbus Southern Power, Ohio Power, and Wheeling Power) provide electricity to 7 million people in 7 midwestern and Appalachian states. Subsidiaries operate a network of 38 coal-fired, nuclear, hydroelectric, and gas turbine generating units. The AEP Service Corp. provides administrative, engineering, legal, and other services to the parent company. Residential electricity sales account for 1/3 of the total; industrial, commercial, and resales account for most of the rest.

AMERICAN EXPRESS COMPANY

200 Vesey St.
New York, NY 10285
Phone: 212-640-2000
Fax: 212-619-9802

CEO: Harvey Golub
CFO: Michael P. Monaco
Symbol: AXP
Exchange: NYSE

1995 Sales: $15,841 million
1995 Profits: $1,564 million
Mkt. Value: $23,433 million
Employees: 70,347

Web site: http://www.americanexpress.com

 53

American Express is one of the US's largest financial services companies and is the largest corporate travel agency. Not only does it offer American Express cards and Travelers Cheques, it also publishes magazines (*Food & Wine*, *Departures*, *Travel & Leisure*), sells life insurance (AMEX Life Assurance), and provides financial advisory services. The company is continuing the drastic makeover that began with its spinoff of Lehman Brothers and is focusing on its corporate-travel credit card business. Investor Warren Buffett owns about 10% of American Express.

While overseas in 1890, **American Express** president **James Fargo** had a rough time using letters of credit to obtain cash. He demanded a solution from underling Marcellus Fleming, who came up with the traveler's cheque. In 1891 the company sold $9,200 worth, a number that ballooned to $6 million within 10 years.

— *Pioneers of American Business*, compiled by Sterling G. Slappey

AMERICAN FINANCIAL GROUP, INC.

1 E. Fourth St.
Cincinnati, OH 45202
Phone: 513-579-6600
Fax: 513-579-2113

CEO: Carl H. Lindner
CFO: Fred J. Runk
Symbol: AFG
Exchange: NYSE

1995 Sales: $3,630 million
1995 Profits: $191 million
Mkt. Value: $1,789 million
Employees: 9,800

345

Diversified company American Financial is an umbrella organization (controlled by Carl Lindner and his family) for a number of insurance businesses, including Great American Insurance Group, which offers multiline property and casualty insurance; American Annuity Group, which sells property and casualty insurance; and American Premier Underwriters, which offers nonstandard auto insurance and California workers' compensation. The company also owns the Golf Center at Kings Island, Provident Travel Corp., Chiquita Brands International (the banana company), and Citicasters, which operates radio and TV stations.

AMERICAN GENERAL CORPORATION

2929 Allen Parkway
Houston, TX 77019
Phone: 713-522-1111
Fax: 713-831-3028

CEO: Harold S. Hook
CFO: Austin P. Young
Symbol: AGC
Exchange: NYSE

1995 Sales: $6,495 million
1995 Profits: $545 million
Mkt. Value: $7,296 million
Employees: 15,300

Web site: http://www.agc.com

American General is a diversified financial services company. Its core business lines are retirement annuities, consumer finance, and life insurance (traditional and interest-sensitive policies). The company owns Western National Corp. and 40% of Franklin Life. To create a distinctive culture for the company, it is instituting a system in which American General sets goals, allocates capital, chooses key personnel, and monitors performance, while its subsidiaries receive the autonomy to carry out the company's programs.

Premarin, the widely prescribed estrogen drug sold by **American Home Products**, is made from the urine of pregnant mares. Demand for the drug, which is used to treat symptoms of menopause and osteoporosis, is expected to grow even more as baby boomers age.

— *Hoover's Guide to the Top New York Companies*

AMERICAN HOME PRODUCTS CORPORATION

5 Giralda Farms
Madison, NJ 07940
Phone: 201-660-5000
Fax: 201-660-5771

CEO: John R. Stafford
CFO: John R. Considine
Symbol: AHP
Exchange: NYSE

1995 Sales: $13,376 million
1995 Profits: $1,680 million
Mkt. Value: $30,841 million
Employees: 64,712

Web site: http://ahpc.com

American Home Products (AHP), a major US pharmaceutical company, also makes consumer health care goods (through its Whitehall Labs and A. H. Robins units), food, and agricultural products. Pharmaceutical subsidiary Wyeth-Ayerst Laboratories produces Premarin (estrogen replacement), one of the most frequently prescribed drugs in America. AHP is also the largest US producer of childhood vaccines and sells the well-known Centrum multivitamins line. Other brands include Advil and Anacin (pain relievers), Chef Boyardee (canned pasta), Preparation H (hemorrhoid ointment), and Jiffy Pop (popcorn).

AMERICAN INTERNATIONAL GROUP, INC.

70 Pine St.
New York, NY 10270
Phone: 212-770-7000
Fax: 212-770-7821

CEO: Maurice R. Greenberg
CFO: Edward E. Matthews
Symbol: AIG
Exchange: NYSE

1995 Sales: $25,874 million
1995 Profits: $2,510 million
Mkt. Value: $43,684 million
Employees: 32,000

Web site: http://www.aig.com

The largest US public property/casualty insurer and one of the largest insurance companies in the world, American International Group (AIG) boasts a well-diversified product line able to stand up to the vagaries of nature and the financial markets. AIG, which also has a strong life insurance operation overseas, has branched into other insurance lines, including personal auto, insurance brokerage, and health care. The company continues to expand overseas by selling insurance in Russia, Uzbekistan, and Pakistan and expanding its operations in China.

AMERICAN PRESIDENT COMPANIES, LTD.

1111 Broadway
Oakland, CA 94607
Phone: 510-272-8000
Fax: 510-272-7941

CEO: Timothy J. Rhein
CFO: L. Dale Crandall
Symbol: APS
Exchange: NYSE

1995 Sales: $2,896 million
1995 Profits: $30 million
Mkt. Value: $549 million
Employees: 5,200

Web site: http://www.apl.com

American President offers an integrated system of ocean, rail, and truck transportation, linking points in North America, Asia, and the Middle East. The company's shipping line, American President Lines, operates about 25 containerships and a network of feeder vessels serving nearly 60 ports in the Pacific and Indian Oceans and the Persian Gulf. The company uses intermodal containers so that freight can be taken off a ship, loaded on a truck or railcar in the same container, and sent onward. American President has transportation operations in 45 countries.

AMERICAN STANDARD COMPANIES INC.

1 Centennial Ave.
Piscataway, NJ 08855
Phone: 908-980-6000
Fax: 908-980-6120

CEO: Emmanuel A. Kampouris
CFO: Fred A. Allardyce
Symbol: ASD
Exchange: NYSE

1995 Sales: $5,222 million
1995 Profits: $112 million
Mkt. Value: $2,193 million
Employees: 43,000

Web site: http://www.trane.com

American Standard makes plumbing products, vehicle braking systems, and air conditioning systems. With 94 plants in 32 countries, the company receives just over half its sales from the US market. Bathroom and kitchen fittings and fixtures are sold under brand names American-Standard, Ideal-Standard, and Standard. The air conditioning products unit makes products under the Trane and American-Standard names and emphasizes service, repair, and replacement over construction. The transportation products unit manufactures air brakes for commercial vehicle industries in Europe and Brazil.

AMERICAN STORES COMPANY

709 E. South Temple
Salt Lake City, UT 84102
Phone: 801-539-0112
Fax: 801-531-0768

CEO: Victor L. Lund
CFO: Teresa Beck
Symbol: ASC
Exchange: NYSE

1995 Sales: $18,309 million
1995 Profits: $317 million
Mkt. Value: $4,318 million
Employees: 121,000

Salt Lake City-based American Stores is the nation's 2nd largest grocery store chain (after Kroger). The company operates its food stores under the names Lucky, Super Saver, Jewel, and Acme and its drugstores under the Osco and Sav-on monikers (about 150 are Jewel Osco combinations). American Stores ranks at or near the top of its markets in several major cities. Its food stores are #1 or #2 in Chicago, Oakland, Orange County (California), Philadelphia, and San Diego, while its drugstores hold the same distinction in Chicago, Indianapolis, Kansas City, Los Angeles, and Phoenix.

AMERISOURCE HEALTH CORPORATION

300 Chester Field Parkway
Malvern, PA 19355
Phone: 610-296-4480
Fax: 610-647-0141

CEO: John F. McNamara
CFO: Kurt J. Hilzinger
Symbol: ASHC
Exchange: Nasdaq

1995 Sales: $4,669 million
1995 Profits: $10 million
Mkt. Value: $698 million
Employees: 2,600

AmeriSource (formerly known as Alco Health Services Corp.) is one of the 5 largest wholesale distributors of branded and generic drugs in the US. It provides goods and services to more than 16,000 customers, including independent and chain pharmacies, hospitals, nursing homes, and clinics. AmeriSource provides discounted pharmaceuticals and general merchandise to smaller buyers, which cannot bargain with manufacturers directly. It also offers such services as merchandising, pricing, and advertising and promotional campaigns. The company owns Liberty Drug Systems, which provides pharmacies with computer hardware and software, allowing them to automate orders, track products, and manage inventory.

AMERITECH CORPORATION

30 S. Wacker Dr.
Chicago, IL 60606
Phone: 312-750-5000
Fax: 312-207-8136

CEO: Richard C. Notebaert
CFO: Oren G. Shaffer
Symbol: AIT
Exchange: NYSE

1995 Sales: $13,428 million
1995 Profits: $2,008 million
Mkt. Value: $30,117 million
Employees: 65,345

Web site: http://www.ameritech.com

Ameritech is the 3rd largest regional Bell operating company (RBOC), at least until the other RBOCs that are planning to merge with each other complete their deals. It focuses on core local telephone and cellular telecommunications services in the 5-state Great Lakes region, operating under the Illinois Bell, Indiana Bell, Michigan Bell, Ohio Bell, and Wisconsin Bell names. The company is developing new services such as long distance and interactive services in an effort to transform itself into a full service telecommunications company. It is working with Walt Disney, BellSouth, and SBC Communications to deliver video programming to consumers' homes.

AMOCO CORPORATION

200 E. Randolph Dr.
Chicago, IL 60601
Phone: 312-856-6111
Fax: 312-856-2460

CEO: H. Laurance Fuller
CFO: John L. Carl
Symbol: AN
Exchange: NYSE

1995 Sales: $27,665 million
1995 Profits: $1,862 million
Mkt. Value: $34,898 million
Employees: 42,689

Web site: http://www.amoco.com

North America's largest natural gas producer, Amoco has confirmed gas reserves of 18.2 trillion cubic feet and oil reserves of 2.2 billion barrels. Not restricting itself to refining and exploration, it is one of the world's largest integrated oil and chemical companies. Amoco is shedding weak product lines, including its oil well chemicals business, and beefing up faster-growing and more profitable areas such as polyester chemicals.

AMP INCORPORATED

470 Friendship Rd.
Harrisburg, PA 17111
Phone: 717-564-0100
Fax: 717-780-6130

CEO: William J. Hudson
CFO: Robert Ripp
Symbol: AMP
Exchange: NYSE

1995 Sales: $5,227 million
1995 Profits: $427 million
Mkt. Value: $9,348 million
Employees: 40,800

Web site: http://www.amp.com

AMP is the world's leading manufacturer of electronic connectors, which are vital to all electrical products. It produces over 100,000 items in facilities in more than 35 countries. They are found in products that range from cars to computers and from aircraft to washing machines. The company also makes circuit boards and specialized electronics equipment such as cabling systems, fiber-optic assemblies, sensors, and terminals. Subsidiary Global Wireless Products makes wireless data and telecommunications interconnection components.

AMR CORPORATION

4333 Amon Carter Blvd.
Fort Worth, TX 76155
Phone: 817-963-1234
Fax: 817-967-9641

CEO: Robert L. Crandall
CFO: Gerard J. Arpey
Symbol: AMR
Exchange: NYSE

1995 Sales: $16,910 million
1995 Profits: $167 million
Mkt. Value: $6,939 million
Employees: 110,000

Web site: http://www.amrcorp.com

High-flying AMR is the holding company for American Airlines, the #1 US airline, and American Eagle, a group of 4 small regional airlines that feed passengers into American's system. AMR also operates the SABRE reservations system and offers a variety of air travel-related services, including management of airport ground services and travel consulting. Cost cutting and service cutbacks have helped the company weather the turbulence of the early 1990s and move financial performance to a higher plane.

ANHEUSER-BUSCH COMPANIES, INC.

1 Busch Place
St. Louis, MO 63118
Phone: 314-577-2000
Fax: 314-577-2900

CEO: August A. Busch III
CFO: Jerry E. Ritter
Symbol: BUD
Exchange: NYSE

1995 Sales: $12,326 million
1995 Profits: $642 million
Mkt. Value: $17,167 million
Employees: 42,529

Web site: http://www.budweiser.com

Anheuser-Busch, the largest beer maker in the US, with almost half the market share, is also the world's largest brewer. The company makes leading brands Budweiser (over 50% of sales), Michelob, and Busch, as well as specialty beers including Elk Mountain, Red Wolf, and O'Doul's. The company has joint ventures in Japan, Italy, Mexico, China, and several Central American countries. It also operates almost a dozen theme parks (Busch Gardens, Sea World). To concentrate on its core business, the King of Beers has exited the snack food and baking businesses and has sold the St. Louis Cardinals baseball team.

Steven Jobs and **Stephen Wozniak** set out to sell circuit boards, but when Jobs came back from his first sales call with an order for 50 units, they switched to selling fully assembled computers. They built the Apple I in Jobs' garage, selling it without a monitor, keyboard, or casing. The name came from Jobs's time spent on an Oregon farm.

— Hoover's Guide to Computer Companies

AON CORPORATION

123 N. Wacker Dr.
Chicago, IL 60606
Phone: 312-701-3000
Fax: 312-701-3100

CEO: Patrick G. Ryan
CFO: Harvey N. Medvin
Symbol: AOC
Exchange: NYSE

1995 Sales: $3,466 million
1995 Profits: $403 million
Mkt. Value: $5,618 million
Employees: 27,000

Web site: http://www.aon.com

Aon -- the name means "oneness" in Gaelic -- unites a wide variety of insurance and insurance brokering and consulting companies that operate worldwide. Aon companies offer a full line of insurance products, including life, accident, health, and specialty property and casualty insurance. Other lines of business include insurance brokerage, consulting, reinsurance, indemnity and cancer insurance, risk management services, Medicare supplements, and disability coverage for individuals and groups.

APPLE COMPUTER, INC.

1 Infinite Loop
Cupertino, CA 95014
Phone: 408-996-1010
Fax: 408-974-2113

CEO: Gilbert F. Amelio
CFO: Fred Anderson
Symbol: AAPL
Exchange: Nasdaq

1995 Sales: $11,062 million
1995 Profits: $424 million
Mkt. Value: $3,200 million
Employees: 15,403

Web site: http://www.apple.com

Apple is one of the world's top computer companies and the pioneer of user-friendly computing with the Macintosh PC. The company also makes the MacOS operating system and peripherals (including printers). Its Claris software unit makes Claris Works and other software packages. Due to its proprietary technology, Apple is facing tough times as archrivals Microsoft and Intel chip away at its market share. Additionally, the company fumbled with its Newton personal digital assistant, and its PowerPC initiative with IBM and Motorola has stalled. In the wake of its troubles, Apple has finally begun licensing its technology to 3rd-party manufacturers.

APPLIED MATERIALS, INC.

3050 Bowers Ave.
Santa Clara, CA 95054
Phone: 408-727-5555
Fax: 408-748-9943

CEO: James C. Morgan
CFO: Gerald F. Taylor
Symbol: AMAT
Exchange: Nasdaq

1995 Sales: $3,062 million
1995 Profits: $454 million
Mkt. Value: $6,208 million
Employees: 10,537

Web site: http://www.amat.com

Applied Materials is the world's largest designer and manufacturer of the machines used to fabricate semiconductor chips. The company's machines perform 6 of the 8 basic semiconductor manufacturing steps (including chemical vapor deposition, plasma etching, and ion implantation), giving it the broadest coverage of any company in the industry. It is looking for more efficient ways to make higher-capacity chips and is developing active-matrix flat panel displays (used in laptop computers and high-definition televisions). In addition, the company has formed a joint venture with SGS-Thomson Microelectronics to research advanced metal deposition processes and develop future generations of chip fabricating equipment.

ARAMARK CORPORATION

1101 Market St.
Philadelphia, PA 19107
Phone: 215-238-3000
Fax: 215-238-3333

CEO: Joseph Neubauer
CFO: James E. Ksansnak
Ownership: Privately Held

1995 Sales: $5,601 million
1995 Profits: $94 million
Employees: 140,000

Web site: http://www.aramark-uniform.com

ARAMARK is a diversified service company. It operates 5 major lines of business: food service, health care, child care, uniform services, and periodical distribution. The company provides food services to *FORTUNE 500* executives, prison inmates, and college students. Its health care services include anesthesia and correctional medical services. It owns Children's World Learning Centers. The company provides uniforms and work clothes through its ARAMARK Uniform Services and WearGuard subsidiaries. It also distributes periodicals to more than 18,000 retail locations nationwide.

A tragic hotel fire did severe damage to **Arrow Electronics**. Thirteen senior managers, including 2 of the 3 founders, were killed in the 1980 fire at the Stouffer Inn in Harrison, New York. The 3rd, **John Waddell**, was spared because he had stayed at corporate headquarters to answer questions about a stock split. He became CEO.

— Hoover's Guide to the Top New York Companies

ARCHER-DANIELS-MIDLAND COMPANY

4666 Faries Parkway
Decatur, IL 62526
Phone: 217-424-5200
Fax: 217-424-5839

CEO: Dwayne O. Andreas
CFO: Douglas J. Schmalz
Symbol: ADM
Exchange: NYSE

1995 Sales: $12,672 million
1995 Profits: $796 million
Mkt. Value: $9,696 million
Employees: 14,833

Archer-Daniels-Midland (ADM) processes raw grain and seed. Products including seed oils, flour, food additives, and meal are sold to just about every major US food company. Oilseed products account for over half of ADM's sales. The company also produces pasta, vitamins, livestock feed, and ethanol. To distribute its products, ADM uses rail, trucks, and ocean-going vessels, and owns and leases almost 2,000 river barges. The company looks to China and the Pacific Rim for sales growth, particularly in the area of vegetable oil. Foreign operations account for about 25% of ADM's revenues.

ARMSTRONG WORLD INDUSTRIES, INC.

313 W. Liberty St.
Lancaster, PA 17604
Phone: 717-397-0611
Fax: 717-396-2787

CEO: George A. Lorch
CFO: Frank A. Riddick III
Symbol: ACK
Exchange: NYSE

1995 Sales: $2,635 million
1995 Profits: $123 million
Mkt. Value: $2,326 million
Employees: 20,500

Web site: http://www.armstrong.com

Armstrong World Industries manufactures floor coverings and building products as well as specialty products for the automotive and textile industries. Besides flooring, its products include industrial adhesives, gaskets, pipe insulation, textile mill supplies, and ceiling and wall systems. Armstrong is expanding globally by pursuing acquisitions, alliances, and joint ventures while divesting underperforming operations. About half of company sales come from the residential repair and remodeling markets; sales to overseas markets account for approximately 1/4 of the total.

ARROW ELECTRONICS, INC.

25 Hub Dr.
Melville, NY 11747
Phone: 516-391-1300
Fax: 516-391-1644

CEO: Stephen P. Kaufman
CFO: Robert E. Klatell
Symbol: ARW
Exchange: NYSE

1995 Sales: $5,919 million
1995 Profits: $203 million
Mkt. Value: $2,353 million
Employees: 7,200

Arrow is the world's largest distributor of electronic components and computer products. The company sells semiconductors (66% of sales), microcomputer boards, desktop computer systems, and peripherals to computer manufacturers and commercial customers. Primary subsidiaries include Arrow/Swerber Electronics Group (semiconductors), Hong Kong-based Components Agent Limited (distribution in Asia), Spoerle Electronic Handelsgesellschaft GmbH and Co. (distribution in Germany), and Zeus Electronics (service to military and high-reliability components markets). Arrow acquired Gates/FA Distributing and Anthem Electronics as part of a strategy to develop a broader customer base.

ASARCO INCORPORATED

180 Maiden Lane
New York, NY 10038
Phone: 212-510-2000
Fax: 212-510-1855

CEO: Richard de J. Osborne
CFO: Kevin R. Morano
Symbol: AR
Exchange: NYSE

1995 Sales: $3,198 million
1995 Profits: $169 million
Mkt. Value: $1,424 million
Employees: 12,200

Web site: http://www.asarco.com

ASARCO is one of the world's leading producers of copper, zinc, silver, and gold. Through its mines in the US, Peru, Australia, and Mexico, the company accounts for almost 15% of the copper mined in the Western world, 15% of the silver, 20% of the lead, and 10% of the zinc. It also provides environmental services and produces specialty chemicals for treating metals. In addition, ASARCO is engaged in a 50/50 joint venture called Silver Valley Resources with Coeur d'Alene Mines, a silver and gold producer, to redevelop silver mines in Idaho idled for several years owing to low silver prices.

ASHLAND INC.

1000 Ashland Dr.
Russell, KY 41169
Phone: 606-329-3333
Fax: 606-329-5274

CEO: John R. Hall
CFO: J. Marvin Quin
Symbol: ASH
Exchange: NYSE

1995 Sales: $11,251 million
1995 Profits: $24 million
Mkt. Value: $2,425 million
Employees: 32,800

Web site: http://www.ashland.com

A worldwide energy and chemical company, Ashland is one of the US's largest independent petroleum refiners through its Ashland Petroleum subsidiary. The company produces and sells natural gas, crude oil, motor oil and car-care products (Valvoline), and specialty chemicals. Subsidiary Ashland Chemical is the largest distributor of plastics and chemicals in the US. The corporation also holds stakes in 2 coal companies, Ashland Coal and Arch Mineral. Ashland brand gasoline and oil products are marketed through its SuperAmerica and Rich retail outlets in 23 states.

ASSOCIATED INSURANCE COMPANIES

120 Monument Circle
Indianapolis, IN 46204
Phone: 317-488-6000
Fax: 317-488-6028

CEO: L. Ben Lytle
CFO: Pat Sheridan
Ownership: Mutual Company

1995 Sales: $6,038 million
1995 Loss: ($98) million
Employees: 16,290

Associated Insurance Companies (now known as Anthem) is a diversified financial services and insurance enterprise. It provides such insurance products and services as health insurance, managed health care, property and casualty insurance, insurance brokerage, and government program administration. Financial services include investment banking market research. Associated's insurance subsidiaries are Acordia, AdminaStar, Anthem Health, and Southeastern Group. Financial subsidiaries include Anthem Companies and Anthem P&C Holdings.

AST RESEARCH, INC.

16215 Alton Parkway
Irvine, CA 92718
Phone: 714-727-4141
Fax: 714-727-8584

CEO: Ian W. Diery
CFO: Bruce C. Edwards
Symbol: ASTA
Exchange: Nasdaq

1995 Sales: $2,468 million
1995 Loss: ($99) million
Mkt. Value: $263 million
Employees: 6,595

Web site: http://www.ast.com

AST Research, one of the world's top 10 makers of personal computers, makes a broad line of desktop (Premmia family) and notebook computers (Ascentia, PowerExec), servers (Premmia and Manhattan SMP series), and monitors (ASTVision), as well as connectivity, graphics, and memory enhancement products. With AST struggling, Samsung Electronics, the world's #1 maker of memory chips and part of the Korea-based Samsung Group, acquired a significant stake in the company in 1995.

AT&T CORP.

32 Sixth Ave.
New York, NY 10013
Phone: 212-387-5400
Fax: 212-841-4715

CEO: Robert E. Allen
CFO: Richard W. Miller
Symbol: T
Exchange: NYSE

1995 Sales: $79,609 million
1995 Profits: $139 million
Mkt. Value: $98,122 million
Employees: 299,300

Web site: http://www.att.com

AT&T, formerly the largest telecommunications company in the world, is still one of the largest even after spinning off its computer products and services (NCR) and network products and R&D unit (Lucent Technologies). AT&T will focus on its telephony services, which include cellular service, online and Internet access, paging, video, and electronic commerce services. It also provides wireless services, air-to-ground telephone services, messaging, electronic mail, and toll-free and "800" calling. AT&T offers consumer credit cards through its Universal Card.

ATLANTIC RICHFIELD COMPANY

515 S. Flower St.
Los Angeles, CA 90071
Phone: 213-486-3511
Fax: 213-486-2063

CEO: Michael R. Bowlin
CFO: Ronald J. Arnault
Symbol: ARC
Exchange: NYSE

1995 Sales: $16,739 million
1995 Profits: $1,376 million
Mkt. Value: $18,094 million
Employees: 22,000

Web site: http://www.arco.com

Oil giant Atlantic Richfield (ARCO) is an integrated oil company engaged in the exploration, production, and marketing of crude oil, natural gas, and natural gas liquids, as well as the refining, marketing, and transportation of petroleum products. The company has exploration and production operations worldwide, including facilities in China, Dubai, Indonesia, the US, and the UK. ARCO has extensive chemical interests, holding large stakes in both Lyondell Petrochemical and ARCO Chemical. Other businesses include coal mines, am/pm convenience stores, and SMOGPROS, an auto emissions testing service in California.

AUTOMATIC DATA PROCESSING, INC.

1 ADP Blvd.	CEO: Joshua S. Weston	1995 Sales: $2,894 million
Roseland, NJ 07068	CFO: Fred D. Anderson Jr.	1995 Profits: $395 million
Phone: 201-994-5000	Symbol: AUD	Mkt. Value: $11,691 million
Fax: 201-994-5387	Exchange: NYSE	Employees: 25,000

436

Automatic Data Processing (ADP) is the largest payroll and tax filing processor in the nation, with over 350,000 accounts. Its tax processing services account for more than 50% of total revenues; ADP files about 10.5 million payroll tax returns with 2,000 different taxing authorities annually. ADP's Brokerage Services -- front-office quotation workstations and back-office record keeping, order entry, and proxy services for brokerage firms -- account for almost 25% of sales. The firm's Dealer Services unit provides accounting, inventory, and other management services to 9,500 auto and truck dealers in the US and Europe. The company also provides accounting and auto collision estimates for insurers.

AVERY DENNISON CORPORATION

150 N. Orange Grove Blvd.	CEO: Charles D. Miller	1995 Sales: $3,114 million
Pasadena, CA 91103	CFO: R. Gregory Jenkins	1995 Profits: $144 million
Phone: 818-304-2000	Symbol: AVY	Mkt. Value: $2,925 million
Fax: 818-792-7312	Exchange: NYSE	Employees: 15,500

394

Avery Dennison manufactures self-adhesive materials and office products. Some of its products are converted into labels through embossing, printing, stamping, and die-cutting, while other products are sold in unconverted form as base materials, films, foils, tapes, and reflective sheeting. The company also manufactures notebooks, 3-ring binders, organizing systems, felt-tip markers, glues, fasteners, business forms, and tags under such name brands as Avery, Marks-A-Lot, Carter's, and HI-LITER. Avery Dennison manufactures and sells its products from some 200 manufacturing facilities and sales offices in over 25 countries.

AVNET, INC.

80 Cutter Mill Rd.	CEO: Leon Machiz	1995 Sales: $4,300 million
Great Neck, NY 11021	CFO: Raymond Sadowski	1995 Profits: $140 million
Phone: 516-466-7000	Symbol: AVT	Mkt. Value: $2,068 million
Fax: 516-466-1203	Exchange: NYSE	Employees: 9,000

Web site: http://www.avnet.com

299

Avnet is the 2nd largest global distributor (after Arrow) of electronic components and computer products. The firm concentrates on industrial, military, and high-tech markets. Subsidiaries include Allied Electronics (electronic components distribution), Hamilton Hallmark (semiconductors), Penstock (RF/microwave components and devices), Time Electronics (interconnect products), Brownell Electro (motor repair and industrial products), and Freeman Products (trophy and award products). Acquisitions such as the Access Group (UK), F.H. Tec Composants (France), and Nortec AB (Scandinavia) give Avnet a strong presence outside the US. The company plans continued expansion, especially in Asia.

AVON PRODUCTS, INC.

9 W. 57th St.
New York, NY 10019
Phone: 212-546-6015
Fax: 212-546-6136

CEO: James E. Preston
CFO: Edwina D. Woodbury
Symbol: AVP
Exchange: NYSE

1995 Sales: $4,492 million
1995 Profits: $257 million
Mkt. Value: $5,896 million
Employees: 31,800

Web site: http://www.avon.com

The world's leading direct seller of cosmetics and beauty-related products, Avon is calling on its traditional means of selling beauty products -- direct sales -- for its expansion into emerging markets. The company manufactures a variety of products, including cosmetics (Avon Color), fragrances (Parfums Creatifs), toiletries (Skin-So-Soft), and accessories (Boutique). It continues to hire "beauty consultants" in emerging markets (Brazil and China) to increase its share of the global market for direct-sales beauty products. Avon promises to remain on top of the global direct-sales beauty products industry with such lines as Far Away (a women's fragrance), the company's first product to be launched worldwide.

BAKER HUGHES INCORPORATED

3900 Essex Lane
Houston, TX 77210
Phone: 713-439-8600
Fax: 713-439-8699

CEO: James D. Woods
CFO: Eric L. Mattson
Symbol: BHI
Exchange: NYSE

1995 Sales: $2,638 million
1995 Profits: $105 million
Mkt. Value: $4,116 million
Employees: 15,200

Web site: http://www.BHI-Net.com

Baker Hughes provides products and services for the global petroleum and continuous process industries. It makes equipment and provides services for drilling, completing, and operating oil and gas wells and for producing, transporting, and refining hydrocarbons. The company is the world's leading maker of rock drilling bits. Other products include vacuum filters, filter presses, belt presses, thickeners, clarifiers, flotation cells, and aeration equipment. Baker Hughes also makes and markets solid bowl, screen bowl, and pusher centrifuges; tilting pan filters; and high-speed drum filters for the minerals, chemical, and petrochemical industries. In addition, it designs water treatment systems for refinery waste streams.

BALL CORPORATION

345 S. High St.
Muncie, IN 47305
Phone: 317-747-6100
Fax: 317-747-6203

CEO: George A. Sissel
CFO: R. David Hoover
Symbol: BLL
Exchange: NYSE

1995 Sales: $2,592 million
1995 Profits: ($19) million
Mkt. Value: $914 million
Employees: 7,424

Web site: http://www.ball.com

Famous for its canning jars, Ball does have a packaging segment that develops, manufactures, and sells rigid packaging products (glass and metal) for the food and beverage industry. But it also has an aerospace and communications segment that provides systems, products, and services to the aerospace, defense, and commercial telecommunications markets. Customers include NASA, the US Department of Defense, and foreign governments as well as packagers of food, juices, and wines and distilled spirits. Subsidiary EarthWatch has entered the satellite-based remote-sensing market.

David McConnell used to sell books. In the 1880s he gave a small bottle of perfume to each housewife who would listen to his book pitch. He found the perfume better received than the books, so he started the California Perfume Company in 1886. The company later adopted the name **Avon**, from the river in England.

— *Hoover's Guide to the Top New York Companies*

BALTIMORE GAS AND ELECTRIC COMPANY

Lexington & Liberty Sts.
Baltimore, MD 21201
Phone: 410-234-5000
Fax: 410-234-5126

CEO: Christian H. Poindexter
CFO: Charles W. Shivery
Symbol: BGE
Exchange: NYSE

1995 Sales: $2,935 million
1995 Profits: $338 million
Mkt. Value: $3,910 million
Employees: 8,156

Web site: http://www.bge.com

424

Baltimore Gas and Electric (BG&E) provides electricity to over one million customers in central Maryland. The company also serves natural gas to nearly 550,000 customers. Subsidiary Constellation Holdings operates wholesale power generation and maintenance projects outside the parent company's utility service territory. Through a chain of 11 BGE Home Products retail stores in Maryland, the firm sells home appliances, electronics, kitchen remodeling, and repair services for appliances and heating and cooling equipment. BG&E and electrical utility company Potomac Electric are merging to form the Constellation Energy Corp., though it is not expected to be finalized until some time in 1997.

BANC ONE CORPORATION

100 E. Broad St.
Columbus, OH 43271
Phone: 614-248-5944
Fax: 614-882-1068

CEO: John B. McCoy
CFO: Michael J. McMennamin
Symbol: ONE
Exchange: NYSE

1995 Sales: $8,971 million
1995 Profits: $1,278 million
Mkt. Value: $14,807 million
Employees: 46,900

Web site: http://www.bankone.com

145

Banc One is a leading superregional banking institution with branches in 13 states, primarily in the Midwest and the Southwest. The company's strategy is to avoid high-risk loans and geographic concentration of loans. It focuses on diversification by acquiring other banks and unifying their product offerings nationally. Banc One customarily avoids wholesale firing of staff when acquiring other banks. It prefers to use incumbent expertise on local conditions to target consumers and small to medium-sized businesses, but the company is restructuring back-office operations at some of its locations to eliminate redundancy. Banc One will continue reducing costs by consolidating subsidiary banks along state lines.

BANK OF BOSTON CORPORATION

100 Federal St.
Boston, MA 01609
Phone: 617-434-2200
Fax: 617-575-2232

CEO: Charles K. Gifford
CFO: William J. Shea
Symbol: BKB
Exchange: NYSE

1995 Sales: $5,411 million
1995 Profits: $541 million
Mkt. Value: $5,310 million
Employees: 17,881

Web site: http://www.bkb.com

243

Bank of Boston operates 3 core lines: Corporate Banking, Global Banking, and Personal Banking. It provides business, retail, trust/asset management, correspondent, leasing, insurance, mortgage banking, real estate, and international investment banking for individual and commercial customers. Its major subsidiaries are Bank of Boston Connecticut, the First National Bank of Boston, and Rhode Island Hospital Trust National Bank. Bank of Boston is shrinking its branch system in northern New England and focusing on the Massachusetts area and on activities such as mortgage banking that can be carried on nationwide without branches.

THE BANK OF NEW YORK COMPANY, INC.

48 Wall St.
New York, NY 10286
Phone: 212-495-1784
Fax: 212-495-1398

CEO: J. Carter Bacot
CFO: Deno D. Papageorge
Symbol: BK
Exchange: NYSE

1995 Sales: $5,327 million
1995 Profits: $914 million
Mkt. Value: $10,102 million
Employees: 15,850

247

The Bank of New York is continuing its strategy of business diversity and regional specialization by dominating the suburban New York and New Jersey retail banking market (with no plans to expand its geographic territory). It is also increasing its role in several fee-generating specialty niches, including factoring, securities transaction processing, trust services, and credit cards. Other business lines include investment management, financial market services, investment banking, and international leasing. Bank of New York is also one of the largest US sponsors of American Depository Receipts and is a leader in government securities and fund clearance.

BANKAMERICA CORPORATION

555 California St.
San Francisco, CA 94104
Phone: 415-622-3456
Fax: 415-622-7915

CEO: David A. Coulter
CFO: Michael E. O'Neill
Symbol: BAC
Exchange: NYSE

1995 Sales: $20,386 million
1995 Profits: $2,664 million
Mkt. Value: $27,149 million
Employees: 95,288

Web site: http://www.bankamerica.com

BankAmerica, the nation's #3 bank (after Citicorp and the combined Chemical and Chase Manhattan), provides business, retail, trust/asset management, correspondent, leasing, insurance, mortgage banking, real estate, and investment services to individual and commercial customers. BankAmerica also offers checking, savings, loans, Mastercard, VISA, and money market deposit accounts. It is focusing on the growth of its investment products and mortgage lending and providing customers with services (cross-selling products) across departmental lines. BankAmerica is also targeting small businesses and experimenting with self-service branches, in-store branches, and electronic banking.

BANKERS TRUST NEW YORK CORPORATION

130 Liberty St.
New York, NY 10017
Phone: 212-250-2500
Fax: 212-454-1704

CEO: Frank Newman
CFO: Richard H. Daniel
Symbol: BT
Exchange: NYSE

1995 Sales: $8,600 million
1995 Profits: $215 million
Mkt. Value: $5,252 million
Employees: 14,000

Web site: http://www.bankerstrust.com

Bankers Trust (BT) is recovering from a few "difficulties" (lawsuits relating to derivatives it sold to 2 long-time clients and a $10 million fine imposed by the SEC). Yet BT remains committed to its specialty of risk management: using derivatives and other strategies to shield itself and its clients from the worst vagaries of the market. It also protects itself from the hazards of risk management with other businesses, such as trading, loan syndications, currency trading, and international merchant banking. BT is trying to cultivate customer relationships and improve communications between departments (to facilitate cross-selling).

BARNETT BANKS, INC.

50 N. Laura St.
Jacksonville, FL 32202
Phone: 904-791-7720
Fax: 904-791-7166

CEO: Charles E. Rice
CFO: Charles W. Newman
Symbol: BBI
Exchange: NYSE

1995 Sales: $3,680 million
1995 Profits: $533 million
Mkt. Value: $5,775 million
Employees: 20,175

Web site: http://www.barnett.com

Barnett operates banks and nonbank subsidiaries in Florida and Georgia. It specializes in mortgage banking (both retail and wholesale) and is attempting to beef up its credit card operations and leasing business. Barnett is instilling a new corporate culture in its employees, emphasizing sales of fee- or commission-generating income (like investment products), and, as part of this effort, it is using its database to target existing customers for new products. The company is looking for new ways to make money, including jumping on board the financial services train.

BAXTER INTERNATIONAL INC.

1 Baxter Parkway
Deerfield, IL 60015
Phone: 847-948-2000
Fax: 847-948-3948

CEO: Vernon R. Loucks Jr.
CFO: H. M. Jansen Kraemer Jr.
Symbol: BAX
Exchange: NYSE

1995 Sales: $9,730 million
1995 Profits: $649 million
Mkt. Value: $12,353 million
Employees: 35,500

Web site: http://www.baxter.com

Although currently the leading US maker and distributor of health care products used in hospitals and other medical facilities, Baxter plans to shrink substantially by splitting into 2 smaller companies. The first, still to be known as Baxter, will include successful high-tech businesses, such as cardiovascular, kidney dialysis, and biotechnology products and its market-leading intravenous-products line. The 2nd, as-yet unnamed, company will include Baxter's lackluster hospital supplies business (hospital gowns and bedpans) and surgical and respiratory therapy supplies. Each company is expected to have about $5 billion in annual sales.

THE BEAR STEARNS COMPANIES INC.

245 Park Ave.
New York, NY 10167
Phone: 212-272-2000
Fax: 212-272-8239

CEO: James E. Cayne
CFO: William J. Montgoris
Symbol: BSC
Exchange: NYSE

1995 Sales: $3,754 million
1995 Profits: $241 million
Mkt. Value: $2,782 million
Employees: 7,481

329

Bear Stearns is one of the US's leading securities trading, investment banking, and brokerage firms. It serves an elite clientele of corporations, financial institutions, governments, and individuals. Services include asset management, clearing and custody, fiduciary, securities lending, and trust. Bear Stearns also has a significant presence overseas, particularly in Latin America, Japan, and China. The company is known for its aggressive trading as well as its dedication to conforming to trading rules.

BECTON, DICKINSON AND COMPANY

1 Becton Dr.
Franklin Lakes, NJ 07417
Phone: 201-847-6800
Fax: 201-847-6475

CEO: Clateo Castellini
CFO: Edward J. Ludwig
Symbol: BDX
Exchange: NYSE

1995 Sales: $2,713 million
1995 Profits: $252 million
Mkt. Value: $5,328 million
Employees: 18,100

461

Becton, Dickinson manufactures and sells medical devices and diagnostic systems. The company's product line includes hypodermic needles and syringes, blood collection equipment, gloves, IV catheters (Becton, Dickinson is the world's #1 supplier), tissue culture lab ware, and immunodiagnostic test kits. It is a leader in clinical diagnostic products for infectious diseases (including AIDS testing). Efforts to improve testing and to protect health care workers from infected blood have fostered demand for the company's products, including its SAFETY-LOK syringes, blood collection systems (Vacutainer is the market leader), and other products.

BELL ATLANTIC CORPORATION

1717 Arch St.
Philadelphia, PA 19103
Phone: 215-963-6000
Fax: 215-963-6470

CEO: Raymond W. Smith
CFO: William O. Albertini
Symbol: BEL
Exchange: NYSE

1995 Sales: $13,430 million
1995 Profits: $1,858 million
Mkt. Value: $26,894 million
Employees: 61,800

Web site: http://www.bel-atl.com

83

Bell Atlantic is the #2 regional Bell operating company. It provides local telephone service to a territory covering 11 million households and 29 million people in 6 mid-Atlantic states and the District of Columbia; it also offers cellular service in many metropolitan and rural areas of the country. It has formed a partnership with NYNEX, U S WEST, and AirTouch to develop a national wireless company called CAI Wireless. This project will enable Bell Atlantic to offer video programming in consumers' homes. Bell Atlantic and Nynex have agreed to a merger that will create the 2nd largest telecommunications company in the US (after AT&T).

In 1877, when he was 7, **Amadeo Giannini** saw his immigrant father, Luigi, shot and killed in a dispute over a $1 debt. Biographers have linked the trauma of that event to Giannini's drive to serve workers and small businesses as he built the **Bank of America**.

— *Breaking the Bank*, by Gary Hector

"Though the per share intrinsic value of our stock has grown at an excellent rate during the past 5 years, its market price has grown still faster."
—CEO Warren Buffett, Berkshire Hathaway

— FORTUNE; April 29, 1996

BELLSOUTH CORPORATION

1155 Peachtree St. N.E.	CEO: John L. Clendenin	1995 Sales: $17,886 million
Atlanta, GA 30309	CFO: Ronald Dykes	1995 Loss: ($1,232) million
Phone: 404-249-2000	Symbol: BLS	Mkt. Value: $36,029 million
Fax: 404-249-5599	Exchange: NYSE	Employees: 87,571

Web site: http://www.bellsouth.com

49

At least until its sisters finish merging, BellSouth is the largest regional bell operating company in the nation, delivering local telephone service to 9 fast-growing states in the Southeast. Its cellular business ranks 2nd in the nation with 2.2 million customers in the southern states. BellSouth's strategy is to buy large segments of the radio spectrum and offer a wide array of wireless communication services. The company is building one of the first personal communications systems in the US with Northern Telecom. It is working with Lotus, Microsoft, and Oracle to develop e-mail and database products and has produced a phone/computer product, called Simon, with IBM.

BERGEN BRUNSWIG CORPORATION

4000 Metropolitan Dr.	CEO: Robert E. Martini	1995 Sales: $8,448 million
Orange, CA 92668	CFO: Neil F. Dimick	1995 Profits: $64 million
Phone: 714-385-4000	Symbol: BBC	Mkt. Value: $979 million
Fax: 714-385-1442	Exchange: NYSE	Employees: 4,770

153

Bergen Brunswig, the 2nd largest pharmaceuticals distributor in the US (after McKesson), counts among its customers Columbia/HCA, the nation's #1 hospital chain. The products it distributes include cosmetics, home health care supplies and equipment, personal health products, pharmaceuticals, sundries, proprietary medicines, and toiletries. Over half of Bergen Brunswig's sales come from hospitals and other managed care facilities, with the rest coming from chain drugstores and independent pharmacies. The company's technological advancements have included AccuSource (an electronic drug information and ordering system for retail pharmacies) and AccuLine (an online pharmacy-management system for hospitals).

BERKSHIRE HATHAWAY INC.

1440 Kiewit Plaza	CEO: Warren E. Buffett	1995 Sales: $4,488 million
Omaha, NE 68131	CFO: Marc D. Hamburg	1995 Profits: $725 million
Phone: 402-346-1400	Symbol: BRK	Mkt. Value: $43,880 million
Fax: 402-536-3030	Exchange: NYSE	Employees: 25,000

Web site: http://www.transarc.com/afs/transarc.com/public/abh/html/brk

293

Berkshire Hathaway is a veritable buffet of businesses. The holding company and investment vehicle for one of the richest men in the world, Warren Buffett, it primarily operates property and casualty insurance and reinsurance businesses through 13 subsidiaries, including National Indemnity, Cypress Insurance, and auto insurer GEICO. Berkshire also owns stakes in a smorgasbord of companies, including gems (Helzberg's Diamond Shops), information (World Book), candy (See's), and shoes (H. H. Brown, Lowell, and Dexter). In addition, the company has accumulated significant minority stakes in American Express, Coca-Cola, Gannett, and Gillette, among others.

BEST BUY CO., INC.

7075 Flying Cloud Dr.
Eden Prairie, MN 55344
Phone: 612-947-2000
Fax: 612-947-2422

CEO: Richard M. Schulze
CFO: Allen U. Lenzmeier
Symbol: BBY
Exchange: NYSE

1995 Sales: $5,080 million
1995 Profits: $58 million
Mkt. Value: $779 million
Employees: 25,300

Best Buy is running neck and neck with archrival Circuit City for the title of #1 consumer electronics retailer in the US. It sells home office products (answering machines, copiers), video products (camcorders, VCRs), audio products (car stereos), entertainment software (videocassettes, compact discs), and appliances (dishwashers, ovens, vacuum cleaners). The company has stores throughout the US, with a heavy concentration in Texas and the Midwest. Best Buy continues to grow with the addition of new stores like its Concept III stores, which offer larger outlets that feature amenities such as interactive answer center kiosks and CD listening posts.

BETHLEHEM STEEL CORPORATION

1170 Eighth Ave.
Bethlehem, PA 18016
Phone: 610-694-2424
Fax: 610-694-6920

CEO: Curtis H. Barnette
CFO: Gary L. Millenbruch
Symbol: BS
Exchange: NYSE

1995 Sales: $4,868 million
1995 Profits: $180 million
Mkt. Value: $1,548 million
Employees: 19,500

Web site: http://www.bethsteel.com

Bethlehem Steel is the 2nd largest US steel producer (after USX-U.S. Steel), the largest steel supplier to the construction industry (15% of sales), and a major supplier to the automotive industry and railroads (25% of sales). The company annually produces almost 10 million tons of steel, constituting 10% of US production. It owns or operates coal mines and coal processing plants in Pennsylvania and West Virginia. The company also owns 5 short line railroads, 2 shipyards, a flatbed trucking company, and stakes in 3 iron mines (Minnesota, Canada, and Brazil). Bethlehem Steel and rival USX-U.S. Steel jointly conduct research on basic ironmaking and steelmaking technologies.

BEVERLY ENTERPRISES, INC.

1200 S. Waldron Rd.
Fort Smith, AR 72903
Phone: 501-452-6712
Fax: 501-452-5131

CEO: David R. Banks
CFO: S. Hollingsworth Jr.
Symbol: BEV
Exchange: NYSE

1995 Sales: $3,229 million
1995 Loss: ($8) million
Mkt. Value: $1,120 million
Employees: 83,000

The largest nursing home chain in the US, Beverly Enterprises also operates retirement homes, rehabilitation services, and specialized nursing services such as hospices, which provide care to terminally ill patients. To tighten its focus on its nursing home business, Beverly spun off its institutional pharmacy subsidiary, Pharmacy Corp. of America. The company continues to expand with outpatient rehabilitation centers, more hospices, and AdviNet, a nationwide referral system that helps people and companies select providers of long-term and other types of care.

BINDLEY WESTERN INDUSTRIES, INC.

10333 N. Meridian St.
Indianapolis, IN 46290
Phone: 317-298-9900
Fax: 317-298-0890

CEO: William E. Bindley
CFO: Thomas J. Salentine
Symbol: BDY
Exchange: NYSE

1995 Sales: $4,673 million
1995 Profits: $16 million
Mkt. Value: $188 million
Employees: 894

Bindley Western is the 5th largest drug wholesaler in the US. The company's customers include Eckerd and Rite Aid (which together account for about 1/3 of company sales). Bindley owns the IV-One Companies (a major drug distribution conglomerate, including IV-1, IV-One, and National Pharmacy Providers) and is under contract to provide medicines to 16 US military facilities in Europe. Subsidiaries include BW Food Distributors, (broker of food and related products), BW Transportation Services (transportation services for the company's divisions and subsidiaries), and First Choice, Inc. of Maine (marketing and distribution of home health care products).

THE BLACK & DECKER CORPORATION

701 E. Joppa Rd.
Towson, MD 21286
Phone: 410-716-3900
Fax: 410-716-2933

CEO: Nolan D. Archibald
CFO: Thomas M. Schoewe
Symbol: BDK
Exchange: NYSE

1995 Sales: $5,566 million
1995 Profits: $224 million
Mkt. Value: $3,230 million
Employees: 34,200

Web site: http://www.blackanddecker.com

Black & Decker is the world's largest producer of power tools and accessories and electric lawn and garden tools. It is also the largest full-line supplier of small household appliances in North America. The company is the world leader in specialty fastening systems, glass container making equipment, steel golf club shafts, and security hardware. Major brands are Alligator, Black & Decker, DeWalt, Dynalite, and Dustbuster. By looking globally and introducing innovative products such as the SnakeLight flexible flashlight, Black & Decker aims for an increase in worldwide sales. The company's products are sold in more than 100 countries (sales outside the US account for over 1/3 of the total).

BOATMEN'S BANCSHARES, INC.

1 BoatmenÆs Plaza
St. Louis, MO 63101
Phone: 314-466-6000
Fax: 314-466-4235

CEO: Andrew B. Craig III
CFO: James W. Kienker
Symbol: BOAT
Exchange: Nasdaq

1995 Sales: $2,996 million
1995 Profits: $419 million
Mkt. Value: $4,997 million
Employees: 17,023

Boatmen's is the largest bank in Missouri, with bank holdings in a number of surrounding states as well as further afield in Texas and New Mexico. The bank offers trust and mortgage banking services. Unlike many banks, which derive a majority of their income from loans and interest, almost half of Boatmen's revenues come from fees (loan, trust, service, and credit card fees). Boatmen's has transferred its small credit card operation to its Albuquerque, New Mexico, offices and is focusing on growing the credit card business from that facility. Boatmen's aggressively pursues a strategy of acquisition (including the purchase of Fourth Financial Corp., the largest bank company in Kansas).

THE BOEING COMPANY

7755 E. Marginal Way S.
Seattle, WA 98108
Phone: 206-655-2121
Fax: 206-655-7004

CEO: Frank A. Shrontz
CFO: Boyd E. Givan
Symbol: BA
Exchange: NYSE

1995 Sales: $19,515 million
1995 Profits: $393 million
Mkt. Value: $27,817 million
Employees: 105,000

Web site: http://www.boeing.com

Boeing is the world's #1 commercial aircraft maker, manufacturing 737s (short-to-medium-range flights, 108-146 seats), 747s (long-range flights, 420-566 seats), 757s (short to medium-range flights, 180-230 seats), and 767s (medium-range flights, 210-250 seats). The company's Defense and Space Group makes the B-2 Bomber and the CH-47 Chinook helicopter. In response to a relatively mature market for commercial aircraft and competition from the European consortium Airbus, Boeing is switching to "just-in-time" inventory control, opening lines of communication with its employees, and giving more responsibility to middle management and workers.

BOISE CASCADE CORPORATION

1111 W. Jefferson St.
Boise, ID 83702
Phone: 208-384-6161
Fax: 208-384-7298

CEO: George J. Harad
CFO: Theodore Crumley
Symbol: BCC
Exchange: NYSE

1995 Sales: $5,058 million
1995 Profits: $352 million
Mkt. Value: $2,028 million
Employees: 17,820

Web site: http://www.bc.com

Boise Cascade is a leading seller of lumber, building supplies, office equipment, paper, and furniture. It is the #3 distributor of full-line building products in the US. The company also makes and sells office products, which account for less than 25% of total revenues. The main products of the paper products division are coated papers, containerboard, forms, corrugated containers, newsprint, and pulp. The building products line includes ceramic tiles, doors, insulation, veneer lumber, paneling, roofing, and windows. The office products division distributes copy paper, office furniture, and office supplies. It operates over 30 mills and 26 office supply distribution centers in the Northwest, South, New England, and the Midwest.

BRISTOL-MYERS SQUIBB COMPANY

345 Park Ave.
New York, NY 10154
Phone: 212-546-4000
Fax: 212-546-4020

CEO: Charles A. Heimbold Jr.
CFO: Michael F. Mee
Symbol: BMY
Exchange: NYSE

1995 Sales: $13,767 million
1995 Profits: $1,812 million
Mkt. Value: $42,636 million
Employees: 48,400

Web site: http://www.bms.com

79

One of the largest pharmaceutical companies in the US, Bristol-Myers Squibb focuses on cardiovascular, anti-infective, and anticancer drugs. It also makes consumer health products (Exedrin), medical devices (surgery products, orthopedic instruments), and toiletries and beauty aids (Ban, Clairol). The company licenses drugs in the final stages of development from other companies, including sorivudine, a shingles treatment, from SmithKline Beecham. Capitalizing on the market for generic drugs, the company has off-patent divisions in the US and Europe.

BROWNING-FERRIS INDUSTRIES, INC.

757 N. Eldridge Rd.
Houston, TX 77079
Phone: 713-870-8100
Fax: 713-870-7844

CEO: Bruce E. Ranck
CFO: Jeffrey E. Curtiss
Symbol: BFI
Exchange: NYSE

1995 Sales: $5,779 million
1995 Profits: $385 million
Mkt. Value: $6,726 million
Employees: 43,000

229

Browning-Ferris Industries (BFI) is the world's #2 waste management firm (after WMX Technologies), operating 104 solid-waste landfills, 32 medical-waste treatment facilities, and 125 recycling facilities in North America. BFI's fleet of 12,400 trucks collects solid waste in 45 states and 14 foreign countries. Anticipating increasing government regulation, BFI nurtured its recycling segment, which has become its fastest-growing business. That segment's revenues soared from $9.6 million in 1990 to $675 million in 1995, representing about 11% of overall revenues. Solid waste transfer and disposal accounts for almost 20% of sales, while medical waste disposal operations bring in less than 5% of the firm's funds.

The first international airmail was delivered between Seattle and Victoria, British Columbia, after WWI when **Boeing Airplane Co.** saw its military sales dry up and decided to start the service using its new B-1 flying boat.

— Hoover's Handbook of American Business 1996

BRUNO'S, INC.

800 Lakeshore Parkway
Birmingham, AL 35211
Phone: 205-940-9400
Fax: 205-940-9534

CEO: William Bolton
CFO: Susan Fitzgibbon
Ownership: Privately Held

1995 Sales: $2,870 million
1995 Profits: $33 million
Employees: 25,600

440

Now owned by Kohlberg Kravis Roberts (KKR), Bruno's runs a chain of some 250 supermarkets under the names Bruno's Food and Pharmacy, FoodMax, Food World, Food Fair, and Piggly Wiggly. The company operates in 6 southeastern states from its base in Birmingham, Alabama. Store formats range from warehouse (FoodMax) to low-volume rural locations (Piggly Wiggly) to its Bruno's upscale stores. After the KKR takeover, chairman Ronald Bruno stepped down and William Bolton, a former American Stores executive, took the helm.

BRUNSWICK CORPORATION

1 N. Field Court	CEO: Peter N. Larsen	1995 Sales: $3,077 million
Lake Forest, IL 60045	CFO: Peter B. Hamilton	1995 Profits: $127 million
Phone: 847-735-4700	Symbol: BC	Mkt. Value: $2,207 million
Fax: 847-735-4765	Exchange: NYSE	Employees: 20,900

Web site: http://www.enw.com/brunswick/index.html

 Brunswick is the leading US maker of recreation and leisure products and the world's leading manufacturer of pleasure boats and equipment. The company also operates one of North America's largest bowling chains and even runs a chain of restaurants (Circus World Pizza). Its marine division accounts for almost 3/4 of total sales. Brand names include Astro, Bayliner, Jazz, Laguna, MonArk, Procraft, Robalo, Sea Ray, Starcraft, and US Marine boats and Mariner, MerCruiser, Quicksilver Marine, and Stealth boat motors. The sporting goods division makes Brunswick, Rhino, and Systems 2000 bowling equipment; Brunswick brand billiards accessories and golf equipment; and Classic, Quantum, and Zebco fishing gear.

 The winter of 1995–96 was so bad it stopped locomotives. After **Burlington Northern** lost more than $1.3 billion in revenue on shipments to western US ports, company CEO **Robert Krebs** decided "we don't have the capacity we need in the locomotive fleet" and vowed to spend $150 million for 75 to 100 more of the huge machines.

— Bloomberg Business News

BURLINGTON NORTHERN SANTA FE CORPORATION

3800 Continental Plaza	CEO: Robert D. Krebs	1995 Sales: $6,183 million
Fort Worth, TX 76102	CFO: Denis E. Springer	1995 Profits: $92 million
Phone: 817-333-2000	Symbol: BNI	Mkt. Value: $12,436 million
Fax: 817-878-2377	Exchange: NYSE	Employees: 45,655

Web site: http://www.bnsf.com

 Burlington Northern Santa Fe (BNSF) is the #3 US railroad. The merged Burlington Northern and Santa Fe Pacific total nearly 31,000 track miles in 27 states and 2 Canadian provinces. The company transports coal (about 1/3 of sales) as well as agricultural commodities, forest products, and other goods. Its intermodal (train-to-truck, train-to-ship, and truck-to-ship) business has been a promising growth sector. In addition to helping control operating and overhead costs, the merger provided improved access to West Coast and Gulf Coast ports.

THE CALDOR CORPORATION

20 Glover Ave.	CEO: Don R. Clarke	1995 Sales: $2,765 million
Norwalk, CT 06856	CFO: John G. Reen	1995 Loss: ($5) million
Phone: 203-846-1641	Symbol: CLD	Mkt. Value: $72 million
Fax: 203-849-2019	Exchange: NYSE	Employees: 24,000

 Bankrupt Caldor is a discount retailer with stores in the Northeast and mid-Atlantic states. Caldor positions itself between traditional discount stores and upscale department stores, emphasizing quality brand-name products. It projects an upscale appearance in its stores and at some locations offers restaurants such as Nathan's Famous hot dog franchises, as opposed to no-name snack bars. The company also locates its stores primarily in high-density urban and suburban markets. The company has sought Chapter 11 protection, citing weak sales, an addiction to short-term financing, lack of credit, and competition from "category killer" Wal-Mart, as well as Target and Kmart.

CALIBER SYSTEM, INC.

3560 W. Market St.
Akron, OH 44333
Phone: 216-384-8184
Fax: 330-665-8898

CEO: Daniel J. Sullivan
CFO: Douglas A. Wilson
Symbol: CBB
Exchange: NYSE

1995 Sales: $2,548 million
1995 Loss: ($27) million
Mkt. Value: $1,713 million
Employees: 25,700

Web site: http://www.calibersys.com

Caliber System, formerly Roadway Services, transports freight and packages world-wide. Among its operating units are RPS, a small-package business-to-business carrier; Viking Freight, a domestic carrier of less-than-truckload (LTL, less than 10,000 lbs.) shipments; Roberts Express, an expediter of high-security, hazardous, and fragile shipments in North America and Europe; Caliber Logistics, a provider of logistics services; and Caliber Technologies, which offers computer services. To reduce its involvement in the less-promising long-haul LTL business, the company spun off its largest subsidiary, Roadway Express, in late 1995.

CAMPBELL SOUP COMPANY

Campbell Place
Camden, NJ 08103
Phone: 609-342-4800
Fax: 609-342-3878

CEO: David W. Johnson
CFO: Basil L. Anderson
Symbol: CPB
Exchange: NYSE

1995 Sales: $7,278 million
1995 Profits: $698 million
Mkt. Value: $15,571 million
Employees: 43,781

Web site: http://www.campbellsoups.com/

Campbell Soup Company is the venerable owner of some of the food industry's best-known brand names -- including the one appearing on almost 80% of all soup cans sold in the US. The company's U.S.A. operating division also includes the Franco-American, Swanson, Pace, V8, Vlasic, Prego, and Mrs. Paul's labels, while its Bakery & Confectionery unit includes brand names Pepperidge Farm, Arnott's, and Godiva. Its 3rd unit, International Grocery, brings in almost 20% of the company's sales. Campbell has made high priorities of acquisitions and overseas growth but is also tweaking its traditional products to spark consumer interest.

CARDINAL HEALTH, INC.

5555 Glendon Court
Dublin, OH 43016
Phone: 614-717-5000
Fax: 614-761-8919

CEO: Robert D. Walter
CFO: David Bearman
Symbol: CAH
Exchange: NYSE

1995 Sales: $7,806 million
1995 Profits: $85 million
Mkt. Value: $2,901 million
Employees: 4,000

Cardinal Health is a national, full-service wholesaler of pharmaceuticals, surgical and hospital supplies, therapeutic plasma and other specialty pharmaceutical products, health and beauty care products, and other items typically sold by hospitals, retail drug-stores, and other health care providers. It provides a variety of support services to its customers, including computerized order entry and order confirmation systems, generic sourcing programs, product movement and management reports, and consultation on store operation and merchandising. Cardinal Health follows an aggressive acquisition strategy, most recently acquiring Medicine Shoppe International, a franchiser of independent retail pharmacies.

CAROLINA POWER & LIGHT COMPANY

411 Fayetteville St.
Raleigh, NC 27601
Phone: 919-546-6111
Fax: 919-546-7678

CEO: Sherwood H. Smith Jr.
CFO: Glenn E. Harder
Symbol: CPL
Exchange: NYSE

1995 Sales: $3,007 million
1995 Profits: $373 million
Mkt. Value: $5,118 million
Employees: 7,203

Carolina Power & Light (CP&L) is a public service corporation that generates and dis-tributes electricity to consumers in North and South Carolina. CP&L retails electricity in about 220 communities and wholesales energy to one municipal power agency, 4 towns, and 2 electric membership corporations. The company has a generating capac-ity of approximately 9,615 MW, the fuel sources of which are 55% coal, 32% nuclear, 2% hydro, and 11% fired by other fuels, including oil, natural gas, and propane. Of CP&L's total revenues, approximately 32% is from residential sales, 21% from commercial sales, 17% from resale, and the remainder from other sources.

CASE CORPORATION

700 State St.
Racine, WI 53404
Phone: 414-636-6011
Fax: 414-636-0483

CEO: Jean-Pierre Rosso
CFO: Theodore R. French
Symbol: CSE
Exchange: NYSE

1995 Sales: $5,105 million
1995 Profits: $337 million
Mkt. Value: $3,795 million
Employees: 15,700

Case Corporation is the world's largest manufacturer of small and medium-sized construction equipment and North America's 2nd largest maker of farm equipment (after Deere). The company makes more than 100 models of farm equipment, including tractors, combines, and plows. It also makes excavators, wheel tractors, loaders, bulldozers, and other construction equipment. Its products are sold through a network of more than 4,000 independent dealers and about 115 company-owned retail stores located throughout the US and in 150 countries. Case was spun off by industrial conglomerate Tenneco in 1994.

CATERPILLAR INC.

100 N.E. Adams St.
Peoria, IL 61629
Phone: 309-675-1000
Fax: 309-675-5948

CEO: Donald V. Fites
CFO: Douglas R. Oberhelman
Symbol: CAT
Exchange: NYSE

1995 Sales: $16,072 million
1995 Profits: $1,136 million
Mkt. Value: $13,969 million
Employees: 54,352

Web site: http://www.caterpillar.com

Caterpillar is the world's #1 maker of earthmoving machinery. Its products are widely renowned for their durability. The company designs and makes a variety of construction, mining, and agricultural machinery as well as engines for trucks, locomotives, and electrical power generation systems. Cat also provides financing and insurance for its dealers and customers. It maintains some 40 plants and nearly 200 dealerships around the world. Foreign sales account for nearly 50% of the company's revenues. With modernized manufacturing systems, a lean labor force, and a reputation for quality, Cat will take advantage of huge investments in physical infrastructure in the developing world to grow its international sales.

CENTERIOR ENERGY CORPORATION

6200 Oak Tree Blvd.
Independence, OH 44131
Phone: 216-447-3100
Fax: 216-447-3240

CEO: Robert J. Farling
CFO: Terrence G. Linnert
Symbol: CX
Exchange: NYSE

1995 Sales: $2,516 million
1995 Profits: $221 million
Mkt. Value: $1,184 million
Employees: 6,532

Web site: http://www.centerior.com

Centerior Energy owns 2 power companies: Cleveland Electric Illuminating (providing electric power to more than 700,000 customers in northeastern Ohio) and Toledo Edison (more than 250,000 customers in northwestern Ohio). It generates more than half its power from fossil fuels and most of the rest from nuclear sources. Centerior also owns a service company that provides administrative, engineering, and legal services for the other 2 firms. The company has interests in 20 generating units at 12 power plants in Ohio and Pennsylvania capable of producing about 6 million kW. Its cost-control efforts have been stymied by depreciation and higher decommissioning costs for its nuclear plants.

CENTEX CORPORATION

3333 Lee Parkway
Dallas, TX 75219
Phone: 214-559-6500
Fax: 214-559-6750

CEO: Laurence E. Hirsch
CFO: David W. Quinn
Symbol: CTX
Exchange: NYSE

1995 Sales: $3,278 million
1995 Profits: $92 million
Mkt. Value: $817 million
Employees: 6,395

Web site: http://www.centex.com

Centex is the nation's #1 home builder. The company survives the boom and bust cycles of the construction industry by operating in nearly 50 geographic markets and several business sectors. Centex has made inroads in almost every state in the continental US and in the UK (where, in a joint venture with the Charles Church Group, it builds luxury homes). It also has entered a joint venture with the Kensington Cottages Corp., in which it will build and operate a facility for people with Alzheimer's disease. The company has interests in mortgage banking, land ownership, commercial real estate development, and construction supply manufacturing.

CENTRAL AND SOUTH WEST CORPORATION

1616 Woodall Rodgers Freeway	CEO: Edgar R. Brooks	1995 Sales: $3,735 million
Dallas, TX 75266	CFO: Glenn D. Rosilier	1995 Profits: $421 million
Phone: 214-777-1000	Symbol: CSR	Mkt. Value: $5,553 million
Fax: 214-777-1033	Exchange: NYSE	Employees: 7,925

Web site: http://www.csw.com

333 Central and South West Corporation (CSW) is a holding company for 4 electric utility subsidiaries: Central Power and Light (South Texas), Public Service Company of Oklahoma, Southwestern Electric Power, and West Texas Utilities. CSW operates 38 generating plants serving more than 1.6 million customers. The company relies on natural gas (60%), coal and lignite (33%), and nuclear power to generate its electricity. CSW also operates a telecommunications company, CSW Communications. Other subsidiaries include CSW Energy (independent power and cogeneration projects), CSW International (foreign independent power and cogeneration projects), and Transok (natural gas pipeline and marketing).

QUOTES

"This is too big a merger.... It would give an all powerful oligarchy a stranglehold on New York banking," said US Representative Emmanuel Celler before the Chase and Manhattan banks joined their $7.6 billion in assets in 1955. **Chase Manhattan** assets hit $300 billion after the1996 Chemical Banking Corp. merger.

— *The Chase*, by John Donald Wilson; *Hoover's Handbook of American Business 1996*

CHAMPION INTERNATIONAL CORPORATION

1 Champion Plaza	CEO: Andrew C. Sigler	1995 Sales: $6,972 million
Stamford, CT 06921	CFO: Frank Kneisel	1995 Profits: $772 million
Phone: 203-358-7000	Symbol: CHA	Mkt. Value: $4,584 million
Fax: 203-358-6444	Exchange: NYSE	Employees: 24,100

Web site: http://www.cha.inch.com

188 Champion is one of the US's largest manufacturers of paper and wood products (linerboard, newsprint, recycled fiber, pulp, turpentine, wood chips, lumber, plywood, veneer, waferboard, and other related goods). It is one of the largest landholders in the country, with over 5 million acres of timberland. The company also has forests and manufacturing facilities in Brazil and Canada. Thanks to an increase in paper prices, Champion is returning to profitability. By modernizing its facilities, selling nonessential assets, and employing innovative money-saving methods (bleach filtrate recycling technology), the company aims to improve its outlook for the future.

CHASE MANHATTAN CORP.

1 Chase Manhattan Plaza	CEO: Walter V. Shipley	1995 Sales: $11,336 million
New York, NY 10081	CFO: Peter J. Tobin	1995 Profits: $1,165 million
Phone: 212-552-2222	Symbol: CMB	Mkt. Value: $12,616 million
Fax: 212-270-2613	Exchange: NYSE	Employees: 33,365

Web site: http://www.chase.com

112 Chase Manhattan (the combination of Chemical Banking and the former Chase Manhattan), is now the 2nd largest bank (after Citicorp) in revenues (the largest measured in assets) in the US. Chemical merged with (some say acquired) Chase and took its name to create a single entity with assets of some $300 billion. After consolidating operations and eliminating up to 12,000 jobs, Chase is focusing on local banking, credit cards and other consumer products, and international banking. Despite its bulk, the bank will still have to contend with increasing competition from nonbanking financial institutions.

CHEMICAL BANKING CORPORATION

270 Park Ave.
New York, NY 10017
Phone: 212-270-6000
Fax: 212-270-2613

CEO: Walter V. Shipley
CFO: Peter J. Tobin
Symbol: CHL
Exchange: NYSE

1995 Sales: $14,884 million
1995 Profits: $1,805 million
Mkt. Value: $16,971 million
Employees: 39,078

Web site: http://www.chase.com

One of the largest banks in the US, Chemical Banking and its subsidiaries operate throughout the US and in 35 other nations. In addition to its retail, credit card, and mortgage activities, Chemical has strong overseas operations, particularly in foreign currency and corporate financing. Other businesses include corporate equity and debt underwriting (it is one of the few US banks currently permitted to do this). It also owns Texas Commerce Bank, which has one of that state's largest banking networks. Chemical Banking became Chase Manhattan in 1996 when it merged with its longtime rival.

CHEVRON CORPORATION

575 Market St.
San Francisco, CA 94105
Phone: 415-894-7700
Fax: 415-894-0348

CEO: Kenneth T. Derr
CFO: Martin R. Klitten
Symbol: CHV
Exchange: NYSE

1995 Sales: $32,094 million
1995 Profits: $930 million
Mkt. Value: $35,791 million
Employees: 43,019

Web site: http://www.chevron.com

One of the largest US-based international oil and gas companies, Chevron has net reserves of 4.2 billion barrels of oil and 10 trillion cubic feet of gas. The largest oil refiner in the US and the 2nd largest natural gas producer, Chevron has operations that run the gamut from exploration to refining to distribution. While sluggish oil markets depressed prices in the early 1990s and forced Chevron to cut costs and improve efficiency, the company is also pursuing an aggressive exploration and production strategy outside the US.

Chiquita Brands has been through several names (including United Fruit and United Brands) as well as at least one nickname, "the Octopus." Hondurans came up with that one during the first half of the century because of the company's broad influence in the country's politics and society.

— *Hoover's Handbook of American Business 1996*

CHIQUITA BRANDS INTERNATIONAL, INC.

250 E. Fifth St.
Cincinnati, OH 45202
Phone: 513-784-8000
Fax: 513-784-8030

CEO: Carl E. Lindner
CFO: Steven G. Warshaw
Symbol: CQB
Exchange: NYSE

1995 Sales: $4,027 million
1995 Profits: $9 million
Mkt. Value: $834 million
Employees: 36,000

Web site: http://www.chiquita.com

Chiquita Brands, best known as the world's largest producer, processor, and distributor of bananas, also sells other fresh fruits and vegetables. The company markets apples, avocados, citrus fruits, grapes, kiwis, mangos, and nectarines (in addition to bananas) under the Chiquita brand name, as well as other fruits and vegetables under the Consul, Chico, Amigo, and Premium names. Additional products include ready-to-eat salads, margarine, shortening, cookies, juices, and other consumer packaged foods.

CHRYSLER CORPORATION

1000 Chrysler Dr.	CEO: Robert J. Eaton	1995 Sales: $53,195 million
Auburn Hills, MI 48326	CFO: Gary C. Valade	1995 Profits: $2,025 million
Phone: 810-576-5741	Symbol: C	Mkt. Value: $23,314 million
Fax: 810-956-3747	Exchange: NYSE	Employees: 126,000

Web site: http://www.chryslercorp.com

By cutting costs, reorganizing, and shaving development time for new car models, Chrysler has become the world's lowest-cost automaker and has the highest profit margin of any US automaker. The #3 US automaker, Chrysler designs and produces Dodge Neon, Intrepid, and Stealth cars; Dodge Ram, Dakota, and Jeep Comanche trucks; and Jeep Cherokee sport utility vehicles. The company also owns Dollar and Thrifty car rental agencies (which it wants to sell) and offers a range of financial services to its dealers and customers. Chrysler's products are sold in more than 100 countries throughout the world, though nearly 90% of sales come from the US.

THE CHUBB CORPORATION

15 Mountain View Rd.	CEO: Dean R. O'Hare	1995 Sales: $6,089 million
Warren, NJ 07061	CFO: Percy Chubb III	1995 Profits: $697 million
Phone: 908-903-2000	Symbol: CB	Mkt. Value: $8,263 million
Fax: 908-580-2027	Exchange: NYSE	Employees: 11,000

Web site: http://www.chubb.com

Not content with plans to become one of the 10 largest property/casualty insurers in the US by the year 2000, Chubb Corporation intends to target overseas markets for further growth. To achieve its goals, the firm is upgrading its technical systems, streamlining operations, and improving customer service so that customers will have one contact within the company, instead of a different contact for each type of insurance. Chubb's products include such niches as winery coverage in France as well as life and health insurance. Its Chubb & Son subsidiary offers insurance company management services, and its Bellemead Development Corp. develops real estate.

CIGNA CORPORATION

1 Liberty Place	CEO: Wilson H. Taylor	1995 Sales: $18,955 million
Philadelphia, PA 19192	CFO: James G. Stewart	1995 Profits: $211 million
Phone: 215-761-1000	Symbol: CI	Mkt. Value: $8,942 million
Fax: 215-761-5505	Exchange: NYSE	Employees: 47,000

Web site: http://www.cigna.com

One of the US's foremost insurance companies, CIGNA saw its property/casualty insurance business in recent years struck by strings of natural disasters, manmade catastrophes, and inefficient operations. To rectify these problems, the company embarked on a program to streamline its direct property/casualty operations and exit property/casualty reinsurance altogether. In contrast, CIGNA's health and financial services operations remain robust. Its HealthCare subsidiary covers some 19 million people and its investment operations are poised to benefit from the graying of America.

CINERGY CORP.

139 E. Fourth St.	CEO: James E. Rogers	1995 Sales: $3,031 million
Cincinnati, OH 45202	CFO: J. Wayne Leonard	1995 Profits: $347 million
Phone: 513-381-2000	Symbol: CIN	Mkt. Value: $4,481 million
Fax: 513-651-9196	Exchange: NYSE	Employees: 8,600

CINergy is the holding company for Cincinnati Gas & Electric (CG&E), PSI Energy, and CINergy Services. CG&E provides electricity to about 710,000 customers and gas service to more than 430,000 in southwestern Ohio and adjacent areas of Kentucky and Indiana. PSI Energy is Indiana's largest electric utility, serving over 635,000 customers in a 22,000-square-mile area of that state. CINergy Services provides administrative, management, and support services to the utilities. The company's international operations include electricity generation and distribution projects in Argentina and the Republic of Kazakhstan.

THE CIRCLE K CORPORATION

3003 N. Central Ave.
Phoenix, AZ 85072
Phone: 602-530-5001
Fax: 602-530-5278

CEO: Robert J. Lavinia
CFO: Jefferson Allen
Symbol: CRK
Exchange: NYSE

1995 Sales: $3,566 million
1995 Profits: $19 million
Mkt. Value: $726 million
Employees: 20,500

Phoenix-based Circle K Corporation operates about 2,500 convenience stores in almost 30 states, mostly in the Sunbelt, and licenses over 800 Circle K stores in nearly 20 other countries. It is the 2nd largest convenience store operation in the nation, trailing only Southland Corporation's 7-Eleven stores. The company derives nearly half its sales from the 1.5 billion gallons of gasoline it sells annually. Other key sale items include beer, cigarettes, soft drinks, and dairy products. Circle K is also testing Blimpie and Taco Bell franchises in its stores, adding pay-at-the-pump credit card readers, and test marketing its own brand of gasoline. Petroleum refiner and marketer Tosco agreed to aquire Circle K in mid-1996.

CIRCUIT CITY STORES, INC.

9950 Mayland Dr.
Richmond, VA 23233
Phone: 804-527-4000
Fax: 804-527-4164

CEO: Richard L. Sharp
CFO: Michael T. Chalifoux
Symbol: CC
Exchange: NYSE

1995 Sales: $5,583 million
1995 Profits: $168 million
Mkt. Value: $2,944 million
Employees: 31,413

Web site: http://www.circuitcity.com

Circuit City is the nation's largest retailer of major appliances and brand-name consumer electronics, including PCs, laptops, printers, cameras, toasters, blenders, and stereos. The company operates in over 30 states, and most of its units are Circuit City Superstores. Its Circuit City Express stores are based in malls. Consumer electronics and appliances are the mainstays of the company, but computers are gaining importance as is home office equipment (PCs, peripherals, and fax machines). To compete in the fierce consumer electronics market, Circuit City focuses on both price and service with ongoing training for salespeople.

CITICORP

399 Park Ave.
New York, NY 10043
Phone: 212-559-1000
Fax: 212-559-5138

CEO: John S. Reed
CFO: Victor J. Menezes
Symbol: CCI
Exchange: NYSE

1995 Sales: $31,690 million
1995 Profits: $3,464 million
Mkt. Value: $33,222 million
Employees: 85,300

Web site: http://www.citicorp.com

Citicorp is the largest US banking company measured in revenues and the world's #1 issuer of credit cards. It has some 3,400 locations worldwide and is actively expanding with new offices in South Africa, Kazakhstan, and Vietnam. It focuses on global retail banking and small companies with up to $20 million in sales and, at the other end of the spectrum, giant international companies. The bank is pulling away from middle-market business and mortgage servicing. Some 32% of its revenues come from banking transaction services and 28% from trading.

CMS ENERGY CORPORATION

330 Town Center Dr.
Dearborn, MI 48126
Phone: 313-436-9200
Fax: 313-436-9225

CEO: Henry C. Duques
CFO: Alan M. Wright
Symbol: CMS
Exchange: NYSE

1995 Sales: $3,890 million
1995 Profits: $204 million
Mkt. Value: $2,597 million
Employees: 10,072

Web site: http://www.cmsenergy.com

CMS Energy is the holding company for Consumers Power (the 4th largest combined electric and gas utility in the US, operating in Michigan's lower peninsula) and CMS Enterprises (nonutility energy-related businesses). The company's energy is produced by coal (44%), oil/gas steam generators (20%), pumped storage (15%), nuclear sources (13%), gas/oil combustion turbines (7%), and hydroelectric sources (1%). CMS Enterprises subsidiary CMS Generation builds and operates nonutility power generation projects in the US and abroad. CMS Energy has 22 projects in various stages of development in the US and 7 other countries.

Like so many of its customers, **Circuit City Stores** is a child of television. **Samuel Wurtzel** started the business in 1949 in Richmond, Virginia, to sell TV sets after learning from a local barber that the South's first station was about to go on the air.

— *Hoover's Handbook of American Business 1996*

THE COASTAL CORPORATION

9 Greenway Plaza	CEO: David A. Arledge	1995 Sales: $10,223 million
Houston, TX 77046	CFO: David A. Arledge	1995 Profits: $270 million
Phone: 713-877-1400	Symbol: CGP	Mkt. Value: $4,122 million
Fax: 713-877-6752	Exchange: NYSE	Employees: 15,500

124 Coastal Corporation is a diversified energy giant whose business segments include natural gas, petroleum, chemicals, power plants, coal mining, and trucking. It engages in exploration, production, refining, and marketing of petroleum and natural gas products worldwide. Interstate transmission of natural gas is the company's most profitable area. Its ANR subsidiary operates over 19,000 miles of natural gas pipeline. Coastal has 1,400 branded retail outlets in 37 states and 3 wholly owned refineries. The company's chairman is the outspoken former corporate raider Oscar Wyatt.

THE COCA-COLA COMPANY

1 Coca-Cola Plaza	CEO: Roberto C. Goizueta	1995 Sales: $18,018 million
Atlanta, GA 30313	CFO: James E. Chestnut	1995 Profits: $2,986 million
Phone: 404-676-2121	Symbol: KO	Mkt. Value: $101,280 million
Fax: 404-676-6792	Exchange: NYSE	Employees: 31,000

Web site: http://www.cocacola.com

48 Coca-Cola, the most famous brand name in the world, is the world's largest soft drink company, with its products available in almost 200 countries around the globe. The company controls over 40% of the US market and 50% of the rest of the world's, with 4 of the top 5 brands in the US: Coca-Cola Classic, Diet Coke, Caffeine-free Diet Coke, and Sprite. Coke continues to emphasize new product development to keep up with changes in consumer tastes (Powerade, Fruitopia), although the company occasionally makes acquisitions as well (Barq root beer). Coke derives almost 2/3 of its revenues and almost 80% of its profits from overseas sales. The company is also the world's largest distributor of juice drinks (Minute Maid, Five Alive, Hi-C).

COCA-COLA ENTERPRISES INC.

2500 Windy Ridge Pkwy	CEO: S. K. Johnston Jr.	1995 Sales: $6,773 million
Atlanta, GA 30339	CFO: John R. Alm	1995 Profits: $82 million
Phone: 770-989-3000	Symbol: CCE	Mkt. Value: $3,728 million
Fax: 770-989-3788	Exchange: NYSE	Employees: 33,000

Web site: http://www.cokecce.com

196 Coca-Cola Enterprises (CCE) is the largest distributor and producer of Coca-Cola products, accounting for over half of all sales of bottled and canned beverages sold by 44% owner the Coca-Cola Company. The firm annually sells the equivalent of over a billion-and-a-half cases (24 eight-ounce servings) of beverage products, over 90% of which are products of the Coca-Cola Company. CCE relies upon the Coca-Cola Company and other beverage companies to supply concentrates and syrups to the firm and to share in advertising and promotional expenses. CCE agreed to buy the Coca-Cola Company's French, Belgian, and UK bottling operations in 1996.

COLGATE-PALMOLIVE COMPANY

300 Park Ave.
New York, NY 10022
Phone: 212-310-2000
Fax: 212-310-3284

CEO: Reuben Mark
CFO: Robert M. Agate
Symbol: CL
Exchange: NYSE

1995 Sales: $8,358 million
1995 Profits: $172 million
Mkt. Value: $11,519 million
Employees: 37,300

Web site: http://www.colgate.com

Colgate-Palmolive is a leading global consumer products company in the oral care (Colgate), personal care (Baby Magic, Irish Spring, Mennen), household and laundry (Ajax, Fab), and pet food (Hill's Science Diet) markets. It focuses aggressively on advertising and product development to compete in the US market as retailers shrink store size and carry only the leading private-label brands. The company is also growing in the international consumer market, particularly in Latin America and Asia. Sales outside the US account for about 70% of total revenues.

COLLEGE RETIREMENT EQUITIES FUND

730 Third Avenue
New York, NY 10017
Phone: 212-490-9000
Fax: 212-916-6231

CEO: John H. Biggs
CFO: Richard L. Gibbs
Ownership: Nonprofit
    Organization

1995 Sales: $7,951 million
Employees: 4,345

Web site: http://www.tiaa-cref.org

College Retirement Equities Fund (CREF), together with its companion organization Teachers Insurance and Annuity Association (TIAA), is the largest private pension system in the world and the largest retirement system serving the nation's education community in the US. The investment arm of the organization, CREF offers several different types of variable annuities for teachers and researchers. Among its investment products are its Stock Account (the nation's largest managed equity fund), Global Equity Account, Bond Market Account, and Money Market Account. CREF's assets total close to $90 billion.

THE COLUMBIA GAS SYSTEM, INC.

20 Montchanin Rd.
Wilmington, DE 19807
Phone: 302-429-5000
Fax: 302-429-5730

CEO: Oliver G. Richard III
CFO: Michael O'Donnell
Symbol: CG
Exchange: NYSE

1995 Sales: $2,635 million
1995 Loss: ($361) million
Mkt. Value: $2,134 million
Employees: 9,981

Web site: http://www.columbiaenergy.com

The Columbia Gas System is the holding company for one of the largest natural gas systems in the US (the Columbia Gas Transmission pipeline, over 23,000 miles). Its subsidiaries' operations range from exploration (Columbia Gas Development, Columbia Natural Resources) to distribution (Columbia Gas of Kentucky, of Maryland, of Ohio, and of Pennsylvania). The company also develops gas-fired cogeneration facilities through its TriStar Ventures subsidiary, sells propane, provides supply and fuel management services, and owns 500 million tons of coal reserves. Columbia emerged from 4 years of Chapter 11 protection in late 1995 and focused on upgrading and expanding its pipeline system to improve efficiency.

COLUMBIA/HCA HEALTHCARE CORPORATION

1 Park Plaza
Nashville, TN 37203
Phone: 615-327-9551
Fax: 615-320-2266

CEO: Richard L. Scott
CFO: David C. Colby
Symbol: COL
Exchange: NYSE

1995 Sales: $17,695 million
1995 Profits: $961 million
Mkt. Value: $23,983 million
Employees: 240,000

Web site: http://www.columbia-hca.com

The largest hospital company in the US, Columbia/HCA specializes in buying hospitals (often church affiliated) and offering local doctors stakes in its facilities. The company has some 350 hospitals to its name. In a joint venture with Blue Cross/Blue Shield of Ohio, it will acquire the medical insurer's businesses, which generate $2 billion annually. The company's holdings, located in the US, the UK, and Switzerland, also include outpatient surgery and diagnostic centers, rehabilitation facilities, and home health care agencies. CEO Richard Scott built the company with financial backing from investor Richard Rainwater.

Three former Texas Instruments employees sketched out a design on a paper place mat in 1982. It was the prototype for **Compaq's** first portable IBM-compatible computer.

— Hoover's Guide to Computer Companies

IDEAS

COMCAST CORPORATION

1500 Market St.	CEO: Ralph J. Roberts	1995 Sales: $3,363 million
Philadelphia, PA 19102	CFO: John R. Alchin	1995 Loss: ($44) million
Phone: 215-665-1700	Symbol: CMCSA	Mkt. Value: $4,340 million
Fax: 215-981-7790	Exchange: Nasdaq	Employees: 12,200

Web site: http://www.comcast.com

369

Comcast Corporation and its subsidiaries run cable and cellular telephone communications systems and produce and distribute cable programming. The company owns 57.45% of home-shopping cable channel QVC Inc., and it has a 2/3 stake in home teams the Philadelphia Flyers (hockey) and the 76ers (basketball). Its domestic cable operations serve more than 3.3 million subscribers. Comcast owns a 50% interest in Garden State Cablevision L.P., a cable company serving approximately 195,000 subscribers. Its UK subsidiary, Comcast UK Cable Partners Limited, is constructing a cable network that will pass approximately 230,000 homes.

COMERICA INCORPORATED

500 Woodward Ave.	CEO: Eugene A. Miller	1995 Sales: $3,113 million
Detroit, MI 48226	CFO: Ralph W. Babb Jr.	1995 Profits: $413 million
Phone: 313-222-3300	Symbol: CMA	Mkt. Value: $4,537 million
Fax: 313-965-4648	Exchange: NYSE	Employees: 13,500

Web site: http://www.comerica.com

395

Comerica is one of the largest banks headquartered in Michigan and focuses on all types of clientele, from the business elite to the individual consumer and small business. The company is strongest in the commercial arena, including international finance, and offers traditional retail banking and loans. It has subsidiaries in widely scattered geographic markets: California, Florida, Michigan, and Texas. Comerica is concentrating on adding fee-based businesses, including insurance, customhouse services (because of its location at the US-Canada border), and leasing to reduce its dependence on loan income, and it continues to diversify by adding new investment products (including mutual funds and annuities).

COMPAQ COMPUTER CORPORATION

20555 State Highway 249	CEO: Eckhard Pfeiffer	1995 Sales: $14,755 million
Houston, TX 77070	CFO: Daryl J. White	1995 Profits: $789 million
Phone: 713-370-0670	Symbol: CPQ	Mkt. Value: $10,613 million
Fax: 713-374-1740	Exchange: NYSE	Employees: 20,470

Web site: http://www.compaq.com

72

Compaq Computer is the world's #1 maker of desktop PCs, portable PCs, and servers. The company's line of desktop PCs includes the Deskpro and ProLinea business series and the Presario home series. Its portable computers include the LTE 5000 and Contura lines, and its servers include the ProSignia and ProLiant families. Compaq also makes modems, monitors, networking products (hubs, interface cards, and switches), storage systems, and software (Insight Manager network and server management tool). Nearly half of Compaq's revenues comes from sales to business customers, but it also markets its products to home users, governments, schools, and students.

COMPUSA INC.

14951 N. Dallas Parkway	CEO: James F. Halpin	1995 Sales: $2,813 million
Dallas, TX 75240	CFO: James E. Skinner	1995 Profits: $23 million
Phone: 214-982-4000	Symbol: CPU	Mkt. Value: $1,034 million
Fax: 214-982-4276	Exchange: NYSE	Employees: 7,963

Web site: http://www.compusa.com

CompUSA is the nation's largest computer retailer. The company sells PCs, laptops, monitors, modems, printers, other peripherals, and software. The company is decreasing the rate of new store openings, emphasizing training and customer services, consolidating inventory and pricing at the corporate level, and focusing on the home market. To make its stores less intimidating to computer neophytes, the company is remodeling and adding informational programs and events. CompUSA is continuing to focus on "nontechie" computer buyers and has introduced to many of its stores a CompKids area, which features hundreds of edutainment software titles that kids can try before they buy.

COMPUTER ASSOCIATES INTERNATIONAL, INC.

1 Computer Associates Plaza	CEO: Charles B. Wang	1995 Sales: $2,623 million
Islandia, NY 11788	CFO: Peter A. Schwartz	1995 Profits: $432 million
Phone: 516-342-5224	Symbol: CA	Mkt. Value: $17,570 million
Fax: 516-342-5329	Exchange: NYSE	Employees: 7,550

Web site: http://www.cai.com

Computer Associates (CA, the #2 independent software company in the world after Microsoft) considers acquisition a major development tool; it paid $1.74 billion in 1995 for competitor Legent Corp. -- just one of the more than 50 companies it has acquired in the past decade. A producer of systems management software (CA-Unicenter), CA also develops information management products and home products such as CA-Simply Tax and Kiplinger's Simply Money. In addition, it provides database and applications development software. CA is moving away from the mainframe market toward software for faster-selling midrange and smaller computer systems.

COMPUTER SCIENCES CORPORATION

2100 E. Grand Ave.	CEO: Van Honeycutt	1995 Sales: $3,373 million
El Segundo, CA 90245	CFO: Leon J. Level	1995 Profits: $111 million
Phone: 310-615-0311	Symbol: CSC	Mkt. Value: $3,977 million
Fax: 310-322-9805	Exchange: NYSE	Employees: 32,900

Web site: http://www.csc.com

Computer Sciences Corporation provides information technology consulting, systems integration, and outsourcing to industry and to government agencies. Among the services provided by the company are account management, system development and engineering, office automation, insurance claims processing, software development, and communication network engineering and operation. The company does much of its work for state and federal governments, such as building a secure data communications network for the Treasury Department and automating the records of the Bureau of Land Management.

CONAGRA, INC.

1 ConAgra Dr.	CEO: Philip B. Fletcher	1995 Sales: $24,109 million
Omaha, NE 68102	CFO: James P. O'Donnell	1995 Profits: $496 million
Phone: 402-595-4000	Symbol: CAG	Mkt. Value: $10,417 million
Fax: 402-595-4595	Exchange: NYSE	Employees: 90,871

ConAgra is the nation's 2nd largest food processor (after Philip Morris). The firm boasts more than 70 operating units spread over 3 segments. The Food Inputs & Ingredients segment provides crop protection chemicals, fertilizers, and seeds. Refrigerated Foods produces beef and pork products, deli meats (Hebrew National), chicken and turkey products (Country Pride, Butterball), and cheese products. Grocery/Diversified Products supplies market shelf-stable foods and frozen foods. Its brands include Hunt's and Healthy Choice tomato-based products, Wesson oils, Orville Redenbacher's popcorn, and Van Camp's canned beans.

CONRAIL INC.

2001 Market St.
Philadelphia, PA 19101
Phone: 215-209-2000
Fax: 215-209-5567

CEO: David M. LeVan
CFO: Timothy T. O'Toole
Symbol: CRR
Exchange: NYSE

1995 Sales: $3,686 million
1995 Profits: $264 million
Mkt. Value: $6,072 million
Employees: 23,510

Web site: http://www.conrail.com

Conrail Inc. is the holding company for Philadelphia-based Consolidated Rail Corp., the dominant freight railroad in the heavily industrialized Northeast. It operates over 15,000 track miles from Massachusetts to Illinois, across the Northeast, Midwest, and Quebec, with connections to the rest of the US. Consolidated Rail is organized into 4 service groups: CORE (petrochemicals, waste, food, metals, and forest products), Intermodal (truck-to-train), Unit Train (coal and ore), and Automotive Service (parts and finished autos). Conrail operates an intermodal services joint venture with Norfolk Southern.

CONSECO, INC.

11825 N. Pennsylvania St.
Carmel, IN 46032
Phone: 317-817-6100
Fax: 317-573-2847

CEO: Stephen C. Hilbert
CFO: Rollin M. Dick
Symbol: CNC
Exchange: NYSE

1995 Sales: $2,861 million
1995 Profits: $220 million
Mkt. Value: $1,401 million
Employees: 3,219

Web site: http://www.conseco.com

A financial services holding company, Conseco is one of the fastest-growing insurance firms in the US. The company's insurance subsidiaries (including Bankers Life and Casualty, Great American Reserve, National Fidelity Life, and Lincoln American Life), provide life insurance, supplemental health insurance, and annuities. Other Conseco subsidiaries offer asset management (Conseco Capital Management), insurance and investment product marketing services (Bankmark) and mortgage services (Conseco Mortgage Capital). Conseco grows by acquiring less efficient insurance companies and then streamlines operations through consolidation.

CONSOLIDATED EDISON COMPANY OF NEW YORK, INC.

4 Irving Place
New York, NY 10003
Phone: 212-460-4600
Fax: 212-982-7816

CEO: Eugene R. McGrath
CFO: Raymond J. McCann
Symbol: ED
Exchange: NYSE

1995 Sales: $6,402 million
1995 Profits: $724 million
Mkt. Value: $7,313 million
Employees: 16,582

Web site: http://www.coned.com

Consolidated Edison (Con Ed) is one of the largest publicly owned gas and electric utilities in the US. Headquartered in New York City, the company provides electric power to more than 8 million people in the 5-borough area (except for parts of Queens). Con Ed also supplies gas in Manhattan, the Bronx, and parts of Queens and Westchester and steam in part of Manhattan. It sells electricity to government customers through the New York Power Authority. Sales of electricity account for about 3/4 of Con Ed's revenues. The company continues to shift the mix of its fuel sources away from oil (which produces about 10% of the company's electricity) toward natural gas, hydroelectric and nuclear power.

Cornelius Vanderbilt, the robber baron who helped assemble what evolved into **Conrail's** rail system, has also been linked to the birth of the potato chip. At Saratoga Springs in 1853, he irritated a cook with complaints that the fried potatoes were too thick. The cook sliced up a batch as thin as he could, deep-fried them to a crisp, and served them up.

— Texas Monthly, January 1996

CONSOLIDATED FREIGHTWAYS, INC.

3240 Hillview Ave.	CEO: Donald E. Moffitt	1995 Sales: $5,281 million
Palo Alto, CA 94304	CFO: Gregory L. Quesnel	1995 Profits: $57 million
Phone: 415-494-2900	Symbol: CNF	Mkt. Value: $1,170 million
Fax: 415-813-0160	Exchange: NYSE	Employees: 41,600

Web site: http://www.cnf.com

251

Consolidated Freightways (CF), the #1 US trucking company, is a diversified freight and package deliverer operating in about 90 countries. Its long-haul division, CF MotorFreight, specializes in less-than-truckload shipments (under 10,000 pounds). Con-Way Transportation Services is a regional trucking and full service truck loading company that offers overnight and 2nd-day delivery to more than 70,000 communities in North America. Emery Worldwide carries international airfreight to more than 500 points. CF also provides contract logistics (clients have included GM, Coca-Cola, Hewlett-Packard, and Sears), customs brokerage, equipment supply, and trailer manufacturing.

CONSOLIDATED NATURAL GAS COMPANY

625 Liberty Ave.	CEO: George A. Davidson Jr.	1995 Sales: $3,307 million
Pittsburgh, PA 15222	CFO: David M. Westfall	1995 Profits: $21 million
Phone: 412-227-1000	Symbol: CNG	Mkt. Value: $4,027 million
Fax: 412-227-1002	Exchange: NYSE	Employees: 6,600

Web site: http://www.cng.com

376

One of the largest natural gas systems in the US, Consolidated Natural Gas explores for, produces, and distributes natural gas to nearly 2 million customers in Ohio, Pennsylvania, Virginia, and West Virginia. Subsidiaries include Consolidated Natural Gas Service Co. (administration, technical services), CNG Producing Co. (exploration and production), CNG Energy Co. (energy marketing), CNG Power Services (electricity resales), CNG Research Co. (research), and CNG Coal Co. (coal mining). The company's CNG Transmission unit operates a regional interstate pipeline system serving each of the company's distribution subsidiaries.

CONTINENTAL AIRLINES, INC.

2929 Allen Parkway	CEO: Gordon Bethune	1995 Sales: $5,825 million
Houston, TX 77019	CFO: Lawrence W. Kellner	1995 Profits: $224 million
Phone: 713-834-5000	Symbol: CAIB	Mkt. Value: $1,130 million
Fax: 713-834-2087	Exchange: NYSE	Employees: 32,300

Web site: http://www.flycontinental.com

226

Continental Airlines and its affiliates serve more than 100 cities in the US and over 50 in Asia, Australia, Europe, and Latin America. It is the #6 US carrier, operating more than 300 aircraft. Principal owners include Air Canada and Air Partners, a limited partnership led by Texan David Bonderman. The company's strategy to end a decade of losses included cutting costs; ending short-haul flights; and focusing on Europe, Micronesia (Continental Micronesia is its major affiliate), and Central and South America, where over 200 flights a week make it a leader among US carriers.

COOPER INDUSTRIES, INC.

1001 Fannin St.	CEO: H. John Riley Jr.	1995 Sales: $4,886 million
Houston, TX 77002	CFO: D. Bradley McWilliams	1995 Profits: $94 million
Phone: 713-739-5400	Symbol: CBE	Mkt. Value: $4,018 million
Fax: 713-739-5555	Exchange: NYSE	Employees: 40,400

Cooper Industries is a diversified manufacturing company. Three divisions make automotive parts, electrical products and tools, and hardware. The automotive sector manufactures and sells Champion spark plugs, ACI electric motors, Anco windshield wipers, Wagner lighting products, and other auto parts. The electrical products division makes Arrow Hart wiring devices, Buss and Edison fuses, Halo lighting systems, and Metalux fluorescent lighting. The tools and hardware division manufactures Apex impact sockets, Crescent wrenches, Plumb hammers, Weller soldering equipment, and Wiss cutting products.

CORESTATES FINANCIAL CORPORATION

Broad & Chestnut Sts.	CEO: Terrence A. Larsen	1995 Sales: $2,868 million
Philadelphia, PA 19101	CFO: David E. Sparks	1995 Profits: $452 million
Phone: 215-973-3100	Symbol: CFL	Mkt. Value: $5,788 million
Fax: 215-786-8294	Exchange: NYSE	Employees: 13,598

CoreStates Financial is the parent company of CoreStates Bank, with operations in Pennsylvania, Delaware, and New Jersey. Its acquisition of Pennsylvania-based Meridian Bancorp creates a combined bank with assets of some $45 billion. Corestates also operates Congress Financial Corporation (factoring and commercial financing), CoreStates Capital Corp. (financing), and Electronic Payment Services, a joint venture with Banc One, PNC Financial Corp., and KeyCorp.

CORNING INCORPORATED

1 Riverfront Plaza	CEO: Roger Ackerman	1995 Sales: $5,346 million
Corning, NY 14831	CFO: Van C. Campbell	1995 Loss: ($51) million
Phone: 607-974-9000	Symbol: GLW	Mkt. Value: $7,928 million
Fax: 607-974-8551	Exchange: NYSE	Employees: 41,000

Web site: http://www.corning.com

Corning manufactures specialty glass. The company produces 60,000 products, including flat-panel displays, liquid crystal glass, optical fiber, and projection-television lenses for the communications industry. Its consumer products division makes Corelle dinnerware, Corning Ware cookware, Pyrex glassware, Serengeti sunglasses, and Steuben crystal. The company also produces specialty materials such as auto pollution control devices, nose cones for spacecraft, and giant mirrors for astronomical telescopes.

COTTER & COMPANY

8600 W. Bryn Mawr Ave.	CEO: Daniel A. Cotter	1995 Sales: $2,437 million
Chicago, IL 60631-3505	CFO: Kerry J. Kirby	Employees: 4,186
Phone: 312-695-5000	Ownership: Cooperative	
Fax: 312-695-6558		

Web site: http://www.cornells.com/cf.htm

Cotter is the largest hardware wholesaler in the US (just ahead of rival Ace). The member-owned cooperative serves over 6,500 True Value hardware and V&S Variety stores in the US and Canada. Almost all of its stock is held by member retailers, who benefit from pooling their buying power. Cotter buys hardware in volume and resells it to members at lower prices. Members also receive annual dividends. Subsidiaries include Baltimore Brush & Roller Co., Inc., Cotter Acceptance, and Cotter Insurance.

CPC INTERNATIONAL INC.

International Plaza
Englewood Cliffs, NJ 07626
Phone: 201-894-4000
Fax: 201-894-2186

CEO: Charles R. Shoemate
CFO: Konrad Schlatter
Symbol: CPC
Exchange: NYSE

1995 Sales: $8,432 million
1995 Profits: $512 million
Mkt. Value: $10,075 million
Employees: 52,502

154 CPC International is a consumer food producer, with such well-known brands as Knorr (soups, sauces, bouillons), Skippy (peanut butter), Karo (corn syrup), Mazola (cooking oil), and Hellmann's (mayonnaise). The company has operations in more than 55 countries, including Britain, Israel, and Mexico. Its corn refining operations, providing corn oil, corn starches, and ethanol for fuel, account for about 15% of sales. CPC plans to fuel future growth with new products (low-fat mayonnaise, reduced-fat peanut butter), markets (Russia, China), and acquisitions (Lesieur, one of France's top salad dressing makers). Almost 2/3 of the company's sales result from foreign operations.

CROWN CORK & SEAL COMPANY, INC.

9300 Ashton Rd.
Philadelphia, PA 19136
Phone: 215-698-5100
Fax: 215-676-7245

CEO: William J. Avery
CFO: Alan W. Rutherford
Symbol: CCK
Exchange: NYSE

1995 Sales: $5,054 million
1995 Profits: $75 million
Mkt. Value: $6,092 million
Employees: 20,409

 266 Crown Cork & Seal (CC&S) is one of the world's top packaging companies and North America's largest. It is a leading worldwide producer of bottle crowns and closures and metal and plastic containers. CC&S is also a leading manufacturer of high-speed filling, handling, and packaging machinery. The company operates over 150 plants worldwide and sells to the food, citrus, brewing, soft drink, oil, drug, antifreeze, chemical, and pet food industries. Its product portfolio consists of aerosol cans, beer and beverage cans, food cans, motor oil cans, paint cans, conveyors, and various types of plastic packaging materials.

CSX CORPORATION

901 E. Cary St.
Richmond, VA 23219
Phone: 804-782-1400
Fax: 804-782-6747

CEO: John W. Snow
CFO: Paul R. Goodwin
Symbol: CSX
Exchange: NYSE

1995 Sales: $10,504 million
1995 Profits: $618 million
Mkt. Value: $9,499 million
Employees: 47,965

Web site: http://www.csx.com

120 CSX, the top US railroad company, also provides ocean shipping, trucking, inland barging, and distribution. Its rail system links 20 US states in the East, the Midwest, and the South. Subsidiary CSX Transportation is the largest coal hauler in the US. CSX's Sea-Land Service, a world leader in container shipping, has about 90 ships serving about 80 countries. In addition, the company operates resorts in West Virginia (the Greenbrier) and Wyoming (Grand Teton Lodge), develops real estate (CSX Real Property Inc.), and has a majority stake in Yukon Pacific, which promotes construction of the Trans-Alaska Gas System.

CUMMINS ENGINE COMPANY, INC.

500 Jackson St.
Columbus, IN 47202
Phone: 812-377-5000
Fax: 812-377-3334

CEO: James A. Henderson
CFO: Kiran M. Patel
Symbol: CUM
Exchange: NYSE

1995 Sales: $5,245 million
1995 Profits: $224 million
Mkt. Value: $1,663 million
Employees: 24,300

Web site: http://www.cummins.com

 253 Cummins Engine Company is the world's largest independent maker of diesel engines. Nearly all major North American truck makers utilize Cummins engines in their vehicles, and they're also used to power school buses, delivery trucks, recreational vehicles, and urban transit systems. The company accounts for about 1/3 of the US market for heavy-duty and midrange truck engines. Its 2nd largest division (around 20% of sales) is its electrical power generation sector, which has footholds in the UK and China. Cummins has manufacturing operations in 14 countries and sells nearly 45% of its products overseas.

CYPRUS AMAX MINERALS COMPANY

9100 E. Mineral Circle
Englewood, CO 80112
Phone: 303-643-5000
Fax: 303-643-5049

CEO: Milton H. Ward
CFO: Gerald J. Malys
Symbol: CYM
Exchange: NYSE

1995 Sales: $3,207 million
1995 Profits: $124 million
Mkt. Value: $2,591 million
Employees: 9,683

Cyprus Amax is the US's largest mining company and one of the world's largest natural resource concerns. It is the US's 2nd largest copper producer, a leading coal producer, and the world's biggest supplier of molybdenum (used in steel making) and lithium (used in plastics, chemicals, and many other products). Cyprus Amax also has significant interests in gold through its 42% stake in Amax Gold. It owns majority stakes in 2 copper properties in Chile (with Codelco, the world's largest copper producer) and Peru (with Sociedad Minera Cerro Verde) and is engaged in joint ventures to produce gold in Chile, Alaska, and Russia.

DANA CORPORATION

4500 Dorr St.
Toledo, OH 43615
Phone: 419-535-4500
Fax: 419-535-4643

CEO: Southwood J. Morcott
CFO: James E. Ayers
Symbol: DCN
Exchange: NYSE

1995 Sales: $7,795 million
1995 Profits: $288 million
Mkt. Value: $3,378 million
Employees: 45,900

Web site: http://www.dana.com

Dana Corporation manufactures components and parts for cars, pickups, vans, trucks, and sport utility vehicles. Its products, including axles, driveshafts, filters, and piston rings are used by auto makers, including Ford and Chrysler (its 2 biggest customers), as well as makers of construction, industrial, and agricultural machinery. The company also sells its products to parts distributors. Dana operates more than 200 manufacturing, assembly, and distribution facilities in nearly 30 countries. Dana Commercial Credit provides leasing and financial services. With 3/4 of sales coming from the US, Dana is looking to boost its international business through acquisitions.

Ready for a stay in the mountains at West Virginia's famed resort, the Greenbrier? If you're an investor in the transportation company **CSX**, you qualify for a 10% discount once a year.

— *Barron's Finance and Investment Handbook*

IDEAS

DAYTON HUDSON CORPORATION

777 Nicollet Mall
Minneapolis, MN 55402
Phone: 612-370-6948
Fax: 612-370-5502

CEO: Robert J. Ulrich
CFO: Douglas A. Scovanner
Symbol: DH
Exchange: NYSE

1995 Sales: $23,516 million
1995 Profits: $311 million
Mkt. Value: $6,049 million
Employees: 214,000

Web site: http://www.dhc.com

Dayton Hudson operates a range of retail formats, including an "upscale discounter" located nationwide (Target), a West Coast midrange department store (Mervyn's), and upscale department stores in the Midwest and Texas (Dayton's, Hudson's, and Marshall Field's). Its department stores division emphasizes brand name fashions and customer service. Target, the company's largest unit, offers more upscale merchandise than competitors such as Wal-Mart and Kmart, but with prices that are still lower than most department stores. Mervyn's continues to be less successful due to a lack of brand-name merchandise, poor promotion, and a heavy concentration of stores in California, which has been slow to recover from its recession.

DEAN FOODS COMPANY

3600 N. River Rd.	CEO: Howard M. Dean	1995 Sales: $2,630 million
Franklin Park, IL 60131	CFO: Dale I. Hecox	1995 Profits: $80 million
Phone: 847-678-1680	Symbol: DF	Mkt. Value: $1,039 million
Fax: 708-928-8621	Exchange: NYSE	Employees: 11,800

Dean Foods manufactures a wide variety of dairy (milk, ice cream, frozen yogurt, and specialty items) and other food items (frozen and canned vegetables, pickles, relishes, sauces, sherbet, and assorted powder products). The company's Bird's Eye brand is carried throughout the country. Dean operates almost 30 regional dairies in over a dozen states, selling a significant number of its milk and ice cream brands under private labels and regional names. The company's products are distributed to retail and food service markets in the US, Europe, Japan, Mexico, and Puerto Rico. Dean also has a small trucking business that concentrates primarily on refrigerated and frozen goods.

Michael Dell, founder of **Dell Computer Company,** ran a successful mail-order stamp trading business when he was 13, grossing over $2,000 in a few months. By age 17 he had bought his first BMW.

— Hoover's Handbook of American Companies 1996

DEAN WITTER, DISCOVER & CO.

2 World Trade Center	CEO: Philip J. Purcell	1995 Sales: $7,934 million
New York, NY 10048	CFO: Thomas C. Schneider	1995 Profits: $856 million
Phone: 212-392-2222	Symbol: DWD	Mkt. Value: $9,120 million
Fax: 212-392-3118	Exchange: NYSE	Employees: 30,779

Web site: http://www.discovercard.com

Dean Witter's current business represents the aftermath of an attempt by Sears to build a financial services empire. Spun off in 1993, the company has activities that are almost evenly balanced between its consumer credit operations (the Discover Card) and the financial services it offers through its Dean Witter Reynolds brokerage and investment operations. The company's credit operations also include credit transaction processing for private-label cards, home mortgage and equity loans, and a cobranded (with NationsBank) MasterCard/Prime Option card. The other half of the business, Dean Witter Reynolds, engages in brokerage, mutual fund sales and management, investment advice, and investment banking.

DEERE & COMPANY

John Deere Rd.	CEO: Hans W. Becherer	1995 Sales: $10,291 million
Moline, IL 61265	CFO: Robert W. Lane	1995 Profits: $706 million
Phone: 309-765-8000	Symbol: DE	Mkt. Value: $11,025 million
Fax: 309-765-4956	Exchange: NYSE	Employees: 33,375

Web site: http://www.deere.com

Deere & Company is the world's largest maker of farm equipment and a leading producer of industrial and lawn care equipment. The Moline, Illinois-based company makes tractors, harvesting machinery, soil preparation machinery, drivetrain components, construction equipment, diesel engines, chain saws, lawn trimmers, leaf blowers, tillers, backhoe loaders, and snowblowers. Deere also provides financing, leasing, and insurance to its dealers and customers. The company makes its products in 9 countries and sells in 120. Farm equipment sales account for about 50% of total revenues. Deere looks to developing markets for sales growth.

DELL COMPUTER CORPORATION

2214 W. Braker Lane
Austin, TX 78758
Phone: 512-338-4400
Fax: 512-728-3653

CEO: Michael S. Dell
CFO: Thomas J. Meredith
Symbol: DELL
Exchange: Nasdaq

1995 Sales: $5,296 million
1995 Profits: $272 million
Mkt. Value: $3,107 million
Employees: 8,400

Web site: http://www.dell.com

Dell Computer is one of the world's top PC makers and the #1 mail-order computer vendor (ahead of Gateway 2000). Led by founder Michael Dell, the company sells a variety of computer products, as well as software and peripheral products through its DellWare and ReadyWare programs. Products include Latitude notebook computers; Dimension, NetPlex, and OptiPlex desktop PCs; and Performance, PowerEdge, and Series servers. Dell also sells 3rd-party products, including CD-ROM drives, modems, monitors, networking hardware, PCMCIA cards, storage devices, printers, and speakers.

DELTA AIR LINES, INC.

1030 Delta Blvd.
Atlanta, GA 30320
Phone: 404-715-2600
Fax: 404-765-2233

CEO: Ronald W. Allen
CFO: Thomas J. Roeck Jr.
Symbol: DAL
Exchange: NYSE

1995 Sales: $12,194 million
1995 Profits: $408 million
Mkt. Value: $4,333 million
Employees: 59,717

Web site: http://www.delta-air.com/index.html

Delta Air Lines is the nation's 3rd largest airline (after American and United). It operates more than 500 jets to reach destinations in nearly every state and about 30 countries (hubs include Atlanta, Dallas, Los Angeles, New York, Orlando, Portland, and Frankfurt, Germany). The company also owns about 40% of WORLDSPAN, a computer reservation system, and has minority stakes in 3 regional carriers: Atlantic Southeast Airlines, Comair, and SkyWest. Delta's efforts to improve profitability have included reduced transatlantic flights, code-sharing reservation agreements with foreign airlines, and pay cuts.

THE DIAL CORP

1850 N. Central Ave.
Phoenix, AZ 85077
Phone: 602-207-4000
Fax: 602-207-5100

CEO: John W. Teets
CFO: Ronald G. Nelson
Symbol: DL
Exchange: NYSE

1995 Sales: $3,575 million
1995 Loss: ($17) million
Mkt. Value: $2,775 million
Employees: 31,356

Web site: http://www.dialcorp.com

Dial makes well-known personal (Breck, Tone) and household consumer (Borateem, Brillo, Purex, Dial soap) products but also has a presence in a hodgepodge of other businesses. Accordingly, the company plans to split into 2 companies with its personal products business remaining under the Dial name. The other will come under the wing of an as yet unnamed company. These units include airline catering (Dobbs International Services), ground-handling services (Aircraft Service International Group), convention services (Exhibitgroup), cruises (Premier Cruise Lines), money orders (Travelers Express), Canadian bus service (Greyhound Lines of Canada), and food services.

DIAMOND SHAMROCK, INC.

9830 Colonnade Blvd.
San Antonio, TX 78269
Phone: 210-641-6800
Fax: 210-641-8687

CEO: Roger R. Hemminghaus
CFO: Robert C. Becker
Symbol: DRM
Exchange: NYSE

1995 Sales: $2,957 million
1995 Profits: $47 million
Mkt. Value: $904 million
Employees: 11,250

Web site: http://www.diasham.com

Diamond Shamrock is the leading independent refiner and marketer of petroleum products in the southwestern US. The company operates 2 crude oil refineries in Texas and is engaged in the wholesale and retail marketing of refined petroleum products. It sells over 1.5 billion gallons of gasoline per year through more than 2,000 independently owned Diamond Shamrock branded retail outlets in Texas, Colorado, Louisiana, New Mexico, and 4 other states; its acquisition of National Convenience Stores (Stop N Go) adds some 700 stores to its stable. The company also owns Northern American InteleCom, a provider of phone service to prison inmates.

DIGITAL EQUIPMENT CORPORATION

111 Powdermill Rd.
Maynard, MA 01754
Phone: 508-493-5111
Fax: 508-493-8780

CEO: Robert B. Palmer
CFO: Vincent J. Mullarkey
Symbol: DEC
Exchange: NYSE

1995 Sales: $13,813 million
1995 Profits: $122 million
Mkt. Value: $9,859 million
Employees: 61,700

Web site: http://www.digital.com

Digital Equipment Corporation (DEC) is one of the world's top suppliers of networked computer systems and components, software, and services. After 4 years of heavy losses, DEC is pulling itself back up with products based on its 64-bit Alpha microprocessor (the industry standard is still 32 bits) and strategic partnerships, including alliances with Microsoft and Oracle. Products include its older VAX family of mainframe computers as well as its newer UNIX-based computers (AlphaServer family), network components (such as adapters and hubs), printers, and peripherals. The company also offers services such as network design and support, systems integration, and project management.

DILLARD DEPARTMENT STORES, INC.

1600 Cantrell Rd.
Little Rock, AR 72201
Phone: 501-376-5200
Fax: 501-376-5917

CEO: William Dillard
CFO: James I. Freeman
Symbol: DDS
Exchange: NYSE

1995 Sales: $6,097 million
1995 Profits: $167 million
Mkt. Value: $4,140 million
Employees: 40,312

Web site: http://www.azstarnet.com/dillards

Operating in 21 Sunbelt and midwestern states, Dillard Department Stores (which sell apparel, shoes, cosmetics, and home furnishings) cater to middle- to upper-middle income consumers. Dillard's growth has been hurt by a weak market for women's apparel, but the company remains steadfast with a marketing strategy it has had since the mid-1980s: merchandising and cost control. Rather than offer frequent advertised sales (an industry standard), Dillard prefers to build customer loyalty with "everyday-low-pricing." It is increasing its mix of private-label brands and is building stores in Mexico. The Dillard family controls the company's voting stock.

DOLE FOOD COMPANY, INC.

31355 Oak Crest Dr.
Westlake Village, CA 91361
Phone: 818-879-6600
Fax: 818-879-6618

CEO: David H. Murdock
CFO: Michael S. Karsner
Symbol: DOL
Exchange: NYSE

1995 Sales: $4,153 million
1995 Profits: $23 million
Mkt. Value: $2,558 million
Employees: 43,000

Web site: http://www.dole5aday.com

With its exit from the real estate business, Dole can now concentrate on being an industry leader in the fresh fruit and vegetable business. Its products include fresh fruits (apples, bananas, cherries, grapefruit, grapes, pineapples, strawberries), packaged foods (canned fruits, snack bars), dried fruits and nuts (dates, almonds, raisins), and fresh vegetables (artichokes, asparagus, broccoli). The company has food operations in North and South America, Asia, and Europe and sells its products worldwide. Dole has exited the real estate business, spinning off its Castle & Cooke home-building operation, along with its other real estate ventures and its resort properties in Hawaii.

DOMINION RESOURCES, INC.

901 E. Byrd St.
Richmond, VA 23219
Phone: 804-775-5700
Fax: 804-775-5819

CEO: Thomas E. Capps
CFO: Unwood Robertson
Symbol: D
Exchange: NYSE

1995 Sales: $4,652 million
1995 Profits: $425 million
Mkt. Value: $6,717 million
Employees: 10,592

Dominion Resources, through its primary subsidiary Virginia Electric and Power, provides electricity to 1.9 million customers in North Carolina, Virginia, and West Virginia. The company's Dominion Capital unit provides financial services to the parent and to other subsidiaries and also makes outside investments. Dominion Energy develops electric power generation projects outside the territory served by Virginia Power, including operations in Argentina and Belize. Dominion Land holds properties in Virginia and North Carolina for future development or sale.

DOVER CORPORATION

280 Park Ave.
New York, NY 10017
Phone: 212-922-1640
Fax: 212-922-1656

CEO: Thomas L. Reece
CFO: John F. McNiff
Symbol: DOV
Exchange: NYSE

1995 Sales: $3,746 million
1995 Profits: $278 million
Mkt. Value: $5,395 million
Employees: 25,332

Best known as a manufacturer of elevators, Dover also owns more than 60 other companies that make products ranging from garbage trucks to manhole covers to pizza ovens. Dover Elevator International is the US's 2nd largest elevator manufacturer (after United Technologies' Otis unit). Dover Industries makes products for the automotive service, bulk transport, commercial food service, machine tool, and waste-handling industries. Dover Resources produces equipment for the fuel handling and petroleum industries; Dover Technologies International makes automated electronics assembly equipment; and Dover Diversified makes industrial assembly and production machinery, compressors, and heat transfer equipment.

Though it took a pounding in the first half of the 1990s, **Digital Equipment** once could do no wrong. Early on, when the company was turning out such innovations as the first interactive computer (PDP-1, 1960), revenue and earnings surged at an average of 30% a year for nearly 2 full decades.

— *Hoover's Guide to Computer Companies*

THE DOW CHEMICAL COMPANY

2030 Dow Center
Midland, MI 48674
Phone: 517-636-1000
Fax: 517-636-1830

CEO: William F. Stavropoulos
CFO: J. Pedro Reinhard
Symbol: DOW
Exchange: NYSE

1995 Sales: $20,957 million
1995 Profits: $2,078 million
Mkt. Value: $23,233 million
Employees: 39,500

Web site: http://www.dow.com

Dow Chemical is a leading manufacturer of chemicals, plastics, and specialty products (agriculture and consumer products). It is the #2 US chemical company after DuPont, manufacturing basic chemicals and plastics (ethylene, butadiene, benzene, caustic soda, and polyethylene). Its consumer products include Fantastik, Saran Wrap, Spray'N Wash, and Ziploc. In response to the poor performance of its 2 spinoffs (prescription drug and over-the-counter health care business Marion Merrell Dow and energy producer Destec) and the breast-implant litigation and subsequent Chapter 11 filing by partner Dow Corning, Dow sold Marion Merrell Dow to pharmaceutical behemoth Hoechst.

DRESSER INDUSTRIES, INC.

2001 Ross Ave.
Dallas, TX 75201
Phone: 214-740-6000
Fax: 214-740-6584

CEO: William E. Bradford
CFO: Bill D. St. John
Symbol: DI
Exchange: NYSE

1995 Sales: $5,629 million
1995 Profits: $197 million
Mkt. Value: $5,198 million
Employees: 31,457

An energy services company, Dresser Industries offers everything from drill bits to gas pumps to pipe coating services to the petroleum industry. Its hydrocarbon processing division manufactures a variety of equipment, including compressors, engines, turbines, generators, and pumps. Dresser's oil field services unit provides drilling fluid and bits, as well as drilling services and pipe coating services. Its Kellogg Oil & Gas unit provides engineering and construction services for hydrocarbon processing plants, including liquefied natural gas (LNG) liquefaction facilities and LNG receiving terminals. Its Dresser-Rand joint venture makes compressors and turbines, and its Ingersoll-Dresser joint venture manufactures pumps.

DTE ENERGY COMPANY

2000 Second Ave.	CEO: John E. Lobbia	1995 Sales: $3,636 million
Detroit, MI 48226	CFO: Larry G. Garberding	1995 Profits: $406 million
Phone: 313-235-8000	Symbol: DTE	Mkt. Value: $4,843 million
Fax: 313-237-8828	Exchange: NYSE	Employees: 8,340

344

DTE Energy is the holding company for Detroit Edison, which generates and sells electricity to nearly 2 million customers in southeast Michigan. Energy sources are fossil fuels (75%), nuclear energy (11%), pumped storage (9%), and oil/gas peaking units (5%). The company has long-term provider contracts with such major industrial customers as Chrysler, Ford, and General Motors. It also provides energy-related services through nonutility subsidiaries such as Bio-mass Energy Systems (landfill gas generation plants), EdVenture Capital Corp. (investments in electrical power controls), and Midwest Energy Resources (transportation of western US coal via railroads and Great Lakes vessels).

DUKE POWER COMPANY

422 S. Church St.	CEO: William H. Grigg	1995 Sales: $4,677 million
Charlotte, NC 28242	CFO: Richard J. Osborne	1995 Profits: $715 million
Phone: 704-594-0887	Symbol: DUK	Mkt. Value: $9,884 million
Fax: 704-382-3814	Exchange: NYSE	Employees: 17,121

Web site: http://www.dukepower.com

280

Duke Power provides electricity to more than 1.7 million customers in North and South Carolina, including Charlotte, Durham, Greenville, and Winston-Salem. In addition, subsidiary Nantahala Power and Light provides electricity to more than 53,000 customers in North Carolina. Duke produces electricity mainly from nuclear sources (60%) and coal (38%). Other subsidiaries include Crescent Resources, Inc. (forest management and real estate development), Duke Energy Group (independent power projects), Duke Merchandising (appliance and electronics sales and service), Duke Water Operations, and DukeNet Communications Inc. (systems management and development).

500 NAMES

George Eastman, who thought the letter "K" was "a strong, incisive sort of letter," experimented with letter combinations starting and ending with "K," finally coming up with **Kodak** in 1892.

— *Hoover's Handbook of American Companies 1996*

THE DUN & BRADSTREET CORPORATION

187 Danbury Rd.	CEO: Robert E. Weissman	1995 Sales: $5,415 million
Wilton, CT 06897	CFO: Nicholas L. Trivisonno	1995 Profits: $321 million
Phone: 203-834-4200	Symbol: DNB	Mkt. Value: $10,119 million
Fax: 203-834-4201	Exchange: NYSE	Employees: 49,500

Web site: http://www.dnb.com

242

Dun & Bradstreet is a business information services company. Dun & Bradstreet Information Services is the world's largest credit reporting agency, with a database covering more than 40 million businesses. Moody's Investor Service publishes business and financial information but is best known for its rating service, which rates debt issued by corporations and governments. Reuben H. Donnelley publishes Yellow Pages directories. Previously a much larger company, Dun & Bradstreet is slimming down. In 1996 it announced plans to split into 3 companies: Dun & Bradstreet, A. C. Nielsen (marketing information), and Cognizant (market research and high-tech advisory services).

EASTMAN CHEMICAL COMPANY

100 N. Eastman Rd.	CEO: Earnest W. Deavenport Jr.	1995 Sales: $5,040 million
Kingsport, TN 37660	CFO: H. Virgil Stephens	1995 Profits: $559 million
Phone: 423-229-2000	Symbol: EMN	Mkt. Value: $5,743 million
Fax: 423-229-1351	Exchange: NYSE	Employees: 17,709

Web site: http://www.eastman.com

267

A former unit of Eastman Kodak, Eastman Chemical is a world leader in polyester plastics for packaging. Sales of polyethylene terephthalate (PET), a plastic used for soft drink, water, and other beverage containers, account for roughly one quarter of total revenues. The company is also a major supplier of cellulose acetate filter tow (a fiber used in cigarette filters) and a leading supplier of specialty chemicals used in the manufacture of inks and resins. Other products include chemicals used in photographic products and pharmaceuticals, cellulose (a fiber used in acetate yarn), and nutritional products (vitamin E).

EASTMAN KODAK COMPANY

343 State St.	CEO: George M.C. Fisher	1995 Sales: $15,269 million
Rochester, NY 14650	CFO: Harry L. Kavetas	1995 Profits: $1,252 million
Phone: 716-724-4000	Symbol: EK	Mkt. Value: $25,293 million
Fax: 716-724-1089	Exchange: NYSE	Employees: 96,600

Web site: http://www.kodak.com

67

Eastman Kodak is remaking the camera business in its own (digital) image. The company is aggressively growing its digital imaging products and services in the US and its film products in the developing world, while continuing to defend its lucrative but mature US film business. It is teaming up with partners in the high-tech industry to develop new products for digital imaging, including Apple Computer (a Mac-compatible digital camera), Microsoft (photo finishing software on PCs), IBM (the marketing of Photo CD products), Hewlett-Packard (image-quality inkjet printers), and Sprint (the sending of images over phone lines).

EATON CORPORATION

Eaton Center	CEO: Stephen R. Hardis	1995 Sales: $6,822 million
Cleveland, OH 44114	CFO: Adrian T. Dillon	1995 Profits: $399 million
Phone: 216-523-5000	Symbol: ETN	Mkt. Value: $4,627 million
Fax: 216-523-4787	Exchange: NYSE	Employees: 52,000

Web site: http://www.eaton.com

191

Eaton makes electrical and electromechanical components for a wide variety of industries. The Vehicle Components division manufactures equipment for the OEM market, including axles, transmissions, and engine components for cars, heavy trucks, and sport utility vehicles. The Electrical and Electronic Controls unit makes components for use in the construction, appliance, aerospace, and defense industries, including controllers, materials-handling systems, and transformers. The company is also the leading maker of ion implanters, which are used in the manufacturing of semiconductors. Amid rising demand for such equipment, this business is one of Eaton's fastest growing.

ECHLIN INC.

100 Double Beach Rd.	CEO: Frederick J. Mancheski	1995 Sales: $2,718 million
Branford, CT 06405	CFO: Richard A. Wisot	1995 Profits: $154 million
Phone: 203-481-5751	Symbol: ECH	Mkt. Value: $2,179 million
Fax: 203-481-6485	Exchange: NYSE	Employees: 23,400

459

Echlin makes products designed to maintain or improve the efficiency and safety of motor vehicles; it also markets those products internationally. The company's brake system parts include shoes, drums, cables, disc pads, rotors and calipers, hoses and controllers, wheel oil seals, spring brakes, and slack adjusters. Its engine system parts include distributors and caps, ignition coils, sensors, voltage regulators, fuel pumps, oxygen sensors, and starter valves. Other products include clutches, bell housings, U-joints, airhorns, mirrors, water pumps, windshield wiper systems, and traction bars. Echlin sells mainly to aftermarket consumers such as professional mechanics and vehicle owners.

ECKERD CORPORATION

8333 Bryan Dairy Rd.	CEO: Frank Newman	1995 Sales: $4,997 million
Largo, FL 34647	CFO: Samuel G. Wright	1995 Profits: $93 million
Phone: 813-399-6000	Symbol: ECK	Mkt. Value: $1,634 million
Fax: 813-399-6409	Exchange: NYSE	Employees: 46,437

Web site: http://www.eckerd.com

Eckerd is the #2 drugstore chain in the US (after Walgreen), with operations in 13 states, mainly in the Sunbelt. Its primary focus is the sale of prescription and over-the-counter drugs, but it has expanded its merchandise offerings to include books and magazines, cosmetics, food, fragrances, greeting cards, and toys. Eckerd is divesting noncore operations (including its extensive photo processing operation, which is among the top 3 US retail photofinishers), investing in new technology, retooling its merchandising strategy, and focusing on 3rd-party marketing and managed care programs. Merrill Lynch owns about 1/3 of the company's stock.

EDISON INTERNATIONAL

2244 Walnut Grove Ave.	CEO: John E. Bryson	1995 Sales: $8,405 million
Rosemead, CA 91770	CFO: Alan J. Fohrer	1995 Profits: $739 million
Phone: 818-302-2222	Symbol: EIX	Mkt. Value: $7,403 million
Fax: 818-302-2517	Exchange: NYSE	Employees: 16,434

Web site: http://www.edisonx.com

Edison International (formerly SCEcorp) is the parent company of Southern California Edison, the 2nd largest (after Pacific Gas & Electric) electric utility in the US. Another subsidiary, Mission Energy, one of the US's largest independent power producers, focuses on providing power projects, such as cogeneration and geothermal plants, in such countries as Australia and India. Mission First Financial is the company's financial arm, providing financing, cash management, and venture capital to the other subsidiaries. The company is also involved in developing real estate for future power projects and building generating plants and transmission systems.

E. I. DU PONT DE NEMOURS AND COMPANY

1007 Market St.	CEO: John A. Krol	1995 Sales: $37,607 million
Wilmington, DE 19898	CFO: Charles L. Henry	1995 Profits: $3,293 million
Phone: 302-774-1000	Symbol: DD	Mkt. Value: $45,120 million
Fax: 302-774-7321	Exchange: NYSE	Employees: 105,000

Web site: http://www.dupont.com

DuPont is the #1 chemical company in the US and intends to stay that way by restructuring and refusing to stick with underperforming operations. It is organized into 5 business segments: chemicals (refrigerants, pigments, and polymer intermediaries), fibers (Lycra, Tyvek, textiles, nylons), polymers (elastomers, nylon resins, film, finishes, packaging materials), petroleum (Conoco, its largest subsidiary), and diversified businesses (agriculture, electronics, and medical products). DuPont plans to expand its Conoco operations through increased offshore drilling. It is also expanding into the women's apparel retail market with a private sportswear line that will highlight its synthetic fiber manufacturing operations.

ELI LILLY AND COMPANY

Lilly Corporate Center	CEO: Randall L. Tobias	1995 Sales: $7,535 million
Indianapolis, IN 46285	CFO: Charles E. Golden	1995 Profits: $2,291 million
Phone: 317-276-2000	Symbol: LLY	Mkt. Value: $33,574 million
Fax: 317-276-2095	Exchange: NYSE	Employees: 26,800

Web site: http://www.lilly.com

Eli Lilly, a major US drug company, researches, produces, and markets pharmaceuticals spanning the entire drug spectrum. Although the company is well known for its life-saving insulin, Humulin, used to treat diabetes, its top-selling drugs are the antidepressant Prozac and the antibiotic Ceclor. Lilly also produces drugs to treat animal diseases and to improve the efficiency of animal food production. The company sells medical and diagnostic devices through its subsidiary, the Guidant Corporation. It owns drug benefit manager PCS Health Systems, which offers prescription discounts to insurance companies and health maintenance organizations.

The Emerson behind **Emerson Electric** had no great technological talent himself, but he knew it when he saw it. **John Emerson**, a former Missouri judge, backed the company in the 1890s based on his faith in the ingenuity of brothers Alexander and Charles Meston in developing uses for the electric motor.

— *Hoover's Handbook of American Business 1996*

EMERSON ELECTRIC CO.

8000 W. Florissant Ave.	CEO: Charles F. Knight	1995 Sales: $10,013 million
St. Louis, MO 63136	CFO: W. J. Galvin	1995 Profits: $908 million
Phone: 314-553-2000	Symbol: EMR	Mkt. Value: $17,895 million
Fax: 314-553-3527	Exchange: NYSE	Employees: 78,900

Electronic component maker Emerson Electric is the world's largest producer of electric motors. It also makes a wide variety of other equipment ranging from compressors and diesel generators to hand tools and welding equipment. Emerson's commercial and industrial control segment makes process control systems, industrial motors and machinery, and other electronic products. Its appliance and construction component business makes appliance components, HVAC equipment, and tools. The company's brand names include Fisher Controls, Rosemount, Wiegand, and Western Forge. Almost 90% of Emerson's electrical products are #1 or #2 in their markets.

ENGELHARD CORPORATION

101 Wood Ave.	CEO: Orin R. Smith	1995 Sales: $2,840 million
Iselin, NJ 08830	CFO: William E. Nettles	1995 Profits: $138 million
Phone: 908-205-5000	Symbol: EC	Mkt. Value: $2,953 million
Fax: 908-321-1161	Exchange: NYSE	Employees: 5,075

Specialty chemicals maker Engelhard is a major producer of catalysts for the petroleum, chemical, and pharmaceutical industries. Products include conductive pastes and powders, electroplating materials, environmental catalysts, paper pigments, petroleum-refining catalysts, temperature-sensing devices, and kaolin (fine-grained) clays that are used for additives and pigments. To fuel sales growth, Engelhard is emphasizing new products (automotive catalysts, calcined paper pigments, and specialty minerals) and international expansion (Asia, Germany, and South Africa).

ENRON CORP.

1400 Smith St.	CEO: Kenneth L. Lay	1995 Sales: $9,189 million
Houston, TX 77002	CFO: Kurt S. Huneke	1995 Profits: $520 million
Phone: 713-853-6161	Symbol: ENE	Mkt. Value: $8,775 million
Fax: 713-853-3129	Exchange: NYSE	Employees: 6,692

Enron, North America's #1 buyer and seller of natural gas, also builds and manages worldwide natural gas transportation, power generation, liquids, and clean fuels facilities. While about 80% of its business is in domestic gas operations and power services, Enron focuses on emerging markets with power plant and pipeline projects (China, Guatemala, and the Philippines). It also operates a natural gas pipeline in Argentina; helps Russia's state-owned gas company, Gazprom, market gas in Europe; and has oil and gas exploration and production operations. Enron wants to become the world's leading natural gas producer.

ENTERGY CORPORATION

639 Loyola Ave.
New Orleans, LA 70113
Phone: 504-569-4000
Fax: 504-569-4265

CEO: Edwin A. Lupberger
CFO: Gerald D. McInvale
Symbol: ETR
Exchange: NYSE

1995 Sales: $6,274 million
1995 Profits: $520 million
Mkt. Value: $6,185 million
Employees: 13,521

Web site: http://www.entergy.com

209

Entergy is the #1 supplier of electricity in the middle South, providing power to about 2.4 million customers through 5 utilities: Arkansas Power & Light, Louisiana Power & Light, Mississippi Power & Light, New Orleans Public Service, and Gulf States Utilities. Subsidiary Entergy Systems and Services handles energy conservation products and services, while Entergy Operations manages the company's 4 nuclear power plants, which provide about 30% of the company's electricity. Entergy generates the remainder of its power from coal and natural gas.

THE ESTÉE LAUDER COMPANIES INC.

767 Fifth Ave.
New York, NY 10153
Phone: 212-572-4200
Fax: 212-572-3941

CEO: Leonard A. Lauder
CFO: Robert J. Bigler
Symbol: EL
Exchange: NYSE

1995 Sales: $2,899 million
1995 Profits: $121 million
Mkt. Value: $4,091 million
Employees: 9,900

Web site: http://www.clinique.com

432

Estée Lauder sells prestige skin care, makeup, and fragrance products. The newly public company markets about 700 products under such brands as Aramis 900, Tuscany, and Aramis Classic fragrances and Aramis Lab Series skin care products. Its Clinique products include aromatics, balanced makeup base, and remoisturizing lipstick. The company's Estée Lauder products include Enlighten and Re-Nutriv Lipstick and White Linen fragrances. Other makeup and skin care brands include Origins, an environmentally safe product line, and Perspectives, aimed at young professional women. Estée Lauder products account for nearly 40% of all US department and specialty store cosmetic sales.

EXXON CORPORATION

5959 Las Colinas Blvd.
Irving, TX 75039
Phone: 214-444-1000
Fax: 214-444-1505

CEO: Lee R. Raymond
CFO: Edgar A. Robinson
Symbol: XON
Exchange: NYSE

1995 Sales: $110,009 million
1995 Profits: $6,470 million
Mkt. Value: $98,093 million
Employees: 82,000

3

The world's largest publicly owned integrated oil company, Exxon has oil reserves of 6.6 billion barrels and gas reserves of 42.2 trillion cubic feet. Its chemical division produces aromatics, solvents, fertilizer, and other products. The company produces and sells petrochemicals and coal worldwide. It explores in more than 25 countries, including former Soviet republics, China's Tarim Basin, Papua New Guinea, and offshore Angola and Nigeria. Lingering legal residue from the 1989 *Exxon Valdez* Alaskan oil spill is keeping the company in court as it fights the $5 billion fine levied by an Alaskan federal jury.

FedEx was the inspiration of **Fred Smith**, who first presented the concept at Yale in a paper that earned him a "C." The idea went over better with investors and bankers, who put up about $130 million in startup money for Federal Express between 1969 and 1971.

— *Hoover's Handbook of American Business 1996*

FARMLAND INDUSTRIES, INC.

3315 N. Oak Trafficway
Kansas City, MO 64116
Phone: 816-459-6000
Fax: 816-459-6979

CEO: Harry D. Cleberg
CFO: John F. Berardi
Ownership: Cooperative

1995 Sales: $7,257 million
Employees: 12,700

Web site: http://www.farmland.com

Farmland Industries is the nation's biggest agricultural cooperative. It provides petroleum, fertilizer, and feed products to help members produce their goods and then processes and markets the beef, pork, and grain grown by its half-million co-op members. Farmland is owned by about 1,400 smaller co-ops throughout the Midwest. It teams with Reuters to operate Market Communications Group, which provides agriculture market news and online information to businesses and other cooperatives. The co-op operates nationwide and in more than 40 foreign countries; about 40% of its sales come from outside the US.

FEDERAL EXPRESS CORPORATION

2005 Corporate Ave.
Memphis, TN 38132
Phone: 901-369-3600
Fax: 901-795-1027

CEO: Frederick W. Smith
CFO: Alan B. Graf Jr.
Symbol: FDX
Exchange: NYSE

1995 Sales: $9,392 million
1995 Profits: $298 million
Mkt. Value: $3,968 million
Employees: 94,201

Web site: http://www.fedex.com

The world leader in the overnight package delivery market, Federal Express (FedEx) delivers more than 2.3 million items each day. It offers next-day, 2nd-day, and international freight delivery to destinations in the US and over 190 countries, including such out-of-the-way locales as Bhutan, Palau, and Suriname. FedEx has the world's largest fleet of cargo delivery planes. Through a joint venture with Network Courier Services, FedEx has entered the US same-day package delivery market. Its business logistics operations include global distribution of Laura Ashley fashion products and operation of a distribution network in Singapore for National Semiconductor.

FEDERAL HOME LOAN MORTGAGE CORPORATION

8200 Jones Branch Dr.
McLean, VA 22102
Phone: 703-903-2000
Fax: 703-903-2447

CEO: Leland C. Brendsel
CFO: John Gibbons
Symbol: FRE
Exchange: NYSE

1995 Sales: $10,915 million
1995 Profits: $1,091 million
Mkt. Value: $14,732 million
Employees: 3,319

Web site: http://www.freddiemac.com

Federal Home Loan Mortgage Corporation (Freddie Mac) is a government-mandated lending company that purchases conventional residential mortgages from banks and mortgage bankers and generates fee and interest income on the mortgages. Freddie Mac uses 2 methods to finance mortgage purchases: purchased mortgages are securitized and sold to investors as guaranteed mortgage securities, or purchased mortgages and mortgage-related securities are held for investment by Freddie Mac and financed with debt and equity capital. The company competes with Federal National Mortgage Association (Fannie Mae), also government mandated, for mortgage purchases.

FEDERAL NATIONAL MORTGAGE ASSOCIATION

3900 Wisconsin Ave. N.W.
Washington, DC 20016
Phone: 202-752-7000
Fax: 202-752-6099

CEO: James A. Johnson
CFO: J. Timothy Howard
Symbol: FNM
Exchange: NYSE

1995 Sales: $22,246 million
1995 Profits: $2,372 million
Mkt. Value: $34,262 million
Employees: 3,300

Web site: http://www.fanniemae.com.

Fannie Mae (the Federal National Mortgage Association) is "showing America a new way home," by extending credit to people who do not fit conventional mortgage criteria but who nevertheless may be good bets (i.e., people with steady jobs who lack the savings for a down payment). Its purpose is to ensure a source of credit for low- and moderate-income home buyers by purchasing the mortgages from the original institutions. Fannie Mae also repackages the mortgages as securities for sale in the US and abroad.

FEDERATED DEPARTMENT STORES, INC.

7 W. Seventh St.	CEO: Allen Questrom	1995 Sales: $15,049 million
Cincinnati, OH 45202	CFO: Ronald W. Tysoe	1995 Profits: $75 million
Phone: 513-579-7000	Symbol: FD	Mkt. Value: $6,660 million
Fax: 513-579-7555	Exchange: NYSE	Employees: 119,000

Web site: http://www.federated-fds.com

 Its acquisition of the venerable R.H. Macy chain makes Federated the largest department store retailer in the US. The list of its retailers contains some of the most prestigious names in the industry, including Jordan Marsh, Lazarus, the Bon Marche, Burdine's, Bloomingdale's, Stern's, Rich's, and Goldsmith's. Federated operates department stores in 35 states, as well as specialty stores (Aeropostale and Charter Club) in 20 states. In 1995 it bought Broadway Stores. Federated is consolidating and streamlining its operations, merging A&S/Jordan Marsh into its Macy's East division and discontinuing its Abraham & Straus name.

FHP INTERNATIONAL CORPORATION

9900 Talbert Ave.	CEO: Wescott W. Price	1995 Sales: $3,909 million
Fountain Valley, CA 92708	CFO: Kenneth S. Ord	1995 Profits: $37 million
Phone: 714-378-5000	Symbol: FHPC	Mkt. Value: $1,316 million
Fax: 714-825-6654	Exchange: Nasdaq	Employees: 13,000

Web site: http://www.fhp.com

 FHP International is one of the nation's largest health insurance companies, providing HMO coverage to 1.7 million members in 11 western and midwestern states and Guam. In addition, FHP provides managed care services, such as outpatient physician care, dental and eye care, home health nursing, and physical therapy. The company also offers group term life, group health, and accident indemnity insurance coverage. Its 24 Hour Managed Care Program provides workers' compensation, HMO plans, and group indemnity medical, dental, and life insurance in a single package. FHP also provides 3rd-party administration and utilization review services and several preferred provider organization (PPO) networks.

FIRST BANK SYSTEM, INC.

601 Second Ave. S.	CEO: John F. Grundhofer	1995 Sales: $3,328 million
Minneapolis, MN 55402	CFO: Susan E. Lester	1995 Profits: $568 million
Phone: 612-973-1111	Symbol: FBS	Mkt. Value: $8,304 million
Fax: 612-973-2351	Exchange: NYSE	Employees: 13,231

Web site: http://www.fbs.com/home.html

 First Bank System is a regional bank holding company serving 11 midwestern and Rocky Mountain states through more than 300 locations. The company has 9 commercial banks and 4 trust companies. It provides commercial and retail banking, asset management, correspondent banking, leasing, insurance, mortgage banking, and investment services to individual and commercial customers. First Bank System offers international customers financing of import and export trade and foreign exchange services.

FIRST CHICAGO NBD CORPORATION

1 First National Plaza	CEO: Verne G. Istock	1995 Sales: $10,681 million
Chicago, IL 60670	CFO: Robert A. Rosholt	1995 Profits: $1,150 million
Phone: 312-732-4000	Symbol: FCN	Mkt. Value: $12,351 million
Fax: 312-732-5976	Exchange: NYSE	Employees: 35,328

Web site: http://www.fcnbd.com

 Now the 7th largest US bank following its acquisition of Detroit's NBD Bancorp, First Chicago NBD is a regional commercial banking company with operations in Illinois, Indiana, Ohio, and Michigan. It provides such services as credit cards, debt trading, leasing, mortgage servicing, trust services, commercial loans, consumer loans, and checking and savings accounts. The company's banking subsidiaries include American National Bank and First National Bank of Chicago. Other subsidiaries include First Chicago Capital Markets, which provides financial management services, and First Chicago International, which provides letters of credit and foreign currency transactions.

FIRST DATA CORPORATION

401 Hackensack Ave.	CEO: Henry C. Duques	1995 Sales: $4,081 million
Hackensack, NJ 07601	CFO: Lee Andrean	1995 Loss: ($84) million
Phone: 201-525-4700	Symbol: FDC	Mkt. Value: $15,743 million
Fax: 770-342-0402	Exchange: NYSE	Employees: 36,000

A leading provider of transaction processing services, First Data is the US's largest 3rd party processor of credit card transactions, providing transaction reporting, billing, and collection services to financial institutions, oil companies, and retailers. Other business units include Western Union (the largest cash transfer agent in the country) and Telecheck (the nation's #1 check authorization service). First Data also provides mutual fund processing (transfer agent services, fund administration, and record keeping), health care claims processing, cost management, document management (data imaging, database management, and printing and distribution), and customized 800 telephone services.

FIRST INTERSTATE BANCORP

633 W. Fifth St.	CEO: William E.B. Siart	1995 Sales: $4,828 million
Los Angeles, CA 90071	CFO: Steven L. Scheid	1995 Profits: $885 million
Phone: 213-614-3001	Symbol: I	Mkt. Value: $12,138 million
Fax: 213-614-3741	Exchange: NYSE	Employees: 27,200

Web site: http://ccseb.com/fi

Once one of the top 3 banks in California, First Interstate is now a part of banking behemoth Wells Fargo, following the latter's successful hostile takeover. After the 2 consolidate their operations, Wells Fargo will have about $100 billion in assets. Wells Fargo gets First Interstate's branches in the US, Brazil, Spain, and the UK and its expanded retail and commercial bank operations in the West and Southwest, with particular emphasis on California and Texas.

FIRST UNION CORPORATION

301 S. Tryon St.	CEO: Edward E. Crutchfield Jr.	1995 Sales: $10,583 million
Charlotte, NC 28288	CFO: Robert T. Atwood	1995 Profits: $1,430 million
Phone: 704-374-6161	Symbol: FTU	Mkt. Value: $16,815 million
Fax: 704-374-2140	Exchange: NYSE	Employees: 44,536

Web site: http://www.firstunion.com/

First Union is a multibank holding company -- one of several North Carolina-based banks that are making that state a regional banking powerhouse. In the past several years, the bank has acquired over a dozen other financial institutions in an effort to expand to the critical mass it thinks it needs to compete. The bank offers the usual array of consumer financial services and products, including checking and savings accounts, mortgage banking, auto and life insurance, and trust and brokerage services. It also offers credit cards, fiduciary services, and commercial and consumer lending. Mutual funds are offered through subsidiary Lieber & Co., which administers the Evergreen family of funds and derivatives.

First Data, the nation's largest processor of credit card transactions, has been singled out as one player likely to capitalize on the transition to "an electronic economy." Weeks before that prediction by a portfolio manager on *Wall Street Week with Louis Rukeyser,* First Data announced it would offer payment services on the Internet using Netscape software.

— **Bloomberg Business News**

Orlando to Miami in about an hour — no plane ticket required. That trip, at a top speed of 220 mph, might be possible in the year 2004 under a $4.8 billion bullet train project planned by **Fluor Corp.** and 3 partners. The contract, awarded by the State of Florida in February 1996, was subject to regulatory review.

— **Bloomberg Business News**

FLAGSTAR COMPANIES, INC.

203 E. Main St.	CEO: James B. Adamson	1995 Sales: $2,894 million
Spartanburg, SC 29319	CFO: C. Robert Campbell	1995 Loss: ($55) million
Phone: 803-597-8000	Symbol: FLST	Mkt. Value: $143 million
Fax: 803-597-8780	Exchange: Nasdaq	Employees: 88,000

435

One of the nation's leading restaurant companies, Flagstar owns or franchises over 1,500 Denny's restaurants (full-service family fare), over 200 Quincy's restaurants (family steakhouses), and more than 200 El Pollo Loco restaurants (quick-serve broiled chicken). It also owns the Coco's and Carrows restaurant chains and is the largest Hardee's franchisee, with nearly 600 units. Investment firm KKR owns a controlling interest in the firm. The company has sold off its food service and lodging service businesses in recent years to concentrate on its restaurant operations.

FLEET FINANCIAL GROUP, INC.

1 Federal St.	CEO: Terrence Murray	1995 Sales: $7,919 million
Boston, MA 02211	CFO: Eugene M. McQuade	1995 Profits: $610 million
Phone: 617-346-4000	Symbol: FLT	Mkt. Value: $10,429 million
Fax: 401-278-5801	Exchange: NYSE	Employees: 30,800

Web site: http://www.fleet.com

166

Fleet provides business, retail, trust/asset management, correspondent, leasing, insurance, mortgage banking, real estate, and investment services. It also offers checking, savings, loans (business, personal, educational, residential, and commercial), Mastercard, VISA, and money market deposit accounts. Fleet has significant consumer, student, and mortgage loan operations as well as strong consumer and small- and middle-market business banking operations. By buying Plaza Home Mortgage (a mortgage servicer), the IBM mutual fund family, Shawmut National, and the commercial operations of National Westminster, the bank hopes to be one of the survivors in this consolidating industry.

FLEETWOOD ENTERPRISES, INC.

3125 Myers St.	CEO: John C. Crean	1995 Sales: $2,856 million
Riverside, CA 92503	CFO: Paul M. Bingham	1995 Profits: $85 million
Phone: 909-351-3500	Symbol: FLE	Mkt. Value: $1,146 million
Fax: 909-351-3690	Exchange: NYSE	Employees: 18,000

448

Fleetwood Enterprises is the nation's #1 maker of both recreational vehicles and manufactured housing. The Riverside, California-based company produces 3 types of RVs: folding trailers, travel trailers, and motor homes. Fleetwood markets its RVs under the brand names American Dream, American Eagle, Jamboree, Pace Arrow, Savanna, Southwind, and Tioga. Subsidiaries in the lumber and fiberglass industries provide materials for RV and housing construction, and Fleetwood Credit Corp. finances customer purchases. CEO John Crean is famous for taking one of the company's RVs out on the road each year for an extended test drive.

FLEMING COMPANIES, INC.

6301 Waterford Blvd.
Oklahoma City, OK 73118
Phone: 405-840-7200
Fax: 405-840-7702

CEO: Robert E. Stauth
CFO: Harry L. Winn Jr.
Symbol: FLM
Exchange: NYSE

1995 Sales: $17,502 million
1995 Profits: $42 million
Mkt. Value: $636 million
Employees: 44,000

Web site: http://www.fleming.com

Fleming is the largest US wholesale grocery distributor, serving more than 10,000 stores in 43 states and several foreign countries. Although it also sells to large chains, including retail titan Wal-Mart, Fleming's main customers are single-store businesses and small chains. The company also operates 350 of its own stores, which account for over 15% of total sales (the goal is to boost it to 25%). Fleming's trade names include Big Star, Big T, Checkers, Festival Foods, Jamboree Foods, Piggly Wiggly, Shop 'n Bag, Super Save, and Super Thrift.

FLORIDA PROGRESS CORPORATION

1 Progress Plaza
St. Petersburg, FL 33701
Phone: 813-824-6400
Fax: 813-824-6751

CEO: Jack B. Critchfield
CFO: Jeffrey R. Heinicka
Symbol: FPC
Exchange: NYSE

1995 Sales: $3,056 million
1995 Profits: $239 million
Mkt. Value: $3,173 million
Employees: 7,174

Florida Progress is a St. Petersburg, Florida-based utility holding company. Primary subsidiary Florida Power is the 2nd largest electric utility in the state (with 13 plants serving some 1.2 million customers). It generates electricity from oil (60%), coal (30%), and nuclear (10%) power plants. Subsidiary Electric Fuels operates coal mines, ships bulk products, maintains drydock facilities, runs a cinderblock factory, and provides railcar services. Subsidiary Mid-Continent Life Insurance offers low-premium insurance policies in 37 states and subsidiary Progress Credit Corp. directs the parent company's interests in aircraft, locomotives, and real estate.

FLUOR CORPORATION

3333 Michelson Dr.
Irvine, CA 92730
Phone: 714-975-2000
Fax: 714-975-5271

CEO: Leslie G. McCraw
CFO: J. Michal Conaway
Symbol: FLR
Exchange: NYSE

1995 Sales: $9,301 million
1995 Profits: $232 million
Mkt. Value: $5,862 million
Employees: 41,678

Web site: http://www.fluor.com

Fluor Corporation provides engineering and construction services to clients in a broad range of markets. Subsidiary Fluor Daniel, which accounts for over 90% of the parent company's revenues, is one of the world's largest engineering and construction firms. It serves customers in the power generation, raw materials processing, petroleum, and industrial markets, as well as government clients. Subsidiary A. T. Massey Coal is one of the US's top 5 coal mining concerns, with 16 facilities in the eastern US. The company has offices worldwide, several foreign joint ventures, and stakes in overseas construction firms.

FMC CORPORATION

200 E. Randolph Dr.
Chicago, IL 60601
Phone: 312-861-6000
Fax: 312-861-6176

CEO: Robert N. Burt
CFO: Michael J. Callahan
Symbol: FMC
Exchange: NYSE

1995 Sales: $4,567 million
1995 Profits: $216 million
Mkt. Value: $2,706 million
Employees: 22,164

Web site: http://www.fmc.com

FMC is a diversified conglomerate organized into 5 main lines of business. The defense systems unit manufactures armament systems, including the Bradley fighting vehicle. The performance chemical operations make products for companies involved in agriculture and in the production of food and pharmaceuticals. FMC's machinery and equipment group makes equipment for the petroleum, airline, and food processing industries. The industrial chemicals unit produces peroxygen, phosphorus, and alkali chemicals. Finally, the FMC Gold unit develops gold and silver mines. FMC also has a soda ash-mining joint venture with Nippon Sheet Glass and Sumitomo Corp.

FOOD 4 LESS HOLDINGS

777 S. Harbor Blvd.
La Habra, CA 90631
Phone: 714-738-2000
Fax: 310-884-2600

CEO: Ronald W. Burkle
CFO: Greg Mays
Ownership: Privately Held

1995 Sales: $3,494 million
1995 Loss: ($216) million
Employees: 14,687

Food 4 Less Holdings controls the supermarket investments of the Yucaipa Companies, a private investment firm. Food 4 Less owns and operates some 500 stores in Southern California, where it is the #1 supermarket company. A $1.5 billion acquisition of Ralphs grocery stores has cemented Food 4 Less's dominance of the market but has also loaded the company with debt. Its grocery stores include Ralphs and Alpha Beta (Southern California), Dominick's (greater Chicago), Smitty's (Arizona), Bell Markets and Cala Foods (Northern California), Falley's (Midwest), and Food 4 Less (California and the Midwest).

FORD MOTOR COMPANY

American Rd.
Dearborn, MI 48121
Phone: 313-322-3000
Fax: 313-390-8929

CEO: Alexander J. Trotman
CFO: John M. Devine
Symbol: F
Exchange: NYSE

1995 Sales: $137,137 million
1995 Profits: $4,139 million
Mkt. Value: $34,908 million
Employees: 346,990

Web site: http://www.ford.com

Ford Motor Company is the world's #2 automaker (after GM). It makes vehicles under the Ford, Jaguar, Lincoln, and Mercury nameplates. Two of its biggest successes are the Ford Taurus and the F-Series Ford trucks. Ford also owns the Hertz car rental operation (#1 in the US) and has stakes in several foreign-based automakers, including an interest giving it effective control of Japanese automaker Mazda. Sales outside the US account for 30% of the total. The company is selling its stake in Associates First Capital Corp., an indirect wholly owned unit that provides finance, leasing, and related services.

FOSTER WHEELER CORPORATION

Perryville Corporate Park
Clinton, NJ 08809
Phone: 908-730-4000
Fax: 908-730-4315

CEO: Richard J. Swift
CFO: David J. Roberts
Symbol: FWC
Exchange: NYSE

1995 Sales: $3,082 million
1995 Profits: $29 million
Mkt. Value: $1,838 million
Employees: 12,650

Foster Wheeler is an engineering and construction company that builds chemical and pharmaceutical plants and refineries and provides management and petroleum development services. Its Energy Equipment Group builds power generation and chemical separation systems and nuclear components. The company's Power Systems Group operates cogeneration and waste-to-energy facilities. Foster Wheeler is targeting emerging nations for new opportunities, especially in power plant construction, and is expanding its environmental remediation business.

FOUNDATION HEALTH CORPORATION

3400 Data Dr.
Rancho Cordova, CA 95670
Phone: 916-631-5000
Fax: 916-631-5149

CEO: Daniel D. Crowley
CFO: Jeffrey L. Elder
Symbol: FH
Exchange: NYSE

1995 Sales: $2,460 million
1995 Profits: $49 million
Mkt. Value: $2,094 million
Employees: 8,896

Foundation Health provides a range of managed health care services. Its subsidiaries offer services including HMO plans, workers' compensation, life insurance, eye care, and administration of Medicaid and other government plans. The Integrated Pharmaceutical Services unit manages pharmacy benefits for various care providers. In line with the industrywide expansion trend, Foundation has pursued acquisitions, extended its reach beyond its California base into more than a dozen other states and the UK, and added 2 DOD contracts worth more than $4 billion.

FOXMEYER HEALTH CORPORATION

1220 Senlac Dr.	CEO: A.J. Butler	1995 Sales: $5,177 million
Carrollton, TX 75006	CFO: Peter B. McKee	1995 Profits: $42 million
Phone: 214-446-4800	Symbol: FOX	Mkt. Value: $268 million
Fax: 214-446-4499	Exchange: NYSE	Employees: 2,823

FoxMeyer Health is one of the largest and oldest pharmaceutical distribution companies in the US. Clients include independent pharmacies, drugstore chains, hospitals and other medical facilities, and managed care companies. FoxMeyer offers a number of pharmacy-related managed care services through its CareStream unit. These services include order, inventory, and billing software; claims processing services; benefits plan management; and drug utilization databases (which are helpful in determining the efficacy of treatment). The company also owns an interest in Ben Franklin Retail Stores, a general merchandise store franchiser.

FPL GROUP, INC.

700 Universe Blvd.	CEO: James L. Broadhead	1995 Sales: $5,593 million
Juno Beach, FL 33408	CFO: Michael W. Yackira	1995 Profits: $553 million
Phone: 407-694-4000	Symbol: FPL	Mkt. Value: $7,980 million
Fax: 407-694-6385	Exchange: NYSE	Employees: 11,353

Web site: http://www.fpl.com

FPL is one of the US's largest publicly owned electric utilities. The Juno Beach, Florida-based company provides electricity for more than 3.4 million customers on Florida's east and lower west coasts (about half that state's population). It produces power from oil (30%), nuclear sources (25%), natural gas (20%), and coal (5%) and purchases the rest.

FPL subsidiaries include ESI Energy (independent energy projects), Turner Foods (one of Florida's largest developers and operators of citrus groves), and Qualtec Quality Services (management consulting and training services).

"**Henry Ford** had no ideas on mass production," wrote Charles Sorenson, a close associate. "He wanted to build a lot of cars. He was determined but, like everyone else at that time, he didn't know how.... He just grew into it, like the rest of us."

QUOTES

— *The Entrepreneurs: An American Adventure*, by Robert Sobel and David B. Sicilia

FRED MEYER, INC.

3800 S.E. 22nd Ave.	CEO: Robert G. Miller	1995 Sales: $3,429 million
Portland, OR 97202	CFO: Kenneth Thrasher	1995 Profits: $30 million
Phone: 503-232-8844	Symbol: FMY	Mkt. Value: $794 million
Fax: 503-797-5609	Exchange: NYSE	Employees: 27,000

Web site: http://www.fredmeyer.com

Retailer Fred Meyer, Inc., operates more than 130 department stores in 7 western states. Most of its stores include food departments, in line with its strategy of enabling customers to do all their household shopping under one roof. The company also operates more than 30 small specialty stores, primarily jewelry stores. It sells name brand merchandise but is increasingly focusing on lower-price, higher-margin, private-label goods under the Fred Meyer, President's Choice, and FMV (Fred Meyer Value) names.

GANNETT CO., INC.

1100 Wilson Blvd.
Arlington, VA 22234
Phone: 703-284-6000
Fax: 703-558-3506

CEO: John J. Curley
CFO: Douglas H. McCorkindale
Symbol: GCI
Exchange: NYSE

1995 Sales: $4,007 million
1995 Profits: $477 million
Mkt. Value: $9,604 million
Employees: 35,300

Web site: http://www.gannett.com

Gannett is the US's largest newspaper publisher. Its flagship paper, *USA Today*, has the highest circulation of any US daily and is available in all 50 states. Gannett also produces an international edition of the paper that is sold in more than 90 countries. The company publishes over 80 daily newspapers and more than 50 nondaily publications. In addition, it has major stakes in broadcasting, owning almost a dozen TV stations (all network affiliates), as well as several radio stations. It also owns North America's largest billboard group and Gannett News Service.

"We are a company whose only answer to the trendy question, 'What do you intend to spin off?' is 'Cash, and lots of it.'"
— **CEO Jack Welch, General Electric**

— FORTUNE; April 29, 1996

THE GAP, INC.

1 Harrison St.
San Francisco, CA 94105
Phone: 415-952-4400
Fax: 415-896-0322

CEO: Millard S. Drexler
CFO: Robert J. Fisher
Symbol: GPS
Exchange: NYSE

1995 Sales: $4,395 million
1995 Profits: $354 million
Mkt. Value: $7,912 million
Employees: 60,000

The Gap, that ubiquitous clothing retailer, operates over 1,500 casual clothing stores in the US, Canada, France, and the UK. The Gap flagship stores offer a wide variety of casual clothing for both men and women. The company also operates GapKids (which includes the babyGap line of infant and toddler apparel), Banana Republic, and Old Navy Clothing. Facing a more competitive market, the Gap is working to broaden its merchandise offerings to appeal to a wider market. All clothing sold by the Gap is private-label merchandise made specifically for the company.

GATEWAY 2000, INC.

610 Gateway Dr.
North Sioux City, SD 57049
Phone: 605-232-2000
Fax: 605-232-2023

CEO: Ted Waitt
CFO: David J. McKittrick
Symbol: GATE
Exchange: Nasdaq

1995 Sales: $3,676 million
1995 Profits: $173 million
Mkt. Value: $2,034 million
Employees: 8,708

Web site: http://www.gw2k.com

Gateway 2000 is the #2 direct marketer (after Dell Computer) of PCs in the US and a leading supplier of Pentium-based computers. The company makes both desktop and portable PCs (including 486-based machines as well as Pentium-based), the HandBook, and advanced ColorBook 2 notebook PCs. Gateway also sells component add-ons such as CD-ROMs. Like rival Dell, the company sells directly to the public. In the US more than 500 salespeople in 3 different locations staff phone banks 16 hours a day. Gateway also has targeted the overseas markets, expanding sales operations in France and Germany and recruiting distributors in Asia and Latin America.

GEICO CORPORATION

1 Geico Plaza
Washington, DC 20076
Phone: 301-986-3000
Fax: 301-986-2851

CEO: Olza M. Nicely
CFO: W. Alvon Sparks Jr.
Ownership: Privately Held

1995 Sales: $3,054 million
1995 Profits: $248 million
Employees: 8,278

Web site: http://www.geico.com

The holding company for Government Employees Insurance Co., GEICO is one of the US's largest auto insurers. One of the few major insurers that still makes auto insurance the backbone of its business, it also offers life and health insurance. It has traditionally marketed its products to low-risk demographic groups, such as government and military employees. However, GEICO has begun to target nonstandard auto markets, including high-risk individuals required by law to buy auto insurance. The company is owned by Warren Buffett's investment firm, Berkshire Hathaway.

GENERAL DYNAMICS CORPORATION

3190 Fairview Park Dr.
Falls Church, VA 22042
Phone: 703-876-3000
Fax: 703-876-3125

CEO: James R. Mellor
CFO: Michael J. Mancuso
Symbol: GD
Exchange: NYSE

1995 Sales: $3,544 million
1995 Profits: $321 million
Mkt. Value: $3,732 million
Employees: 27,700

General Dynamics is a military systems manufacturer with 2 main areas of operation: nuclear submarines and artillery systems. Its Electric Boat division builds the Seawolf-class attack submarines and the Trident ballistic missile submarine, and its Land Systems division builds the M1 Series Main Battle Tank. It is also part of a team developing an advanced artillery system for the US Army. After downsizing in the early 1990s to cope with military spending cutbacks, General Dynamics has begun making some new acquisitions, including ship builder Bath Iron Works and the vehicle systems division on Teledyne.

GENERAL ELECTRIC COMPANY

3135 Easton Turnpike
Fairfield, CT 06431
Phone: 203-373-2211
Fax: 203-373-2071

CEO: John F. Welch Jr.
CFO: Dennis D. Dammerman
Symbol: GE
Exchange: NYSE

1995 Sales: $70,028 million
1995 Profits: $6,573 million
Mkt. Value: $126,523 million
Employees: 222,000

Web site: http://www.ge.com

Industrial behemoth GE operates a wide array of businesses, from TV network NBC to power plant parts manufacturing. The manufacturer is #1 among US electronics firms, and it produces aircraft engines, appliances (kitchen and laundry equipment), industrial products and systems (lighting, electrical distribution, and control equipment), and materials (plastics, silicones, laminates, and abrasives). Financial services arm GE Capital Corp. is one of the largest financial services companies in the US. The company has almost 150 manufacturing plants throughout the US and Puerto Rico and over 100 plants in 25 other countries.

GENERAL INSTRUMENT CORPORATION

8770 W. Bryn Mawr Ave.
Chicago, IL 60631
Phone: 312-695-1000
Fax: 312-695-1001

CEO: Richard S. Friedland
CFO: Charles T. Dickson
Symbol: GIC
Exchange: NYSE

1995 Sales: $2,432 million
1995 Profits: $124 million
Mkt. Value: $3,162 million
Employees: 12,300

Web site: http://www.gi.com

General Instrument is a leading developer of products that deliver interactive data, video, and voice information. Subsidiary GI Communications, its primary revenue source, is a top world supplier of interactive TV cable boxes and other technology used by cable system operators to package and deliver programming. The company also has a subsidiary, CommScope, that is a major provider of coaxial and fiber-optic cable, as well as a semiconductor division. GI licenses its cable box technology to such manufacturers as Hewlett-Packard and Zenith. It purchased Next Level Communications, a maker of digital telephone equipment, to increase its market base.

GENERAL MILLS, INC.

1 General Mills Blvd.	CEO: Stephen W. Sanger	1995 Sales: $8,394 million
Minneapolis, MN 55426	CFO: Leslie M. Frecon	1995 Profits: $367 million
Phone: 612-540-2311	Symbol: GIS	Mkt. Value: $9,188 million
Fax: 612-540-4925	Exchange: NYSE	Employees: 9,900

General Mills is the #2 cereal producer in the US (after Kellogg) and the leading maker of dessert mixes, dinner mixes, fruit snacks, and other consumer foods. Products include Cheerios cereal, Betty Crocker dessert mixes, Hamburger Helper dinner mixes, Gold Medal flour, Yoplait yogurt, and Bisquick baking mix. Now focused solely on its food lines after the 1995 spinoff of its casual dining business (Red Lobster, the Olive Garden) as Darden Restaurants, the company is expanding overseas through joint ventures with Nestlé, PepsiCo, and CPC International.

GENERAL MOTORS CORPORATION

3044 W. Grand Blvd.	CEO: John F. Smith Jr.	1995 Sales: $168,829 million
Detroit, MI 48202	CFO: J. Michael Losh	1995 Profits: $6,881 million
Phone: 313-556-5000	Symbol: GM	Mkt. Value: $39,309 million
Fax: 313-556-5108	Exchange: NYSE	Employees: 709,000

Web site: http://www.gm.com

Detroit-based General Motors is the #1 automaker in the world. GM produces nearly 80 different vehicle models marketed under the Buick, Chevrolet, Pontiac, Oldsmobile, Cadillac, GMC, and Saturn nameplates. GM has approximately 9,200 motor vehicle dealers in the US and 5,500 such outlets overseas. Almost 30% of its sales come from foreign countries. GM owns Hughes Electronics, which makes automotive, defense, and commercial electronics, including antilock brakes modules, engine controls, radar systems, air traffic control systems, and satellites. The automaker has announced plans to spin off its data processing subsidiary, Electronic Data Systems (EDS), one of the largest such companies in the US.

GENERAL PUBLIC UTILITIES CORPORATION

100 Interpace Parkway	CEO: James R. Leva	1995 Sales: $3,805 million
Parsippany, NJ 07054	CFO: John G. Graham	1995 Profits: $440 million
Phone: 201-263-6500	Symbol: GPU	Mkt. Value: $3,800 million
Fax: 201-263-6822	Exchange: NYSE	Employees: 10,310

Web site: http://www.gpu.com

General Public Utilities is the holding company for Jersey Central Power & Light (JCP&L), Metropolitan Edison (Met-Ed), and Pennsylvania Electric (Penelec), which provide electricity to nearly 2 million customers in New Jersey and Pennsylvania. Another subsidiary, GPU Nuclear, operates and maintains the utilities' nuclear units, including the infamous Three Mile Island plant. GPU generates power from coal (30%), nuclear sources (14%), gas/oil combustion (11%), gas/oil steam (4%), pumped storage (3%), and hydroelectric sources (1%) and purchases the rest. The company is concentrating on expanding business internationally, including the development of power generation projects in Central America.

GENERAL RE CORPORATION

695 E. Main St.	CEO: Ronald E. Ferguson	1995 Sales: $7,210 million
Stamford, CT 06904	CFO: Joseph P. Brandon	1995 Profits: $825 million
Phone: 203-328-5000	Symbol: GRN	Mkt. Value: $11,679 million
Fax: 203-328-5329	Exchange: NYSE	Employees: 3,426

General Re is the parent company of General Reinsurance, the largest property/casualty reinsurer in the US and one of the 3 largest in the world. General Re writes most of its business on an excess-of-loss basis, which pays only after the primary insurer's losses exceed a specific sum. Other lines of business include insurance consulting, aviation insurance, and asset management. Facing a mature US reinsurance market, General Re is expanding overseas to countries such as Germany, where new business is on the rise.

GENUINE PARTS COMPANY

2999 Circle 75 Parkway	CEO: Larry L. Prince	1995 Sales: $5,262 million
Atlanta, GA 30339	CFO: Jerry W. Nix	1995 Profits: $309 million
Phone: 770-953-1700	Symbol: GPC	Mkt. Value: $5,451 million
Fax: 770-956-2212	Exchange: NYSE	Employees: 22,500

252

Genuine Parts Company (GPC) is the nation's top aftermarket auto parts distributor, wholesaling parts from 150 suppliers to retail stores (such as Midas and Montgomery Ward) and job shops (which sell to garages) in the US, Canada, and Mexico. The company offers more than 150,000 replacement parts. The largest member of the National Automotive Parts Association (NAPA), it distributes parts to over 5,100 independently owned NAPA retail stores and operates 64 NAPA parts distribution centers and over 700 NAPA stores in the US. Other operations include remanufacturing auto parts (Raylock), office supply distribution (S. P. Richards), and industrial parts distribution (Berry Bearing, Motion Industries).

"If I had a spare $1 billion in cash, would I put it into the auto business? I doubt it."

— VC Harry Pearce, GM

— Fortune; April 29, 1996

QUOTES

GEORGIA-PACIFIC CORPORATION

133 Peachtree St. N.E.	CEO: A.D. Correll	1995 Sales: $14,292 million
Atlanta, GA 30303	CFO: John F. McGovern	1995 Profits: $1,018 million
Phone: 404-652-4000	Symbol: GP	Mkt. Value: $6,485 million
Fax: 404-521-4422	Exchange: NYSE	Employees: 47,500

75

Georgia-Pacific is the top US manufacturer, distributor, and wholesaler of building products and #2 in forest and paper products. Its manufacturing facilities in the US, Canada, and Mexico produce lumber, siding, doors, and drywall as well as containers, paper, bathroom tissue, paper towels, envelopes, pulp, adhesives, and other items. The company's consumer product brands include Angel Soft, Coronet, Delta, and Sparkle. Georgia-Pacific controls over 6 million acres of timberland in the US and Canada and seeks to expand its softwood forest holdings overseas.

GIANT FOOD INC.

6300 Sheriff Rd.	CEO: Pete L. Manos	1995 Sales: $3,696 million
Landover, MD 20785	CFO: David B. Sykes	1995 Profits: $94 million
Phone: 301-341-4100	Symbol: GFSA	Mkt. Value: $1,894 million
Fax: 301-341-4804	Exchange: AMEX	Employees: 25,000

336

Giant Food operates more than 160 stores in the mid-Atlantic region, primarily Baltimore and Washington, DC. Most are located in shopping centers, 16 of which the company owns through subsidiary GFS Realty. It plans to expand with more than 10 new stores in Delaware, New Jersey, and Pennsylvania. The company also plans to open another 7 stores in its existing markets. Giant Food differs from other grocery retailers in its uncommon degree of vertical integration. Subsidiaries perform site analysis, buy real estate, plan and construct stores, and design advertisements. UK-based food retailer J. Sainsbury owns a stake in the company and may purchase the rest.

THE GILLETTE COMPANY

Prudential Tower Building
Boston, MA 02199
Phone: 617-421-7000
Fax: 617-421-7123

CEO: Alfred M. Zeien
CFO: Thomas F. Skelly
Symbol: G
Exchange: NYSE

1995 Sales: $6,795 million
1995 Profits: $824 million
Mkt. Value: $23,075 million
Employees: 33,500

195

Although best known for its razors and blades (Sensor, Good News, Atra, Trac II), consumer products manufacturer Gillette is also a leader in dental care products (Oral-B), writing instruments (Parker Pen, Paper Mate), and coffee makers (Braun). The company also makes other small appliances (Braun blenders, shavers, and juicers), toiletries (Right Guard, Dry Idea), and stationery products (Liquid Paper). Gillette derives more than 2/3 of its revenues from outside the US and manufactures its products in 28 countries. Gillette invests heavily in R&D to bring a steady stream of new products to market.

GOLDEN WEST FINANCIAL CORPORATION

1901 Harrison St.
Oakland, CA 94612
Phone: 510-446-3420
Fax: 510-446-4259

CEO: H.M. Sandler
CFO: J. L. Helvey
Symbol: GDW
Exchange: NYSE

1995 Sales: $2,470 million
1995 Profits: $235 million
Mkt. Value: $2,903 million
Employees: 4,165

491

Golden West's World Savings & Loan Association, with branches in 7 states (mostly in California and Colorado), is the nation's #3 S&L and one of the nation's strongest financial institutions, with a very low rate of nonperforming loans. Golden West is managed conservatively, providing only savings accounts and residential mortgages and keeping expenses low (branches are small and spartan). It originates home loans throughout the US and owns Atlas Assets, an investment company, and 2 other service corporations (primarily serving Atlas Assets): Atlas Advisors and Atlas Securities.

"Growth: that's what our investors expect of us. If they had wanted security, they would have bought a utility."

—CEO Al Zeien, Gillette

FORTUNE; April 29, 1996

THE GOODYEAR TIRE & RUBBER COMPANY

1144 E. Market St.
Akron, OH 44316
Phone: 330-796-2121
Fax: 330-796-6502

CEO: Samir F. Gibara
CFO: Robert W. Tieken
Symbol: GT
Exchange: NYSE

1995 Sales: $13,166 million
1995 Profits: $611 million
Mkt. Value: $7,868 million
Employees: 87,390

Web site: http://www.goodyear.com

88

The world's largest rubber manufacturer, Goodyear is also the #1 maker of car and truck tires in the US, and the 3rd ranked tire maker in the world. Other products include auto hoses and belts, shoe soles, and industrial chemicals. It operates more than 70 plants in the US and other countries, oversees 6 rubber plantations in Guatemala and Indonesia, and has 1,800 retail stores in the US. Its Celeron subsidiary operates the longest crude oil pipeline in the US (All American Pipeline), which runs between California and Texas. Goodyear sells its Aquatred, Eagle, Intrepid, Tracker ATT, and Workhorse tires to the replacement tire market as well as to automakers and agricultural equipment makers.

GRAYBAR ELECTRIC COMPANY, INC.

34 N. Meramec	CEO: Carl L. Hall	1995 Sales: $2,774 million
St. Louis, MO 63105	CFO: John W. Wolf	1995 Profits: $37 million
Phone: 314-512-9200	Ownership: Privately Held	Employees: 6,200
Fax: 314-512-9453		

Graybar Electric is the world's largest independent distributor of electrical, telephone, and communications equipment. The employee-owned company is divided into 2 business segments: one distributes electrical products such as ballasts, conduits, raceways, lamps and lighting tools, and the other distributes communications and data products including broadband, connectivity, and fiber-optic products. Suppliers include industrial behemoth General Electric and electronics manufacturer Comdial, which provide telecommunications products and services. The company has a minority stake in R.E.D. Electronics, a Canadian computer networking company.

GREAT WESTERN FINANCIAL CORPORATION

9200 Oakdale Ave.	CEO: John Maher	1995 Sales: $3,556 million
Chatsworth, CA 91311	CFO: Carl F. Geuther	1995 Profits: $261 million
Phone: 818-775-3411	Symbol: GWF	Mkt. Value: $3,092 million
Fax: 818-775-3434	Exchange: NYSE	Employees: 14,393

Great Western provides retail banking in California and Florida and offers financial services as well as mortgage banking nationwide. The company's retail banking operation offers financial products and services, including checking and savings accounts, residential mortgage lending, commercial real estate loans, construction and land loans, business loans, and consumer loans. In addition to its retail banking division, it also operates real estate and consumer finance units. The company is actively reducing its dependence on the California market by growing its mortgage business outside the state.

GTE CORPORATION

1 Stamford Forum	CEO: Charles R. Lee	1995 Sales: $19,957 million
Stamford, CT 06904	CFO: J. Michael Kelly	1995 Loss: ($2,144) million
Phone: 203-965-2000	Symbol: GTE	Mkt. Value: $40,465 million
Fax: 203-965-2277	Exchange: NYSE	Employees: 106,000

Web site: http://www.gte.com

GTE is the leading local telephone company in the US and provides traditional wireline telephone services in 28 states. GTE also provides cellular service through its Mobilnet and Contel subsidiaries. The company's Tele-Go personal communications service combines standard telephone service with cellular service and is the first of its kind. Through an alliance with regional Bell operating company SBC Communications, GTE offers both wireline and wireless services in Texas. The company is extending its wireless services in several markets by purchasing broadband spectrum licenses in Atlanta, Seattle, Cincinnati, and Denver.

THE GUARDIAN LIFE INSURANCE COMPANY OF AMERICA

201 Park Ave. S.	CEO: Joseph D. Sargent	1995 Sales: $6,172 million
New York, NY 10003	CFO: Peter L. Hutchings	1995 Profits: $125 million
Phone: 212-598-8000	Ownership: Mutual Company	Employees: 5,322
Fax: 212-598-8813		

The Guardian Life Insurance Company of America offers group and individual life and health insurance; disability, medical, and dental coverage through indemnity policies, HMOs, and PPOs; and variable annuities. Its Guardian Asset Management and Guardian Investor Services units offer a variety of financial services, including the flagship Guardian Park Avenue Fund, the Baillie Gifford International Fund (an international investment fund), and a variety of other equity, money market, and bond funds. The company also provides life, credit, and annuity reinsurance to other insurers. Guardian Life operates in all 50 states and the District of Columbia.

HALLIBURTON COMPANY

3600 Lincoln Plaza	CEO: Richard B. Cheney	1995 Sales: $5,951 million
Dallas, TX 75201	CFO: David J. Lesar	1995 Profits: $168 million
Phone: 214-978-2600	Symbol: HAL	Mkt. Value: $6,611 million
Fax: 214-978-2611	Exchange: NYSE	Employees: 57,300

Web site: http://www.halliburton.com

Halliburton is one of the world's largest energy, engineering, and construction services companies. Subsidiary Halliburton Energy Services provides equipment and services for oil exploration, development, and production, as well as construction and mainte- nance of oil refineries. Its Brown & Root unit provides engineering and construction services, including technical and economic feasibility studies, site evaluation, engi- neering, construction management, and environmental consulting. Its Highland Insurance unit pro- vides property and casualty insurance, but Halliburton has announced that it will exit this business by spinning off Highland to shareholders.

HANNAFORD BROS. CO.

145 Pleasant Hill Rd.	CEO: Hugh G. Farrington	1995 Sales: $2,568 million
Scarborough, ME 04074	CFO: Blyth McGarvie	1995 Profits: $70 million
Phone: 207-883-2911	Symbol: HRD	Mkt. Value: $1,152 million
Fax: 207-885-3165	Exchange: NYSE	Employees: 20,438

Web site: http://www.hannaford.com

Food retailer Hannaford has more than 130 stores in Maine, New Hampshire, New York, Massachusetts, Vermont, North Carolina, South Carolina, and Virginia. Its stores are op- erated under the names Shop 'n Save, Sun Foods, and Wilson's. Of Hannaford's nearly 100 stores in the northeastern US, more than 75% are either new or have been remod- eled in the past 10 years. More than 60 company stores are combination stores, with tra- ditional supermarket departments along with much-expanded general merchandise sections. Hannaford bought 28 stores in Virginia and North and South Carolina in 1994 and 1995.

HARCOURT GENERAL, INC.

27 Boylston St.	CEO: Robert J. Tarr Jr.	1995 Sales: $3,242 million
Chestnut Hill, MA 02167	CFO: John R. Cook	1995 Profits: $166 million
Phone: 617-232-8200	Symbol: H	Mkt. Value: $3,351 million
Fax: 617-278-5397	Exchange: NYSE	Employees: 16,935

Web site: http://www.harcourtbrace.com

Harcourt General is a publishing, specialty retail, and professional services company. It owns Harcourt Brace & Company, which publishes scientific, technical, and profes- sional books and journals as well as children's books and general adult fiction and non- fiction. It also owns several other publishers, including Holt, Rinehart and Winston, the Psychological Corp., and WB Saunders. Harcourt General derives roughly 2/3 of its rev- enues from its 67% interest in the Neiman Marcus Group, which operates fashion and specialty re- tailers Neiman Marcus and Bergdorf Goodman. The company offers outplacement consulting through its Drake Beam Morin subsidiary.

HARRIS CORPORATION

1025 W. NASA Blvd.	CEO: Phillip W. Farmer	1995 Sales: $3,481 million
Melbourne, FL 32919	CFO: Bryan R. Roub	1995 Profits: $155 million
Phone: 407-727-9100	Symbol: HRS	Mkt. Value: $2,578 million
Fax: 407-727-9344	Exchange: NYSE	Employees: 26,600

Web site: http://www.harris.com

Defense electronics manufacturer Harris Corporation has 4 main lines of business: electronic systems, information management equipment, semiconductors, and com- munications equipment. Products include air traffic control systems, avionics, energy management systems, mobile radio networks, office products (Lanier), integrated cir- cuits, semiconductors, 2-way radios, digital telephone switches, and microwave systems. The company relies heavily on R&D to produce innovative products such as the CyberGuard Firewall, a computer system that protects networks against intruders attempting to gain access from the Internet.

Derry Church, Pennsylvania has been known by its most influential business's name since 1906 when the company's name was adopted for the town. The company? **Hershey Foods Corporation.** The town — Hershey, Pennsylvania.

— *Hoover's Handbook of American Business 1996*

HASBRO, INC.

1027 Newport Ave.	CEO: Alan G. Hassenfeld	1995 Sales: $2,858 million
Pawtucket, RI 02862	CFO: John T. O'Neill	1995 Profits: $156 million
Phone: 401-431-8697	Symbol: HAS	Mkt. Value: $3,091 million
Fax: 401-431-8535	Exchange: AMEX	Employees: 13,000

Web site: http://www.gijoe.com/

Hasbro is the #2 toy manufacturer in the US (after Mattel) and the maker of such childhood favorites as G.I. Joe, Play-Doh, Monopoly, and Trivial Pursuit. The company is organized into a Toy Group, which includes its Playskool, Playskool Baby, Hasbro, Kid Dimension, and Kenner lines, and a Games Group, which includes its 2 games companies, Milton Bradley and Parker Brothers. Hasbro is looking to regain its #1 position in the toy industry through acquisitions (Western Publishing's puzzle and board game line) and by introducing new toys based on movies, comics, and TV shows (*Batman Forever, The Mask*).

HEALTH SYSTEMS INTERNATIONAL, INC.

21600 Oxnard St.	CEO: M.M. Hasan	1995 Sales: $2,732 million
Woodland Hills, CA 91367	CFO: E. Keith Hovland	1995 Profits: $90 million
Phone: 719-542-0500	Symbol: HQ	Mkt. Value: $1,787 million
Fax: 719-542-8402	Exchange: NYSE	Employees: 2,500

Health Systems International provides managed health care services primarily in the western and northwestern US. The company operates health maintenance organizations (HMOs) through subsidiaries Health Net (one of California's top HMOs), QualMed, and M.D. Enterprises of Connecticut; a preferred provider organization (PPO) network; 2 health and life insurance companies (Health Net Life and QualMed Health & Life Insurance); and a reinsurance company (HN Reinsurance). A proposed merger with Wellpoint Health Networks that would have formed the nation's largest for-profit HMO fell apart in late 1995 when neither side could agree on who would control the new entity.

HERSHEY FOODS CORPORATION

100 Crystal A Dr.	CEO: Kenneth L. Wolfe	1995 Sales: $3,691 million
Hershey, PA 17033	CFO: William F. Christ	1995 Profits: $282 million
Phone: 717-534-4000	Symbol: HSY	Mkt. Value: $5,700 million
Fax: 717-534-4078	Exchange: NYSE	Employees: 13,300

Web site: http://www.hersheys.com

The market leader in the US candy business (ahead of Mars), Hershey produces such confections as Hershey's Kisses, Reese's peanut butter cups, York peppermint patties, Twizzlers licorice, and Kit Kat, Oh Henry!, and Skor candy bars. It also makes chocolate and chocolate-related baking products, ice cream toppings, and chocolate syrup. However, Hershey is not all sweetness and chocolate. The company is also the biggest seller of pasta in the US (ahead of Borden) with brand names such as Skinner, Ronzoni, Delmonico, and American Beauty. Other grocery items include peanut butter and milk products.

HEWLETT-PACKARD COMPANY

3000 Hanover St.	CEO: Lewis E. Platt	1995 Sales: $31,519 million
Palo Alto, CA 94304	CFO: Robert P. Wayman	1995 Profits: $2,433 million
Phone: 415-857-1501	Symbol: HWP	Mkt. Value: $50,932 million
Fax: 415-857-5518	Exchange: NYSE	Employees: 102,300

Web site: http://www.hp.com

Hewlett-Packard is one of the world's most innovative and consistently successful high-tech companies. HP products include servers, computers, and workstations for home and business (Pavilion and Vectra PCs, HP OmniGo handheld computers, HP 9000 servers), networking software and equipment (HP-UX UNIX), storage devices (SureStore series), printers (LaserJet, DeskJet), measurement and testing equipment (acceSS7 network performance monitoring software), and medical products (CareVue computerized medical information system, i-STAT blood analysis equipment). Its products and services are used in industry, business, engineering, science, medicine, and education.

H.F. AHMANSON & COMPANY

4900 Rivergrade Rd.	CEO: Charles Rinehart	1995 Sales: $4,398 million
Irwindale, CA 91706	CFO: Kevin M. Twomey	1995 Profits: $216 million
Phone: 818-960-6311	Symbol: AHM	Mkt. Value: $2,702 million
Fax: 818-814-3675	Exchange: NYSE	Employees: 9,344

H.F. Ahmanson is the holding company for Home Savings of America, the US's largest savings institution and one of the largest mortgage lenders and servicers. Ahmanson provides a variety of financial products and services to its customers, including annuities, deposit services, consumer loans, life insurance, mortgage loans, mutual funds, and property and casualty insurance. Stung by mortgage losses, the company is adding significantly to its nonmortgage income by offering home equity and consumer loans and by increasing sales of investment products and insurance offered through its Griffin Financial Services subsidiary.

H.J. HEINZ COMPANY

600 Grant St.	CEO: Anthony J.F. O'Reilly	1995 Sales: $8,087 million
Pittsburgh, PA 15219	CFO: David R. Williams	1995 Profits: $591 million
Phone: 412-456-5700	Symbol: HNZ	Mkt. Value: $12,615 million
Fax: 412-237-7883	Exchange: NYSE	Employees: 42,200

Web site: http://www.hjheinz.com

Best known for its ubiquitous ketchup, H. J. Heinz is one of the leading food processors in the world. Through its Heinz and other well-known brand names — among them Ore-Ida, Star-Kist, and 9 Lives — the company has strong market position in the US in several areas, including ketchup (52%), frozen potatoes (49%), tuna (45%), and canned cat food (32%). Its Weight Watchers diet program is also a US market leader. Heinz has a strong international presence, deriving more than 40% of its revenues from foreign operations. The company has boosted its sales recently with over a billion dollars in domestic and foreign acquisitions and is emphasizing its expansion in developing markets.

One of the first customers of **Hewlett-Packard** (founded in 1938) was Walt Disney Studios, which purchased 8 of the company's oscillators to use in the making of *Fantasia*.

— Hoover's Guide to Computer Companies

THE HOME DEPOT, INC.

2727 Paces Ferry Rd. N.W.
Atlanta, GA 30339
Phone: 770-433-8211
Fax: 770-431-2707

CEO: Bernard Marcus
CFO: Marshall L. Day
Symbol: HD
Exchange: NYSE

1995 Sales: $15,470 million
1995 Profits: $732 million
Mkt. Value: $23,603 million
Employees: 80,000

Web site: http://www.homedepot.com

The Home Depot caters to both do-it-yourselfers and professional contractors. It is the largest home center retailer in the US and continues to expand by adding more outlets across the US and Canada. The typical store contains more than 100,000 square feet of space and stocks 40,000-50,000 kinds of home improvement materials, including lumber, floor and wall coverings, plumbing supplies, hardware, tools, and paint. The company's strategy stresses superior customer service, low prices, and broad product assortment.

HONEYWELL INC.

Honeywell Plaza
Minneapolis, MN 55408
Phone: 612-951-1000
Fax: 612-951-0137

CEO: Michael R. Bonsignore
CFO: William M. Hjerpe
Symbol: HON
Exchange: NYSE

1995 Sales: $6,731 million
1995 Profits: $334 million
Mkt. Value: $6,793 million
Employees: 50,100

Web site: http://www.honeywell.com/

Honeywell is one of the world's leading makers of control systems and components for buildings, homes, industry, space, and aviation. Its home and building control products include building automation systems, energy management equipment, fire protection and security control devices, and the Duracraft line of heaters and humidifiers. Honeywell's industrial products division makes automation and control products, field instrumentation, and vision-based sensors. The space and aviation division manufactures commercial, military, and space avionics equipment. The company, which has operations in nearly 100 countries, is looking for further international expansion to help fuel future growth.

HORMEL FOODS CORPORATION

1 Hormel Place
Austin, MN 55912
Phone: 507-437-5611
Fax: 507-437-5489

CEO: Joel W. Johnson
CFO: Don J. Hodapp
Symbol: HRL
Exchange: NYSE

1995 Sales: $3,046 million
1995 Profits: $120 million
Mkt. Value: $1,956 million
Employees: 10,600

Web site: http://www.webauthor.com/corp/hrl_6.htm

Hormel Foods is a diversified food producer. Perhaps best known for its SPAM canned meat, the company also offers Farm Fresh catfish, Jennie-O turkey roast, Dinty Moore beef stew, Quick Meal frozen foods, and Hormel chili. Other products include Peloponnese olive oil and stuffed grape leaves, Chi-Chi's salsa, and House of Tsang oils, marinades, and sauces. Meat products are still the biggest revenue generators at Hormel, constituting over half its sales. The company operates processing and packaging facilities in 12 states and sells its products in more than 40 countries.

HOUSEHOLD INTERNATIONAL, INC.

2700 Sanders Rd.
Prospect Heights, IL 60070
Phone: 708-564-5000
Fax: 847-205-7490

CEO: William F. Aldinger III
CFO: David A. Schoenholz
Symbol: HI
Exchange: NYSE

1995 Sales: $5,144 million
1995 Profits: $453 million
Mkt. Value: $6,537 million
Employees: 13,066

Household International is a leading provider of consumer loans. It also makes secured (home equity) and unsecured consumer loans through its primary subsidiary, Household Finance. One of the top issuers of credit cards in the US, Household International's credit card business is booming on the strength of private and affinity cards (like the GM Card, which allows users to earn points toward buying a car). The company offers life and credit insurance and commercial vehicle and equipment leasing. It also provides commercial loans in a joint venture with Dominion Resources.

HOUSTON INDUSTRIES INCORPORATED

1111 Louisiana	CEO: Don D. Jordan	1995 Sales: $4,388 million
Houston, TX 77002	CFO: William Cropper	1995 Profits: $1,124 million
Phone: 713-207-3000	Symbol: HOU	Mkt. Value: $5,746 million
Fax: 713-207-0206	Exchange: NYSE	Employees: 8,891

Houston Industries is a holding company for Houston Lighting & Power (HL&P), which provides electric service to more than 1.4 million customers in a 5,000-square-mile area along the Texas Gulf Coast. The company's Houston Industries Energy (HI Energy) subsidiary pursues domestic and international independent natural gas power projects and invests in privatized foreign electric utilities, particularly in fast-growing markets such as Asia and Latin America. HI Energy owns a controlling interest in Argentina's Santiago del Estero electric utility system, which serves more than 100,000 customers in that country.

HUMANA INC.

500 W. Main St.	CEO: David A. Jones	1995 Sales: $4,702 million
Louisville, KY 40202	CFO: W. Roger Drury	1995 Profits: $190 million
Phone: 502-580-1000	Symbol: HUM	Mkt. Value: $3,885 million
Fax: 502-580-3615	Exchange: NYSE	Employees: 16,800

Web site: http://www.Humana.com

A managed health care company, Humana offers a range of health maintenance organizations (HMOs), preferred-provider organizations (PPOs), and Medicare supplement insurance to more than 3.8 million members in 22 states and the District of Columbia, primarily in the South and Midwest. Humana controls health care costs by various means, including requiring preadmission approval for hospital inpatient services and preauthorization of outpatient surgical procedures. A significant portion of its revenues comes from Medicare payments. Humana's HMO and PPO products are marketed primarily to employers and other groups and Medicare-eligible individuals.

IBP, INC.

IBP Ave.	CEO: Robert L. Peterson	1995 Sales: $12,668 million
Dakota City, NE 68731	CFO: Lonnie O. Grigsby	1995 Profits: $258 million
Phone: 402-494-2061	Symbol: IBP	Mkt. Value: $2,286 million
Fax: 402-241-2063	Exchange: NYSE	Employees: 34,000

The world's largest producer of fresh beef and pork, IBP processes more than 9 billion pounds of meat per year, almost 15% of the US total. Products include boxed beef and pork, deli meats, cooked hams, hides, and animal by-products (used for animal feeds, cosmetics, pharmaceuticals, and other applications). IBP sells to grocery chains, meat distributors, wholesalers, restaurant chains, and food processors. It also owns Lakeside Farm Industries, Canada's 2nd largest slaughterhouse. The company markets low-cost meats in Eastern Europe and Russia and produces pork through a joint venture with Japan's Nippon Meat Packers.

ILLINOIS TOOL WORKS INC.

3600 W. Lake Ave.	CEO: W. James Farrell	1995 Sales: $4,152 million
Glenview, IL 60025	CFO: Michael W. Gregg	1995 Profits: $388 million
Phone: 708-724-7500	Symbol: ITW	Mkt. Value: $7,861 million
Fax: 847-657-4261	Exchange: NYSE	Employees: 21,200

Illinois Tool Works (ITW) makes an extensive range of equipment for the automotive, construction, food and beverage, and general industry markets worldwide. The company operates in 2 business segments: Engineered Components and Industrial Systems and Consumables. The Engineered Components unit produces adhesives, polymers, arc welding equipment, automobile door handles, nails, staples, and screws. Its Industrial Systems and Consumables unit makes spray guns, hot stamp imprinters, paint curing systems, paper packaging systems, and strapping machinery. ITW uses small, decentralized business units to be more responsive to its customers.

INGERSOLL-RAND COMPANY

200 Chestnut Ridge Rd.	CEO: James E. Perrella	1995 Sales: $5,729 million
Woodcliff Lake, NJ 07675	CFO: Thomas F. McBride	1995 Profits: $270 million
Phone: 201-573-0123	Symbol: IR	Mkt. Value: $4,492 million
Fax: 201-573-3448	Exchange: NYSE	Employees: 41,133

Web site: http://www.ingersoll-rand.com

Ingersoll-Rand is a leading worldwide manufacturer of nonelectrical industrial machinery and air compression systems, antifriction bearings, construction equipment, air tools, and water pumps. Other products include locks and lock sets for industrial, commercial, and residential applications; steel doors, primarily for commercial buildings; drivetrain components for off-highway vehicles; and golf carts and utility vehicles. More than half of Ingersoll-Rand's 100 manufacturing facilities are located outside the US, and about 40% of the company's sales come from overseas. The company is continuing its overseas expansion, with an emphasis on the Asia/Pacific region.

INLAND STEEL INDUSTRIES, INC.

30 W. Monroe St.	CEO: Robert J. Darnall	1995 Sales: $4,782 million
Chicago, IL 60603	CFO: Earl L. Mason	1995 Profits: $147 million
Phone: 312-346-0300	Symbol: IAD	Mkt. Value: $1,256 million
Fax: 312-899-3197	Exchange: NYSE	Employees: 15,410

Web site: http://www.inland.com

Inland Steel Industries is a holding company with 3 operating units that make and sell steel (Inland Steel Co.), distribute industrial materials nationally (Inland Materials Distribution Group), and trade steel and other industrial materials internationally (Inland International, Inc.). Inland Steel annually produces more than 5.5 million tons of steel, which it sells to automobile, appliance, and office furniture makers. Inland Materials Distribution Group, the largest metals distributor in the US, operates more than 50 US steel service centers and metals distribution and processing centers. Inland International sells, trades, and distributes steel products and other industrial materials worldwide.

INTEL CORPORATION

2200 Mission College Blvd.	CEO: Andrew S. Grove	1995 Sales: $16,202 million
Santa Clara, CA 95052	CFO: Andy D. Bryant	1995 Profits: $3,566 million
Phone: 408-765-8080	Symbol: INTC	Mkt. Value: $48,348 million
Fax: 408-765-1402	Exchange: Nasdaq	Employees: 41,600

Web site: http://www.intel.com

Intel is the world's #1 maker of microprocessors. Its x86, Pentium, and Pentium Pro microprocessors have provided the brains for personal computers since 1981. The company also makes computer microcontrollers, random access memory (RAM) cards, networking products like EtherExpress adapters, FastEthernet cards and servers, and conferencing equipment such as the ProShareVideo System. Intel is expanding and updating its facilities to meet desktop computing demands and to fight off upstart chip maker Cyrix as well as old nemesis Advanced Micro Devices.

Extendicare, now known as **Humana**, shifted its focus from old age to illness in the late 1960s and, as a result, got very healthy very fast. By selling off its 40 nursing homes to finance expansion into hospitals, the company pushed sales from $7.7 million in 1968 to $106 million in 1973.

— Hoover's Handbook of American Business 1996

For the 3rd year running, **IBM** won the crown for bright ideas in 1995, qualifying for a total of 1,383 US patents (that's more than 5 per working day). The company, as far down as No. 9 in 1990, had a hefty lead over Canon, the runner-up at 1,088. Rounding out the top 5 were Motorola, NEC, and Mitsubishi.

— *Business Week;* March 25, 1996

INTELLIGENT ELECTRONICS, INC.

411 Eagleview Blvd.	CEO: Richard D. Sanford	1995 Sales: $3,475 million
Exton, PA 19341	CFO: Edward A. Meltzer	1995 Loss: ($19) million
Phone: 610-458-5500	Symbol: INEL	Mkt. Value: $216 million
Fax: 610-458-6702	Exchange: Nasdaq	Employees: 3,500

Web site: http://www.intelect.com

358 Intelligent Electronics (IE) sells computers, workstations, networking and telecommunications equipment, and software to corporate customers, educational institutions, and government agencies nationwide. It is one of the leading wholesaler/resellers of technology products and services in the US. IE also provides financing and marketing programs and configuration, promotion, and technical support to more than 2,500 network integrators, including Intelligent Systems Group, Entre Computer Centers, Todays Computers Business Centers, and Connecting Point of America. IE operates 4 distribution centers, one in Memphis and 3 in the Denver area.

INTERNATIONAL BUSINESS MACHINES CORPORATION

Old Orchard Rd.	CEO: Louis V. Gerstner Jr.	1995 Sales: $71,940 million
Armonk, NY 10504	CFO: G. Richard Thoman	1995 Profits: $4,178 million
Phone: 914-765-1900	Symbol: IBM	Mkt. Value: $68,257 million
Fax: 914-288-1147	Exchange: NYSE	Employees: 252,215

Web site: http://www.ibm.com

6 The world's top computer company, IBM has broadened its focus from strictly mainframes (System/390) and minicomputers (AS/400) to open systems. Its offerings include PCs, software, networking (LAN Server network operating system, SystemView systems management software) and client/server products (DB2, a relational database management system). The most notable result of this change in strategy was IBM's acquisition of software pioneer Lotus, developer of the Lotus Notes messaging system. Other IBM products include AIX (IBM's flavor of UNIX), UNIX-based servers (RISC System/6000), and OS/2, IBM's failing answer to the Windows operating system. The company has also set up 2 separate Internet information services, infoSage and infoMarket.

INTERNATIONAL PAPER COMPANY

2 Manhattanville Rd.	CEO: John T. Dillon	1995 Sales: $19,797 million
Purchase, NY 10577	CFO: Marianne M. Parrs	1995 Profits: $1,153 million
Phone: 914-397-1500	Symbol: IP	Mkt. Value: $10,244 million
Fax: 914-397-1928	Exchange: NYSE	Employees: 81,500

Web site: http://www.ipaper.com

39 New York-based International Paper is the world's leading producer of forest products and a leading distributor of paper and office supplies. More diverse (and less international) than its name suggests, the company's nonpaper offerings include chemicals (Arizona Chemical), nonwoven fabrics (Veratec), oil and gas, and photographic films (Anitec, Horsell, Ilford). It is trying to live up to its name by acquiring overseas companies and forming joint ventures abroad. The US market accounts for nearly 80% of the company's sales.

ITT CORPORATION

1330 Sixth Ave.	CEO: Rand V. Araskog	1995 Sales: $6,346 million
New York, NY 10020	CFO: Ann N. Reese	1995 Profits: $147 million
Phone: 212-258-1000	Symbol: ITT	Mkt. Value: $7,099 million
Fax: 212-258-1297	Exchange: NYSE	Employees: 38,000

Web site: http://www.ittinfo.com

ITT Corp. operates in the hospitality, gambling, and sports entertainment industries. It owns the 425-hotel Sheraton chain and the 3 Caesars World hotel/casinos, including the flagship Caesars Palace in Las Vegas. ITT's sports entertainment holdings include a 50% stake in Madison Square Garden, comprising the arena, the 5,600-seat Paramount Theater, the MSG Network (cable sports), and the New York Knicks and New York Rangers. The company's focus on hospitality and entertainment is part of a restructuring carried out in late 1995 that included the spin-off of its insurance unit and its electronics and defense business.

ITT HARTFORD GROUP, INC.

Hartford Plaza	CEO: Donald Frahm	1995 Sales: $12,150 million
Hartford, CT 06115	CFO: David K. Zwiener	1995 Profits: $559 million
Phone: 860-547-5000	Symbol: HIG	Mkt. Value: $5,518 million
Fax: 860-547-3799	Exchange: NYSE	Employees: 21,000

Web site: http://www.itthartford.com

ITT Hartford Group's primary operating unit, Hartford Fire Insurance, offers a variety of personal and commercial property/casualty insurance products, including homeowners, auto, and workers' compensation. Hartford Life offers individual and group life insurance, annuities, employee benefits administration, and asset management. ITT Hartford has also joined with Health Net, a California-based HMO, to design a new workers' compensation management plan. The company has emerged as a result of the breakup of parent company ITT Corporation into 3 companies; the other 2 are ITT Industries (manufacturing) and the new ITT Corp. (hospitality, gambling, and sports entertainment).

ITT INDUSTRIES, INC.

4 West Red Oak Lane	CEO: D. Travis Engen	1995 Sales: $8,884 million
White Plains, NY 10604	CFO: Heidi Kunz	1995 Profits: $708 million
Phone: 914-641-2000	Symbol: IIN	Mkt. Value: $2,971 million
Fax: 914-696-2950	Exchange: NYSE	Employees: 58,000

ITT Industries is a holding company with subsidiaries that manufacture and market automotive, defense electronic, and fluid technology products. The ITT Automotive subsidiary makes brake and chassis systems, including antilock brakes, fluid-handling components, and foundation brake components. ITT Defense & Electronics makes electronic warfare systems, interconnect products, night-vision devices, and radar equipment. ITT Fluid Technology makes fluid controls, mixers, pumps, and valves. The company was created in late 1995 when ITT Corporation restructured, splitting into 3 companies: ITT Industries, ITT Corp. (hospitality, gambling, and sports entertainment), and ITT Hartford (insurance).

JAMES RIVER CORPORATION OF VIRGINIA

120 Tredegar St.	CEO: Miles L. Marsh	1995 Sales: $6,800 million
Richmond, VA 23219	CFO: Stephen E. Hare	1995 Profits: $126 million
Phone: 804-644-5411	Symbol: JR	Mkt. Value: $2,385 million
Fax: 804-649-4428	Exchange: NYSE	Employees: 27,250

Web site: http://www.jrc.com

A major international paper manufacturer, James River is one of the top 4 US makers of paper towel and tissue products, manufacturing products under such brand names as Chelsea, Nice 'n Soft, Quilted Northern, Vanity Fair, and Brawny. It also produces paper and plastic beverage and food service products (Dixie plates and cups, #1 in the commercial food service industry), and it makes cereal boxes, ice cream cartons, potato chip bags, and plastic sandwich wrapping for the retail food and consumer products market. James River owns 86% of Jamont, Europe's #3 paper producer.

J. C. PENNEY COMPANY, INC.

6501 Legacy Dr.
Plano, TX 75024
Phone: 214-431-1000
Fax: 214-431-1977

CEO: James E. Oesterreicher
CFO: Donald A. McKay
Symbol: JCP
Exchange: NYSE

1995 Sales: $21,419 million
1995 Profits: $838 million
Mkt. Value: $11,212 million
Employees: 205,000

Web site: http://www.jcpenney.com

J. C. Penney is the US's #5 retailer. It sells clothing, home furnishings, jewelry, shoes, and accessories. In addition, it operates an insurance company (JCPenney Insurance), a credit bank (JCPenney National Bank), and drug stores (Thrift Drug). CEO James Oesterreicher is working to boost Penney's market share by cutting costs to keep prices down. At the same time he is strengthening the company's emphasis on private-label products (Arizona, Stafford, and Worthington), which account for approximately half of Penney's merchandise. J. C. Penney operates 1,233 JCPenney retail stores and 526 drugstores throughout all 50 states and Puerto Rico, as well as 6 distribution centers.

JEFFERSON SMURFIT CORPORATION

8182 Maryland Ave.
St. Louis, MO 63105
Phone: 314-746-1100
Fax: 314-746-1281

CEO: James E. Terrill
CFO: John R. Funke
Symbol: JJSC
Exchange: Nasdaq

1995 Sales: $4,093 million
1995 Profits: $243 million
Mkt. Value: $1,263 million
Employees: 16,200

Jefferson Smurfit is the #3 producer of newsprint in the US, the #4 corrugated container maker, and the #1 producer of newsprint made from more than 40% recycled content. It also makes folding cartons, labels, and paper tubes and cores. In addition, the company has diversified into making fragranced advertising products, punch-card election ballots, and patented building material made from recycled paper (Cladwood siding and WindowMate shutters). It is recovering from the early 1990s slump in paper prices and is focusing on innovative ways to use recycled paper to manufacture consumer products.

JOHN HANCOCK MUTUAL LIFE INSURANCE COMPANY

John Hancock Place
Boston, MA 02117
Phone: 617-572-6000
Fax: 617-572-6451

CEO: Stephen Lee Brown
CFO: Thomas E. Moloney
Ownership: Mutual Company

1995 Sales: $5,846 million
1995 Profits: $341 million
Employees: 7,996

John Hancock Mutual Life Insurance is an insurance and financial services company. In addition to its traditional life insurance products and annuities, the firm offers health plans (including long-term care plans) and accelerated death benefits options known as viatical settlements, which provide income to terminally ill people to cover their medical expenses. The corporation has been acquiring investment firms, brokerages, and mutual fund companies, and it recently launched a new holding company, John Hancock Asset Management, for these businesses and older units such as its timber and agricultural funds. John Hancock operates throughout the US and in Belgium, Canada, Indonesia, and the UK.

JOHNSON & JOHNSON

1 J&J Plaza
New Brunswick, NJ 08933
Phone: 908-524-0400
Fax: 908-524-3300

CEO: Ralph S. Larsen
CFO: Clark H. Johnson
Symbol: JNJ
Exchange: NYSE

1995 Sales: $18,842 million
1995 Profits: $2,403 million
Mkt. Value: $62,630 million
Employees: 82,300

Web site: http://www.jnj.com

Johnson & Johnson (J&J) is a diversified health care manufacturer, whose products range from a leading pain reliever (Tylenol) to the world's #1 contact lens brand (Acuvue). The company operates in 3 sectors: consumer products (with brands like Reach toothbrushes and Band-Aid bandages), professional products (ranging from surgical instruments to joint replacements), and pharmaceuticals (including Hismanal antihistamine and Ergamisol cancer treatment). J&J created Johnson and Johnson Health Care Systems to help its managed care customers better serve their clients. In addition, the company continues to focus on international expansion.

JOHNSON CONTROLS, INC.

5757 N. Green Bay Ave.	CEO: James H. Keyes	1995 Sales: $8,330 million
Milwaukee, WI 53209	CFO: Stephen A. Roell	1995 Profits: $196 million
Phone: 414-228-1200	Symbol: JCI	Mkt. Value: $2,910 million
Fax: 414-228-2302	Exchange: NYSE	Employees: 59,200

Web site: http://www.jci.com

160

Johnson Controls has operations in building controls, automotive products, plastics, and batteries. Its Automotive Division is the world's largest independent auto seating supplier to US and foreign automakers. The Controls Division makes, installs, and services control systems and offers on-site facility management in nonresidential buildings. The Plastics Technology Group makes plastic containers for beverages, food, personal care, and household items and also manufactures, installs, and services plastics blowmolding systems. The Battery Group makes auto batteries for the replacement and original equipment markets as well as specialty batteries for telecommunications and uninterruptible power supplies.

J.P. MORGAN & CO. INCORPORATED

60 Wall St.	CEO: Douglas A. Warner III	1995 Sales: $13,838 million
New York, NY 10260	CFO: John A. Meyer	1995 Profits: $1,296 million
Phone: 212-483-2323	Symbol: JPM	Mkt. Value: $15,004 million
Fax: 212-648-5193	Exchange: NYSE	Employees: 15,600

Web site: http://www.jpmorgan.com

76

J.P. Morgan is one of the US's premier international banking companies, with offices in 7 US cities and 35 other countries. Its primary subsidiary is Morgan Guaranty Trust, a major dealer in government securities, derivatives, and currencies for a worldwide clientele. J.P. Morgan also offers asset and liability management, sales and trading, and equity investment. It has traditionally been a client-centered bank, but it is also increasing efforts to derive a greater amount of income from trading for its own account.

The first wheat flakes were made in 1894 by **William Kellogg** and his brother, **Dr. John Kellogg**, at Battle Creek's famed homeopathic sanitarium. While experimenting with grains for patients' diets they were interrupted, and a dough they had been preparing absorbed too much water. They toasted the dough, and voila: cereal.

— Hoover's Handbook of American Companies 1996

KELLOGG COMPANY

1 Kellogg Square	CEO: Arnold G. Langbo	1995 Sales: $7,004 million
Battle Creek, MI 49016	CFO: John R. Hinton	1995 Profits: $490 million
Phone: 616-961-2000	Symbol: K	Mkt. Value: $16,688 million
Fax: 616-961-2871	Exchange: NYSE	Employees: 14,487

Web site: http://www.kelloggs.com

187

Kellogg is the world's largest maker of ready-to-eat cereals (ahead of #2 General Mills), with a market share of more than 40%. Among the company's famous brand names are Kellogg's Frosted Flakes, Special K, Rice Krispies, Product 19, Froot Loops, Apple Jacks, and All-Bran. It also produces frozen foods (Eggo Waffles), snack foods (Nutri-Grain Bars), other breakfast foods (Pop Tarts), and health foods (Healthy Choice). The company, which manufactures its products in 20 countries and sells them in nearly 160, continues to expand its overseas markets.

KELLY SERVICES, INC.

999 W. Big Beaver Rd.
Troy, MI 48084
Phone: 810-362-4444
Fax: 810-244-4853

CEO: Terence E. Adderley
CFO: Paul K. Geiger
Symbol: KELYA
Exchange: Nasdaq

1995 Sales: $2,690 million
1995 Profits: $70 million
Mkt. Value: $1,140 million
Employees: 5,600

Web site: http://www.kellyservices.com

One of the top 3 temporary personnel companies (with Manpower and Olsten), Kelly Services provides more than 650,000 employees to some 200,000 customers. Kelly's primary subsidiary, Temporary Services, has benefited from structural economic changes that have made it preferable for some companies to keep employment rolls lean and use temps when demand surges. Once a business dealing primarily with clerical help, it has expanded to include technical and professional employees, which Kelly provides in addition to light-industry workers. Another subsidiary, Kelly Assisted Living Services, provides personal care and daily living assistance to people who need care at home.

The first throw-away handkerchief appeared in 1924 when **Kimberly & Clark Co.** introduced its Kleenex tissue.

— Hoover's Guide to the Top Texas Companies

IDEAS

KERR-MCGEE CORPORATION

123 Robert S. Kerr Ave.
Oklahoma City, OK 73102
Phone: 405-270-1313
Fax: 405-270-3029

CEO: Frank A. McPherson
CFO: John C. Linehan
Symbol: KMG
Exchange: NYSE

1995 Sales: $2,928 million
1995 Loss: ($31) million
Mkt. Value: $3,244 million
Employees: 3,976

Kerr-McGee is an international energy and chemicals company, with operations in oil and gas, coal, and inorganic chemicals. It explores for and produces oil and natural gas in Canada, the Gulf of Mexico, the North Sea (where 50% of its oil is produced), and the South China Sea, and it has low-sulfur coal mining activities in Illinois, West Virginia, and Wyoming. The company also produces industrial and specialty chemicals, railroad crossties (45% of the US market), and heavy minerals at plants in the US, Australia, and Saudi Arabia.

KEYCORP

127 Public Square
Cleveland, OH 44114
Phone: 216-689-6300
Fax: 216-689-0519

CEO: Robert W. Gillespie
CFO: K. Brent Somers
Symbol: KEY
Exchange: NYSE

1995 Sales: $6,054 million
1995 Profits: $825 million
Mkt. Value: $8,671 million
Employees: 28,905

KeyCorp is active in insurance, investment management, and corporate and retail banking. Services include checking and savings accounts, loans (consumer, commercial, mortgage, and auto), credit cards, leasing, mortgage banking, securities brokerage, and trust services. One of the US's more geographically diverse banking companies, with branches from Alaska to Florida, most of Keycorp's branches are located in the Northeast and Midwest. KeyCorp is focusing on increasing its market share in the small-business lending market and stepping up sales of investment products (including mutual funds) in small towns that are underserved by other financial companies.

KIMBERLY-CLARK CORPORATION

351 Phelps Dr.
Irving, TX 75038
Phone: 214-281-1200
Fax: 214-281-1490

CEO: Wayne R. Sanders
CFO: John W. Donehower
Symbol: KMB
Exchange: NYSE

1995 Sales: $13,789 million
1995 Profits: $33 million
Mkt. Value: $21,271 million
Employees: 55,341

78

Kimberly-Clark is one of the world's top 2 providers of personal paper products (the other is Procter & Gamble) and ranks 3rd nationally in forest and paper products (behind International Paper and Georgia-Pacific). Its products include Huggies disposable diapers and Kleenex tissues (both US market leaders); Kotex, New Freedom, and Lightdays feminine hygiene products; Hi-Dri paper towels; Neenah papers; and newsprint. Kimberly-Clark has plants in about 2 dozen countries and 700,000 acres of timberland. It has focused more on its core business by acquiring Scott Paper for $9.4 billion and moving to sell its stake in Midwest Air Holdings.

KMART CORPORATION

3100 W. Big Beaver Rd.
Troy, MI 48084
Phone: 810-643-1000
Fax: 810-643-5249

CEO: Floyd Hall
CFO: Martin E. Welch III
Symbol: KM
Exchange: NYSE

1995 Sales: $34,654 million
1995 Loss: ($571) million
Mkt. Value: $4,709 million
Employees: 250,000

Web site: http://www.kmart.com

16

Kmart, the nation's #3 retailer, is struggling to keep up with Sears and Wal-Mart in the retail trade. The company sells general merchandise (clothing, appliances, furniture, and toys), groceries, and home improvement supplies (through its Builders Square unit). It operates retail stores throughout the US and in Canada, Mexico, Puerto Rico, and Singapore. In order to focus on its core discount operations, Kmart has spun off 3 of its specialty retailers (OfficeMax, Sports Authority, and Borders Group). Kmart is modernizing facilities and fixing an inefficient distribution system, and it is counting on Super Kmart stores, which combine discount merchandise and groceries, to rescue its sinking fortunes.

KNIGHT-RIDDER, INC.

1 Herald Plaza
Miami, FL 33132
Phone: 305-376-3800
Fax: 305-376-3828

CEO: P. Anthony Ridder
CFO: Ross Jones
Symbol: KRI
Exchange: NYSE

1995 Sales: $2,752 million
1995 Profits: $160 million
Mkt. Value: $3,348 million
Employees: 21,022

Web site: http://www.phillynews.com

456

Knight-Ridder is the #2 newspaper publisher in the US, with such heavy hitters as the *Detroit Free Press, Philadelphia Inquirer,* and *Miami Herald* in its stable. Newspapers generate more than 80% of the company's revenues, but Knight-Ridder is also a player in the electronic information industry. It owns an interest in Internet communications company Netscape and also delivers online information via SourceOne (patents and business articles), DIALOG (online and CD-ROM information services), and Technimetrics (global investor information). The company is one of 8 major publishers forming the New Century Network, an online information and advertising service.

THE KROGER CO.

1014 Vine St.
Cincinnati, OH 45202
Phone: 513-762-4000
Fax: 513-762-4454

CEO: Joseph A. Pichler
CFO: Rodney McMullen
Symbol: KR
Exchange: NYSE

1995 Sales: $23,938 million
1995 Profits: $303 million
Mkt. Value: $4,516 million
Employees: 200,000

Web site: http://www.foodcoop.com/kroger

27

The biggest supermarket chain in the US, Kroger operates over 1,300 stores in 24 Midwest and Sunbelt states primarily under the Kroger and Dillon names. It also runs some 800 convenience stores. Kroger has almost 40 processing facilities that provide milk, ice cream, juice, bread, deli items, and other grocery products. Kroger's more than 6,000 private-label items constitute about 20% of the grocery business. Like other large chains, Kroger operates several innovative stores, with such novelties as fast-food franchises in-store, extensive arrays of produce and gourmet items, and self-service checkout lanes. The company is also testing its shop-at-home service through an interactive cable TV network in the Dallas area.

LEAR CORPORATION

21557 Telegraph Rd.
Southfield, MI 48034
Phone: 810-746-1500
Fax: 810-746-1722

CEO: Kenneth L. Way
CFO: James H. Vanderberghe
Symbol: LEA
Exchange: NYSE

1995 Sales: $4,714 million
1995 Profits: $92 million
Mkt. Value: $1,828 million
Employees: 35,600

Web site: http://www.lear.com

278 Lear is the world's #1 supplier of automotive seating products, with about a 1/4 market share. It manufactures complete seat systems, seat covers, seat frames, and seat components and related products, including armrests, headrests, and molded foam cushions. The company, which has operations in more than 15 countries, sells to automakers, both in the US (Chrysler, Ford, General Motors) and overseas (BMW, Fiat, Mazda, Saab, Volkswagen, and others). Lear's seat systems are used in light trucks, sport utility vehicles, and midsize, luxury, full-size, sport, and compact vehicles. The company produces approximately 30 million seat systems each year.

LEHMAN BROTHERS HOLDINGS INC.

3 World Financial Center
New York, NY 10285
Phone: 212-526-7000
Fax: 212-526-5952

CEO: Richard S. Fuld Jr.
CFO: Charles B. Hintz
Symbol: LEH
Exchange: NYSE

1995 Sales: $13,476 million
1995 Profits: $242 million
Mkt. Value: $2,482 million
Employees: 7,800

82 Lehman Brothers is a leader in investment banking, with offices in the US, Latin America, Europe, the Middle East, and Asia. Spun off by American Express in 1994 to stockholders and the public, it has continued to raise money for corporate, institutional, and government clients through underwriting and placing securities. It also provides a variety of advisory and investment management services. In addition, Lehman Brothers trades stocks, currency, derivatives, and commodities. The firm has cut costs (through massive layoffs, among other tactics) and is expanding into such emerging markets as China and India. It is also anticipating more growth in Europe.

LEVI STRAUSS ASSOCIATES INC.

1155 Battery St.
San Francisco, CA 94111
Phone: 415-544-6000
Fax: 415-544-3939

CEO: Robert D. Haas
CFO: George B. James
Ownership: Privately Held

1995 Sales: $6,708 million
1995 Profits: $735 million
Employees: 37,700

Web site: http://www.levi.com

198 Levi Strauss is synonymous with blue jeans. The company is the world's #1 maker of brand-name clothing and is 2nd only to VF (makers of Wrangler and Lee jeans) in US jeans sales. Brands include its signature line of jeans and denim clothing and Docker's casual wear. The company advertises heavily, using radio, billboards, and television, and it also takes part in cooperative advertising with retailers. Its clothing is carried in department stores and other shops, and Levi also has begun operating company-owned Original Levi's Stores and Docker's Shops in upscale urban locations and high-visibility regional malls.

LIBERTY MUTUAL COMPANIES

175 Berkeley St.
Boston, MA 02117
Phone: 617-357-9500
Fax: 617-350-7648

CEO: Gary L. Countryman
CFO: Robert H. Gruhl
Ownership: Mutual Company

1995 Sales: $9,308 million
1995 Profits: $410 million
Employees: 23,000

139 Liberty Mutual is the #1 workers' compensation insurer in the US. In addition, the company offers homeowners, auto, group life, and disability insurance, and it provides loss prevention services (analyzing work sites and work practices to make them safer in order to prevent losses). It also operates rehabilitation facilities and has a number of alliances with health care providers to manage disability care. Liberty Mutual's financial services companies, grouped under the Liberty Financial umbrella, provide investment management services and sell fixed and variable annuities and mutual funds. The company operates throughout the US, Canada, Mexico, and the UK.

THE LIMITED, INC.

3 Limited Parkway
Columbus, OH 43230
Phone: 614-479-7000
Fax: 614-479-7080

CEO: Leslie H. Wexner
CFO: Kenneth B. Gilman
Symbol: LTD
Exchange: NYSE

1995 Sales: $7,881 million
1995 Profits: $962 million
Mkt. Value: $6,930 million
Employees: 104,000

Specialty retailer the Limited operates more than 4,000 stores across the US, focusing primarily on clothing for women. The company's women's apparel stores include the Limited, Express, Lerner, Henri Bendel, and Lane Bryant. The Limited's other stores offer children's clothing (Limited Too), sportswear (Abercrombie & Fitch, Structure) and sporting goods (Galyan's). The company also owns a majority stake in Intimate Brands, operator of Victoria's Secret (lingerie stores and catalog), Cacique (lingerie stores), and Bath & Body Works and Penhaligon (personal care product stores).

On a fishing trip during the 1930s, **Levi Strauss** president **Walter Haas** had a sudden revelation about the famous rivets used in his company's pants. After squatting by a campfire for a few minutes, he decided the one in the crotch was one too many.

— Levi's: The Shrink to Fit Business that Stretched to Cover the World, by Ed Cray

LINCOLN NATIONAL CORPORATION

200 E. Berry St.
Fort Wayne, IN 46802
Phone: 219-455-2000
Fax: 219-455-1590

CEO: Ian M. Rolland
CFO: Richard C. Vaughan
Symbol: LNC
Exchange: NYSE

1995 Sales: $6,633 million
1995 Profits: $482 million
Mkt. Value: $5,274 million
Employees: 10,250

Web site: http://www.lnc.com

Lincoln National is the #1 writer of individual annuities and the world's largest life and health reinsurer. Lincoln National Life Insurance sells individual annuities, pension products, and life insurance. Its health reinsurance operations, Lincoln National Life Reinsurance and Lincoln National Reassurance, sell coverage and risk management services to other insurers, HMOs, and self-insurance programs. Lincoln National sells property/casualty insurance through American States Insurance, which covers personal auto and homeowners insurance. It also provides workers' compensation, fire, inland marine, and machinery coverage. Lincoln National Specialty Insurance serves the sports and entertainment markets.

LITTON INDUSTRIES, INC.

21240 Burbank Blvd.
Woodland Hills, CA 91367
Phone: 818-598-5000
Fax: 818-598-5940

CEO: John M. Leonis
CFO: Rudolph E. Lang Jr.
Symbol: LIT
Exchange: NYSE

1995 Sales: $3,320 million
1995 Profits: $135 million
Mkt. Value: $2,260 million
Employees: 29,100

Web site: http://www.littoncorp.com

Litton Industries has operations in defense electronics and shipbuilding. Subsidiary Ingalls Shipbuilding is a leading maker of surface combat ships for the US Navy, manufacturing amphibious assault ships, cruisers, and destroyers (Aegis). It also provides overhaul, repair, modernization, design, and engineering services. Litton's electronics products include command, control, communications, and intelligence systems; electronic warfare systems; inertial navigation and guidance systems; airborne computers; avionics; Doppler radar; lasers; and night vision systems. The company's operations are located primarily in the US, Canada, Germany, and Italy. About 3/4 of Litton's sales are to the US government.

LOCKHEED MARTIN CORPORATION

6801 Rockledge Drive
Bethesda, MD 20817
Phone: 301-897-6000
Fax: 301-897-6704

CEO: Norman Augustine
CFO: Marcus C. Bennett
Symbol: LMT
Exchange: NYSE

1995 Sales: $22,853 million
1995 Profits: $682 million
Mkt. Value: $15,136 million
Employees: 160,000

Web site: http://www.lockheed.com

Lockheed Martin is the largest defense contractor in the US. Lockheed Martin's government products include the Trident II submarine-launched ballistic missile, external fuel tanks for the space shuttle, and the Titan IV space launch vehicle. Commercial products include spacecraft for Motorola's satellite communication network. The company is the product of a merger between Lockheed and Martin Marietta. Lockheed Martin is downsizing in response to dwindling US defense budgets and is concentrating on obtaining contracts in the Middle East and Asia.

LOEWS CORPORATION

667 Madison Ave.
New York, NY 10021
Phone: 212-545-2000
Fax: 212-545-2525

CEO: L.A Tisch
CFO: Roy E. Posner
Symbol: LTR
Exchange: NYSE

1995 Sales: $18,770 million
1995 Profits: $1,766 million
Mkt. Value: $9,279 million
Employees: 7,500

Web site: http://www.loewshotels.com

Insurance forms Loews' main business, and after acquiring Continental Corp. and Alexsis, it is one of the 10 largest insurance providers in the US. Insurance subsidiaries also include CNA Financial, Continental Assurance, and Continental Casualty. Loews' wholly owned subsidiary Lorillard makes Kent, Newport, and True cigarettes. The holding company for brothers Larry and Bob Tisch, Loews also owns Loews Hotels, which operates in markets such as New York City and Monte Carlo; watchmaker Bulova; and oil drilling subsidiary Diamond Offshore Drilling. The company also owns stakes in a crude oil transportation company, Hellespont.

QUOTES

After **Loews**'s Lorillard unit lost a tobacco liability verdict in March 1996, one legal activist said it should be "abundantly clear to everyone that the legal tide is finally turned against the tobacco industry." Declining to run up the white flag, Lorillard and 3 other producers said a week later that they "have no intention of settling ... pending tobacco cases out of court."

— Bloomberg Business News

LONG ISLAND LIGHTING COMPANY

175 Old Country Rd.
Hicksville, NY 11801
Phone: 516-755-6000
Fax: 516-931-3165

CEO: William J. Catacosinos
CFO: Anthony Nozzolillo
Symbol: LIL
Exchange: NYSE

1995 Sales: $3,075 million
1995 Profits: $303 million
Mkt. Value: $2,039 million
Employees: 5,688

Long Island Lighting (Lilco) generates electricity for more than one million customers on Long Island. It also sells natural gas to about 450,000 customers in the same area. Lilco owns 5 steam electric plants and 42 internal combustion units on Long Island, and generates its power primarily from oil and gas. The company also has a minority interest in the Nine Mile Point nuclear plant (Unit 2) near Oswego, New York. Lilco charges about twice the national average for electrical power, and to defend itself against the threat of competition, it is working to cut costs.

LONGS DRUG STORES CORPORATION

141 N. Civic Dr.	CEO: Robert M. Long	1995 Sales: $2,644 million
Walnut Creek, CA 94596	CFO: Clay E. Selland	1995 Profits: $46 million
Phone: 510-937-1170	Symbol: LDG	Mkt. Value: $930 million
Fax: 510-210-6886	Exchange: NYSE	Employees: 16,000

Longs is a leading drugstore chain with stores in Alaska, California, Colorado, Hawaii, and Nevada. The company prides itself on its decentralized management style, which gives managers considerable independence in running their stores and ties their salaries to their location's performance. It does not attempt to compete on price with large discount drug chains and megaretailers like Wal-Mart. Instead, Longs stresses service and upscale products. Longs stores are larger than the industry average, allowing for more nonpharmacy merchandise, which accounts for more than half of sales. Longs has begun to concentrate more intensively on its pharmacy operations, which are less vulnerable to consumer buying cycles.

LORAL CORPORATION

600 Third Ave.	CEO: Bernard L. Schwartz	1995 Sales: $5,484 million
New York, NY 10016	CFO: Michael P. DeBlasio	1995 Profits: $288 million
Phone: 212-697-1105	Symbol: LOR	Mkt. Value: $8,090 million
Fax: 212-661-8988	Exchange: NYSE	Employees: 28,900

Loral is a leading manufacturer of defense electronics and telecommunications and space systems. The company's defense electronics business includes radar-jamming devices and weapons guidance systems. Loral also makes air traffic control systems, builds large computer systems for government agencies, and provides electronic reconnaissance and satellite tracking systems for the Department of Defense. Loral also holds about a 30% interest in Globalstar, a wireless voice and data communications company. In early 1996, as part of the continuing merger activity in the defense industry, defense giant Lockheed Martin acquired most of Loral's assets.

LOUISIANA-PACIFIC CORPORATION

111 S.W. Fifth Ave.	CEO: Mark A. Suwyn	1995 Sales: $2,843 million
Portland, OR 97204	CFO: William L. Hebert	1995 Loss: ($52) million
Phone: 503-221-0800	Symbol: LPX	Mkt. Value: $2,711 million
Fax: 503-796-0204	Exchange: NYSE	Employees: 13,000

Web site: http://www.lpx.com

Louisiana-Pacific produces lumber and building products and owns more than 1.6 million acres of timberland (primarily in California and Texas). The company makes a wide range of building products, including gypsum fiber wallboard, cellulose insulation, cement fiber, hardboard, glass, medium-density fiberboard, particleboard, and softwood plywood panels. Another product, inner-seal oriented strand board (OSB) — a substitute for plywood and marketed for a variety of uses, including house siding — accounts for about 1/4 of total revenues. The company also produces pulp at 3 mills in the US and Canada.

LOWE'S COMPANIES, INC.

State Highway 268 E.	CEO: Leonard G. Herring	1995 Sales: $7,075 million
North Wilkesboro, NC 28659	CFO: Harry B. Underwood II	1995 Profits: $226 million
Phone: 910-651-4000	Symbol: LOW	Mkt. Value: $5,669 million
Fax: 910-651-4766	Exchange: NYSE	Employees: 44,500

Web site: http://www.lowes.com

Lowe's is the #2 US building supplies/home center chain (after the Home Depot), with stores in 21 states, mostly in the Southeast. The company sells building commodities and millwork, home decorating and lighting, structural lumber, tools, heating and cooling systems, paints, carpeting, and wallpaper, as well as major appliances and consumer electronics. Most of the company's outlets are located in small towns, where mom-and-pop stores have trouble competing with the large selection and prices offered by Lowe's. The company continues to add more stores and is eyeing major expansion in the Midwest.

THE LTV CORPORATION

25 W. Prospect Ave.
Cleveland, OH 44115
Phone: 216-622-5000
Fax: 216-622-4610

CEO: David H. Hoag
CFO: Arthur W. Huge
Symbol: LTV
Exchange: NYSE

1995 Sales: $4,283 million
1995 Profits: $185 million
Mkt. Value: $1,380 million
Employees: 14,400

300 The LTV Corporation is the 3rd largest US steelmaker (after USX-U.S. Steel and Bethlehem Steel). A leading supplier to the automotive, appliance, and electrical equipment industries, LTV produces mostly sheet and tubular steel. Automaker General Motors is LTV's largest customer. LTV's energy company, Continental Emsco, is one of the largest oil- and gas-drilling equipment suppliers in North America. LTV operates 2 integrated steel plants, the Cleveland Works and Indiana Harbor Works (East Chicago, IN); 2 electro-galvanizing plants; various finishing and processing facilities; and tubular and tin mill operations. It also has offices in Mexico and Japan.

LYONDELL PETROCHEMICAL COMPANY

1221 McKinney St.
Houston, TX 77010
Phone: 713-652-7200
Fax: 713-652-7430

CEO: Bob G. Gower
CFO: Russell S. Young
Symbol: LYO
Exchange: NYSE

1995 Sales: $4,936 million
1995 Profits: $389 million
Mkt. Value: $2,520 million
Employees: 2,732

270 Lyondell, among the top US petrochemical companies, makes ethylene, propylene, butadiene, methanol, and other substances used in products from trash bags to paint and tires. It is about half-owned by Atlantic Richfield, from which Lyondell was spun off. Its LYONDELL-CITGO unit (a joint venture with CITGO) refines petrochemical products, including aromatics, gasoline, heating oil, jet fuel, and motor oil. The company stepped up its capacity to produce high-density polyethylene (used in milk containers and a variety of other common plastic products) with the acquisition of Occidental Chemical's Alathon operations.

MANPOWER INC.

5301 N. Ironwood Rd.
Milwaukee, WI 53217
Phone: 414-961-1000
Fax: 414-961-7081

CEO: Mitchell S. Fromstein
CFO: Jon F. Chait
Symbol: MAN
Exchange: NYSE

1995 Sales: $5,484 million
1995 Profits: $128 million
Mkt. Value: $2,698 million
Employees: 8,719

Web site: http://www.randles.com/infomall/ehtml/manpower

241 Manpower is the world's largest temporary-employment company. It employs more than 1.5 million people worldwide, supplying temporary office and clerical, industrial trade, and medical employees. In addition to temporary services, the company provides permanent-employment services, including employee testing and training. About 50% of the company's revenues come from contracts to fulfill the worldwide staffing needs of multinational companies. Like other temporary agencies, Manpower is benefiting from structural economic changes that have made the use of temporary employees more attractive to businesses.

MANVILLE

717 17th St.
Denver, CO 80202
Phone: 303-978-2000
Fax: 303-978-2363

CEO: W. Thomas Stephens
CFO: Robert E. Cole
Symbol: GLS
Exchange: NYSE

1995 Sales: $2,734 million
1995 Profits: $116 million
Mkt. Value: $1,568 million
Employees: 7,500

Web site: http://www.schuller.com

457 Manville (now known as Schuller) is a holding company for Schuller International, a leading manufacturer of building and insulation products. It makes aerospace insulation, air duct components, automotive molding, building insulation, filter cartridges, roofing products, and other fiberglass building products. As part of a strategy of focusing on building products, the company sold its majority stake in paperboard packaging maker Riverwood International, which had accounted for nearly half of its annual revenues. The company is on the lookout for acquisitions to expand its product line, and it is also looking into expansion opportunities in Asia and Eastern Europe.

Hotel and food services giant **Marriott International** started out as a root beer stand set up in 1927 by **John and Alice Marriott** in Washington, DC.

— Hoover's Handbook of American Business 1996

ORIGINS

MAPCO INC.

1800 S. Baltimore	CEO: James E. Barnes	1995 Sales: $3,310 million
Tulsa, OK 74119	CFO: Philip W. Baxter III	1995 Profits: $75 million
Phone: 918-581-1800	Symbol: MDA	Mkt. Value: $1,630 million
Fax: 918-581-1534	Exchange: NYSE	Employees: 6,204

Web site: http://www.mapcoinc.com

MAPCO refines and markets petroleum products and mines coal. The company operates one refinery in Tennessee and one in North Pole, Alaska. It also operates gas gathering and pipeline systems in the Midwest and Rocky Mountain states and markets natural gas liquids, farm fertilizers, and chemicals. The company owns 7 US coal mines. It sells steam coal to electrical utilities and industrial clients and metallurgical coal to steel and coke producers. In addition, MAPCO is one of the largest natural gas liquids and ammonia pipeline operators in the US and the country's 4th largest retail propane distributor.

MARRIOTT INTERNATIONAL, INC.

Marriott Dr.	CEO: J. Willard Marriott Jr.	1995 Sales: $8,961 million
Washington, DC 20058	CFO: Michael A. Stein	1995 Profits: $247 million
Phone: 301-380-3000	Symbol: MAR	Mkt. Value: $6,212 million
Fax: 301-897-9014	Exchange: NYSE	Employees: 179,400

Web site: http://www.marriott.com

Marriott International operates or franchises more than 850 hotels in 50 states and 22 countries. It is one of the largest US providers of food and services management to businesses, hospitals, and schools. Hotel chains include Courtyard, Residence Inn, Fairfield Inn, and Marriott Hotels and Resorts. One of the leading hotel operators in the world, Marriott traditionally focuses on middle- and upper-middle-level hotels, but with 49% of Ritz-Carlton (which manages 31 luxury hotels around the world, including New York, Chicago, and Cancun) Marriott also offers upscale luxury accommodations.

MARSH & MCLENNAN COMPANIES, INC.

1166 Sixth Ave.	CEO: A.J.C. Smith	1995 Sales: $3,770 million
New York, NY 10036	CFO: Frank J. Borelli	1995 Profits: $403 million
Phone: 212-345-5000	Symbol: MMC	Mkt. Value: $6,822 million
Fax: 212-345-4838	Exchange: NYSE	Employees: 27,100

Marsh & McLennan is the world's leading insurance brokerage service. Other business units include Guy Carpenter & Company (reinsurance), the Mercer Consulting Group (management consulting in Europe and North America), and Putnam Investments (money management). The company's Frizzell Financial Services is the UK's #1 provider of group insurance programs and offers insurance, finance, and financial planning programs for affinity groups; Seabury & Smith, which offers insurance program management services, is the US counterpart. The company's Marsh & McLennan Risk Capital Corp. provides insurance industry investment and advisory services.

MASCO CORPORATION

21001 Van Born Rd.
Taylor, MI 48180
Phone: 313-274-7400
Fax: 313-374-6787

CEO: Richard A. Manoogian
CFO: Richard G. Mosteller
Symbol: MAS
Exchange: NYSE

1995 Sales: $4,779 million
1995 Loss: ($442) million
Mkt. Value: $4,778 million
Employees: 20,500

Web site: http://homesights.com

276 Masco is a leading manufacturer of kitchen and bathroom products. The company produces more than one out of every 3 faucets made in the US under such brand names as Delta, Peerless, and Sherle Wagner. It is also the nation's largest manufacturer of cabinets (KraftMaid, Fieldstone, Merillat, StarMark), producing 20 lines. The company also markets cooktops, ovens, ranges (Thermador), bath and shower units and whirlpools (Aqua Glass), and spas and hot tubs (Hot Spring Spa). The company has more than 150 manufacturing plants in 23 states and 17 countries.

MASSACHUSETTS MUTUAL LIFE INSURANCE COMPANY

1295 State St.
Springfield, MA 01111
Phone: 413-788-8411
Fax: 413-744-8889

CEO: Thomas B. Wheeler
CFO: Daniel J. Fitzgerald
Ownership: Mutual Company

1995 Sales: $6,804 million
1995 Profits: $229 million
Employees: 9,395

Web site: http://www.massmutual.com

193 Massachusetts Mutual Life Insurance is a diversified financial services and insurance company that targets wealthy individuals and small businesses. Mass Mutual operates in 4 core areas: Insurance and Financial Management (life insurance and investment and asset management), Life and Health Benefits Management (health coverage and managed care and case review services), Pension Management (401(k) and other pension programs), and Investment Management. Mass Mutual merged with Connecticut Mutual Life Insurance in March 1996.

MATTEL, INC.

333 Continental Blvd.
El Segundo, CA 90245
Phone: 310-252-2000
Fax: 310-252-4423

CEO: John W. Amerman
CFO: Francesca Luzuriaga
Symbol: MAT
Exchange: NYSE

1995 Sales: $3,639 million
1995 Profits: $358 million
Mkt. Value: $7,557 million
Employees: 25,000

343 Mattel is the #1 toy maker in the US. The company focuses on 4 principal toy brands (Barbie, Fisher-Price, Disney entertainment lines, and Hot Wheels). Its other toy brands include Cabbage Patch Kids, Wham-O (frisbees), and Hacky Sack. Games include Skip-Bo and UNO. Mattel believes that children everywhere like the same toys, so it designs products with worldwide appeal and markets them globally. It sells toys in more than 35 countries, and about half of its revenues come from outside the US. The company's primary manufacturing facilities are in China, Indonesia, Italy, Malaysia, and Mexico.

HISTORY

Early in the 20th century, the trend was for the middle class either to send laundry out or bring a laundress in; **Maytag**'s agitator washer (invented in 1922 by **L. B. Maytag**, son of the founder, and **Howard Snyder**, head of the development department) turned the middle-class woman of the house back into the washerwoman.

— Hoover's Handbook of American Companies 1996, Overworked American, and More Work for Mother

MAXXAM INC.

5847 San Felipe
Houston, TX 77057
Phone: 713-975-7600
Fax: 713-267-3703

CEO: Charles E. Hurwitz
CFO: Paul N. Schwartz
Symbol: MXM
Exchange: AMEX

1995 Sales: $2,565 million
1995 Profits: $58 million
Mkt. Value: $381 million
Employees: 12,000

The holding company for corporate raider Charles Hurwitz, MAXXAM deals primarily in aluminum mining and production, timber products, real estate investment, and horse racing. MAXXAM's top revenue source is 58.9%-owned Kaiser Aluminum, a publicly traded company. MAXXAM's timber subsidiary, Pacific Lumber, owns about 198,000 acres of old-growth redwood and Douglas fir timberlands in Humboldt County, California. Among MAXXAM's real estate interests are commercial and residential properties in Arizona, California, and Texas, and Palmas del Mar, a Puerto Rican resort. MAXXAM also has a stake in the Sam Houston Race Park, a Thoroughbred and quarter horse track near Houston.

THE MAY DEPARTMENT STORES COMPANY

611 Olive St.
St. Louis, MO 63101
Phone: 314-342-6300
Fax: 314-342-4461

CEO: David C. Farrell
CFO: John L. Dunham
Symbol: MA
Exchange: NYSE

1995 Sales: $12,187 million
1995 Profits: $752 million
Mkt. Value: $12,542 million
Employees: 130,000

Web site: http://www.maycompany.com

May Department Stores is the US's #2 upmarket department store operator (after Federated), with about 350 stores. The company operates units in 29 states under such well-known names as Lord & Taylor (New York), Foley's (Houston), Filene's (Boston), Hecht's (Washington, DC), Robinsons-May (Los Angeles), Famous-Barr (St. Louis), Meier & Frank (Portland, Oregon), and Kaufmann's (Pittsburgh). In 1996 it spun off to shareholders its Payless Shoe Source, the nation's #1 self-service family shoe store chain. May agreed to buy all 13 Philadelphia-based Strawbridge & Clothier stores in 1996.

MAYTAG CORPORATION

403 W. Fourth St. N.
Newton, IA 50208
Phone: 515-792-8000
Fax: 515-791-6209

CEO: Leonard A. Hadley
CFO: Gerald J. Pribanic
Symbol: MYG
Exchange: NYSE

1995 Sales: $3,040 million
1995 Loss: ($21) million
Mkt. Value: $2,161 million
Employees: 16,595

Web site: http://www.maytag.com

Maytag is the 4th largest manufacturer of large appliances in the US (after Whirlpool, GE, and Electrolux). The company's high-end brands include Maytag (washers, dryers, dishwashers, refrigerators, and cooking appliances) and Jenn-Air (cooking appliances, dishwashers, and refrigerators). Its midrange brands include Admiral (washers, dryers, dishwashers, refrigerators, and cooking appliances) and Magic Chef (cooking appliances, refrigerators, dishwashers, laundry equipment, and microwave ovens). The company also makes Hoover vacuum cleaners (#1 in North America), utility cleaners, floor polishers, and shampooers. Subsidiary Dixie-Narco makes vending machines and equipment.

MBNA CORPORATION

400 Christiana Rd.
Newark, DE 19713
Phone: 302-453-9930
Fax: 302-456-2280

CEO: Alfred Lerner
CFO: M. Scot Kaufman
Symbol: KRB
Exchange: NYSE

1995 Sales: $2,565 million
1995 Profits: $353 million
Mkt. Value: $6,543 million
Employees: 11,171

MBNA Corp., through its subsidiary, MBNA America Bank, is the leading issuer of affinity credit cards, marketed primarily through endorsements of membership associations and financial institutions. Among the names that show up on MBNA cards are the Chicago Bulls, Columbia University, the American Bar Association, and Ducks Unlimited. The company also offers demand and time deposits, money market deposits, individual retirement accounts, certificates of deposit, home equity loans, and mortgages. MBNA Corp. has banking facilities in the UK that offer a full range of consumer banking services, in addition to providing international financing, merchant banking, and letters of credit.

MCDONALD'S CORPORATION

McDonald's Plaza
Oak Brook, IL 60521
Phone: 708-575-3000
Fax: 708-575-3392

CEO: Michael R. Quinlan
CFO: Jack M. Greenberg
Symbol: MCD
Exchange: NYSE

1995 Sales: $9,795 million
1995 Profits: $1,427 million
Mkt. Value: $35,684 million
Employees: 212,000

Web site: http://www.mcdonalds.com.

131

McDonald's is the largest global food service retailer. The company's brand name is the world's 2nd most familiar (after Coca-Cola). McDonald's operates more than 15,000 restaurants (2nd only to PepsiCo) and has more than 20% of the US fast-food restaurant market. The company stays competitive by redesigning its menus to stress value and choice and by maintaining product awareness through a $1.4 billion advertising budget. International expansion is important to the company, and overseas restaurants (1/3 of the total) contribute half its profits. McDonald's has outlets in 79 countries, with further expansion on the table.

MCDONNELL DOUGLAS CORPORATION

McDonnell Blvd. at Airport Rd.
Berkeley, MO 63134
Phone: 314-232-0232
Fax: 314-234-3826

CEO: Harry C. Stonecipher
CFO: James F. Palmer
Symbol: MD
Exchange: NYSE

1995 Sales: $14,332 million
1995 Loss: ($416) million
Mkt. Value: $10,180 million
Employees: 63,612

Web site: http://pat.mdc.com

74

McDonnell Douglas is the world's #1 maker of military aircraft, #2 among US defense contractors (after Lockheed Martin), and #3 globally in commercial aircraft (after Boeing and Airbus). It makes the F/A-18 Hornet, the F-15 Eagle, the MD 500 helicopter, the C-17 transport, and the Harrier II Plus warplane. Its commercial aircraft unit builds MD-80s, MD-90s (twin jets), and MD-11s (trijets). The company also makes components for the space station, the Delta launch vehicle, and Tomahawk missiles. After years of plant closings and layoffs related to defense cutbacks, it is focusing on building its commercial aircraft business, with emphasis on the proposed 100-seat MD-95, for short- and medium-range flights.

THE MCGRAW-HILL COMPANIES, INC.

1221 Sixth Ave.
New York, NY 10020
Phone: 212-512-2000
Fax: 212-512-3514

CEO: Joseph L. Dionne
CFO: Robert J. Bahash
Symbol: MHP
Exchange: NYSE

1995 Sales: $2,935 million
1995 Profits: $227 million
Mkt. Value: $4,434 million
Employees: 15,004

Web site: http://www.mcgraw-hill.com

423

McGraw-Hill is an information provider. The company publishes *Business Week*, computer trade magazine *BYTE*, and other consumer and trade magazines. Subsidiary Standard & Poor's is a leading provider of credit ratings and also publishes directories of corporate information. Besides print media, McGraw-Hill also serves the business, professional, consumer, government, and education markets through electronic networks, software, and CD-ROMs, and via broadcasting (the company owns 4 TV stations). McGraw-Hill's acquisition of full control over joint venture Macmillan/McGraw-Hill School Publishing from Macmillan has helped make McGraw-Hill the nation's #1 school textbook publisher.

MCI COMMUNICATIONS CORPORATION

1801 Penn. Ave. N.W.
Washington, DC 20006
Phone: 202-872-1600
Fax: 202-887-3140

CEO: Bert C. Roberts Jr.
CFO: Douglas L. Maine
Symbol: MCIC
Exchange: Nasdaq

1995 Sales: $15,265 million
1995 Profits: $548 million
Mkt. Value: $19,161 million
Employees: 50,367

Web site: http://www.mci.com

68

MCI is the US's #2 long distance provider (after AT&T and ahead of Sprint). Besides long distance, other communications services include paging (Friends & Family Paging and networkMCI PAGING) and an Internet service (internetMCI). NetworkMCI BUSINESS is the company's business software package, integrating e-mail, fax messaging, and desktop videoconferencing. For consumers it offers Friends & Family Connections (paging, e-mail, personal 800 service, and calling card). A major investment in Rupert Murdoch's media company News Corp. should allow MCI to develop and distribute communications products that may include pay-per-view movies and business information services.

MCKESSON CORPORATION

1 Post St.	CEO: Alan J. Seelenfreund	1995 Sales: $13,326 million
San Francisco, CA 94104	CFO: Kevin B. Ferrell	1995 Profits: $405 million
Phone: 415-983-8300	Symbol: MCK	Mkt. Value: $2,450 million
Fax: 415-983-7160	Exchange: NYSE	Employees: 12,200

McKesson is the largest wholesale drug distributor in the US and Canada, providing pharmaceuticals to hospitals and drugstores, and distributing health and beauty products to retail stores. It owns Armor All Products, maker of the nation's #1 automotive protectant, and McKesson Water Products, the US's 2nd largest bottled water company, with brands such as Aqua-Vend and Sparkletts. Subsidiary McKesson Health Systems provides pharmaceuticals, computer services, and delivery services to health care facilities. McKesson owns about 1/4 of Nadro S.A. de C.V., Mexico's leading drug distributor.

THE MEAD CORPORATION

Courthouse Plaza N.E.	CEO: Steven C. Mason	1995 Sales: $5,179 million
Dayton, OH 45463	CFO: William R. Graber	1995 Profits: $350 million
Phone: 513-495-6323	Symbol: MEA	Mkt. Value: $2,824 million
Fax: 513-461-2424	Exchange: NYSE	Employees: 15,200

The Mead Corporation is a pulp and paper producer and the #1 manufacturer and distributor of school supplies. The company produces corrugated containers, coated paperboard, and papers and distributes paper, plastic products, packaging equipment, and school and office supplies. Products include envelopes, filler paper, legal pads, binders, portfolios, stationery, notebooks, and greeting card stock. Mead controls 1.35 million acres of US timberlands and holds a half-interest in Northwood Forest, a lumber and pulp producer. It operates facilities throughout the US and in Argentina, Canada, Chile, France, Germany, Hong Kong, Italy, Japan, Mexico, the Netherlands, Spain, and the UK.

MELLON BANK CORPORATION

1 Mellon Bank Center	CEO: Frank V. Cahouet	1995 Sales: $4,514 million
Pittsburgh, PA 15258	CFO: Steven G. Elliott	1995 Profits: $691 million
Phone: 412-234-5000	Symbol: MEL	Mkt. Value: $7,477 million
Fax: 412-234-6265	Exchange: NYSE	Employees: 24,300

Web site: http://www.mellon.com

Mellon provides full-scale banking services in 15 states throughout the US and in 5 foreign countries. It offers checking and savings accounts, loans (business, personal, educational, residential, and commercial), MasterCard, VISA, money market deposit accounts, and wholesale banking (corporate and middle-market) services. Its other primary businesses are trust and investment management and information services. Mellon is also one of the US's largest mortgage servicers. The company is focusing on its trust operations and investment services, particularly its recently acquired mutual fund business Dreyfus and asset manager Boston Company. It is also expanding its foreign-exchange operations.

Ray Kroc, who made **McDonald's** a fast-food giant, was drawn to the original store in San Bernardino, Calif., by milkshake Multimixers — about 10 of them. Kroc, who held rights to the 5-spindle machines, couldn't imagine why a single store would order so many. He dropped by one day in 1954, witnessed a lunch rush like he'd never seen before, and wanted in.

ORIGINS

— *McDonald's: Behind the Golden Arches*, by John F. Love

Founded as the Byte Shop in Tempe, Arizona, in the late 1970s, **MicroAge** became the nation's largest computer retailer-wholesaler by 1979. Then came the fall; by 1982, a national recession had helped put it in Chapter 11. MicroAge finally got back on its feet with the help of a $5 million investment by an Olivetti subsidiary .

— Hoover's Guide to Computer Companies

MELVILLE CORPORATION

1 Theall Rd.
Rye, NY 10580
Phone: 914-925-4000
Fax: 914-925-4026

CEO: Stanley P. Goldstein
CFO: Carlos E. Alberini
Symbol: MES
Exchange: NYSE

1995 Sales: $11,516 million
1995 Loss: ($657) million
Mkt. Value: $3,626 million
Employees: 96,832

110

Melville Corporation's primary focus is its CVS drugstores. With most of its stores in strip shopping centers, Melville positions itself primarily as a discount retailer. It also provides pharmacy services and managed-care drug programs through PharmaCare Management Services. As it has struggled in a difficult retail environment, Melville has restructured to slim down. In late 1995 it announced plans to spin off its shoe stores and sell its Marshall discount clothing stores to TJX. In 1996 Melville announced plans to sell its Kay-Bee toy stores to Consolidated Stores and to sell or spin off its Linens 'n Things (housewares) and Bob's (casual apparel) stores.

MERCANTILE STORES COMPANY, INC.

9450 Seward Rd.
Fairfield, OH 45014
Phone: 513-881-8000
Fax: 513-881-8689

CEO: David L. Nichols
CFO: James M. McVicker
Symbol: MST
Exchange: NYSE

1995 Sales: $2,944 million
1995 Profits: $123 million
Mkt. Value: $2,128 million
Employees: 19,500

Web site: http://www.mercstores.com

421

Mercantile is a department store retailer operating 13 separate chains in 17 states, mostly in the South and Midwest. Some of the larger and better-known of Mercantile's chains are Gayfers (Alabama), Maison Blanche (Louisiana), Castner Knott (Nashville), and McAlpin's (Cincinnati). The company's stores specialize in fashion apparel (dresses, slacks, shirts, sweaters, suits, blouses, and footwear), accessories (jewelry, purses, and hand bags), and fashion home furnishings (lighting, picture frames, and clocks) for middle- and upper-middle-class shoppers. Mercantile carries such brand names as Ralph Lauren, Guess, Izod, and Nautica.

MERCK & CO., INC.

1 Merck Dr.
Whitehouse Station, NJ 08889
Phone: 908-423-1000
Fax: 908-735-1813

CEO: Raymond V. Gilmartin
CFO: Judy C. Lewent
Symbol: MRK
Exchange: NYSE

1995 Sales: $16,681 million
1995 Profits: $3,335 million
Mkt. Value: $76,496 million
Employees: 45,200

Web site: http://www.merck.com

56

Merck & Co. is a research-oriented pharmaceutical products and services company. It develops and markets a wide variety of products for humans, animals, and plants. The Merck-Medco Managed Care Division manages pharmacy benefits and provides disease management programs for more than 40 million people. Human health products include therapeutic and preventive agents, generally sold by prescription, for the treatment of human disorders. Among these are cardiovasculars, antiulcerants, and antibiotics. Animal health protection products include animal medicinals used for the control of disease in livestock, small animals, and poultry. Insecticides and miticides are its largest-selling crop protection products.

MERISEL, INC.

200 Continental Blvd.	CEO: Dwight Sterffensen	1995 Sales: $5,802 million
El Segundo, CA 90245	CFO: James J. Brill	1995 Loss: ($9) million
Phone: 310-615-3080	Symbol: MSEL	Mkt. Value: $80 million
Fax: 310-615-1270	Exchange: Nasdaq	Employees: 3,250

Web site: http://www.merisel.com

The world's #1 publicly held wholesale computer hardware and software distributor, Merisel sells 25,000 hardware (computer systems, disk drives, modems, monitors, printers) and software products (desktop publishing and graphics, operating systems, spreadsheets, and word processing) from more than 850 manufacturers to over 65,000 resellers worldwide. The company also sells its products at more than 750 ComputerLand franchises and Datago resellers. In addition, Merisel puts together complete customized computer systems. Hardware and accessories account for 3/4 of the company's sales; software accounts for the rest. Merisel has offices in Australia, Europe, and North and South America.

MERRILL LYNCH & CO., INC.

250 Vesey St.	CEO: Daniel P. Tully	1995 Sales: $21,513 million
New York, NY 10281	CFO: Joseph T. Willett	1995 Profits: $1,114 million
Phone: 212-449-1000	Symbol: MER	Mkt. Value: $9,769 million
Fax: 212-236-4384	Exchange: NYSE	Employees: 46,000

Web site: http://www.ml.com

Merrill Lynch, the US's leading brokerage firm and the leader in US and foreign equities underwriting, combines retail brokerage and cash management with investment banking. Other lines include clearing services, retail banking, and insurance. It also has a recognized presence overseas and provides investment and financing services to companies outside the US and Canada. Its combined asset management arms make up one of the largest mutual fund managers in the world. Merrill Lynch also deals in government bonds and derivatives and provides insurance services.

METROPOLITAN LIFE INSURANCE COMPANY

1 Madison Ave.	CEO: Harry P. Kamen	1995 Sales: $27,977 million
New York, NY 10010	CFO: Stewart G. Nagler	1995 Loss: ($559) million
Phone: 212-578-2211	Ownership: Mutual Company	Employees: 40,797
Fax: 212-578-3320		

Web site: http://www.metlife.com

Metropolitan Life Insurance (MetLife) is the largest North American life insurer, with over $1.2 trillion in life insurance in force. In addition, the company offers health, property, and casualty insurance, as well as savings, retirement, and other financial services for groups and individuals. Its insurance affiliates include Albany Life Assurance, Farmers National, MetLife Limited (UK), Metropolitan Property and Casualty, and Metropolitan Tower. Primarily an insurance provider to middle-income consumers, MetLife's merger with New England Mutual gives it access to that company's upper-income customers and higher profit margins.

MICROAGE, INC.

2400 S. MicroAge Way	CEO: Jeffrey D. McKeever	1995 Sales: $2,941 million
Tempe, AZ 85282	CFO: James R. Daniel	1995 Profits: $0.2 million
Phone: 602-804-2000	Symbol: MICA	Mkt. Value: $135 million
Fax: 602-966-7339	Exchange: Nasdaq	Employees: 2,088

Web site: http://www.microage.net

MicroAge distributes more than 25,000 high-tech products from top names such as Apple, Compaq, Hewlett-Packard, Packard Bell, and IBM. It also provides such services as systems integration, technical support, and electronic ordering and product information. MicroAge Service Solutions offers telephone services to businesses, including inbound and outbound call management, 800 numbers, and simple order taking. The company sells directly to large corporations, government agencies, and educational institutions. MicroAge is focusing on its international business (distributing its products to US corporations with overseas operations) and has been designated international reseller for IBM and Hewlett-Packard.

MICRON TECHNOLOGY, INC.

8000 S. Federal Way	CEO: Steven R. Appleton	1995 Sales: $2,953 million
Boise, ID 83707	CFO: Wilber G. Stover Jr.	1995 Profits: $844 million
Phone: 208-368-4400	Symbol: MU	Mkt. Value: $6,754 million
Fax: 208-368-4435	Exchange: NYSE	Employees: 8,080

Web site: http://www.micron.com

Micron Technology designs dynamic and static random access memory chips (DRAMs and SRAMs) used to store data in computers. The company is the 3rd largest DRAM maker in the US (after Texas Instruments and IBM). Instead of focusing on R&D to beat other makers to market with more powerful chips, Micron tries to be the low-cost provider. The company has begun developing a wider range of products, including a radio frequency identification chip and a flat panel display. Micron also holds a majority interest in PC maker and contract manufacturer Micron Electronics.

MICROSOFT CORPORATION

1 Microsoft Way	CEO: William H. Gates III	1995 Sales: $5,937 million
Redmond, WA 98052	CFO: Michael W. Brown	1995 Profits: $1,453 million
Phone: 206-882-8080	Symbol: MSFT	Mkt. Value: $60,811 million
Fax: 206-883-8101	Exchange: Nasdaq	Employees: 17,801

Web site: http://www.microsoft.com

The largest independent software company in the world, Microsoft has replaced IBM as the behemoth everybody loves to hate. Despite US Justice Department inquiries into a variety of alleged anticompetitive activities, billionaire brainiac Bill Gates and Microsoft forge ahead. Gates is broadening his company's scope from PC operating software (Windows 95, Windows NT) and applications (Word, Excel, Microsoft Office) to online services (Microsoft Network), online banking (Money personal finance software), and multimedia. Deals with companies such as NBC, DreamWorks SKG, and Reader's Digest position Microsoft to capitalize on entertainment software and multimedia development.

MINNESOTA MINING AND MANUFACTURING COMPANY

3M Center	CEO: Livio D. DeSimone	1995 Sales: $16,105 million
St. Paul, MN 55144	CFO: Giulio Agostini	1995 Profits: $976 million
Phone: 612-733-1110	Symbol: MMM	Mkt. Value: $26,588 million
Fax: 612-733-9973	Exchange: NYSE	Employees: 70,687

Web site: http://www.mmm.com

Minnesota Mining and Manufacturing (3M), the Post-it Note company, is a diversified manufacturer with 3 main sectors: Industrial and Consumer; Information, Imaging, and Electronics; and Life Sciences. With about 16% of the scouring-pad market, the Never Rust Wool Soap Pad (made of recycled plastic bottles) is one of 3M's successful new products. Other lines include tape, fax machines, and film. The company actively invests in R&D, and it encourages creativity in its technical and engineering staff, allowing them to spend about 15% of their workday (called "bootleg time") tinkering with new products. 3M derives 50% of its sales from overseas and continues to expand outside the US, particularly in the Pacific Rim.

MOBIL CORPORATION

3225 Gallows Rd.	CEO: Lucio R. Noto	1995 Sales: $66,724 million
Fairfax, VA 22037	CFO: Thomas C. DeLoach Jr.	1995 Profits: $2,376 million
Phone: 703-846-3000	Symbol: MOB	Mkt. Value: $44,192 million
Fax: 703-846-4669	Exchange: NYSE	Employees: 50,400

Web site: http://www.mobil.com

The 2nd largest oil company in the US and 3rd largest in the world, Mobil has reserves of 6.6 billion barrels of oil equivalent. It sells its Mobil brand gasoline in more than 50 countries. The company also operates a fully integrated chemicals operation, which produces petrochemicals, wood/polymer building materials, and other products. Mobil continues to cut costs and restructure its operations (selling its plastic films operations to auto parts producer Tenneco) to become more profitable, mainly with job cuts in the US and abroad.

MONSANTO COMPANY

800 N. Lindbergh Blvd.
St. Louis, MO 63167
Phone: 314-694-1000
Fax: 314-694-6572

CEO: Robert B. Shapiro
CFO: Robert B. Hoffman
Symbol: MTC
Exchange: NYSE

1995 Sales: $8,962 million
1995 Profits: $739 million
Mkt. Value: $17,703 million
Employees: 28,514

Web site: http://www.monsanto.com

146

The #4 chemical company in the US (after DuPont, Dow Chemical, and Occidental Petroleum), Monsanto makes a range of products for the agricultural, home furnishings, automobile, construction, and personal care markets. Products include aspartame, control valves, pharmaceuticals, phosphates, plastics, resins, and rubber products. Its chemicals unit makes detergents, nylon carpet fiber, and laminated glass (Saflex), while its Nutrasweet unit controls more than half of the US tabletop sweeteners market. The Nutrasweet division also markets a fat substitute (Simplesse). Monsanto is looking to agricultural biotechnology products (such as Posilac, which improves milk production in cows) for growth.

MORGAN STANLEY GROUP INC.

1251 Sixth Ave.
New York, NY 10020
Phone: 212-703-4000
Fax: 212-761-0086

CEO: Richard B. Fisher
CFO: Philip N. Duff
Symbol: MS
Exchange: NYSE

1995 Sales: $10,949 million
1995 Profits: $720 million
Mkt. Value: $7,527 million
Employees: 9,238

Web site: http://www.ms.com

116

Investment banking firm Morgan Stanley offers a full range of financial services for institutional clients. Services include asset management, foreign-exchange trading, futures trading, corporate financing, securities trading and underwriting, and stock brokerage. The investment banking and brokerage house operates in the US, Europe, and Asia and is increasing its numbers, primarily overseas, by adding new offices in Beijing, Geneva, Johannesburg, Montreal, and Sydney. Morgan Stanley is upgrading its status in Europe (specifically in Germany, France, and Italy). The firm's mergers and acquisitions, merchant banking, custody and clearing, and asset management businesses continue to grow.

At 15, **Microsoft** chairman **Bill Gates** and school buddy Paul Allen made $20,000 by selling roadway traffic programs. At 17, Gates was offered $30,000 by TRW to design power allocation software for the Bonneville Dam. After arranging to have the project counted as senior year high school credit, young Bill took the salaried position — his last.

— *Profiles of Genius*, by Gene N. Landrum

MORRISON KNUDSEN CORPORATION

720 Park Blvd.
Boise, ID 83729
Phone: 208-386-5000
Fax: 208-386-7186

CEO: Robert A. Tinstman
CFO: Denis M. Slavich
Symbol: MRN
Exchange: NYSE

1995 Sales: $2,531 million
1995 Loss: ($484) million
Mkt. Value: $50 million
Employees: 4,887

484

Morrison Knudsen is one of the largest engineering and construction firms in the US. The company provides industrial, heavy civil and marine, mechanical, pipeline, building, and underground construction for both public and private customers. Morrison Knudsen also provides hazardous waste abatement services, operations and maintenance services for military and commercial facilities, and mines for coal in the US and Germany. As a result of cost overruns and the cancellation of construction projects, including a transit system in Honolulu and the superconducting supercollider in Texas, the company ran into serious financial trouble. It has announced it will be acquired by Washington Construction.

MORTON INTERNATIONAL, INC.

100 N. Riverside Plaza
Chicago, IL 60606
Phone: 312-807-2000
Fax: 312-807-2241

CEO: S. Jay Stewart
CFO: Thomas F. McDevitt
Symbol: MII
Exchange: NYSE

1995 Sales: $3,355 million
1995 Profits: $294 million
Mkt. Value: $5,680 million
Employees: 13,800

Morton, the salt maker with the "Umbrella Girl," manufactures specialty chemicals for a variety of applications. The company's other products include adhesives for food packaging, liquid plastic coatings for autos, electronic materials used in printing circuit boards, and dyes used in inks. Morton's table salt remains #1 in the US, and the company sells salt for water conditioning, highway/ice control, and industrial and chemical uses. Its Automotive Safety Products division is the US's leading driver and passenger-side air bag maker and is expanding in Europe with the acquisition of production facilities in Germany and the Netherlands.

Fred, Edgar, and **Willis Nash** were small retailers with 2 stores in the Dakota Territory before an unclaimed boxcar full of peaches took their business (now known as **Nash Finch**) in a different direction in 1889. They bought the entire load and turned a quick profit, giving them a taste of the fruits of wholesaling.

— *Hoover's Handbook of American Business 1996*

MOTOROLA, INC.

1303 E. Algonquin Rd.
Schaumburg, IL 60196
Phone: 708-576-5000
Fax: 847-576-8003

CEO: Gary L. Tooker
CFO: Carl F. Koenemann
Symbol: MOT
Exchange: NYSE

1995 Sales: $27,037 million
1995 Profits: $1,781 million
Mkt. Value: $32,872 million
Employees: 142,000

Web site: http://www.motorola.com

Motorola manufactures computer, communications, and networking products. Product lines include the PowerPC microprocessor and HP Laserjet printer chip. The Schaumburg, Illinois, company's core business is semiconductors and wireless communications. It also makes electronic controls for the aerospace, automotive, lighting, and transportation industries. Motorola controls 30% of the Iridium project that is ringing the earth with low-orbit communications satellites to provide instant global telecommunications services such as fax, paging, and mobile phones. The company is also manufacturing Apple clones based on the joint PowerPC technology developed by Motorola, Apple, and IBM.

MUTUAL OF OMAHA COMPANIES

Mutual of Omaha Plaza
Omaha, NE 68175
Phone: 402-351-7600
Fax: 402-978-2775

CEO: John William Weekly
CFO: John W. Sturgeon
Ownership: Mutual Company

1995 Sales: $4,134 million
1995 Profits: $71 million
Employees: 8,152

Mutual of Omaha provides property, casualty, life, health, and accident insurance. The company's Mutual of Omaha Insurance subsidiary provides nearly 6.3 million individuals with accident coverage under some 2 million group and individual insurance policies. The subsidiary also provides over 6,600 group policies providing health, life, and dental coverage to 4.7 million people. The United of Omaha Life Insurance subsidiary has over $74 billion in life insurance in force. Mutual of Omaha Investor Services, another subsidiary, manages mutual funds, which it sells through Mutual of Omaha's agency sales system.

NASH FINCH COMPANY

7600 France Ave. S.
Minneapolis, MN 55435
Phone: 612-832-0534
Fax: 612-844-1234

CEO: Alfred N. Flaten Jr.
CFO: John R. Scherer
Symbol: NAFC
Exchange: Nasdaq

1995 Sales: $2,889 million
1995 Profits: $17 million
Mkt. Value: $177 million
Employees: 11,500

Nash Finch is a grocery wholesaler and retailer that serves approximately 700 affiliated and other independent retail supermarkets in the US. The company also distributes food and other groceries to approximately 5,000 convenience stores, military bases, schools, and hospitals. Nash Finch distributes fresh fruits and vegetables, frozen foods, fresh and processed meat and dairy products, and nonfood products, including health and beauty aids, tobacco products, and paper products. The company's affiliated and company-owned stores operate under the names Econofoods, Sun Mart, Easter Foods, and Jack & Jill.

NATIONAL CITY CORPORATION

1900 E. Ninth St.
Cleveland, OH 44114
Phone: 216-575-2000
Fax: 216-575-3332

CEO: Edward B. Brandon
CFO: Robert G. Siefers
Symbol: NCC
Exchange: NYSE

1995 Sales: $3,450 million
1995 Profits: $465 million
Mkt. Value: $4,912 million
Employees: 20,767

Web site: http://www.webauthor.com/corp/ncc_1.htm

National City is one of the of the largest bank holding companies in the Midwest, operating through more than 600 banking offices in Indiana, Kentucky, Ohio, and Pennsylvania. It offers commercial and retail banking, trusts, item processing, mortgage servicing, and credit card processing. Through subsidiary NatCity Investments the company has expanded into investment banking and brokerage services. To boost its retail banking business, National City is working to reach its customers in new ways, such as providing 24-hour telephone service centers and opening branches in supermarkets. The company continues to look for acquisitions in order to compete in the rapidly consolidating banking industry.

NATIONSBANK CORPORATION

100 N. Tryon St.
Charlotte, NC 28255
Phone: 704-386-5000
Fax: 704-386-1709

CEO: Hugh L. McColl Jr.
CFO: James H. Hance Jr.
Symbol: NB
Exchange: NYSE

1995 Sales: $16,298 million
1995 Profits: $1,950 million
Mkt. Value: $20,296 million
Employees: 58,322

Web site: http://www.nationsbank.com

NationsBank is a superregional bank (in the South) and a national presence, with more than 2,000 locations in 34 states. It provides commercial and retail banking services and also operates globally from offices in Colombia, Germany, Singapore, the UK, and other countries. NationsBank also offers investment and brokerage services, insurance, and mutual funds. The bank has expanded aggressively through acquisitions, usually setting its sights on bargain buys, but it has also gone after bigger targets, including Atlanta-based Bank South.

NATIONWIDE INSURANCE ENTERPRISE

1 Nationwide Plaza
Columbus, OH 43215
Phone: 614-249-7111
Fax: 614-249-9071

CEO: D. Richard McFerson
CFO: Robert A. Oakley
Ownership: Mutual Company

1995 Sales: $11,702 million
1995 Profits: $183 million
Employees: 27,983

Web site: http://www.nationwide.com

Nationwide Insurance Enterprise provides property/casualty insurance, life and health insurance, and financial services. It operates in 4 core areas: exclusive agency lines (proprietary insurance policies sold through its own agencies), long-term savings (annuities and pension plans for individuals and groups), commercial services (insurance for businesses), and investments (companies in which it owns interests). Operating units include Nationwide Mutual, which provides auto insurance, Nationwide Mutual Fire, and the Wausau Group, which provides a range of insurance to businesses. Nationwide also has interests in 12 radio stations in 7 states.

NAVISTAR INTERNATIONAL CORPORATION

455 N. Cityfront Plaza Dr.
Chicago, IL 60611
Phone: 312-836-2000
Fax: 312-836-2192

CEO: John R. Horne
CFO: Robert C. Lannert
Symbol: NAV
Exchange: NYSE

1995 Sales: $6,342 million
1995 Profits: $164 million
Mkt. Value: $802 million
Employees: 16,079

208 Navistar is the US's #1 maker of medium-sized and heavy trucks (with about 1/4 of the market) and the leading supplier of school bus frames. It also builds diesel engines, provides replacement parts, and offers financing and insurance to its dealers and customers. After several years of hard times, the company has rebounded somewhat. To stay on the right track, Navistar is simplifying its products, using fewer parts, improving its engines, and reducing development times. It sells its products through over 950 dealers in North America and exports trucks and parts to more than 75 countries around the world.

NEW YORK LIFE INSURANCE COMPANY

51 Madison Ave.
New York, NY 10010
Phone: 212-576-7000
Fax: 212-576-8145

CEO: Harry G. Hohn
CFO: Howard I. Atkins
Ownership: Mutual Company

1995 Sales: $16,202 million
1995 Profits: $625 million
Employees: 7,867

62 New York Life Insurance offers a variety of life, health, and disability insurance policies; annuities; mutual funds and other investments; and health care management services. The company's investment services are sold through NYLIFE Securities. NYLCare handles the company's health benefits business, offering preferred provider coverage, HMO coverage, and physician practice management. Outside the US, the company has operations in Argentina, Bermuda, China, Hong Kong, Indonesia, Mexico, South Korea, Taiwan, and the UK. It continues to look for expansion opportunities overseas, particularly in less-developed countries, where it sees a huge untapped market for insurance products.

NEWELL CO.

29 E. Stephenson St.
Freeport, IL 61032
Phone: 815-235-4171
Fax: 815-233-8060

CEO: William P. Sovey
CFO: William T. Alldredge
Symbol: NWL
Exchange: NYSE

1995 Sales: $2,498 million
1995 Profits: $223 million
Mkt. Value: $4,321 million
Employees: 23,000

488 A diversified consumer products maker, Newell manufactures housewares (Mirro cookware and kitchen utensils, Anchor Hocking glassware), home furnishings (Levolor blinds), office products (Sanford markers, Stuart Hall school supplies), and hardware (Amerock cabinet and window hardware, EZ Paintr paint brushes and rollers, BernzOmatic propane torches). It sells to discount chains, superstores, warehouse clubs, home centers, and other retailers. Retailing leviathan Wal-Mart is Newell's biggest customer, accounting for about 15% of its revenues. Always on the lookout for acquisitions, the company seeks businesses with well-established product lines and dominant market positions.

NGC CORPORATION

13430 Northwest Freeway
Houston, TX 77040
Phone: 713-507-6400
Fax: 713-507-6405

CEO: C.L. Watson
CFO: H. Keith Kaelber
Symbol: NGL
Exchange: NYSE

1995 Sales: $3,666 million
1995 Profits: $93 million
Mkt. Value: $1,206 million
Employees: 1,100

341 NGC is a leading natural gas and natural gas liquids gathering firm; after its merger with Chevron's gas gathering, processing, and marketing operations, it will be the #1 gas marketer in North America. Subsidiaries include Accord Energy (a UK energy marketer jointly owned by British Gas), Electric Clearinghouse (an electric power marketer), NGC Oil Trading and Transportation (a crude oil marketer), and Novagas Clearinghouse (a Canadian natural gas and natural gas liquids marketer, jointly owned by NOVA Corp.). The company also owns Ozark Gas Transmission System, a 266-mile pipeline connecting Arkansas and Oklahoma. British Gas and NOVA each hold 33% of NGC.

NIAGARA MOHAWK POWER CORPORATION

300 Erie Blvd. W.
Syracuse, NY 13202
Phone: 315-474-1511
Fax: 315-428-5101

CEO: William E. Davis
CFO: John W. Powers
Symbol: NMK
Exchange: NYSE

1995 Sales: $3,917 million
1995 Profits: $248 million
Mkt. Value: $974 million
Employees: 8,800

Web site: http://www.nimo.com

317

Niagara Mohawk sells electricity to about 1.5 million customers in New York State. More than half of the company's power is purchased; it also generates power from coal, nuclear sources, hydroelectric, oil, and natural gas. Niagara Mohawk also sells and transports natural gas to about 500,000 customers; in addition, it owns a Canadian subsidiary, Opinac Energy. The company's long-term contracts with power providers (which are mandated by state and federal regulations) have put it in a financial bind. To find relief, it is exploring a number of options, including splitting its generation business from its transmission business.

500 QUOTES

"Not just a little better year, but the kind of year that makes you want to spike the ball in the end zone, take a victory lap pointing to the sky ... and do a little trash talkin' into the next fiscal year."
— **CEO Phil Knight, NIKE**

— FORTUNE, April 29, 1996

NIKE, INC.

1 Bowerman Dr.
Beaverton, OR 97005
Phone: 503-671-6453
Fax: 503-671-6300

CEO: Philip H. Knight
CFO: Robert S. Falcone
Symbol: NKE
Exchange: NYSE

1995 Sales: $4,761 million
1995 Profits: $400 million
Mkt. Value: $11,406 million
Employees: 14,240

277

Athletic shoe maker NIKE is a powerhouse in the world of sports. It is the world's #1 shoe company and controls about 1/3 of the US athletic shoe market. The company makes shoes for just about every activity imaginable, including baseball, basketball, football, volleyball, cheerleading, and wrestling. NIKE also makes casual shoes and a line of athletic wear, including caps, leotards, running clothes, shirts, shorts, and uniforms. It operates NIKE TOWN shoe and sportswear stores in several cities, including Boston, New York, and Seattle. NIKE sells its products in more than 80 countries.

NORAM ENERGY CORP.

1600 Smith
Houston, TX 77002
Phone: 713-654-5699
Fax: 713-654-7511

CEO: T. Milton Honea
CFO: Michael A. Creel
Symbol: NAE
Exchange: NYSE

1995 Sales: $2,862 million
1995 Profits: $66 million
Mkt. Value: $1,121 million
Employees: 6,703

Web site: http://www.noram.com

443

NorAm has the 3rd largest base of natural gas customers in the US, and its services cover the country from the Canadian to the Mexican border. Its 3 natural gas distribution divisions are Entex (Louisiana, Mississippi, Texas), Arkla (Arkansas, Louisiana, Oklahoma, and Texas), and Minnegasco (Minnesota). NorAm also transports chemical and petroleum products. The company has partnered with Mexican gas gathering firm Grupo Gutsa to develop local distribution companies and regional pipelines in Mexico, and it has applied for permission from state authorities to branch into the telecommunications business in Arkansas and Oklahoma.

NORDSTROM, INC.

1501 Fifth Ave.
Seattle, WA 98101
Phone: 206-628-2111
Fax: 206-628-1795

CEO: J. Whitacre
CFO: John A. Goesling
Symbol: NOBE
Exchange: Nasdaq

1995 Sales: $4,114 million
1995 Profits: $165 million
Mkt. Value: $4,008 million
Employees: 34,700

Nordstrom is a leading upscale apparel and shoe chain. Its merchandise includes dresses, skirts, shirts, sweaters, blouses, jewelry, menswear, childrenswear, and cosmetics. Nordstrom, which has developed a strong reputation for top-notch customer service, operates department stores in 10 states, leases shoe departments in 12 department stores, and operates 19 clearance stores (Last Chance, Nordstrom Rack). The chain is closely supervised by 3rd-generation members of the Nordstrom family, who own about 1/4 of the company's stock and are working to expand beyond the company's base on the West Coast to the Northeast and Midwest.

NORFOLK SOUTHERN CORPORATION

3 Commercial Place
Norfolk, VA 23510
Phone: 804-629-2600
Fax: 804-629-2798

CEO: David R. Goode
CFO: Henry C. Wolf
Symbol: NSC
Exchange: NYSE

1995 Sales: $4,668 million
1995 Profits: $713 million
Mkt. Value: $11,014 million
Employees: 26,944

Web site: http://www.nscorp.com

Transportation titan Norfolk Southern owns a major freight railway (Norfolk Southern Railway), a motor carrier (North American Van Lines), and coal, natural gas, and timber holdings (Pocahontas Land). The company owns almost 15,000 track miles in 20 midwestern and southeastern states and Ontario, Canada. Together with rival Conrail in a project called Triple Crown Services, it operates an intermodal network (freight transported in the same container by train, truck, or ship) that covers the entire Eastern Seaboard. North American Van Lines offers services through nearly 700 US locations and has agents in Canada, Germany, Panama, and the UK.

Aircraft designer **John "Jack" Northrop** left his mark across much of his industry. In addition to starting what is now **Northrop Grumman**, he was a founder of Lockheed Aircraft, Avion Corp. (bought by the forerunner of UAL), and an earlier Northrop Corp. (absorbed by Douglas Aircraft).

— Hoover's Guide to the Top Southern California Companies

NORTHEAST UTILITIES

107 Selden St.
Berlin, CT 06037
Phone: 860-665-5000
Fax: 860-665-5885

CEO: Bernard M. Fox
CFO: Robert E. Busch
Symbol: NU
Exchange: NYSE

1995 Sales: $3,749 million
1995 Profits: $282 million
Mkt. Value: $2,627 million
Employees: 8,800

New England's largest electric utility, Northeast Utilities is the parent company of a group of operating subsidiaries that provide electricity to approximately 1.7 million retail customers in Connecticut, Massachusetts, and New Hampshire. It also provides power to wholesale consumers, including the town of Wallingford, Massachusetts, and several other municipalities in that state. The company's utility companies include Connecticut Light and Power (which accounts for more than half its sales), Holyoke Water Power, Public Service Co. of New Hampshire, and Western Massachusetts Electric. Subsidiary Charter Oak Energy is an independent power producer for customers outside the utilities' service territory.

NORTHERN STATES POWER COMPANY

414 Nicollet Mall
Minneapolis, MN 55401
Phone: 612-330-5500
Fax: 612-330-2900

CEO: James J. Howard
CFO: Edward J. McIntyre
Symbol: NSP
Exchange: NYSE

1995 Sales: $2,569 million
1995 Profits: $276 million
Mkt. Value: $3,269 million
Employees: 7,495

Web site: http://www.nspco.com

476

Northern States Power, a utility holding company, generates, transmits, and distributes electricity to about 3 million customers throughout a 49,000-square-mile area that includes Minnesota and the Dakotas. NSP draws electricity from coal (59%), nuclear plants (36%), and other sources and has a generating capacity of 8,942 MW. Subsidiary Viking Gas Transmission is a regulated natural gas transmission company that operates a 500-mile interstate natural gas pipeline and provides gas to customers in the same region. Subsidiary NRG Energy develops and operates unregulated energy businesses.

NORTHROP GRUMMAN CORPORATION

1840 Century Park E.
Los Angeles, CA 90067
Phone: 310-553-6262
Fax: 310-553-2076

CEO: Kent Kresa
CFO: Richard B. Waugh, Jr.
Symbol: NOC
Exchange: NYSE

1995 Sales: $6,818 million
1995 Profits: $252 million
Mkt. Value: $3,005 million
Employees: 37,300

192

Northrop Grumman, among the US leaders in the aerospace and defense industries, makes B-2 Stealth bombers and E-2C Hawkeyes as well as components for F/A-18 and F-14 fighters and for commercial customers including Boeing, Airbus, and Gulfstream. The aircraft segment accounts for about 2/3 of company revenue. Northrop Grumman also produces electronics (sensors and radar-jamming equipment), missile systems, and computer systems for the government and private industry. The company is focusing on consolidating operations and cutting its workforce to pay down debt from acquisitions, which included the $3 billion purchase of Westinghouse Electric's defense electronics unit in 1996.

NORTHWEST AIRLINES CORPORATION

5101 Northwest Dr.
St. Paul, MN 55111
Phone: 612-726-2111
Fax: 612-727-7617

CEO: John H. Dasburg
CFO: Mickey Foret
Symbol: NWAC
Exchange: Nasdaq

1995 Sales: $9,085 million
1995 Profits: $392 million
Mkt. Value: $4,657 million
Employees: 45,124

Web site: http://www.nwa.com

143

Northwest is the nation's 4th largest airline, serving 150 cities worldwide with hubs at Detroit, Memphis, Minneapolis/St. Paul, and Tokyo. Operating more than 300 aircraft, it is unique among US airlines as one of the world's top air cargo carriers (about 10% of revenues). The company combines services with KLM in a joint venture serving more than 100 destinations in the US and abroad. Among its other interests are the WORLDSPAN computer reservation system (32% share) and subsidiaries such as MLT Inc. (wholesale travel and tour programs) and Northwest Aerospace Training Corp. (pilot training).

NORTHWESTERN MUTUAL LIFE INSURANCE COMPANY

720 E. Wisconsin Ave.
Milwaukee, WI 53202
Phone: 414-271-1444
Fax: 414-299-7022

CEO: James D. Ericson
CFO: Mark G. Doll
Ownership: Mutual Company

1995 Sales: $11,483 million
1995 Profits: $459 million
Employees: 3,344

Web site: http://www.northwesternmutual.com

111

Northwestern Mutual Life Insurance is a diversified insurance and financial services company. It offers such insurance products and services as disability insurance, mortgage insurance, and permanent and term life insurance. The company's financial services include annuities and securities brokerage. It markets its products through a network of 7,300 exclusive agents, many of whom the company hires through an innovative internship program that funnels young agents into the company directly from college. Northwestern Mutual Life holds interests in Robert W. Baird, a Milwaukee securities firm.

NORWEST CORPORATION

Sixth St. & Marquette Ave.
Minneapolis, MN 55479
Phone: 612-667-1234
Fax: 612-667-7680

CEO: Richard M. Kovacevich
CFO: John T. Thornton
Symbol: NOB
Exchange: NYSE

1995 Sales: $7,582 million
1995 Profits: $956 million
Mkt. Value: $12,269 million
Employees: 45,404

Web site: http://www.norwest.com

170

Norwest offers community banking through more than 700 branches in a 16-state region. Through its other operations, including mortgage banking and servicing, consumer finance, title services, asset and investment management, and leasing, it operates in every state and territory of the US and throughout Canada. The company also has offices in Asia, the Caribbean, and Central and South America. Norwest places a strong emphasis on customer service, and because of this ethic, it is one of the few banking companies that are bucking the industry trend toward automated banking and reduced branch networks.

NUCOR CORPORATION

2100 Rexford Rd.
Charlotte, NC 28211
Phone: 704-366-7000
Fax: 704-362-4001

CEO: John D. Correnti
CFO: Samuel Siegel
Symbol: NUE
Exchange: NYSE

1995 Sales: $3,462 million
1995 Profits: $275 million
Mkt. Value: $5,391 million
Employees: 6,200

Web site: http://www2.nue.com/nbs

359

The US's 4th largest steelmaker and one of the lowest-cost steel producers in the world, Nucor pioneered minimills, which make steel at a fraction of the time and cost of conventional steelmaking by melting scrap metal in electric arc furnaces. The company makes steel and steel products, including steel bearing components, metal buildings and components, cold-finished steel bars, structural bolts, pilings, beams, deck, and joist girders. Using new technology, nonunion labor, and hefty bonuses, Nucor has kept its mills running 7 days a week at close to 100% capacity.

NYNEX CORPORATION

1095 Sixth Ave.
New York, NY 10036
Phone: 212-395-2121
Fax: 212-921-2917

CEO: Ivan Seidenberg
CFO: Alan Z. Senter
Symbol: NYN
Exchange: NYSE

1995 Sales: $13,407 million
1995 (Loss): ($1,850) million
Mkt. Value: $21,080 million
Employees: 65,800

Web site: http://www.nynex.com

85

NYNEX is the 4th largest regional Bell operating company; it provides local telecommunications services in New York and New England. Together with U S WEST, AirTouch, and Bell Atlantic, the New York City-based company is creating a national cellular network (the foursome already has licenses to offer personal communications services in a dozen markets). NYNEX has been improving its cost structure (by cutting jobs) and its system infrastructure (by initiating capital improvement projects) to prepare for increased competition in the telecommunications market. The company's merger with Bell Atlantic will create a telecomunications behemoth with operations stretching from Maine to Virginia.

OCCIDENTAL PETROLEUM CORPORATION

10889 Wilshire Blvd.
Los Angeles, CA 90024
Phone: 310-208-8800
Fax: 310-824-2372

CEO: Ray R. Irani
CFO: Anthony R. Leach
Symbol: OXY
Exchange: NYSE

1995 Sales: $10,423 million
1995 Profits: $511 million
Mkt. Value: $8,120 million
Employees: 17,280

121

Occidental Petroleum makes chemicals (#3 in the US after DuPont and Dow Chemical), fertilizers, and plastics; it also explores for, produces, and markets gas and crude oil. Its Occidental Chemical subsidiary is the #6 US producer of ethylene, which it uses in plastics, solvents, fibers, and detergents. The MidCon subsidiary carries about 10% of the natural gas transmissions in the US market; it seeks to expand domestically and overseas, with a focus on Asia. The company's strategy has included cutting costs, divesting noncore assets (shrinking the workforce by about 2/3 to fewer than 20,000 during the 1990s), and boosting reserves.

Office Depot, **OfficeMax**, and **Staples** have quickly turned their niche into a sizable nest. None had a store open before 1986; 10 years later they had more than 1,200 combined.

— Hoover's Handbook of American Business 1996

OFFICE DEPOT, INC.

2200 Old Germantown Rd.	CEO: David I. Fuente	1995 Sales: $5,313 million
Delray Beach, FL 33445	CFO: Barry J. Goldstein	1995 Profits: $132 million
Phone: 407-278-4800	Symbol: ODP	Mkt. Value: $3,163 million
Fax: 407-265-4403	Exchange: NYSE	Employees: 30,000

Web site: http://www.officedepot.com

Office Depot sells high-quality, brand-name products in large volume and at steep discounts through warehouse-style superstores, primarily to small and medium-sized businesses. It is the largest office supply retail chain in the US, with stores throughout the US and Canada. Each store offers an array of services, including printing, faxing, copying, and discount long-distance services; computer hardware and software; and art and engineering supplies. Office Depot's Business Services Division combines its contract stationer units with its telemarketing and delivery services. Its Images outlet offers a one-stop shop for printing, graphic design, layout, and mailing services.

OFFICEMAX, INC.

3605 Warrensville Ctr. Rd.	CEO: Michael Feuer	1995 Sales: $2,543 million
Shaker Heights, OH 44122	CFO: John C. Belknap	1995 Profits: $126 million
Phone: 216-921-6900	Symbol: OMX	Mkt. Value: $2,006 million
Fax: 216-491-4040	Exchange: NYSE	Employees: 20,000

Web site: http://www2.pcy.mci.net/marketplace/omax

OfficeMax is the #3 office product superstore chain (behind Office Depot and Staples), selling brand-name goods at discount prices. The Kmart spin-off has increased its number of delivery centers to raise the percentage of its business that comes from delivery services. It is also focusing on FurnitureMax, a 10,000-square-foot store-within-a-store concept offering office furniture; CopyMax, a copy center connected to OfficeMax stores; and OfficeMax OnLine, a service allowing customers to order office products through various online services.

OHIO EDISON COMPANY

76 S. Main St.	CEO: Willard R. Holland	1995 Sales: $2,466 million
Akron, OH 44308	CFO: H. Peter Burg	1995 Profits: $317 million
Phone: 216-384-5151	Symbol: OEC	Mkt. Value: $3,395 million
Fax: 216-384-5791	Exchange: NYSE	Employees: 4,812

Web site: http://www.ohioedison.com

Ohio Edison generates, distributes, and sells electricity to more than 1 million customers in Ohio and Pennsylvania. Facing increased competition, it has adopted a simple strategy of freezing rates, cutting expenses (including construction and workforce), and improving customer service (partly by adding major account representatives). In addition, it has changed its marketing approach by segmenting commercial and industrial customers by type of business and has made productivity improvements at its Sammis and New Castle generating plants.

OLIN CORPORATION

501 Merritt 7	CEO: Donald W. Griffen	1995 Sales: $3,150 million
Norwalk, CT 06856	CFO: Anthony W. Ruggiero	1995 Profits: $140 million
Phone: 203-750-3000	Symbol: OLN	Mkt. Value: $2,159 million
Fax: 203-750-3292	Exchange: NYSE	Employees: 13,000

Web site: http://www.olincorp.com

392

A diversified manufacturer, Olin makes a range of wares, such as metals, chemicals, defense-related products, and ammunition. Metal products include copper and copper alloy sheets, strips, rods, wires, tubes, clad metal (Posit-Bond), foil (Copperbond), and stainless steel strips. The company's chemicals unit makes flexible urethanes, pool chemicals (HTH, Sock-It, Pulsar, and Duration), biocides, acids, urethanes, surfactants, chlor-alkali products and bleaches, image-forming specialty chemicals, and electronic interconnect materials. Defense and ammunition products include small-, medium-, and large-caliber military ammunition and components (Ball Powder propellant) and sporting ammunition (Winchester).

THE OLSTEN CORPORATION

175 Broad Hollow Rd.	CEO: Frank N. Liguori	1995 Sales: $2,519 million
Melville, NY 11747	CFO: Anthony J. Puglisi	1995 Profits: $91 million
Phone: 516-844-7800	Symbol: OLS	Mkt. Value: $1,994 million
Fax: 516-844-7011	Exchange: NYSE	Employees: 8,800

Web site: http://www.olsten.com

485

Olsten is the nation's 3rd largest employment agency. Its 1,200 offices provide some 500,000 temporary employees to more than 90,000 North American businesses. The company supplies office and clerical workers, accountants and other professionals, and health care workers for hospitals and in-home care. It also operates a clinical pharmacy network and conducts pre-employment and insurance medical exams through its ASB Meditest unit. Although most of Olsten's offices are company-owned, it franchises or licenses offices in less-competitive markets. Stuart Olsten, son of founder William Olsten, remains active in company management, and family members own over 20% of the company.

ORACLE CORPORATION

500 Oracle Parkway	CEO: Lawrence J. Ellison	1995 Sales: $2,967 million
Redwood City, CA 94065	CFO: Jeffrey O. Henley	1995 Profits: $442 million
Phone: 415-506-7000	Symbol: ORCL	Mkt. Value: $21,276 million
Fax: 415-506-7200	Exchange: Nasdaq	Employees: 16,882

Web site: http://www.oracle.com

417

Oracle is the leading developer (ahead of #2 Sybase and #3 Informix) of database management systems (DBMS) software, which allows multiple users and applications to use the same data at the same time. The company's flagship database software runs on everything from notebook computers to mainframes and accounts for nearly 3/4 of the company's sales. It also makes applications development productivity tools, computer-automated software engineering products, and document automation products. Oracle has an alliance with computer manufacturer DEC to build a hardware/software package based on DEC's Alpha microprocessor used in its Unix systems.

Michael Owens didn't seem cut out to be the founder of an industry. A coal miner's son, he was a union agitator in his youth and never learned to use decimals or blueprints. But in 1898, at a glassblowing shop in Toledo, Ohio, he began to devise the mass-production machinery upon which **Owens-Illinois** and the rest of today's glass business were built.

— *Pioneers of American Business*, compiled by Sterling G. Slappey

OWENS & MINOR, INC.

4800 Cox Rd.
Richmond, VA 23060
Phone: 804-747-9794
Fax: 804-273-0232

CEO: G. Gilmer Minor III
CFO: Glenn J. Dozier
Symbol: OMI
Exchange: NYSE

1995 Sales: $2,977 million
1995 Loss: ($11) million
Mkt. Value: $351 million
Employees: 3,350

Web site: http://www.webauthor.com/corp/omi_1.htm

416

The US's 2nd largest wholesale distributor of medical and surgical supplies (after Baxter International), Owens & Minor carries more than 160,000 products from about 3,000 manufacturers (including Abbott Labs, Johnson & Johnson, Sherwood, and Kimberly-Clark). Products include medical dressings, blood collection devices, endoscopic products, incontinence products, and syringes. The company serves hospitals, integrated health care systems, nursing homes, physician offices, and surgical centers. Its primary customers are not-for-profit hospitals under the Volunteer Hospitals of America umbrella. Other customers include Columbia/HCA Healthcare, the US Department of Defense, and University Hospital Consortium.

OWENS CORNING

Fiberglas Tower
Toledo, OH 43659
Phone: 419-248-8000
Fax: 419-248-5337

CEO: Glen H. Hiner
CFO: David W. Devonshire
Symbol: OCF
Exchange: NYSE

1995 Sales: $3,612 million
1995 Profits: $231 million
Mkt. Value: $2,184 million
Employees: 17,300

Web site: http://www.owens-corning.com

346

Owens Corning is the world's #1 maker of glass fiber and composite materials and a major producer of polyester resins. Using the Pink Panther cartoon character as its pitchman, it sells fiberglass insulation and other products under the Fiberglas and Miraflex PinkPlus brand names. Owens Corning also manufactures piping and roofing materials, asphalt, specialty foams, windows, patio doors, and yarns. The company operates manufacturing facilities in the US and 11 foreign countries, and it is focusing on international expansion, with a particular eye on Asia. It is also working to improve R&D to speed development of new products.

OWENS-ILLINOIS, INC.

1 SeaGate
Toledo, OH 43666
Phone: 419-247-5000
Fax: 419-247-2839

CEO: Joseph H. Lemieux
CFO: Lee A. Wesselman
Symbol: OI
Exchange: NYSE

1995 Sales: $3,763 million
1995 Profits: $169 million
Mkt. Value: $1,883 million
Employees: 30,100

Web site: http://www.owens-ill.com

327

Owens-Illinois is the world's leading producer of glass containers, with a market share approaching 50%, and it is one of the largest manufacturers of packaging products. The company makes glass beverage bottles, jars, and food containers; plastic containers and closures, trigger sprayers, finger pumps, and prescription medicine containers; glass pharmaceutical containers; and packaging materials. It also owns a minority interest in specialized glass company Kimble Glass, which makes laboratory ware such as beakers, culture tubes, flasks, and pipettes. Owens-Illinois is looking for growth opportunities in expanding international markets such as Latin America and Eastern Europe.

PACCAR INC

777 106th Ave. N.E.
Bellevue, WA 98004
Phone: 206-455-7360
Fax: 206-453-5959

CEO: Charles M. Pigott
CFO: T. Ronald Morton
Symbol: PCAR
Exchange: Nasdaq

1995 Sales: $4,848 million
1995 Profits: $253 million
Mkt. Value: $1,914 million
Employees: 14,200

273

PACCAR is the world's 2nd largest heavy-duty truck maker (after Daimler-Benz's Freightliner). The company makes Kenworth, Peterbilt, and Foden trucks worldwide and also handles truck leasing and financing. In addition, it makes Kobe and Trico oilfield pumps; Braden, Carco, and Gearmatic winches; and medium-duty trucks. PACCAR sells automotive parts and accessories in the western US through more than 120 Al's Auto Supply and Grand Auto retailers. The company has plants in 7 US states and in Australia, Canada, Mexico, and the UK, as well as a joint venture with ZiL, Russia's largest truck manufacturer.

PACIFIC GAS AND ELECTRIC COMPANY

77 Beale St.
San Francisco, CA 94105
Phone: 415-973-7000
Fax: 415-543-7830

CEO: Stanley T. Skinner
CFO: Gordon R. Smith
Symbol: PCG
Exchange: NYSE

1995 Sales: $9,622 million
1995 Profits: $1,339 million
Mkt. Value: $9,988 million
Employees: 21,000

Web site: http://www.pge.com

133 Pacific Gas & Electric (PG&E) is the nation's largest publicly owned electric and gas utility. It serves almost 4.5 million electric customers and 3.5 million gas customers in northern and central California. The company obtains electricity from a nuclear power plant, fossil-fuel plants, hydroelectric and geothermal systems, and such renewable sources as wind power and solar power. Major subsidiaries include PG&E Properties, which develops real estate for future power projects; Alberta and Southern Gas Co. Ltd., a Canada-based gas supplier; and U.S. Operating Services Company, a partnership with Bechtel Group that operates and maintains power facilities outside PG&E's utility service territory.

PACIFIC MUTUAL LIFE INSURANCE COMPANY

700 Newport Center Dr.
Newport Beach, CA 92660
Phone: 714-640-3011
Fax: 714-640-7614

CEO: Thomas C. Sutton
CFO: Glenn S. Schafer
Ownership: Mutual Company

1995 Sales: $3,161 million
1995 Profits: $85 million
Employees: 2,700

 Pacific Mutual is the largest life and health insurer headquartered in California. Its insurance products include life, medical, dental, vision, prescription drug, disability, and stop-loss insurance. The company also offers administrative and managed care services and pension management assistance as well as investment, asset management, and estate planning services. These services are sold through a force of more than 5,000 independent brokers. Pacific Mutual also provides securities brokerage services through a network of more than 1,200 independent financial planners and managers and insurance agents. Its products include fixed and variable annuities, mutual funds, and unit investment trusts.

PACIFIC TELESIS GROUP

130 Kearny St.
San Francisco, CA 94108
Phone: 415-545-1900
Fax: 415-394-3312

CEO: Philip J. Quigley
CFO: William E. Downing
Symbol: PAC
Exchange: NYSE

1995 Sales: $9,042 million
1995 Loss: ($2,312) million
Mkt. Value: $11,300 million
Employees: 48,062

Web site: http://www.pactel.com

144 Baby Bell Pacific Telesis provides telephone service to about 3/4 of California's population (through Pacific Bell) and about 1/3 of Nevada's (through Nevada Bell). In addition to its core telephone service operations, Pacific Telesis provides information services (such as Internet service—marketed through a partnership with Sun Microsystems, Cisco Systems, and Netscape Communications—and voice mail) and personal communications services (such as wireless communications systems for cellular phones and pagers). Subsidiaries offer mobile phone service, wireless broadband services, and voice mail. The company has announced plans to merge with one of its Baby Bell siblings, SBC Communications.

PACIFICARE HEALTH SYSTEMS, INC.

5995 Plaza Dr.
Cypress, CA 90630
Phone: 714-952-1121
Fax: 714-220-3725

CEO: Alan R. Hoops
CFO: Wayne B. Lowell
Symbol: PHSYA
Exchange: Nasdaq

1995 Sales: $3,731 million
1995 Profits: $108 million
Mkt. Value: $3,038 million
Employees: 4,438

Web site: http://www.phs.com

 One of the largest health maintenance organizations in the US, PacifiCare gets more than half of its revenues from its Secure Horizons Medicare program, which has more than 1.7 million members and is the largest risk-contract Medicare program in the nation. In addition, the company's pharmacy benefit management unit, Preferred Solutions, serves about one million members. PacifiCare also provides Medi-Cal (California's Medicaid system) with HMO services. Although most of PacifiCare's customers live on the West Coast, it operates in nearly all 50 states (through a deal with Affordable Medical Networks) to form a preferred provider organization for multistate employers.

PACIFICORP

700 N.E. Multnomah St.	CEO: Fred Buckman	1995 Sales: $3,401 million
Portland, OR 97232	CFO: Richard T. O'Brien	1995 Profits: $505 million
Phone: 503-731-2000	Symbol: PPW	Mkt. Value: $5,757 million
Fax: 503-731-2136	Exchange: NYSE	Employees: 12,621

Web site: http://www.upl.com

PacifiCorp owns Pacific Power and Utah Power, which generate and sell electricity to more than 1 million customers in 7 western states, making it the #1 investor-owned power wholesaler in the West. The company primarily generates power from coal but also uses hydroelectric sources and gas steam. Another subsidiary, Pacific Telecom, provides local telephone service in Alaska, 7 western states, and 3 midwestern states. Through subsidiaries PacifiCorp Power Marketing and PacifiCorp Energy, the company competes for wholesale power customers outside the utility's primary territory. In addition, subsidiary Pacific Generation develops and operates independent power and cogeneration projects.

PAINE WEBBER GROUP INC.

1285 Sixth Ave.	CEO: Donald B. Marron	1995 Sales: $5,320 million
New York, NY 10019	CFO: Regina A. Dolan	1995 Profits: $81 million
Phone: 212-713-2000	Symbol: PWJ	Mkt. Value: $2,058 million
Fax: 212-713-4924	Exchange: NYSE	Employees: 15,900

Web site: http://www.pwcm.com

Paine Webber is one of the nation's largest full-service securities firms. The company provides retail brokerage services, investment banking, municipal securities underwriting, real estate services, institutional stock and bond trading, asset management (through Mitchell Hutchins), and transaction services. Its more than 2 million clients include individuals, institutions, corporations, state and local governments, and public agencies. Paine Webber is expecting growing demand for its products and services from aging baby boomers with the means and need to seek investment help. The company has more than 300 offices in the US and 7 other countries.

PANENERGY CORPORATION

5400 Westheimer Court	CEO: Paul Anderson	1995 Sales: $4,968 million
Houston, TX 77056	CFO: Paul F. Ferguson	1995 Profits: $304 million
Phone: 713-627-5400	Symbol: PEL	Mkt. Value: $4,391 million
Fax: 713-627-4145	Exchange: NYSE	Employees: 5,000

PanEnergy (formerly Panhandle Eastern), the nation's #2 natural gas transmission company, also gathers, processes, stores, and markets natural gas, natural gas liquids, and crude oil. Its more than 34,000 miles of pipeline serve mostly northeastern and midwestern states. The company also imports and regasifies Algerian liquefied natural gas for sale in the US through subsidiary Trunkline LNG. Deregulation of the gas industry was a major reason for the company's merger with Associated Natural Gas, whose gas gathering operations were less regulated than is gas transportation. PanEnergy is now among the top US natural gas gatherers.

Back in the era when it used wood-fired boilers to run its generators, Pacific Power & Light, later to become part of **PacifiCorp**, helped jump-start its electricity sales by peddling appliances to homeowners.

— *Hoover's Handbook of American Business 1996*

PARKER-HANNIFIN CORPORATION

17325 Euclid Ave.	CEO: Duane E. Collins	1995 Sales: $3,214 million
Cleveland, OH 44112	CFO: Michael J. Hiemstra	1995 Profits: $218 million
Phone: 216-531-3000	Symbol: PH	Mkt. Value: $2,790 million
Fax: 216-383-9414	Exchange: NYSE	Employees: 30,590

Parker-Hannifin is a leading US maker of fluid power systems and components, with over 1,000 product lines for hydraulic, pneumatic, and electromechanical applications in 1,200 industrial and aerospace markets. Customers include Sea World and the US Air Force. Products include actuators, connectors, filters, hoses, and pumps. Parker-Hannifin has a presence in Europe through subsidiaries Telemecanique Electro-pneumatic, a French maker of valves and actuators; Polyflex, a leading European maker of thermoplastic hose; and Chomerics, the world's #1 maker of electromagnetic interference-shielding materials and thermal interface products.

PAYLESS CASHWAYS, INC.

2300 Main St.	CEO: David Stanley	1995 Sales: $2,686 million
Kansas City, MO 64108	CFO: Stephen A. Lightstone	1995 Loss: ($129) million
Phone: 816-234-6000	Symbol: PCS	Mkt. Value: $160 million
Fax: 816-234-6361	Exchange: NYSE	Employees: 18,100

Payless Cashways is one of the top 5 US retailers of building materials and home improvement products. It operates more than 200 full-line retail stores in 24 states (primarily in the Southwest, California, and the Boston area) under the names Payless Cashways Building Materials, Furrow Building Materials, Lumberjack Building Materials, Hugh M. Woods Building Materials, Knox Lumber, and Somerville Lumber. Designed as one-stop sources of home improvement products and services, the stores stock about 24,000 products including lumber and building materials, millwork, tools, hardware, electrical and plumbing products, paint, lighting, home decor products, and seasonal items.

PECO ENERGY CO.

2301 Market St.	CEO: Corbin A. McNeill Jr.	1995 Sales: $4,186 million
Philadelphia, PA 19101	CFO: Kenneth G. Lawrence	1995 Profits: $610 million
Phone: 215-841-4000	Symbol: PE	Mkt. Value: $5,860 million
Fax: 215-841-4188	Exchange: NYSE	Employees: 7,217

Web site: http://www.libertynet.org:80/peco

PECO Energy is an operating utility that provides electric and gas service to the public in southeastern Pennsylvania. It supplies electricity to residential, small and large commercial, and industrial users. The company provides electric service to a 2,340-square-mile area with a population of about 3.7 million, including 1.6 million in Philadelphia. Approximately 95% of the electric service area and 63% of the retail kilowatt hour sales are in the suburbs around Philadelphia and in northeastern Maryland.

THE PENN TRAFFIC COMPANY

1200 State Fair Blvd.	CEO: John Dixon	1995 Sales: $3,537 million
Syracuse, NY 13221	CFO: Eugene R. Sunderhaft	1995 Loss: ($80) million
Phone: 315-453-7284	Symbol: PNF	Mkt. Value: $169 million
Fax: 315-461-2474	Exchange: NYSE	Employees: 28,000

352 Penn Traffic is a leading food retailer in the eastern US, operating more than 250 supermarkets in Pennsylvania, upstate New York, Ohio, and northern West Virginia under the names Riverside Markets, Bi-Lo Foods, Insalaco's, Quality Markets, P&C Foods, and Big Bear and Big Bear Plus. The company also operates general merchandise discount chain Harts and a wholesale food distribution business that serves about 125 licensed franchises and more than 100 independent operators. In addition, Penn Traffic runs full-service dairy businesses under the names Sani-Dairy, Penny Curtiss, and Big Bear Bakeries.

PENNZOIL COMPANY

700 Milam St.	CEO: James L. Pate	1995 Sales: $2,490 million
Houston, TX 77252	CFO: David P. Alderson II	1995 Loss: ($305) million
Phone: 713-546-4000	Symbol: PZL	Mkt. Value: $1,751 million
Fax: 713-546-6639	Exchange: NYSE	Employees: 9,758

Web site: http://www.pennzoil.com

489 Oiling up for the future, Pennzoil sold ailing businesses to refocus on 3 core areas: motor oil, Jiffy Lube oil change outlets (it leads both markets), and oil and gas exploration. Taking advantage of brand-name prominence, the company has partnered with Prestone, the #1-selling antifreeze, in a joint marketing agreement, and with Sears to expand its Jiffy Lube operations. Pennzoil is looking for growth in oil and exploration from international projects in places including the Caspian Sea, Egypt, and Qatar.

PEPSICO, INC.

700 Anderson Hill Rd.	CEO: Roger Enrico	1995 Sales: $30,421 million
Purchase, NY 10577	CFO: Robert G. Dettmer	1995 Profits: $1,606 million
Phone: 914-253-2000	Symbol: PEP	Mkt. Value: $49,147 million
Fax: 914-253-2070	Exchange: NYSE	Employees: 480,000

Web site: http://www.pepsi.com

21 PepsiCo is the perennial #2 in the cola wars behind archrival Coca-Cola. But beverages (Pepsi, 7Up, Slice, Mountain Dew) make up just over 1/3 of sales for the diversified food and drink company. Snack foods (Cheetos, Doritos, Fritos, Lay's) constitute almost 30% of revenues while dominating the world market (25% share; over 50% in the US). The company produces 8 of the 10 best-selling snacks in the nation. PepsiCo's largest division, fast-food restaurants, accounts for nearly 40% of company sales. Each of the firm's 3 restaurant chains—Taco Bell, Pizza Hut, and KFC—is #1 in its food specialty. PepsiCo's restaurant brands, with almost 29,000 units, make up the largest restaurant system in the world.

PETER KIEWIT SONS', INC.

1000 Kiewit Plaza	CEO: Walter Scott Jr.	1995 Sales: $2,902 million
Omaha, NE 68131	CFO: Eric Mortensen	1995 Profits: $244 million
Phone: 402-342-2052	Ownership: Privately Held	Employees: 14,300
Fax: 402-271-2829		

431 Employee-owned Peter Kiewit Sons' is one of the largest general construction companies in the US. It derives nearly 3/4 of its revenues from wholly owned Kiewit Construction Group. Kiewit also has interests in coal mining (through joint ownership of 3 US mines), power plant construction and operation (California Energy), and cable television (C-TEC Corp.). Through United Infrastructure (a joint venture with another big construction firm, Bechtel), the company is also investing heavily in private infrastructure projects (such as toll roads) that it helps fund and operate.

PFIZER INC.

235 E. 42nd St.
New York, NY 10017
Phone: 212-573-2323
Fax: 212-573-7851

CEO: William C. Steere Jr.
CFO: David L. Shedlarz
Symbol: PFE
Exchange: NYSE

1995 Sales: $10,021 million
1995 Profits: $1,573 million
Mkt. Value: $39,998 million
Employees: 43,800

Web site: http://www.pfizer.com

126

A research-based, international health care company, Pfizer gets nearly 3/4 of its revenues from pharmaceuticals. These include cardiovascular agents, anti-infectives, central nervous system drugs, anti-inflammatories, and diabetes treatments. The company makes Procardia XL (a leading heart drug), Cefobid (antibiotic), Diflucan (antifungal), Feldene (antiarthritic), and Zoloft (antidepressant). Pfizer is one of the world's leading veterinary drug makers, producing vaccines, antiparasitics, and antibiotics. It also manufactures medical products such as pumps and catheters, and consumer health products Barbasol shaving cream, Ben-Gay analgesic cream, and Plax dental rinse.

PHARMACIA & UPJOHN, INC.

1209 Orange St.
Wilmington, DE 19801
Phone: 616-323-4000
Fax: 616-323-4077

CEO: John L. Zabriskie
CFO: Robert C. Salisbury
Symbol: PNU
Exchange: NYSE

1995 Sales: $7,095 million
1995 Profits: $739 million
Mkt. Value: $20,968 million
Employees: 34,000

Web site: http://www.pharmacia.se

183

One of the largest pharmaceutical companies in the world, Pharmacia & Upjohn develops prescription products for the human and animal health fields. The company makes a broad line of prescription drugs, mainly central nervous system agents, nonsteroidal anti-inflammatory and analgesic agents, antibiotics, cancer drugs, steroids, oral antidiabetes agents, and a hair growth product. It also produces nonprescription drugs, pharmaceutical chemicals for use in its own products and for bulk sales, and generic versions of some of its own drugs. The company was formed by the transatlantic merger of the Upjohn Co. (US) and Pharmacia AB (Sweden) in 1995.

PHELPS DODGE CORPORATION

2600 N. Central Ave.
Phoenix, AZ 85004
Phone: 602-234-8100
Fax: 602-234-8337

CEO: Douglas C. Yearley
CFO: Thomas M. St. Clair
Symbol: PD
Exchange: NYSE

1995 Sales: $4,185 million
1995 Profits: $747 million
Mkt. Value: $4,644 million
Employees: 15,343

303

Phelps Dodge is the largest copper producer in the US (ranked by domestic output) and also mines gold, silver, molybdenum, and other minerals. While copper is the company's biggest revenue generator, Phelps Dodge's manufacturing businesses bring in nearly half its sales. The company is the world's #1 maker of magnet wire (used in electrical equipment), its Columbian Chemicals subsidiary is the 2nd largest producer globally of carbon black (used in tires), and the Hudson International Conductors subsidiary is the world's leading maker of high-performance conductors (used in aerospace, automobiles, and electronics).

PHILIP MORRIS COMPANIES INC.

120 Park Ave.
New York, NY 10017
Phone: 212-880-5000
Fax: 212-878-2167

CEO: Geoffrey C. Bible
CFO: Hans G. Storr
Symbol: MO
Exchange: NYSE

1995 Sales: $53,139 million
1995 Profits: $5,450 million
Mkt. Value: $79,613 million
Employees: 151,000

10

Best known for its tobacco products (including Marlboro, the #1-selling cigarette in the world), Philip Morris is the world's largest tobacco company, with a 45% share of the US market. It also has the world's 2nd largest food business (after Nestle). The Miller Brewing subsidiary is the 2nd largest brewer in the US, after Anheuser-Busch. Through subsidiaries such as Kraft, General Foods, and Oscar Mayer, the firm produces Budget Gourmet frozen dinners, Louis Rich lunch meats, and Jell-O. Its Freia Marabou candy subsidiary (Skor candy bars) has 15% of the European candy market. About 2/3 of revenues come from domestic operations. Food accounts for 50% of sales, tobacco for over 40%, and beer for less than 10%.

PHILLIPS PETROLEUM COMPANY

Phillips Building
Bartlesville, OK 74004
Phone: 918-661-6600
Fax: 918-661-7636

CEO: W. Wayne Allen
CFO: Tom C. Morris
Symbol: P
Exchange: NYSE

1995 Sales: $13,521 million
1995 Profits: $469 million
Mkt. Value: $10,221 million
Employees: 17,400

Phillips is a fully integrated petroleum company, conducting exploration, production, refining, transportation, and marketing of oil products and natural gas. It has 3 US oil refineries and sells Phillips 66 gasoline through more than 8,500 service stations in 26 states; it also owns about 300 Phillips 66 convenience stores. The chemicals unit produces petrochemicals and plastics such as ethylene, polyethylene, polypropylene, and K-Resin and is a leading producer of cyclohexane (the feedstock for nylon). The company has recently built its oil and gas reserves to their highest levels in more than a decade.

PITNEY BOWES INC.

1 Elmcroft Rd.
Stamford, CT 06926
Phone: 203-356-5000
Fax: 203-351-6835

CEO: George B. Harvey
CFO: Carmine F. Adimando
Symbol: PBI
Exchange: NYSE

1995 Sales: $3,861 million
1995 Profits: $583 million
Mkt. Value: $7,390 million
Employees: 27,723

Web site: http://www.pitneybowes.com

Pitney Bowes is the world's largest producer of mailing equipment and postage meters. It makes copiers and fax machines and provides shipping and weighing systems. The company also has a management services division, which provides litigation support, records management, and document services. With the sale of its Dictaphone Corp. (voice processing systems) to Stonington Partners, a New York investment group; the divestiture of its Monarch Marking Systems subsidiary (bar code equipment); and the reorganization of its German operations, Pitney Bowes is restructuring its operations to focus on its core business of mailing systems and office products.

"As determined as we are to grow our business and increase shareholder returns, we are equally determined to fight those who would unfairly impede our progress."
— CEO Geoffrey Bible, Philip Morris
— FORTUNE; April 29, 1996

PITTSTON COMPANY

100 First Stamford Place
Stamford, CT 06912
Phone: 203-978-5200
Fax: 203-978-5315

CEO: Joseph C. Farrell
CFO: James B. Hartough

1995 Sales: $2,926 million
1995 Profits: $98 million
Employees: 23,900

Web site: http://www.pittston.com

The Pittston Company is a single corporate entity with 3 separate classes of stock representing its 3 lines of business: freight transportation, securities services, and mining. Pittston Burlington Group provides overnight air freight and sea freight forwarding, logistics management, and international customs brokering through Burlington Air Express. Pittston Brinks Group offers armored, bulletproof vehicles for currency and deposit processing; ATM servicing; and air courier services through Brink's Inc. It also installs, maintains, and monitors home electronic security systems through Brink's Home Security. Pittston Minerals Group mines for coal through Pittston Coal and for gold through the Pittston Mineral Ventures.

PNC BANK CORP.

249 Fifth Ave.
Pittsburgh, PA 15222
Phone: 412-762-2000
Fax: 412-762-6238

CEO: Thomas H. O'Brien
CFO: Robert L. Haunschild
Symbol: PNC
Exchange: NYSE

1995 Sales: $6,390 million
1995 Profits: $408 million
Mkt. Value: $9,938 million
Employees: 26,757

Web site: http://www.pncbank.com

205

PNC operates 10 banking subsidiaries in Delaware, Indiana, Kentucky, Massachusetts, New Jersey, Ohio, and Pennsylvania and more than 80 nonbanking subsidiaries. The company offers credit cards, mortgage banking, institutional investment management, leasing, and trust services. Its BlackRock Financial Management subsidiary provides asset management, Provident Capital Management provides institutional investment management, and PFPC Inc. manages mutual funds. The company is reducing its number of branches and is utilizing telebanking, where appropriate, in an effort to cut personnel costs, allow customers to conduct their banking around the clock, and pave the way for electronic banking.

Linde Air Products, now known as **Praxair**, started experimenting in 1911 with production of acetylene, though its use as a gaslight fuel had been largely eclipsed by the electric lightbulb. But when a French researcher mixed acetylene and oxygen to produce a metal-cutting flame, Linde had a hot item.

IDEAS

— *Hoover's Guide to the Top New York Companies*

PP&L RESOURCES, INC.

2 N. Ninth St.
Allentown, PA 18101
Phone: 610-774-5151
Fax: 610-774-4198

CEO: William F. Hecht
CFO: Ronald E. Hill
Symbol: PPL
Exchange: NYSE

1995 Sales: $2,650 million
1995 Profits: $350 million
Mkt. Value: $3,758 million
Employees: 6,661

Web site: http://www.papl.com

466

PP&L Resources provides electrical service to about 1.2 million homes and businesses throughout a 10,000-square-mile area in 29 counties in central eastern Pennsylvania. The company generates electricity by operating nuclear-fueled, coal-fired, and oil-fired steam stations; combustion turbines and diesel units; and hydroelectric plants. It also operates coal mines, refined-petroleum pipelines, and commercial and industrial construction operations. PP&L serves Allentown, Bethlehem, Harrisburg, Hazleton, Lancaster, Scranton, and Wilkes-Barre.

PPG INDUSTRIES, INC.

1 PPG Place
Pittsburgh, PA 15272
Phone: 412-434-3131
Fax: 412-434-2448

CEO: Jerry E. Dempsey
CFO: William H. Hernandez
Symbol: PPG
Exchange: NYSE

1995 Sales: $7,058 million
1995 Profits: $768 million
Mkt. Value: $9,237 million
Employees: 31,200

Web site: http://www.ppg.com

185

PPG is a diversified manufacturer. It is the nation's #1 glass producer, making windows for homes and businesses and windshields for autos and jets. The company is also the global leader in supplying automotive and industrial paints, as well as a leader in the residential and commercial coatings business. It is the world's #2 producer of continuous-strand fiberglass and the #3 producer of chlorine and caustic soda. PPG also makes a range of other products, including sulfur chemicals, phosgene derivatives, vinyl chloride monomers, flame retardants, silica products, and water treatment chemicals.

PRAXAIR, INC.

39 Old Ridgebury Rd.
Danbury, CT 06810
Phone: 203-837-2000
Fax: 203-837-2731

CEO: H. William Lichtenberger
CFO: John A. Clerico
Symbol: PX
Exchange: NYSE

1995 Sales: $3,146 million
1995 Profits: $262 million
Mkt. Value: $5,420 million
Employees: 18,822

Web site: http://www.praxair.com

393

Praxair is the largest supplier of gases in North and South America and is the 3rd largest gas producer in the world, after the French gas giant L'Air Liquide and the British company BOC. Praxair produces industrial gases used in a wide range of industries (chemicals, food processing, electronics, petroleum refining, and pulp). The company's products also include wear-resistant metallic and ceramic powders and coatings as well as commercialized noncryogenic technologies used for air separation. Praxair is focusing on international growth, looking for growth in Asia and further expansion in South America.

PREMARK INTERNATIONAL, INC.

1717 Deerfield Rd.
Deerfield, IL 60015
Phone: 847-405-6000
Fax: 847-405-6013

CEO: James M. Ringler
CFO: Lawrence B. Skatoff
Symbol: PMI
Exchange: NYSE

1995 Sales: $3,574 million
1995 Profits: $238 million
Mkt. Value: $3,206 million
Employees: 24,300

348

Premark is a major consumer and commercial products manufacturer, producing a range of goods including food service equipment, decorative building products, and small appliances. Its Food Equipment Group is the world's #1 supplier of commercial food equipment, manufacturing products that include dishwashers, ovens, refrigerators, and deep fryers which it sells under the brand names Vulcan, Foster, and Adamatic. Its Consumer and Decorative Products division sells laminates (Wilsonart), glazed ceramic wall and floor tile (Florida Tile), small appliances and stainless steel cookware (West Bend), and physical-fitness equipment (Precor). Premark has announced plans to spin off plastic container maker Tupperware.

PRICE/COSTCO, INC.

999 Lake Drive
Issaquah, WA 98027
Phone: 206-313-8100
Fax: 206-313-8103

CEO: James D. Sinegal
CFO: Richard A. Galanti
Symbol: PCCW
Exchange: Nasdaq

1995 Sales: $18,247 million
1995 Profits: $134 million
Mkt. Value: $3,686 million
Employees: 52,000

Web site: http://www.pricecostco.com

46

Price/Costco is the 2nd largest wholesale club operator in the US, after Wal-Mart's Sam's Clubs. It features apparel, appliances, automotive supplies, cameras, electronics, furniture, office supplies, pharmaceuticals, tobacco, tools, and video and audio tape. The company operates more than 230 warehouse stores using the Price Club and Costco Wholesale names. The stores average about 120,000 square feet and offer discount prices on a limited number of products (3,500-4,000, compared to 40,000-60,000 items at traditional discount retailers). Price/Costco was created from the 1993 merger of the Price Company and Costco Wholesale.

THE PRINCIPAL FINANCIAL GROUP

711 High St.
Des Moines, IA 50392
Phone: 515-247-5111
Fax: 515-247-5930

CEO: David J. Drury
CFO: Jerry G. Wisgerhof
Ownership: Privately Held

1995 Sales: $10,561 million
1995 Profits: $554 million
Employees: 17,392n

Web site: http://www.principal.com

119

The Principal Financial Group is a diversified financial services and insurance company. Its main subsidiary, Principal Mutual Life Insurance, offers individual and group life, health care (through a number of HMO and PPO companies operating in the Midwest and South), and dental and disability insurance. This unit also sells annuities and other pension products. The company's financial services subsidiaries (Princor, Principal Financial Securities, Hamilton Investments) offer investment management and securities brokerage services. Another subsidiary, Principal Residential Mortgage, originates residential mortgages and buys both mortgages and servicing rights.

THE PROCTER & GAMBLE COMPANY

1 P&G Plaza
Cincinnati, OH 45202
Phone: 513-983-1100
Fax: 513-983-9369

CEO: John E. Pepper
CFO: Erik G. Nelson
Symbol: PG
Exchange: NYSE

1995 Sales: $33,434 million
1995 Profits: $2,645 million
Mkt. Value: $57,058 million
Employees: 99,200

Web site: http://www.pg.com

17

Procter & Gamble is the #1 manufacturer of household products in the world. Its well-known brands include Tide and Cheer detergents, Safeguard and Ivory soaps, Crest toothpaste, Pampers diapers, Charmin toilet paper, Mr. Clean and Dawn dishwashing liquids, Crisco vegetable oil, Head & Shoulders and Vidal Sassoon shampoos, Sunny Delight Florida citrus punch, and Folgers coffee. More than 1/2 of the company's sales come from outside the US.

THE PROGRESSIVE CORPORATION

6300 Wilson Mills Rd.
Mayfield Village, OH 44143
Phone: 216-461-5000
Fax: 216-446-7481

CEO: Peter B. Lewis
CFO: Charles B. Chokel
Symbol: PGR
Exchange: NYSE

1995 Sales: $3,012 million
1995 Profits: $251 million
Mkt. Value: $3,216 million
Employees: 7,970

Web site: http://www.auto-insurance.com

413

A leader in nonstandard, high-risk personal auto insurance, Progressive Corp. has motored beyond its traditional lines into standard-risk auto insurance. The company also now sells coverage for motorcycles, recreational vehicles, and small commercial accounts. Progressive's nonvehicle coverage includes collateral insurance for lenders, director and officer insurance, and employee misconduct insurance. The company operates through 13 divisional headquarters that oversee some 30,000 independent agents in the US and Canada. It has upgraded its claims adjustment and processing procedures, in which accident reports are taken around the clock and referred to roving adjusters.

PROVIDENT COMPANIES, INC.

1 Fountain Square
Chattanooga, TN 37402
Phone: 423-755-1011
Fax: 423-755-7013

CEO: J. Harold Chandler
CFO: Thomas R. Watjen
Symbol: PVB
Exchange: NYSE

1995 Sales: $2,555 million
1995 Profits: $116 million
Mkt. Value: $1,498 million
Employees: 1,848

481

Provident is an insurance holding company that sells life and disability insurance products in the US, Puerto Rico, and Canada. Primary subsidiaries Provident Life & Accident Insurance and Provident Health Care Plans offer individual and group accident, health, disability, and life insurance products such as ordinary life, fixed and variable premium interest-sensitive life, and individual single-premium annuities and services. The company also offers group pension and employee benefit products such as group long-term disability, group life, and medical stop-loss coverage to businesses with more than 150 employees.

PROVIDIAN CORPORATION

400 W. Market St.
Louisville, KY 40202
Phone: 502-560-2000
Fax: 502-560-3975

CEO: Irving W. Bailey II
CFO: Robert L. Walker
Symbol: PVN
Exchange: NYSE

1995 Sales: $3,388 million
1995 Profits: $345 million
Mkt. Value: $4,142 million
Employees: 9,000

366

Providian is a diversified financial services and insurance company, operating throughout the US. Much of the company's revenue comes from insurance, including life, personal, and property/casualty, through subsidiaries such as Academy Life Insurance, Capital Security Insurance, and Veterans Life Insurance. Other lines include homeowners, auto, and medical insurance. The company has expanded into the financial services market by offering retail banking services, including checking and savings accounts, through its subsidiary Providian Bancorp. Providian also offers secured credit cards, a program that allows people with poor or nonexistent credit to obtain credit cards by depositing security funds.

THE PRUDENTIAL INSURANCE COMPANY OF AMERICA

751 Broad St.
Newark, NJ 07102
Phone: 201-802-6000
Fax: 201-802-6092

CEO: Arthur F. Ryan
CFO: Mark Grier
Ownership: Mutual Company

1995 Sales: $41,330 million
1995 Profits: $579 million
Employees: 92,966

Web site: http://www.prudential.com

Prudential is a diversified financial services company that offers life, health, and property insurance, estate and financial planning, credit card services, and annuities. It also provides asset management, as well as health care management and other benefit programs for employees and group members. The company is returning to profitability, though it is still hampered by continuing investigation into and publicity about its scandal-plagued Prudential Securities unit, which sold high-risk real estate limited partnerships as low-risk investments.

"Are you certain that the plate you eat and the cup you drink from have not been washed with soap made of diseased cattle?" Not to worry, counseled **Procter & Gamble**, which sold its vegetable oil product Ivory soap starting in 1879. P&G cleaned up during that era with ads that, like those of its competitors, were sometimes less than 99 and 44/100 percent pure.

— *The Entrepreneurs: An American Adventure,* by Robert Sobel and David B. Sicilia

PUBLIC SERVICE ENTERPRISE GROUP INCORPORATED

80 Park Plaza
Newark, NJ 07101
Phone: 201-430-7000
Fax: 201-430-5983

CEO: E. James Ferland
CFO: Robert C. Murray
Symbol: PEG
Exchange: NYSE

1995 Sales: $6,164 million
1995 Profits: $662 million
Mkt. Value: $6,332 million
Employees: 11,452

Public Service Enterprise Group is the parent company of Public Service Electric and Gas Company (PSE&G), New Jersey's largest electric and natural gas utility. PSE&G provides service to about 300 cities and towns, including Newark, Trenton, and Camden. Through subsidiary Enterprise Diversified Holdings, the company is also involved in nonutility businesses. Subsidiaries include Public Service Conservation Resources Corporation (energy management products and services), Community Energy Alternatives (investment in and development of cogeneration and small power plants), and Energy Development Corporation (oil and gas exploration, development, and production).

PUBLIX SUPER MARKETS, INC.

1936 George Jenkins Blvd.
Lakeland, FL 33801
Phone: 941-688-1188
Fax: 914-680-5257

CEO: Howard M. Jenkins
CFO: William H. Vass
Ownership: Privately Held

1995 Sales: $9,471 million
1995 Profits: $242 million
Employees: 95,000

Publix is one of the nation's 10 largest supermarket chains. Most of its approximately 500 stores are in Florida, but it also has stores in Georgia and South Carolina and is expanding rapidly, working to expand throughout the Southeast. The company produces its own deli, bakery, and dairy goods. It also provides fresh flowers, health and beauty care, photo processing, video rental, and housewares products and services. Publix is private; relatives of its founder own 35% of the company, while the other 65% is owned by employees.

THE QUAKER OATS COMPANY

321 N. Clark St.	CEO: William D. Smithburg	1995 Sales: $6,365 million
Chicago, IL 60610	CFO: Robert S. Thomason	1995 Profits: $802 million
Phone: 312-222-7111	Symbol: OAT	Mkt. Value: $4,617 million
Fax: 312-222-8532	Exchange: NYSE	Employees: 17,300

Web site: http://www.quaker-oats.com

206 The Quaker Oats Company, long known as the leader in hot cereals (with nearly 2/3 of the US market), also quenches more athletes' thirst than any other company. Its Gatorade brand has more than 85% of the roughly $1 billion sports drink market and accounts for almost 15% of sales. Quaker has a diverse product line, including pet food (Ken-L Ration and Gaines), juices (Snapple and Ardmore Farms), and pancake mixes and syrups (Aunt Jemima). Its breakfast foods segment (more than 25% of revenues) encompasses dry cereals (Cap'n Crunch), rice cakes (Chico-San), and granola bars (Quaker Chewy Granola Bars) as well as hot cereals. International grocery products constitute nearly 1/3 of the company's sales.

QUANTUM CORPORATION

500 McCarthy Blvd.	CEO: William J. Miller	1995 Sales: $3,368 million
Milpitas, CA 95035	CFO: Joseph T. Rodgers	1995 Profits: $82 million
Phone: 408-894-4000	Symbol: QNTM	Mkt. Value: $1,027 million
Fax: 408-894-3218	Exchange: Nasdaq	Employees: 7,265

Web site: http://www.quantum.com

368 Quantum is the world's leading supplier of computer hard disks. Products include the Trailblazer hard disk (for low-end PCs) and the Fireball (for high-performance PCs) as well as high-capacity drives, such as the Atlas II and Empire II, which have more than 9 gigabytes of memory. It also makes QCard flash memory cards with embedded drivers, high-capacity minilibraries designed for data backup, and tape drives. Quantum sells its hard drives through original equipment manufacturers and commercial and industrial distribution channels. Its products are also sold as optional equipment on Compaq and Silicon Graphics high-end systems.

The friendly Quaker Man image was first used as a trademark in 1877 by **Henry Crowell** at his Quaker Mill in Ravenna, Ohio. The image was a key to the early success of **Quaker Oats** as Crowell, an advertising innovator, used it nationwide to push oatmeal sold by the company he formed with 7 other millers.

— Hoover's Guide to the Top Chicago Companies

RALSTON PURINA COMPANY

Checkerboard Square	CEO: William P. Stiritz	1995 Sales: $7,210 million
St. Louis, MO 63164	CFO: James R. Elsesser	1995 Profits: $296 million
Phone: 314-982-1000	Symbol: RAL	Mkt. Value: $7,126 million
Fax: 314-982-2134	Exchange: NYSE	Employees: 31,837

180 Ralston Purina is the world's largest producer of dry dog food, soft-moist cat food, and dry-cell battery products (Eveready and Energizer). It makes dog and cat food under labels such as Dog Chow, Cat Chow, Chuck Wagon, and Kit'N Kaboodle, as well as several brands of cat litter. It also sells Chow livestock and poultry feeds outside the US. Ralston Purina's battery products include alkaline, carbon zinc, miniature, and rechargeable batteries, along with battery-powered lights. The company also makes dietary soy protein, fiber food ingredients, and polymer products.

RAYTHEON COMPANY

141 Spring St.	CEO: Dennis J. Picard	1995 Sales: $11,716 million
Lexington, MA 02173	CFO: Peter D'Angelo	1995 Profits: $793 million
Phone: 617-862-6600	Symbol: RTN	Mkt. Value: $12,513 million
Fax: 617-860-2172	Exchange: NYSE	Employees: 76,000

Web site: http://www.raytheon.com

Raytheon, among the leading US defense contractors, has 4 segments: electronics, aircraft, engineering and construction (focusing on industrial projects), and appliances (including Amana, Caloric, and Speed Queen). The largest segment is electronics, where Raytheon ranks #6 nationwide; products include semiconductors, air traffic control systems, Patriot missile systems, and marine electronics. The company is the top US manufacturer of small passenger aircraft, under such names as Beech, King Air, and Baron. The acquisition of E-Systems for $2.3 billion and an agreement to buy Chrysler's aerospace and defense holdings reflect Raytheon's commitment to defense technology.

THE READER'S DIGEST ASSOCIATION, INC.

Reader's Digest Rd.	CEO: James P. Schadt	1995 Sales: $3,069 million
Pleasantville, NY 10570	CFO: Stephen R. Wilson	1995 Profits: $264 million
Phone: 914-238-1000	Symbol: RDA	Mkt. Value: $4,977 million
Fax: 914-238-4559	Exchange: NYSE	Employees: 6,200

The Reader's Digest Association is a publishing powerhouse. Its flagship publication, *Reader's Digest*, is the world's most widely read magazine; it's published in nearly 20 languages and has a circulation of more than 25 million. The company also produces a wide range of books (Reader's Digest Condensed Books, how-to, reference, cookbooks), music (original and licensed recordings), videos (videocassettes and original video productions), and special-interest magazines (*Travel Holiday*, *New Choices for Retirement Living*, *American Health*). It markets its products through sophisticated direct mailings and an extensive consumer database that is considered one of the best in the world.

REEBOK INTERNATIONAL LTD.

100 Technology Center Dr.	CEO: Paul B. Fireman	1995 Sales: $3,482 million
Stoughton, MA 02072	CFO: Kenneth Watchmaker	1995 Profits: $165 million
Phone: 617-341-5000	Symbol: RBK	Mkt. Value: $2,182 million
Fax: 617-341-7402	Exchange: NYSE	Employees: 6,700

Web site: http://www.planetreebok.com

Reebok is the 2nd largest athletic shoemaker in the US, a couple of steps behind NIKE. It makes a variety of athletic shoes for everything from basketball and volleyball to aerobics and rock climbing and also makes sportswear for running, aerobics, and swimming as well as accessories such as duffel bags and socks. The company's Rockport subsidiary makes casual and dress shoes. In an effort to catch NIKE, Reebok is aggressively pursuing endorsements from sports stars (Shaquille O'Neal, Emmitt Smith, Greg Norman) and licensing Reebok's technology or name for various sporting goods or products.

RELIANCE GROUP HOLDINGS, INC.

55 E. 52nd St.	CEO: Saul P. Steinberg	1995 Sales: $2,906 million
New York, NY 10055	CFO: Lowell C. Freiberg	1995 Profits: $88 million
Phone: 212-909-1100	Symbol: REL	Mkt. Value: $921 million
Fax: 212-909-1864	Exchange: NYSE	Employees: 8,775

Web site: http://RelianceNational.com

Reliance Group is a holding company for a collection of insurance companies that focus primarily on commercial clients. Through its subsidiaries—Reliance National, Reliance Insurance, Reliance Reinsurance, and Reliance Surety—the company provides a wide range of property/casualty coverages for *FORTUNE 500* businesses, including specialty lines and nonstandard risks. The firm offers reinsurance services primarily to small to midmarket specialty insurers, and it provides surety bonds for contractors and financial institutions. The company's Commonwealth Land Title subsidiary is one of the 3 largest title insurers in the US. Reliance has operations in the US, Argentina, Canada, Mexico, the Netherlands, Spain, and the UK.

REPUBLIC NEW YORK CORPORATION

452 Fifth Ave.
New York, NY 10018
Phone: 212-525-6100
Fax: 212-525-5678

CEO: Walter H. Weiner
CFO: Kenneth F. Cooper
Symbol: RNB
Exchange: NYSE

1995 Sales: $2,860 million
1995 Profits: $289 million
Mkt. Value: $3,218 million
Employees: 4,900

Web site: http://www.rnb.com

445

Republic New York's main subsidiary is Republic National Bank, which offers banking services to individuals and institutions from nearly 70 branches in the New York City area. The company also operates offices in Asia, the Caribbean, Europe, and Latin America, where it provides foreign exchange transactions and credit and transaction processing. Subsidiary Republic Bank for Savings is a New York-based thrift, and another subsidiary, Republic Factors, buys receivables, primarily from the retail clothing trade. The company also provides investment and asset management and brokerage services through Republic New York Securities, Republic Asset Management, and Republic New York Securities International.

REVCO D.S., INC.

1925 Enterprise Parkway
Twinsburg, OH 44087
Phone: 216-425-9811
Fax: 216-487-6539

CEO: D. Dwayne Hoven
CFO: James J. Hagan
Symbol: RXR
Exchange: NYSE

1995 Sales: $4,432 million
1995 Profits: $58 million
Mkt. Value: $1,867 million
Employees: 32,000

Web site: http://www.revco.com

295

One of the largest drugstore chains in the US, Revco operates more than 2,100 outlets in 14 eastern and midwestern states. It offers prescription drugs (which account for about half its revenues) and over-the-counter drugs as well as general merchandise such as beauty care products, cosmetics, personal hygiene products, vitamins, book, magazines, stationery, and snack food. In keeping stride with the changing health care industry, Revco has created a pharmacy benefits management company, RxCONNECTIONS, to provide services for managed-care payers. The company also continues to add new stores.

REYNOLDS METALS COMPANY

6601 W. Broad St.
Richmond, VA 23230
Phone: 804-281-2000
Fax: 804-281-3695

CEO: Richard G. Holder
CFO: Henry S. Savedge Jr.
Symbol: RLM
Exchange: NYSE

1995 Sales: $7,252 million
1995 Profits: $389 million
Mkt. Value: $3,713 million
Employees: 29,800

Web site: http://www.rmc.com

179

Reynolds is the world's #3 aluminum producer (after Canada's Alcan and the US's Alcoa). Best known for Reynolds Wrap aluminum foil, it also makes soft drink and beer cans, other aluminum packaging and consumer products, and materials for the transportation, building, and construction industries. The company also makes nonaluminum packaging and consumer products, such as plastic containers and wax papers. Reynolds has extensive mineral mining and marketing operations, as well as metal recycling and distribution businesses. To boost sales, the company is exploring new markets around the world (especially in Asia, Central America, and South America).

RITE AID CORPORATION

30 Hunter Lane
Camp Hill, PA 17011
Phone: 717-761-2633
Fax: 717-975-5871

CEO: Martin Grass
CFO: Frank Bergonzi
Symbol: RAD
Exchange: NYSE

1995 Sales: $4,534 million
1995 Profits: $141 million
Mkt. Value: $2,722 million
Employees: 36,700

290

With over 2,700 stores, Rite Aid has more retail drugstores in the US than any other chain. The company operates stores under the names Gray Drug Fair, Lane Drug, Life-Aid Services, and Name Rite in 21 eastern states. Stores offer prescription drugs and a wide selection of health, beauty care, and seasonal merchandise, as well as a large private-label product line. Rite Aid also operates Eagle Managed Care, a wholly owned subsidiary designed to market prescription benefit programs. The company is undertaking an aggressive expansion plan, including building more than 75 new stores in New York City.

When demand for his company's gunpowder canisters dropped after WWI, **Richard Reynolds** turned to a family connection: a tobacco outfit founded by his uncle R. J. needed tinfoil for cigarette packages. The two companies formed US Foil, which became part of **Reynolds Metals** in 1929.

— Hoover's Handbook of American Business 1996

RJR NABISCO HOLDINGS CORP.

1301 Sixth Ave.
New York, NY 10019
Phone: 212-258-5600
Fax: 212-969-9173

CEO: Steven F. Goldstone
CFO: Robert S. Roath
Symbol: RN
Exchange: NYSE

1995 Sales: $16,008 million
1995 Profits: $611 million
Mkt. Value: $9,105 million
Employees: 76,000

65

RJR Nabisco Holdings Corp. is the parent of separately traded subsidiary Nabisco, Inc., a leading US food company. RJR is also the #2 cigarette maker (after Philip Morris) in the US. Product lines include cigarettes (Camel, Winston, Salem); candy, gum, and nuts (Breath Savers, Care Free, Planters); cookies, crackers, and cereals (Nilla Wafers, Cheese Nips, Cream of Wheat); and a myriad of other brands (A-1 steak sauce, Blue Bonnet margarine, and Ortega Mexican food products). Almost 3/4 of RJR's revenues come from domestic operations; sales are split almost evenly between food products and tobacco products.

ROCKWELL INTERNATIONAL CORPORATION

2201 Seal Beach Blvd.
Seal Beach, CA 90740
Phone: 310-797-3311
Fax: 310-797-5690

CEO: Donald R. Beall
CFO: W. Michael Barnes
Symbol: ROK
Exchange: NYSE

1995 Sales: $13,009 million
1995 Profits: $742 million
Mkt. Value: $12,410 million
Employees: 82,671

Web site: http://www.rockwell.com

90

Rockwell International makes products for the electronics, automotive, aerospace, and graphics industries at facilities worldwide. It ranks #5 among US manufacturers of electronics and electrical equipment (roughly half of Rockwell's business) and leads the world in producing both microchips for modems and web offset press equipment. It is also a leading supplier of vehicle components. Rockwell has built its Allen-Bradley unit into the top US industrial automation company. Yet about 1/3 of sales still go to the government; the aerospace division makes propulsion systems for Atlas and Delta rockets, and the company is in a joint venture with Lockheed Martin to negotiate a sole-source contract to run the space shuttle program.

ROHM AND HAAS COMPANY

100 Independence Mall W.
Philadelphia, PA 19106
Phone: 215-592-3000
Fax: 215-592-3377

CEO: J. Lawrence Wilson
CFO: Fred W. Shaffer
Symbol: ROH
Exchange: NYSE

1995 Sales: $3,884 million
1995 Profits: $292 million
Mkt. Value: $4,677 million
Employees: 11,670

Web site: http://www.rohmhaas.com

322

Rohm and Haas is a multinational producer of specialty polymers and biological compounds. These products range from automotive fluids and biocides to acrylic plastics, including Plexiglas, a glass substitute used in outdoor signs, industrial lighting, skylights, and boat windshields. Rohm and Haas also makes resins and monomers for industrial applications as well as agricultural applications and chemicals. The company has a joint venture with pharmaceutical firm American Home Products to develop a new insecticide. Nearly half of Rohm and Haas's profits come from outside North America, and it is looking for continued growth overseas, particularly in Asia.

ROUNDY'S, INC.

23000 Roundy Dr.
Pewaukee, WI 53072
Phone: 414-547-7999
Fax: 414-547-4540

CEO: Gerald F. Lestina
CFO: Robert D. Ranus
Ownership: Cooperative

1995 Sales: $2,488 million
Employees: 4,839

Roundy's distributes food and other items to more than 900 grocery stores in 12 states, mostly in the Midwest. The company itself owns and operates a handful of stores, including Pick 'n Save warehouse stores used to test new concepts for customer stores. Franchisees own about 55 additional Pick 'n Saves. Product lines include bakery goods, dairy products, dry groceries, fresh produce, frozen foods, and meats. Roundy's is a cooperative that is about 2/3-owned by its members (the owners of more than 100 Wisconsin and Illinois stores) and 1/3-owned by employees and former members. Roundy's offers members and customer stores a host of support services, including insurance and group advertising.

R. R. DONNELLEY & SONS COMPANY

77 W. Wacker Dr.
Chicago, IL 60601
Phone: 312-326-8000
Fax: 312-326-8543

CEO: John R. Walter
CFO: Cheryl A. Francis
Symbol: DNY
Exchange: NYSE

1995 Sales: $6,512 million
1995 Profits: $299 million
Mkt. Value: $5,677 million
Employees: 41,000

Web site: http://www.rrdonnelley.com

R. R. Donnelley & Sons is the #1 supplier of commercial print and related services in the US. Its Commercial Print division covers magazine, catalog, newspaper insert, and CD-ROM and print directories. Networked Services handles the company's book publishing, computer documentation, CD-ROM and diskette replication, and financial printing operations. Information Resources, through its Metromail unit, manages consumer mailing lists and offers cross-reference and online services. Its information services unit offers digital and on-demand printing, graphics design and management, and CD-ROM production.

RYDER SYSTEM, INC.

3600 N.W. 82nd Ave.
Miami, FL 33166
Phone: 305-593-3726
Fax: 305-593-3336

CEO: M. Anthony Burns
CFO: Edwin A. Huston
Symbol: R
Exchange: NYSE

1995 Sales: $5,167 million
1995 Profits: $148 million
Mkt. Value: $2,168 million
Employees: 44,503

Web site: http://ryder.inter.net/ryder

Ryder provides full-service leasing and short-term rental of trucks, tractors, and trailers. Major clients include the Home Depot, GM, Ford, Toyota, and Honda. In addition, Ryder daily transports more than 400,000 students by school bus in some 20 states and manages or operates about 90 public transit systems. It also operates a dedicated logistics services segment (Ryder Dedicated Logistics) for transportation that uses state-of-the-art technology for information systems and logistics tracking. Ryder offers truck rentals in Canada, Germany, Mexico, Poland, the UK, and the US and operates a fleet of nearly 200,000 vehicles.

R.R. Donnelley & Sons, with roots reaching back to the 1860s, has had a hand in a number of landmark print industry developments. By 1900 it was printing telephone books and the Montgomery Ward catalog. It began printing the "Encyclopædia Britannica" in 1910, won the contract to print "Time" in 1927, and influenced Henry Luce's 1936 decision to start "Life" by coming up with innovations in high-speed press operations.

— Hoover's Handbook of American Business 1996

SAFECO CORPORATION

Safeco Plaza
Seattle, WA 98185
Phone: 206-545-5000
Fax: 206-545-5995

CEO: Roger H. Eigsti
CFO: Boh A. Dickey
Symbol: SAFC
Exchange: Nasdaq

1995 Sales: $3,723 million
1995 Profits: $399 million
Mkt. Value: $4,409 million
Employees: 7,466

Web site: http://www.safeco.com/home2.html

Known primarily for its auto insurance lines, SAFECO also offers other insurance products. Its property/casualty operations, which include SAFECO Insurance Co. of America, General Insurance Co. of America, First National Insurance Co. of America, and SAFECO National Insurance, offer personal and commercial insurance to individuals and businesses. The life and health segment, which includes SAFECO Life Insurance, SAFECO Administrative Services, and First SAFECO National Life Insurance Co. of New York, offers individual and group life and health insurance, pension and annuity products, and benefit-plan administration. Other lines of business include real estate development and financial services.

SAFEWAY INC.

201 Fourth St.
Oakland, CA 94660
Phone: 510-891-3000
Fax: 510-891-3603

CEO: Steven A. Burd
CFO: Julian C. Day
Symbol: SWY
Exchange: NYSE

1995 Sales: $16,398 million
1995 Profits: $326 million
Mkt. Value: $5,863 million
Employees: 113,000

Safeway is one of the nation's largest food retailers, with over 1,000 stores located mostly in the western and mid-Atlantic regions of the US and western Canada. The company owns 35% of the Vons Companies, the largest supermarket chain in southern California, and almost 50% of Casa Ley, S.A. de C.V., which operates food/variety and wholesale stores in western Mexico. It also manufactures and sells private-label merchandise. Safeway is building larger stores and remodeling its older stores to accommodate a wider selection of food and general merchandise. Kohlberg Kravis Roberts owns about 60% of Safeway.

THE ST. PAUL COMPANIES, INC.

385 Washington St.
St. Paul, MN 55102
Phone: 612-310-7911
Fax: 612-221-8294

CEO: Douglas W. Leatherdale
CFO: Patrick A. Thiele
Symbol: SPC
Exchange: NYSE

1995 Sales: $5,410 million
1995 Profits: $521 million
Mkt. Value: $4,565 million
Employees: 12,300

Web site: http://www.stpaul.com

St. Paul is a leading diversified financial services company. Through its subsidiaries the firm offers property/casualty insurance, reinsurance, and investment services. St. Paul Fire and Marine sells commercial insurance (including general liability, customized coverage, and workers' compensation) and personal lines (including home and auto coverage). St. Paul Re offers reinsurance for property/liability insurance companies; Minet provides retail, wholesale, and reinsurance brokering and risk advisory services to major corporations; and the John Nuveen Co. develops and manages tax-free investment products. St. Paul sells its products through independent agents and brokers.

SALOMON INC

7 World Trade Center
New York, NY 10048
Phone: 212-783-7000
Fax: 212-783-2110

CEO: Robert E. Denham
CFO: Jerome H. Bailey
Symbol: SB
Exchange: NYSE

1995 Sales: $8,933 million
1995 Profits: $457 million
Mkt. Value: $3,857 million
Employees: 8,439

Web site: http://www.salomon.com

Salomon is one of Wall Street's leading investment banking firms. It is also a major trader of oil and other commodities. The company provides asset and money management, financial research and advice, mutual funds, and securities underwriting. Salomon is focusing on client services and providing stricter compensation to client-side personnel (while leaving the firm's proprietary traders untouched). Investor Warren Buffett owns a significant interest in the company.

SARA LEE CORPORATION

3 First National Plaza
Chicago, IL 60602
Phone: 312-726-2600
Fax: 312-726-3712

CEO: John H. Bryan
CFO: Judith A. Sprieser
Symbol: SLE
Exchange: NYSE

1995 Sales: $17,719 million
1995 Profits: $804 million
Mkt. Value: $15,974 million
Employees: 149,100

50

Sara Lee is a multiline consumer products manufacturer. Its Packaged Foods segment turns out packaged meats (Ball Park franks, Jimmy Dean sausage) and bakery items (Sara Lee cheesecake). The company also distributes dry, refrigerated, and frozen foods, along with paper supplies and equipment, to the food service industry under the PYA/Monarch name. The Packaged Consumer Products segment makes leather accessories (Coach, Mark Cross), knit products (Champion underwear), hosiery (Hanes and L'Eggs), and personal care products (Brylcreem hair grooming cream). It operates plants in 27 states and 35 other nations and is increasing its presence overseas, particularly in Europe.

SBC COMMUNICATIONS INC.

175 E. Houston
San Antonio, TX 78205
Phone: 210-821-4105
Fax: 210-351-2071

CEO: Edward E. Whitacre Jr.
CFO: Donald E. Kiernan
Symbol: SBC
Exchange: NYSE

1995 Sales: $12,670 million
1995 Loss: ($930) million
Mkt. Value: $31,154 million
Employees: 59,300

Web site: http://www.sbc.com

93

Forsaking a name that spanned nearly the entire century, Southwestern Bell became SBC Communications in 1994. Perhaps SBC was just preparing for its 1996 announcement that it would acquire fellow RBOC, Pacific Telesis. If the deal goes through, SBC will be the primary provider of local telephone service in Arkansas, California, Kansas, Missouri, Nevada, Oklahoma, and Texas and cellular service in 61 cities, including Albany, Austin, Boston, Buffalo, Chicago, Dallas, El Paso, Houston, St. Louis, and Syracuse. Internationally, SBC has a 10% stake in a national cellular carrier in France; 10% of Mexico's telephone company, Telefonos de Mexico, or TelMex; and a 40% stake in a Chilean telecommunications company.

SCHERING-PLOUGH CORPORATION

1 Giralda Farms
Madison, NJ 07940
Phone: 201-822-7000
Fax: 201-822-7447

CEO: Richard Kogan
CFO: Jack L. Wyszomierski
Symbol: SGP
Exchange: NYSE

1995 Sales: $5,151 million
1995 Profits: $887 million
Mkt. Value: $21,127 million
Employees: 20,100

259

Schering-Plough develops and markets prescription drugs, vision care products, animal health products, over-the-counter drugs, and foot care and sun care products. Its pharmaceuticals include Claritin (antihistamine), its top-selling product, as well as Vanceril (antiasthmatic) and Lotrimin (antifungal treatment). Over-the-counter brand names include Afrin (nasal sprays), Coppertone (sun care), and Dr. Scholl's (foot care). The company has a joint venture with Canji to research new cancer treatments based on Canji's new p53 gene therapy technology and an agreement with Corvas to develop oral antithrombotic drugs to treat cardiovascular disorders.

SCI SYSTEMS, INC.

2101 W. Clinton Ave.
Huntsville, AL 35805
Phone: 205-882-4800
Fax: 205-882-4804

CEO: Olin B. King
CFO: Ronald G. Sibold
Symbol: SCIS
Exchange: Nasdaq

1995 Sales: $2,674 million
1995 Profits: $45 million
Mkt. Value: $1,047 million
Employees: 13,185

465

SCI Systems is the #1 contract electronic components manufacturer in the world. It builds finished PCs and hundreds of other products, including circuit boards, subassemblies, video terminals, computer networking modems, digital television reception units, and local- and wide-area network interfaces. Customers include Dell, Conner Peripherals, Hewlett-Packard, and IBM as well as original equipment manufacturers in the aerospace, defense, telecommunications, medical, and entertainment industries. Though its past focus has been on components, the company views the trend toward outsourcing of finished products as a key factor in its future.

SEAGATE TECHNOLOGY, INC.

920 Disc Dr.	CEO: Alan F. Shugart	1995 Sales: $4,540 million
Scotts Valley, CA 95066	CFO: Donald L. Waite	1995 Profits: $260 million
Phone: 408-438-6550	Symbol: SEG	Mkt. Value: $5,888 million
Fax: 408-438-6172	Exchange: NYSE	Employees: 65,000

Web site: http://www.seagate.com

Seagate makes rigid magnetic disk drives for notebook computers, desktop PCs, workstations, and supercomputers. The company also provides disk drives for such multimedia applications as digital video and video-on-demand. Its products include approximately 100 rigid disc drive models with capacities from 170 MB to 9 GB. Seagate's $1 billion acquisition of leading drive manufacturer Conner Peripherals gives it Conner's roster of some 40 hardware and software storage products.

SEARS, ROEBUCK AND CO.

3333 Beverly Rd.	CEO: Arthur C. Martinez	1995 Sales: $35,181 million
Hoffman Estates, IL 60179	CFO: Allen J. Lacy	1995 Profits: $1,801 million
Phone: 847-286-2500	Symbol: S	Mkt. Value: $19,571 million
Fax: 847-875-8351	Exchange: NYSE	Employees: 275,000

Sears, the nation's #2 retailer (after Wal-Mart), has shed much of its noncore operations (including its Allstate insurance business and Homart real estate business). The company is focusing on its Merchandise Group, which operates mall-based department stores and freestanding stores in Canada, Mexico, and the US. Sears operates an automotive division, including Western Auto (which operates Tire America and NTW stores), hardware stores (Sears Hardware), and furniture stores (Sears Homelife). Sears recently sold its 50% stake in the Prodigy online service to an investor group that includes Prodigy's management.

SERVICE MERCHANDISE COMPANY, INC.

7100 Svc. Merchandise Dr.	CEO: Raymond Zimmerman	1995 Sales: $4,019 million
Brentwood, TN 37027	CFO: S. Cusano	1995 Profits: $50 million
Phone: 615-660-6000	Symbol: SME	Mkt. Value: $561 million
Fax: 615-660-3319	Exchange: NYSE	Employees: 26,850

Web site: http://www.servicemerchandise.com

Service Merchandise is the nation's largest catalog showroom retailer, with stores in 37 states. The company sells more jewelry, cameras, and electric razors than any retailer in the US and is 2nd only to J. C. Penney in the sale of luggage. Its products also include housewares, small appliances, TVs, lawn and garden accessories, and toys. Service Merchandise hopes to increase sales by adding more promotional items and displaying its products to create opportunities for impulse buying without detracting from the company's main focus: catalog operations.

Many **Sears** store managers got an intimidating introduction to the Information Age in 1982, when **Edward Brennan**, then CEO for merchandising, was pushing to revive the business. Brennan would call managers to his office to show off his new computer screen, which revealed daily sales figures from every department in every store nationwide.

— *The Big Store*, by Donald R. Katz

For **ServiceMaster**, cleanliness is next to godliness. The leading provider of professional cleaning services (whose first principle is "to honor God in all we do") uses Christian values as a guide in its efforts to motivate workers by treating them with dignity.

HISTORY

— Hoover's Guide to the Top Chicago Companies

SERVICEMASTER LIMITED PARTNERSHIP

1 ServiceMaster Way	CEO: Carlos H. Cantu	1995 Sales: $3,203 million
Downers Grove, IL 60515	CFO: Ernest J. Mrozek	1995 Profits: $106 million
Phone: 708-271-1300	Symbol: SVM	Mkt. Value: $3,017 million
Fax: 708-271-5753	Exchange: NYSE	Employees: 34,000

Web site: http://www.svm.com

388 ServiceMaster is a leading provider of professional cleaning services (ServiceMaster and Res/Com), termite and pest control (Terminix), maid services (Merry Maids), lawn care (TruGreen-ChemLawn), and home appliance repair warranties (American Home Shield). These consumer services are offered through a worldwide network of company-owned and franchised branches. ServiceMaster also provides health care, educational, and industrial facilities with management support services, such as maintenance, housekeeping and custodial services, laundry and linen services, and grounds and landscaping services. The company also operates child care centers and provides food services for schools.

SHAW INDUSTRIES, INC.

616 E. Walnut Ave.	CEO: Robert E. Shaw	1995 Sales: $2,870 million
Dalton, GA 30721	CFO: William C. Lusk Jr.	1995 Profits: $52 million
Phone: 706-278-3812	Symbol: SHX	Mkt. Value: $1,580 million
Fax: 706-275-1040	Exchange: NYSE	Employees: 24,608

Web site: http://www.shawinds.com

439 The world's #1 carpet manufacturer, Shaw Industries makes some 2,500 styles of carpets and rugs for residential and commercial use under such brand names as Abingdon, Cabin Crafts, Crossley, Minster, Redbook, Shawmark, and Terza. Shaw, which holds more than 1/3 of the US residential market, sells to more than 40,000 retailers and wholesalers across the US and Canada. Also the #1 carpet manufacturer in Australia and the UK, the company is continuing its international expansion. It has stakes in Mexican carpet makers Tapetes Luxor and Corporacion Santa Rosa.

THE SHERWIN-WILLIAMS COMPANY

101 Prospect Ave. N.W.	CEO: John G. Breen	1995 Sales: $3,274 million
Cleveland, OH 44115	CFO: Larry J. Pitorak	1995 Profits: $201 million
Phone: 216-566-2000	Symbol: SHW	Mkt. Value: $3,710 million
Fax: 216-566-2947	Exchange: NYSE	Employees: 18,458

382 Sherwin-Williams is North America's largest manufacturer of paints and varnishes. It also makes chemical and automotive coatings and equipment for applying paint. The firm's paints are marketed under the brand names Acme, Color Works, Dutch Boy, EverClean, Kem-Tone, Martin-Senour, Rust Tough, Sherwin-Williams, SuperPaint, and others. The company operates more 2,000 Sherwin-Williams paint stores nationwide and also supplies paint for the private-label brands of Sears and Kmart. Sherwin-Williams has expanded into Mexico and continues to be on the lookout for acquisitions in the highly fragmented paint industry.

SMITH'S FOOD & DRUG CENTERS, INC.

1550 S. Redwood Rd.	CEO: Jeffrey P. Smith	1995 Sales: $3,084 million
Salt Lake City, UT 84104	CFO: Matthew G. Tezak	1995 Loss: ($41) million
Phone: 801-974-1400	Symbol: SFD	Mkt. Value: $608 million
Fax: 801-974-1662	Exchange: NYSE	Employees: 20,277

Smith's Food & Drug Centers operates regional supermarkets and drug stores in Arizona, California, Idaho, Nevada, New Mexico, Texas, Utah, and Wyoming. The company runs approximately 140 food and drug centers ranging from 54,000 to 81,000 sq. ft. The stores offer such food products as groceries, meat, poultry, produce, dairy products, delicatessen items, prepared foods, bakery products, frozen foods, take-out foods, fresh juices, and specialty fish, meat, and cheese. Other offerings include prescription and over-the-counter drugs, health and beauty aids, videos, housewares, toys, cameras, photo processing, and cosmetics.

SONOCO PRODUCTS COMPANY

N. Second St.	CEO: Charles W. Coker	1995 Sales: $2,706 million
Hartsville, SC 29550	CFO: F. Trent Hill Jr.	1995 Profits: $165 million
Phone: 803-383-7000	Symbol: SON	Mkt. Value: $2,494 million
Fax: 803-339-6078	Exchange: NYSE	Employees: 19,000

Web site: http://www.sonoco.com

Sonoco is a global manufacturer of packaging products. The company's products include pressure-sensitive labels, flexible packaging, plastic containers, composite cans, fiber partitions, tubes, cores, paperboard cones, and wire and cable reels. It sells its products to industrial markets (papermakers, chemical and pharmaceutical producers, textile manufacturers, and the construction industry) and consumer markets (food and beverage processors, the personal care and health care industries, food stores, household goods makers, and consumer electronics manufacturers). Sonoco has offices in the US and 22 other countries. It has joint venture alliances in China and Indonesia and continues to build its international business.

THE SOUTHERN COMPANY

64 Perimeter Center E.	CEO: A.W. Dahlberg	1995 Sales: $9,180 million
Atlanta, GA 30346	CFO: W. L. Westbrook	1995 Profits: $1,103 million
Phone: 404-393-0650	Symbol: SO	Mkt. Value: $15,405 million
Fax: 770-668-2674	Exchange: NYSE	Employees: 31,882

Web site: http://www.southernco.com

The Southern Company is one of the largest independent power producers in the world, providing service to more than 3.5 million customers in 4 southeastern states. Southern's 5 operating companies are Alabama Power, Georgia Power, Gulf Power, Mississippi Power, and Savannah Electric and Power. Subsidiary Southern Electric International designs, builds, and runs cogeneration power plants and provides power for the independent power market both in the US and abroad. In addition, subsidiary Southern Communications Services provides wireless communications services within the company and to outside businesses.

SOUTHERN PACIFIC RAIL CORPORATION

1 Market Plaza	CEO: Jerry R. Davis	1995 Sales: $3,151 million
San Francisco, CA 94105	CFO: Lawrence C. Yarberry	1995 Loss: ($3) million
Phone: 415-541-1000	Symbol: RSP	Mkt. Value: $3,864 million
Fax: 415-541-1033	Exchange: NYSE	Employees: 19,049

Southern Pacific is one of the largest US freight rail companies. It has 5 main routes along more than 16,000 miles of primary track through 16 states in the West, Southwest, and Midwest. The company also serves markets in Mexico through an agreement with that country's national railroad. Southern Pacific transports intermodal (truck-to-train) freight, chemicals, forest products, coal, metals, construction materials, and automobiles. It has been investing in upgrading its system with the proceeds from several real estate sales. Rival railroad Union Pacific has made a bid to acquire the company.

SOUTHWEST AIRLINES CO.

2702 Love Field Dr.
Dallas, TX 75235
Phone: 214-904-4000
Fax: 214-904-4200

CEO: Herbert D. Kelleher
CFO: Gary C. Kelly
Symbol: LUV
Exchange: NYSE

1995 Sales: $2,873 million
1995 Profits: $183 million
Mkt. Value: $4,480 million
Employees: 19,933

Web site: http://www.iflyswa.com

Southwest Airlines, which refined the low-cost, no-frills, no-reserved seats, no-meals approach to air travel, is the country's 8th largest airline. The carrier serves more than 40 cities in 24 states and is frequently expanding its destinations. To curb maintenance and pilot training costs, the airline uses only fuel-efficient Boeing 737s, of which the company operates more than 200. Southwest offers a "ticketless" travel system to trim travel agents' commissions. It is also using a new computer reservation system for automated booking of passengers after 3 airline reservation systems partially owned by rivals bumped Southwest off their computer systems.

SPARTAN STORES INC.

850 76th St. S.W.
Grand Rapids, MI 49518
Phone: 616-878-2000
Fax: 616-878-2775

CEO: Patrick M. Quinn
CFO: James B. Meyer
Ownership: Cooperative

1995 Sales: $2,512 million
Employees: 3,200

Spartan Stores is one of the nation's leading wholesale food cooperatives, serving approximately 500 supermarket chains in Indiana, Ohio, and Michigan. It distributes bakery products, dairy products, fresh fruits and vegetables, meats, frozen foods, and other grocery items and also provides accounting, advertising, and insurance to its member retailers from two distribution centers in Michigan. The company also owns one grocery store, which it runs through its Valueland subsidiary. Other subsidiaries conduct Spartan's insurance and real estate businesses. Shares in the cooperative are owned by employees and by member stores.

SPRINT CORPORATION

2330 Shawnee Mission Pkwy.
Westward, KS 66205
Phone: 913-624-3000
Fax: 913-624-3281

CEO: William T. Esrey
CFO: Arthur B. Krause
Symbol: FON
Exchange: NYSE

1995 Sales: $13,600 million
1995 Profits: $395 million
Mkt. Value: $12,397 million
Employees: 48,300

Web site: http://www.sprint.com

The #3 long-distance telephone service provider in the US (after AT&T and MCI), Sprint also provides local exchange and cellular telephone services. Sprint Spectrum, a partnership with 3 of the US's largest cable TV operators, has the ability to provide wireless communications service to more than 180 million people. Global One, a joint venture with Deutsche Telekom and France Telecom, gives Sprint a foothold on 6 continents. In addition, subsidiary North Supply Co. is a wholesale distributor of telecommunications equipment, security and alarm systems, and electrical products. Expansion in Europe, Mexico, and China plays a key role in Sprint's strategy.

THE STANLEY WORKS

1000 Stanley Dr.
New Britain, CT 06053
Phone: 860-225-5111
Fax: 203-827-3895

CEO: Richard H. Ayers
CFO: Richard Huck
Symbol: SWK
Exchange: NYSE

1995 Sales: $2,624 million
1995 Profits: $59 million
Mkt. Value: $2,438 million
Employees: 19,784

Stanley Works offers a comprehensive range of hardware and tools, which it makes and sells around the world. Its major product lines include consumer tools (carpentry tools, toolboxes, masonry tools), industrial tools (hand tools, electronic diagnostic tools, cabinets), engineered tools (pneumatic nailers, staplers, office products), hardware (hinges, brackets, bolts), and specialty hardware (door systems, power-operated gates, garage door openers). Brand names include Bostitch, Jensen, Leverlock, MAC Tools, Monarch, Powerlock, Stanley, and Vidmar. The company operates more than 110 manufacturing and major distribution facilities in the US and 19 other countries.

STAPLES, INC.

100 Pennsylvania Ave.
Framingham, MA 01701
Phone: 508-370-8500
Fax: 508-370-8955

CEO: Thomas G. Stemberg
CFO: John B. Wilson
Symbol: SPLS
Exchange: Nasdaq

1995 Sales: $3,068 million
1995 Profits: $74 million
Mkt. Value: $3,043 million
Employees: 10,332

Web site: http://www.staples.com

One of the Big 3 office supply superstores (along with Office Depot and OfficeMax), Staples is one of the fastest-growing specialty retailers in the US. Staples sells office products, business services, furniture, and computers through some 450 stores in the eastern US, California, and Canada (the latter under the name Business Depot). The company also has joint ventures in Germany and the UK. Staples superstores are located primarily in suburban areas; it operates smaller Staples Express stores in downtown Boston, Manhattan, and Washington, DC. The company continues an aggressive expansion plan and is also experimenting with larger stores.

STATE FARM MUTUAL AUTOMOBILE INSURANCE COMPANY

1 State Farm Plaza
Bloomington, IL 61710
Phone: 309-766-2311
Fax: 309-766-6169

CEO: Edward B. Rust Jr.
CFO: Roger S. Joslin
Ownership: Mutual Company

1995 Sales: $40,810 million
1995 Profits: $1,271 million
Employees: 71,437

Web site: http://www.statefarm.com

State Farm is the nation's largest auto insurance company. The company provides casualty insurance and reinsurance through its State Farm Fire and Casualty affiliate. It offers life, accident, and health insurance through its State Farm Life & Accident Assurance and State Farm Life affiliates. Other affiliates State Farm Investment Management and State Farm International Services provide investment management and other financial services. State Farm operates throughout the US and Canada.

Herb Kelleher, the flamboyant CEO of **Southwest Airlines**, had one of the company's Boeing 737s painted up to look like Shamu the killer whale in 1988, when Southwest became the official airline of Sea World.

— Hoover's Guide to the Top Texas Companies

STATE STREET BOSTON CORPORATION

225 Franklin St.
Boston, MA 02110
Phone: 617-786-3000
Fax: 617-654-4006

CEO: Marshall N. Carter
CFO: Ronald L. O'Kelley
Symbol: STT
Exchange: NYSE

1995 Sales: $2,446 million
1995 Profits: $247 million
Mkt. Value: $3,879 million
Employees: 11,324

State Street Boston is a holding company for State Street Bank and Trust. The bank primarily offers investment management services and is the largest US mutual-fund custodian. It also focuses on international investment and has offices in some 16 countries. State Street's commercial lending segment specializes in lending to businesses and other financial institutions. The bank also provides short-term loans to its investment customers to support their trading activities.

STONE CONTAINER CORPORATION

150 N. Michigan Ave.
Chicago, IL 60601
Phone: 312-346-6600
Fax: 312-580-4919

CEO: Roger W. Stone
CFO: Randolph C. Read
Symbol: STO
Exchange: NYSE

1995 Sales: $7,351 million
1995 Profits: $256 million
Mkt. Value: $1,425 million
Employees: 25,900

175 Stone Container is the world's top producer of paperboard and paper packaging materials and is among the US leaders in forest and paper products overall. With 180 plants around the world, it makes containerboard, corrugated containers, bags, folding cartons, kraft paper, newsprint, white paper and pulp, uncoated paper, lumber, veneer, and related products. The Stone family holds roughly 15% of the stock. The company is looking to the expanding demand for boxes in Europe and Asia to boost sales; higher paper prices, along with sales of assets and debt restructuring, helped end a string of annual losses.

HISTORY While innovators steal much of the high-tech limelight, **Sun Microsystems** did quite well as a startup by blending in. Because it adopted AT&T's UNIX operating system in the early 1980s, its workstations ran easily with hardware and software of other vendors. Sales blew past $500 million within 5 years.

— Hoover's Guide to Computer Companies

THE STOP & SHOP COMPANIES, INC.

1385 Hancock St.
Quincy, MA 02169
Phone: 617-380-8000
Fax: 617-380-5915

CEO: Robert G. Tobin
CFO: Joseph D. McGlinchey
Symbol: SHP
Exchange: NYSE

1995 Sales: $4,116 million
1995 Profits: $68 million
Mkt. Value: $1,330 million
Employees: 37,000

309 Stop & Shop operates the largest supermarket chain in New England. The company runs more than 125 supermarkets under the Stop & Shop name in Connecticut, Massachusetts, New York, and Rhode Island. Almost 100 of the stores, representing nearly 90% of the company's revenues, are superstores called Super Stop & Shops. The company's superstores offer a wider variety of food and nonfood items than traditional grocery stores and have a large number of specialty departments with products that provide increased profit margins. Dutch retailer Royal Ahold has announced plans to acquire Stop & Shop for about $3 billion.

STUDENT LOAN MARKETING ASSOCIATION

1050 T. Jefferson St. N.W.
Washington, DC 20007
Phone: 202-333-8000
Fax: 202-298-3160

CEO: Lawrence A. Hough
CFO: Denise B. McGlone
Symbol: SLM
Exchange: NYSE

1995 Sales: $3,917 million
1995 Profits: $496 million
Mkt. Value: $5,252 million
Employees: 4,741

Web site: http://www.slma.com

318 The Student Loan Marketing Association (Sallie Mae) is a publicly mandated private company designed to keep loan money flowing and to protect student loans from the ups and downs of the credit market. Sallie Mae has the advantage of an implicit guarantee of US government support and protection from the costs of defaulted loans by state and federal guarantees. However, legislation designed to turn 60% of its student loans over to the federal government has Sallie Mae looking for ways to sever its links with Uncle Sam and give up its preferential position, which would allow it to diversify into new areas.

SUN COMPANY, INC.

1801 Market St.	CEO: Robert H. Campbell	1995 Sales: $8,370 million
Philadelphia, PA 19103	CFO: Robert M. Aiken Jr.	1995 Profits: $140 million
Phone: 215-977-3000	Symbol: SUN	Mkt. Value: $2,156 million
Fax: 215-977-3409	Exchange: NYSE	Employees: 11,995

157

One of the largest oil refiners in the US, Sun markets SUNOCO gasoline in 17 states through its SUNOCO service stations, ULTRA SERVICE CENTER service stations, and APLUS convenience stores. The company, which operates 5 refineries as well as domestic pipelines and terminals, gets almost all its revenues from its refining and marketing operations. It conducts limited exploration activities in Canada, and crude oil and natural gas production in Canada and the North Sea. Sun's products include SUNOCO Super C diesel engine oil and ULTRA and OPTIMA gasoline. Its chemical operations make petrochemicals for use in plastics and other industries.

SUN MICROSYSTEMS, INC.

2550 Garcia Ave.	CEO: Scott G. McNealy	1995 Sales: $5,902 million
Mountain View, CA 94043	CFO: Michael E. Lehman	1995 Profits: $336 million
Phone: 415-960-1300	Symbol: SUNW	Mkt. Value: $8,409 million
Fax: 415-969-9131	Exchange: Nasdaq	Employees: 14,498

Web site: http://www.sun.com

222

Sun Microsystems is the leading manufacturer of network-based distributed computing systems and is the #1 maker of UNIX-based workstations (with about 1/3 of the market). The company's line includes microprocessors (SPARC, UltraSPARC—a competitor to the PowerPC and Pentium chips), software (Solaris UNIX), and systems (SPARCstation, SPARCserver). Its SunService Division provides system support, education, consulting, systems integration, and system and network management services. In response to the rapidly growing interest in the Internet, the company has beefed up its offerings for the global computer network with its Hot Java Internet browser and its Netra Internet server.

SUNTRUST BANKS, INC.

25 Park Place	CEO: James B. Williams	1995 Sales: $3,740 million
Atlanta, GA 30303	CFO: John W. Spiegel	1995 Profits: $566 million
Phone: 404-588-7711	Symbol: STI	Mkt. Value: $7,923 million
Fax: 404-827-6001	Exchange: NYSE	Employees: 19,415

332

SunTrust operates 29 banking subsidiaries in 4 southeastern states. It continues to grow through the acquisition of banks in the affluent retirement markets of Florida, where it does more business than in its home state of Georgia. In addition to standard retail and commercial banking services (including checking and savings accounts), SunTrust offers credit cards, mortgage banking, mutual funds, asset and investment management, and securities underwriting and dealing. It operates over 650 offices in Alabama, Florida, Georgia, and Tennessee.

SUPERMARKETS GENERAL HOLDINGS CORPORATION

301 Blair Rd.	CEO: John Boyle	1995 Sales: $4,182 million
Woodbridge, NJ 07095	CFO: Ron Marshall	1995 Profits: $76 million
Phone: 908-499-3000	Ownership: Privately Held	Employees: 30,000
Fax: 908-499-3072		

304

Supermarkets General Holdings operates nearly 150 Pathmark supermarkets in Connecticut, Delaware, New Jersey, New York, and Pennsylvania. The grocery chain has responded to customer interest in grocery superstores by opening more than 100 Super Centers, which average more than 60,000 square feet. Supermarkets General also runs some 30 "Pathmark 2000" supermarkets, which provide a more upscale store format and grocery selection. It operates only 6 conventional grocery stores, as well as 6 deep-discount drugstores in Connecticut. The company sells a line of more than 3,000 private-label groceries, one of the largest of such programs in the nation.

SUPERVALU INC.

11840 Valley View Rd.
Eden Prairie, MN 55344
Phone: 612-828-4000
Fax: 612-828-8998

CEO: Michael W. Wright
CFO: Jeffrey C. Girard
Symbol: SVU
Exchange: NYSE

1995 Sales: $16,564 million
1995 Profits: $43 million
Mkt. Value: $2,136 million
Employees: 43,500

SUPERVALU is among the US's top food distributors, supplying its 4,600 (primarily independent) supermarkets in 48 states with thousands of grocery and nongrocery items, including produce, meat, dairy products, paper goods, and clothes. The company uses such "value added" services as store design, insurance, and payroll services to help offset shrinking profits from the sale of its products. SUPERVALU has realigned its operations into 4 logistical and 6 marketing regions and opened new distribution centers to increase operating efficiency and profitability. The company also operates 296 of its own supermarkets under the Cub Foods, Shop-N-Save, and other names.

SYSCO CORPORATION

1390 Enclave Parkway
Houston, TX 77077
Phone: 713-584-1390
Fax: 713-584-1245

CEO: Bill M. Lindig
CFO: John K. Stubblefield Jr.
Symbol: SYY
Exchange: NYSE

1995 Sales: $12,118 million
1995 Profits: $252 million
Mkt. Value: $6,052 million
Employees: 28,100

Web site: http://www.sysco.com

SYSCO is the #1 food service distributor in the US, providing products and services to nearly 250,000 restaurants, schools, hotels, and hospitals. The company distributes frozen foods, fresh meat and produce, imported specialties, canned and dry goods, paper products, and tableware. It offers national brand names as well as its own Imperial, Classic, and Reliance labels. The SYGMA subsidiary serves more than 20 restaurant chains. The company also distributes restaurant and kitchen equipment, cleaning supplies, and medical supplies. SYSCO's market area includes the entire US, Mexico, and the Pacific Coast area of Canada.

TANDY CORPORATION

1800 One Tandy Center
Fort Worth, TX 76102
Phone: 817-390-3700
Fax: 817-390-3500

CEO: John V. Roach
CFO: Dwain H. Hughes
Symbol: TAN
Exchange: NYSE

1995 Sales: $5,839 million
1995 Profits: $212 million
Mkt. Value: $2,969 million
Employees: 45,300

Web site: http://www.tandy.com

Tandy, one of the US's leading electronics retailers, operates Radio Shack, Computer City, and Incredible Universe. The company's flagship, Radio Shack, sells private-label electronic parts, computers, telephones, and audio and video equipment through more than 4,800 stores. Computer City sells computers, peripherals, software, and related products in about 100 stores. The company's newest concept is Incredible Universe, a chain of about 20 "gigastores" that sell an array of electronics (including appliances, cameras, and computers) and software and that also provide child-care facilities, fast food, live entertainment, and a recording studio.

TEACHERS INSURANCE AND ANNUITY ASSOCIATION

730 Third Ave.
New York, NY 10017
Phone: 212-490-9000
Fax: 212-916-6231

CEO: John H. Biggs
CFO: Richard L. Gibbs
Ownership: Nonprofit
Organization

1995 Sales: $11,646 million
1995 Profits: $752 million
Employees: 4,345

Web site: http://www.tiaa-cref.org

Teachers Insurance and Annuity Association (TIAA) is the traditional annuity arm of the world's largest private pension system. TIAA and its sibling organization, College Retirement Equitites Fund (CREF, the variable annuity arm), have assets of $160 billion. TIAA invests the retirement savings of its members (teachers and researchers) in bonds, commercial mortgages, and real estate. One of the nation's largest life insurance companies, TIAA provides portable insurance and retirement benefits to the often transient employees of educational and research organizations. It gains new clients primarily as new institutions adopt its services as part of an increasing menu of benefit plans.

TECH DATA CORPORATION

5350 Tech Data Dr.
Clearwater, FL 34620
Phone: 813-539-7429
Fax: 813-538-7050

CEO: Steven A. Raymund
CFO: Jeffery P. Howells
Symbol: TECD
Exchange: Nasdaq

1995 Sales: $3,087 million
1995 Profits: $22 million
Mkt. Value: $573 million
Employees: 2,625

Tech Data is one of the world's largest full-line wholesale distributors of PCs, computer software (including complete lines from Lotus and Claris Corp.), hardware (printers, modems), and supplies (mouse pads, speakers). The company distributes products from more than 350 manufacturers (such as Apple, IBM, Intel, Microsoft, and Novell) to 50,000 resellers in North and South America. Tech Data practices volume discounting, often selling products at less than manufacturers' wholesale list prices. It also offers advertising assistance, favorable credit terms, product support (including a staff of engineers to provide technical advice by phone), and training.

HISTORY

Like Texas, its home state, **Tandy** has moved from the Old West to high-tech. Founded in 1919 as a leather business in the cow town of Fort Worth, the company turned to craft and hobby retailing before hitting on electronics with the 1963 purchase of Radio Shack. By 1977 Tandy had introduced the first mass-market PC, the TRS-80.

— *Hoover's Guide to the Top Texas Companies*

TELE-COMMUNICATIONS, INC.

5619 DTC Parkway
Englewood, CO 80111
Phone: 303-267-5500
Fax: 303-779-1228

CEO: John C. Malone
CFO: Donne F. Fisher
Symbol: TCOMA
Exchange: Nasdaq

1995 Sales: $6,851 million
1995 Loss: ($171) million
Mkt. Value: $12,893 million
Employees: 39,000

Web site: http://www.tcinc.com

Tele-Communications, Inc. (TCI), is the largest US cable TV systems operator, serving over 11 million basic subscribers. TCI has joined with other businesses, including media, cable, and long-distance companies (Cox Communications, Comcast, and Sprint) to develop the technology of 500-channel interactive TV systems integrated with telephone service. Its TCI Communications handles cable TV service in the US; Liberty Media invests in entertainment, educational, and informational programs for TV and other media; Tele-Communications International is a leading operator of cable TV outside the US; and TCI Technology Ventures develops new technologies (such as electronic games).

TELEDYNE, INC.

2049 Century Park E.
Los Angeles, CA 90067
Phone: 310-277-3311
Fax: 310-551-4366

CEO: William P. Rutledge
CFO: Douglas J. Grant
Symbol: TDY
Exchange: NYSE

1995 Sales: $2,568 million
1995 Profits: $162 million
Mkt. Value: $1,618 million
Employees: 18,000

Web site: http://www.tbe.com/teledyne

Teledyne is a diversified company that provides aviation, electronics, specialty metals, and defense technologies. It has sold more than 25 subsidiaries and consolidated its operating companies to focus on areas where it can maintain leadership. These areas include water filtration for home use (Water Pik products) and encryption, where the company draws on its experience in the defense industry to develop commercial products for preventing program piracy on cable television networks. Other products include dentist and dental lab equipment and Laars swimming pool and spa heaters. After resisting takeover attempts by WHX, Teledyne agreed in 1996 to merge with steelmaker Allegheny Ludlum.

TEMPLE-INLAND INC.

303 S. Temple Dr.
Diboll, TX 75941
Phone: 409-829-5511
Fax: 409-829-1366

CEO: Clifford J. Grum
CFO: Kenneth M. Jastrow II
Symbol: TIN
Exchange: NYSE

1995 Sales: $3,460 million
1995 Profits: $281 million
Mkt. Value: $2,545 million
Employees: 15,400

360

Temple-Inland is a leading producer of paper and building products. The company manufactures containerboard and corrugated boxes as well as gypsum items, hardboard paneling, lumber, particleboard, and plywood. It owns or leases nearly 2 million acres of timberland in Alabama, Georgia, Louisiana, and Texas. Through Guaranty Federal Bank (which has more than 120 branches in Texas), the company is involved in financial services. Temple-Inland also has real estate, mortgage, and insurance subsidiaries. A joint venture with Massuh S.A. of Buenos Aires and its Inland-Chile joint venture have increased the company's production of boxes and corrugated containers in South America.

TENET HEALTHCARE CORPORATION

3820 Stone Street
Santa Barbara, CA 93105
Phone: 805-563-7000
Fax: 805-563-7070

CEO: Jeffrey C. Barbakow
CFO: Trevor Fetter
Symbol: THC
Exchange: NYSE

1995 Sales: $3,318 million
1995 Profits: $165 million
Mkt. Value: $4,260 million
Employees: 69,050

373

Tenet Healthcare is the nation's #2 hospital chain (after Columbia/HCA). Previously known as National Medical Enterprises, the company operates about 70 US acute-care hospitals in California, Florida, and Texas as well as long-term care facilities. It also owns one hospital in Barcelona, Spain. The company runs psychiatric and rehabilitation facilities but has sold off most of its operations in those areas. Tenet's long-term care affiliates include the Hillhaven Corporation and the UK's Westminster Health Care Holdings PLC. The company plans to expand its network of hospitals through acquisitions as the health care industry consolidates.

---

500 HISTORY

Texaco has been known to come up a bit short in upholding big oil's gold-plated image, say some people in the industry. One story has the company taking advantage of cheaper nighttime rates to cable the Libyan government with information about price changes worth millions of dollars.

— *The Seven Sisters*, by Anthony Sampson

TENNECO INC.

1275 King St.
Greenwich, CT 06831
Phone: 203-863-1000
Fax: 203-863-1018

CEO: Dana G. Mead
CFO: Robert T. Blakely
Symbol: TEN
Exchange: NYSE

1995 Sales: $8,899 million
1995 Profits: $735 million
Mkt. Value: $9,558 million
Employees: 60,000

Web site: http://www.tenneco.com

150

Tenneco is a holding company for a diversified collection of businesses. It makes automotive parts (Walker exhaust systems and Monroe ride control products) and packaging materials, transports natural gas from Texas to New England and the Upper Midwest via a 16,000-mile pipeline, and makes plastic products (Hefty and Baggie brands) for the consumer market. The company has announced plans to spin off its Newport News Shipbuilding facilities to shareholders and may spin off or sell its natural gas transportation division to concentrate on its auto parts and packaging operations. It previously spun off Case Corporation, its construction and farm equipment subsidiary.

TEXACO INC.

2000 Westchester Ave.	CEO: Alfred C. DeCrane Jr.	1995 Sales: $36,787 million
White Plains, NY 10650	CFO: William C. Bousquette	1995 Profits: $607 million
Phone: 914-253-4000	Symbol: TX	Mkt. Value: $21,888 million
Fax: 914-253-7753	Exchange: NYSE	Employees: 28,247

Web site: http://www.texaco.com

Texaco, the #3 oil company on the *FORTUNE 500*, is an integrated petroleum company with worldwide operations. The company produces and refines petroleum and markets petroleum products through Texaco stations nationwide. Its Gulf Coast Star Center is a natural gas subsidiary that offers transportation, storage, processing, and marketing operations. Texaco also produces lubricant additives and antifreeze products. Its Caltex Petroleum joint venture with Chevron operates in 61 countries. The company is exploring areas in China, Colombia, and Russia and is investing in high technology to increase output in North Sea oil fields.

TEXAS INSTRUMENTS INCORPORATED

13500 N. Central Expressway	CEO: Jerry R. Junkins	1995 Sales: $13,128 million
Dallas, TX 75265	CFO: William A. Aylesworth	1995 Profits: $1,088 million
Phone: 214-995-2011	Symbol: TXN	Mkt. Value: $9,943 million
Fax: 214-995-4360	Exchange: NYSE	Employees: 59,574

Web site: http://www.ti.com

A leading electronics manufacturer, Texas Instruments (TI) is one of the world's biggest makers of laptop computers and computer chips. It produces digital signal processors (DSPs, used in computer sound cards and cellular phones), dynamic random-access memory (DRAM) chips, speech recognition products, defense electronics, and personal productivity products such as calculators, printers, and electrical control devices. It also makes audio encoders, avionics systems, navigation systems, radar systems, and other products for the government and private sectors. It has several joint ventures, including 2 Asian fabs (with Acer and Kobe Steel).

TEXAS UTILITIES COMPANY

1601 Bryan St.	CEO: Jerry S. Farrington	1995 Sales: $5,639 million
Dallas, TX 75201	CFO: H. Dan Farell	1995 Loss: ($139) million
Phone: 214-812-4600	Symbol: TXU	Mkt. Value: $8,836 million
Fax: 214-812-4651	Exchange: NYSE	Employees: 11,729

Web site: http://www.tu.com

Texas Utilities (TU) is a holding company for one of the largest utilities in the country, TU Electric, which provides electricity to about 1/3 of the population of Texas. TU Electric generates power from lignite, oil and gas, and nuclear sources. Other TU subsidiaries support TU Electric by providing lignite coal (Texas Utilities Mining) and natural gas and oil (TU Fuel) for the company's generating plants. TU Fuel owns half of a 395-mile natural gas pipeline linking the Dallas/Fort Worth area to West Texas producing fields. The company has announced plans to acquire national gas distribution company ENSERCH.

TEXTRON INC.

40 Westminster St.	CEO: James F. Hardymon	1995 Sales: $9,973 million
Providence, RI 02903	CFO: Stephen L. Key	1995 Profits: $479 million
Phone: 401-421-2800	Symbol: TXT	Mkt. Value: $6,701 million
Fax: 401-421-2878	Exchange: NYSE	Employees: 57,000

Web site: http://www.textron.com

One of America's oldest industrial companies, Textron manufactures a wide range of transportation products, from airplanes to golf carts (E-Z-GO). It is a widely diversified company with operations in aircraft (Cessna Aircraft and Bell Helicopter), finance (Avco Financial Services), automotive (McCord Winn windshield washer systems), defense systems and components, and industrial products. The company's products range from Cone Drive gear motors to watchbands (Speidel). Textron is the largest supplier of automotive interiors in the US and its Cessna unit is the world leader in light and midsize business jets. It has announced plans to sell its Paul Revere insurance unit.

THRIFTY PAYLESS HOLDINGS, INC.

9275 S.W. Peyton Lane
Wilsonville, OR 97070
Phone: 503-682-4100
Fax: 503-685-6140

CEO: Gordon Barker
CFO: David R. Jessick
Ownership: Privately Held

1995 Sales: $4,659 million
1995 Loss: ($35) million
Employees: 31,200

One of the largest drugstore chains in the US, Thrifty Payless operates more than 1,000 stores under the Thrifty and Payless names, primarily on the West Coast. The company's merchandise includes prescription and over-the-counter drugs as well as health and beauty aids, candy, tobacco, stationery, and magazines. Thrifty Payless also operates about 40 Bi-Mart discount membership stores in Oregon and Washington. Investment firm Leonard Green & Partners owns about 1/2 of the enterprise; retailer Kmart owns the rest. The company is focusing on building sales in its pharmacy and health care lines.

TIME WARNER INC.

75 Rockefeller Plaza
New York, NY 10019
Phone: 212-484-8000
Fax: 212-484-8734

CEO: Gerald M. Levin
CFO: Richard J. Bressler
Symbol: TWX
Exchange: NYSE

1995 Sales: $8,067 million
1995 Loss: ($166) million
Mkt. Value: $16,855 million
Employees: 35,800

Web site: http://www.pathfinder.com/Corp

Time Warner's portfolio contains such giants as Time Inc. (the US's #1 magazine publisher), Warner Bros. (the world's #1 producer and distributor of movies, TV programs, and videos), Home Box Office (the #1 premium cable TV service), Little, Brown and Co. and Warner Books (leading book publishers), and Time Warner Cable (the #2 US cable system). If its impending acquisition of Turner Broadcasting is approved, it will aquire the news and entertainment giant's complementary holdings in cable (CNN, TNT), movies (Castle Rock Entertainment), and its sports teams. Time Warner also owns stakes in cable channels Cinemax, Court TV, Comedy Central, the Sega Channel, and others.

THE TIMES MIRROR COMPANY

Times Mirror Square
Los Angeles, CA 90053
Phone: 213-237-3700
Fax: 213-237-3800

CEO: Mark Willis
CFO: Thomas Unterman
Symbol: TMC
Exchange: NYSE

1995 Sales: $3,491 million
1995 Profits: $1,227 million
Mkt. Value: $4,003 million
Employees: 21,877

Web site: http://www.latimes.com

The nation's 3rd largest newspaper company, the Times Mirror Company publishes the prestigious *Los Angeles Times*. It also publishes other dailies, among them the highly respected Connecticut newspaper the *Hartford Courant*, and several weekly papers. Specialty magazines include *Field & Stream*, *Popular Science*, and *Outdoor Life*, and the company also owns several specialty book publishers (Richard D. Irwin, Matthew Bender, Mosby-Year Book). The company is controlled by descendants of cofounder Harry Chandler. Their demand for management changes led to the hiring of CEO Mark Willes, known for his cost cutting (one of his first acts was to close the New York edition of Long Island's *Newsday*).

THE TJX COMPANIES, INC.

770 Cochituate Rd.
Framingham, MA 01701
Phone: 508-390-1000
Fax: 508-390-3635

CEO: Bernard Cammarata
CFO: Donald G. Campbell
Symbol: TJX
Exchange: NYSE

1995 Sales: $4,448 million
1995 Profits: $26 million
Mkt. Value: $1,892 million
Employees: 63,000

TJX is the #1 off-price specialty apparel retailer in North America. The company's largest chain is T.J. Maxx, which sells family apparel, accessories, women's shoes, domestics, giftware, and jewelry at 20-60% off full price. It also operates Winners Apparel, a Canadian chain of family clothing stores; Chadwick's of Boston, a women's apparel catalog company; and HomeGoods, a chain of off-price home fashion stores. TJX is concentrating on improving operations and service to respond to increased competition, a weak clothing market, and image problems (waffling between career and casual clothing).

TOSCO CORPORATION

72 Cummings Point Rd.	CEO: Thomas D. O'Malley	1995 Sales: $7,284 million
Stamford, CT 06902	CFO: Jefferson F. Allen	1995 Profits: $77 million
Phone: 203-977-1000	Symbol: TOS	Mkt. Value: $1,705 million
Fax: 203-964-3187	Exchange: NYSE	Employees: 3,750

Tosco is the 2nd largest independent refiner of unbranded petroleum products in the US (after Sun). The company, which has refineries in California, New Jersey, Pennsylvania, and Washington, also sells gasoline through more than 1,000 gas stations, about 1/3 of them company-owned, in the Pacific Northwest and Northern California under the BP brand name and in Arizona under the Exxon brand. Tosco continues to expand its marketing business. It has agreed to purchase Circle K, the #2 convenience store chain in the US with some 2,500 outlets. The purchase will at least double Tosco's daily retail gasoline volume.

TOYS "R" US, INC.

461 From Rd.	CEO: Michael Goldstein	1995 Sales: $9,427 million
Paramus, NJ 07652	CFO: Louis Lipschitz	1995 Profits: $148 million
Phone: 201-262-7800	Symbol: TOY	Mkt. Value: $7,442 million
Fax: 201-262-7606	Exchange: NYSE	Employees: 59,973

Web site: http://www.tru.com

Toys "R" Us is the world's #1 toy retailer. Not only does the company carry toys and games, it also has furniture, bikes, cribs, diapers, and sporting goods. It has to contend with competitors, like Wal-Mart, that have expanded their toy business. The enterprise continues to grow, but with the US market saturated, Toys "R" Us is focusing its efforts on overseas expansion. In addition to opening corporate-owned stores, the company is franchising abroad. Toys "R" Us is cutting prices, increasing advertising and promotions, and adding computer software to its product mix. It is also adding several in-store specialty shops, including Books "R" Us children's book stores, the Lego Store, and the Learning Center.

TRANS WORLD AIRLINES, INC.

515 N. Sixth St.	CEO: Jeffrey H. Erickson	1995 Sales: $3,317 million
St. Louis, MO 63101	CFO: Robert A. Peiser	1995 Loss: ($228) million
Phone: 314-589-3000	Symbol: TWA	Employees: 22,927
Fax: 314-589-3129	Exchange: NYSE	

Web site: http://www.twa.com

Troubled Trans World Airlines (TWA) flies to cities in the US, Europe, and the Middle East. From its primarily domestic St. Louis hub (Lambert International Airport), the airline offers more than 300 scheduled flights daily. TWA operates a domestic/international hub at JFK International Airport in New York from which its wholly owned subsidiary, Trans World Express, Inc., provides service to several cities on the East Coast. The company has cut back its offerings of international flights as it has struggled to cut expenses. TWA emerged from bankruptcy in 1995.

TRANSAMERICA CORPORATION

600 Montgomery St.
San Francisco, CA 94111
Phone: 415-983-4000
Fax: 415-983-4234

CEO: Frank C. Herringer
CFO: George B. Sundby
Symbol: TA
Exchange: NYSE

1995 Sales: $6,101 million
1995 Profits: $471 million
Mkt. Value: $5,205 million
Employees: 10,400

Web site: http://www.transamerica.com

213

Transamerica is a leading provider of life insurance and financial services. The company's operations include consumer lending (home equity and unsecured loans), commercial lending (financing inventories and consumer goods), and leasing (it has one of the world's largest fleets of transportation containers for rail, motor, and steamship carriers and is the world's 2nd largest container lessor). It also offers real estate services (property-tax monitoring and real estate development and management) and is the largest life reinsurer in the US. TransAmerica is cutting back staff and centralizing management.

THE TRAVELERS INC.

388 Greenwich St.
New York, NY 10013
Phone: 212-816-8000
Fax: 212-816-8913

CEO: Sanford I. Weill
CFO: Heidi G. Miller
Symbol: TRV
Exchange: NYSE

1995 Sales: $16,583 million
1995 Profits: $1,834 million
Mkt. Value: $19,692 million
Employees: 48,000

57

Travelers provides insurance and banking services. Since it was acquired by Sanford Weill's Primerica, which took the Travelers name, the company has survived a period of cost cutting and streamlining to emerge with several core insurance and financial businesses: Smith Barney provides investment services, Commercial Credit offers consumer finance, Travelers Bank issues credit cards, and Primerica Financial Services handles mutual funds. Insurance operations include Travelers Insurance and Travelers Indemnity, which sell property/casualty and other types of insurance and retirement products.

TRIBUNE COMPANY

435 N. Michigan Ave.
Chicago, IL 60611
Phone: 312-222-9100
Fax: 312-222-0449

CEO: John W. Madigan
CFO: Donald C. Grenesko
Symbol: TRB
Exchange: NYSE

1995 Sales: $2,864 million
1995 Profits: $278 million
Mkt. Value: $4,207 million
Employees: 10,500

Web site: http://www.tribune.com

442

Tribune Company is a newspaper and entertainment behemoth. It publishes 3 major daily newspapers (*Chicago Tribune*, Ft. Lauderdale's *Sun-Sentinel*, and the *Orlando Sentinel*) and owns several TV stations in Chicago, Los Angeles, New York, and other cities and a handful of radio stations, also in large urban markets. The company owns various book publishers (including NTC and Contemporary Books); produces and syndicates TV, radio, and online programming; and owns a major league baseball team (Chicago Cubs). It also owns other newspapers, has a stake in cable TV, and has investments in such new media companies as America Online, Peapod (online shopping), and Excite (Internet search engine).

Travelers Insurance (now **The Travelers Inc.**), founded in 1864, sold the world's first auto insurance policy in 1897 and the first air travel insurance policy in 1919 (to President Woodrow Wilson).

— *Hoover's Guide to the Top New York Companies*

TRW INC.

1900 Richmond Rd.
Cleveland, OH 44124
Phone: 216-291-7000
Fax: 216-291-7629

CEO: Joseph T. Gorman
CFO: Ronald D. Sugar
Symbol: TRW
Exchange: NYSE

1995 Sales: $10,172 million
1995 Profits: $446 million
Mkt. Value: $5,770 million
Employees: 66,500

Web site: http://www.trw.com

TRW supplies advanced technology products and services to the automotive and space and defense markets. The company's auto products include air bags, power rack-and-pinion steering, and multivalve engines. Space and defense products include spacecraft and satellite technology, defense communications, and complex systems integration. To concentrate on its automotive, space and defense units, TRW has announced plans to sell most of its Information Systems and Services unit (credit information, direct marketing services, imaging systems engineering and integration services) for about $1 billion to a buyout group led by Thomas H. Lee Co. and Bain Capital.

TURNER BROADCASTING SYSTEM, INC.

1 CNN Center
Atlanta, GA 30348
Phone: 404-827-1700
Fax: 404-827-2437

CEO: R.E. Turner
CFO: Wayne H. Pace
Symbol: TBSA
Exchange: AMEX

1995 Sales: $3,437 million
1995 Profits: $103 million
Mkt. Value: $5,828 million
Employees: 6,000

Web site: http://www.turner.com

Turner Broadcasting System is a global entertainment and news empire built around cable TV and movies. TBS owns 4 cable TV entertainment networks (Turner Network Television, TBS SuperStation, the Cartoon Network, and Turner Classic Movies) in the US and 4 abroad. The company also owns New Line Cinema, Castle Rock Entertainment, Turner Pictures, and Fine Line Features. Its ownership of Cable News Network (CNN) makes it a major international news source. TBS also owns a major league baseball team (Atlanta Braves), a professional basketball team (Atlanta Hawks), and stakes in other cable networks. Media conglomerate Time Warner has agreed to purchase TBS.

THE TURNER CORPORATION

375 Hudson St.
New York, NY 10014
Phone: 212-229-6000
Fax: 212-229-6390

CEO: Alfred T. McNeill
CFO: David J. Smith
Symbol: TUR
Exchange: AMEX

1995 Sales: $3,282 million
1995 Profits: $1 million
Mkt. Value: $48 million
Employees: 2,500

The Turner Corporation is one of the world's leading commercial construction companies, with the United Nations Secretariat and Plaza and the Madison Square Garden among its credits. The company provides construction and project management services and primarily constructs commercial and multifamily buildings; correctional, entertainment, and manufacturing facilities; airports; and stadiums. It operates 35 offices nationwide, and works to maintain strong ties to local communities. It has a presence outside the US through Turner Steiner International, a joint venture with Karl Steiner Holding AG, the largest general builder in Switzerland, and through a joint venture with Birmann SA of Brazil.

TYCO INTERNATIONAL LTD.

1 Tyco Park
Exeter, NH 03833
Phone: 603-778-9700
Fax: 603-778-7700

CEO: L. Dennis Kozlowski
CFO: Mark H. Swartz
Symbol: TYC
Exchange: NYSE

1995 Sales: $4,535 million
1995 Profits: $214 million
Mkt. Value: $5,452 million
Employees: 34,000

Tyco International is the world's #1 manufacturer and provider of fire protection systems. It also makes electrical and electronic components, flow control materials, and disposable medical, adhesive, and other packaging products. Tyco's fire protection subsidiaries include Wormald and Grinnel. Those companies' products include sprinklers, fire extinguishers, fire hydrants, fire detection systems, valves, pipes, fittings, and meters. Subsidiary Simplex is the world's leading producer of undersea fiber-optic cable. The company also owns Kendall International, a maker of medical supplies and adhesive products, and Professional Medical Products, which supplies medical products to nursing homes.

TYSON FOODS, INC.

2210 W. Oaklawn Dr.
Springdale, AR 72762
Phone: 501-290-4000
Fax: 501-290-4061

CEO: Leland E. Tollett
CFO: Gerald Johnston
Symbol: TYSNA
Exchange: Nasdaq

1995 Sales: $5,511 million
1995 Profits: $219 million
Mkt. Value: $3,261 million
Employees: 64,000

The nation's #1 poultry processor, Tyson Foods operates food production and distribution facilities in 20 states and 12 other countries. The company breeds, raises, processes, and markets chickens and also produces beef, pork, and Cornish game hens. Almost half of sales are to food service companies (catering accounts) and clients such as KFC and McDonald's. It also sells Mexican food products (under the Mexican Original brand) and seafood, raises swine, and produces animal feed and pet food. Tyson exports to 43 countries and is responsible for more than half of the chickens exported to Japan. The company has announced plans to exit the pork and beef business.

U S WEST, INC.

7800 E. Orchard Rd.
Englewood, CO 80111
Phone: 303-793-6500
Fax: 303-793-6654

CEO: Richard D. McCormick
CFO: James T. Anderson

1995 Sales: $11,746 million
1995 Profits: $1,317 million
Mkt. Value: $14,419 million
Employees: 61,047

Web site: http://www.uswest.com

U S WEST, Inc., is made up of 2 operating units, each represented by its own class of stock. U S WEST Communications Group provides local phone service to 25 million customers in 14 western and midwestern states. U S WEST Media Group has interests in cable and wireless networks, directory publishing, and interactive media services. In a deal that will place it among the nation's largest cable television providers, U S WEST Media has agreed to aquire Continental Cablevision. The company also owns about a quarter of Time Warner Entertainment, which includes cable holdings and content providers (HBO, Warner Bros. Studios).

UAL CORPORATION

1200 E. Algonquin Rd.
Elk Grove Tnshp., IL 60007
Phone: 847-952-4000
Fax: 847-952-7578

CEO: Gerald Greenwald
CFO: Douglas A. Hacker
Symbol: UAL
Exchange: NYSE

1995 Sales: $14,943 million
1995 Profits: $349 million
Mkt. Value: $2,495 million
Employees: 79,410

Web site: http://www.ual.com

UAL is a holding company for United Airlines, the #2 air carrier in the US (after American). United flies more than 500 jets to more than 150 cities in about 30 countries (with hubs in Chicago, Denver, San Francisco, Washington, London, and Tokyo). UAL's United Express marketing program feeds passengers from regional carriers into United's system in exchange for the carriers' participation in United's reservation system. The company also operates Shuttle by United, offering about 400 low-fare, short-haul flights per day. UAL is over 50% employee-owned after a buyout intended partly to meet fierce competition by cutting labor costs.

ULTRAMAR CORPORATION

2 Pickwick Plaza
Greenwich, CT 06830
Phone: 203-622-7000
Fax: 203-622-7007

CEO: Jean Gaulin
CFO: H. Pete Smith
Symbol: ULR
Exchange: NYSE

1995 Sales: $2,714 million
1995 Profits: $70 million
Mkt. Value: $1,265 million
Employees: 2,800

Ultramar is an independent refiner and marketer of petroleum products. The company and subsidiaries Ultramar Inc. and Canadian Ultramar Ltd. market gasoline under the Ultramar, Beacon, Sergaz, and XL brand names at more than 300 retail outlets in Central and Northern California and over 1,300 in eastern Canada. Some of the outlets are company-owned or -leased while others are independent stations. The company also sells gasoline and diesel fuel to about 260 unbranded wholesale customers in Arizona, California, and Nevada, and home heating oil to more than 173,000 Canadian households. Ultramar's refineries in Los Angeles and Quebec produce unleaded gasoline, diesel fuel, jet fuel, and petroleum coke.

UNICOM CORPORATION

1 First National Plaza	CEO: James J. O'Connor	1995 Sales: $6,910 million
Chicago, IL 60603	CFO: John C. Bukovski	1995 Profits: $640 million
Phone: 312-394-7399	Symbol: UCM	Mkt. Value: $6,713 million
Fax: 312-394-7251	Exchange: NYSE	Employees: 17,100

189

Unicom is the parent company of Commonwealth Edison and Unicom Enterprises. ComEd produces, purchases, distributes, and sells electricity to 8.2 million people in northern Illinois, including Chicago. It relies on nuclear power for about 70% of its electricity. Unicom sells its electricity to residential users (about 35%), small commercial and industrial companies (30%), large commercial and industrial companies (20%), and public authorities. Unicom Enterprises handles the company's other energy service businesses, including Unicom Thermal Technologies, which uses chilled water to provide cooling services to offices and other buildings.

UNION CAMP CORPORATION

1600 Valley Rd.	CEO: W. Craig McClelland	1995 Sales: $4,212 million
Wayne, NJ 07470	CFO: James M. Reed	1995 Profits: $451 million
Phone: 201-628-2000	Symbol: UCC	Mkt. Value: $3,607 million
Fax: 201-628-2848	Exchange: NYSE	Employees: 18,258

Web site: http://www.uccden.com

301

A diversified manufacturer, Union Camp makes paper, packaging products, chemicals, and wood products. The company's packaging products division makes kraft paper and packaging, linerboard, corrugated containers, and flexible packaging and folding cartons for the US and international markets. Its uncoated free sheet products include paper for copiers, laser printers, envelopes, desktop publishing, direct mail, and similar applications. Union Camp's chemical products division is a majority shareholder in Bush Boake Allen, an international manufacturer of flavors, fragrances, and aroma chemicals. Its forest resources division manages a woodlands base of over 1.5 million acres.

UNION CARBIDE CORPORATION

39 Old Ridgebury Rd.	CEO: William H. Joyce	1995 Sales: $5,888 million
Danbury, CT 06817	CFO: John K. Wulff	1995 Profits: $925 million
Phone: 203-794-2000	Symbol: UK	Mkt. Value: $6,537 million
Fax: 203-794-4336	Exchange: NYSE	Employees: 11,521

223

Union Carbide is the world's #1 producer of ethylene oxide and ethylene glycol (used to make antifreeze and polyester fibers, respectively). It is also one of the largest manufacturers of polyethylene (the most widely used plastic in the world) and makes solvents, coatings, latex, resins, emulsions, and plasticizers. The company is thinking globally. It is expanding its presence in the Asian plastics market, has a joint venture with France's Elf Aquitaine to produce specialty polyethylene resins and products for the wire, cable, and pipe industries, and is building a major petrochemical plant in Kuwait.

Without the benefit of refrigerated trucking, **Tyson Foods** founder **John Tyson** in 1935 figured out a way to move chickens long distances from farm to market. He kept them alive for the trip, equipping a trailer with a food-and-water trough and nailing up small feed cups, enabling him to get his birds from Arkansas to Chicago.

— *Hoover's Handbook of American Business 1996*

UNION PACIFIC CORPORATION

Eighth & Eaton Aves.	CEO: Andrew L. Lewis Jr.	1995 Sales: $8,942 million
Bethlehem, PA 18018	CFO: L. White Matthews III	1995 Profits: $946 million
Phone: 610-861-3200	Symbol: UNP	Mkt. Value: $14,442 million
Fax: 610-861-3220	Exchange: NYSE	Employees: 51,200

Web site: http://www.unionpacific.com

Union Pacific (UP), the #2 US railroad company (after CSX), moves goods across North America using trucks as well as trains. Its more than 23,000 miles of track reach the East, the West, the Midwest, and the Gulf Coast region. The company has an intermodal (truck-to-train) business and strong ties to Mexico's national railway. Besides truck and rail shipping, UP is involved in oil and gas (Union Pacific Resources), computer technology (Union Pacific Technologies), and passenger rail (Chicago and North Western). Seeking to become the largest US railroad, the company proposed a merger with Southern Pacific.

UNISYS CORPORATION

Township Line & Union Mtg.	CEO: James A. Unruh	1995 Sales: $6,460 million
Blue Bell, PA 19424	CFO: Edward Blechschmidt	1995 Loss: ($625) million
Phone: 215-986-4011	Symbol: UIS	Mkt. Value: $1,114 million
Fax: 215-986-2312	Exchange: NYSE	Employees: 37,400

Web site: http://www.unisys.com

A systems integrator for business and government, Unisys offers such computer-related products and services as departmental servers and desktop systems (including U 6000 UNIX network and document-imaging services), enterprise systems and servers, and equipment maintenance. Software services include database management and transaction processing. Unisys sells its products and services to airlines, financial services companies, transportation companies, communications providers, government agencies, and health care providers worldwide. Government contracts play a major role in the company's business, but it is trying to boost its presence in the commercial client/server market.

UNITED HEALTHCARE CORPORATION

9900 Bren Rd. E.	CEO: William W. McGuire	1995 Sales: $5,670 million
Minnetonka, MN 55343	CFO: David P. Koppe	1995 Profits: $286 million
Phone: 612-936-1300	Symbol: UNH	Mkt. Value: $11,107 million
Fax: 612-935-1471	Exchange: NYSE	Employees: 25,000

One of the US's largest and most geographically diverse health maintenance organizations (HMOs), United HealthCare (UHC) offers services from Alaska to Puerto Rico. The company owns or manages more than 20 HMOs serving more than 3 million members, with most of its HMOs ranked #1 or #2 in their markets. It offers a variety of specialized services, including geriatric care, management mental health and substance abuse services, workers' compensation, and casualty services. Known for its low premiums and rapid enrollment growth, UHC plans to expand its Medicaid coverage into states that are enrolling Medicaid-eligible patients in HMOs.

UNITED PARCEL SERVICE OF AMERICA, INC.

55 Glenlake Parkway N.E.
Atlanta, GA 30328
Phone: 404-828-6000
Fax: 404-828-6593

CEO: Oz Nelson
CFO: Robert J. Clanin
Ownership: Privately Held

1995 Sales: $21,045 million
1995 Profits: $1,043 million
Employees: 337,000

Web site: http://www.ups.com

United Parcel Service of America (UPS) is the world's #1 package delivery company. It offers air and ground delivery services, including early morning, next day air, consignee billing, worldwide expedited, and authorized return services. The company has also launched same-day and next-flight-out delivery services through the acquisition of the shipper SonicAir. Same-day delivery prices start from $160 a package. UPS stock is owned primarily by its employees and their families and heirs. The company is noted for its philanthropy, supporting efforts to stock soup kitchens and collecting relief supplies for Bosnian refugee schoolchildren.

UNITED TECHNOLOGIES CORPORATION

1 Financial Plaza
Hartford, CT 06101
Phone: 203-728-7000
Fax: 860-728-7979

CEO: George David
CFO: Stephen F. Page
Symbol: UTX
Exchange: NYSE

1995 Sales: $22,802 million
1995 Profits: $750 million
Mkt. Value: $13,543 million
Employees: 170,600

Web site: http://www.utc.com

United Technologies Corporation (UTC) makes a variety of products, from elevators to air conditioners. Subsidiary Carrier is the world's largest heating and air-conditioning systems maker. It manufactures and services heating, ventilating, and refrigeration equipment. UTC's Otis, the world's #1 elevator manufacturer, also makes and services escalators, moving sidewalks, and shuttle systems. Subsidiary Hamilton Standard makes Sikorsky helicopters and parts as well as engine controls, environmental systems, propellers, and other flight systems. Subsidiary Pratt & Whitney makes gas turbine engines and parts for aircraft.

UNIVERSAL CORPORATION

1501 N. Hamilton St.
Richmond, VA 23230
Phone: 804-359-9311
Fax: 804-254-3584

CEO: Henry H. Harrell
CFO: Hartwell H. Roper
Symbol: UVV
Exchange: NYSE

1995 Sales: $3,281 million
1995 Profits: $26 million
Mkt. Value: $951 million
Employees: 30,000

Universal is the world's largest buyer and processor of leaf tobacco. The company selects, ships, and packs air-cured, burley, chewing, cigar, dark fired, flue-cured, Maryland, and dark air-cured tobacco to tobacco product makers. Its main customer, Philip Morris, maker of Marlboro and Virginia Slims cigarettes, accounts for nearly half of the company's sales. Universal's other operations, handled through its Deli Universal division, include lumber; agricultural products such as rubber, tea, dried fruit, and sunflower seeds; and canned meat. The firm owns a controlling share of the Nyiregyhaza Tobacco Processing Company, Hungary's largest leaf processor.

UNOCAL CORPORATION

2141 Rosecrans Ave.
El Segundo, CA 90245
Phone: 310-726-7600
Fax: 310-726-7806

CEO: Roger C. Beach
CFO: Neal E. Schmale
Symbol: UCL
Exchange: NYSE

1995 Sales: $7,527 million
1995 Profits: $260 million
Mkt. Value: $7,878 million
Employees: 12,509

Unocal is a vertically integrated oil and gas company with operations from exploration for crude oil and natural gas to marketing of petroleum products. It owns 3 refineries in California and is co-owner of another in Chicago (as part of a joint venture with Petroleos de Venezuela). The company markets gasoline and other products under the Unocal 76 brand name. Unocal is also the world's #1 producer of geothermal energy and manufactures chemicals for the agricultural and industrial markets. It has extensive exploration and development projects in North and South America, the Middle East, and Asia.

UNUM CORPORATION

2211 Congress St.	CEO: James F. Orr III	1995 Sales: $4,123 million
Portland, ME 04122	CFO: Robert F. Crispin	1995 Profits: $281 million
Phone: 207-770-2211	Symbol: UNM	Mkt. Value: $4,267 million
Fax: 207-770-6933	Exchange: NYSE	Employees: 6,900

UNUM is a disability and special-risk insurance holding company that provides coverage to customers in the US, the UK, Canada, and the Pacific Rim. Subsidiaries UNUM Life Insurance Co. of America, First UNUM Life Insurance, UNUM Limited, Colonial Life & Accident Insurance, and UNUM Japan Accident Insurance offer long-term and short-term disability, group life, accidental death and dismemberment, dental, and other insurance lines. Subsidiary Commercial Life Insurance sells travel accident, group universal life, and group life insurance. Duncanson & Holt offers accident and health reinsurance underwriting to insurance companies in the US, Canada, Europe, and Asia.

U. S. BANCORP

111 S.W. Fifth Ave.	CEO: Gerry B. Cameron	1995 Sales: $2,897 million
Portland, OR 97204	CFO: Steven P. Erwin	1995 Profits: $329 million
Phone: 503-275-6111	Symbol: USBC	Mkt. Value: $4,865 million
Fax: 503-275-3452	Exchange: Nasdaq	Employees: 14,081

Web site: http://www.usbank.com

U. S. Bancorp is a regional multibank holding company with more than 500 offices in the western and northwestern US. Its principal subsidiaries are United States Bank of Oregon, U.S. Bank of Washington, and West One Bancorp. The company offers individuals, businesses, institutions, and government agencies a full range of banking services, including savings and demand deposits; commercial, consumer, and real estate financing; bank credit cards; safe deposit services; brokerage and investment management; credit life insurance; asset-based lending; and trust services. Its international services include letters of credit, loans, and acceptances.

U.S. HEALTHCARE, INC.

980 Jolly Rd.	CEO: Leonard Abramson	1995 Sales: $3,518 million
Blue Bell, PA 19422	CFO: James Bickerson	1995 Profits: $381 million
Phone: 215-628-4800	Symbol: USHC	Mkt. Value: $7,178 million
Fax: 215-283-6579	Exchange: Nasdaq	Employees: 4,980

Web site: http://www.ushc.com

U.S. Healthcare provides comprehensive managed health care services through health maintenance organizations (HMOs) to employer groups. The company offers both HMO and indemnity-type plans and provides prepaid medical, dental, vision, and other health care services. Emphasizing preventive care, its wellness programs include special programs for women's care (including free routine mammograms when indicated) and a variety of aggressive disease management programs for such conditions as congestive heart failure and diabetes. The programs are designed to keep employees healthy and save the company money. Insurance giant Aetna Life & Casualty has announced plans to acquire U.S. Healthcare.

U.S. INDUSTRIES, INC.

101 Wood Avenue S.	CEO: David H. Clarke	1995 Sales: $2,908 million
Iselin, NJ 08830	CFO: Frank R. Reilly	1995 Loss: ($89) million
Phone: 908-767-0700	Symbol: USN	Mkt. Value: $1,107 million
Fax: 908-767-2222	Exchange: NYSE	Employees: 18,640

A diversified manufacturer, U.S. Industries has 3 business segments: building products, consumer products, and industrial products. The company's subsidiaries include whirlpool maker Jacuzzi and toolmaker Ames as well as Bear (archery equipment), Piedmont Moulding, Ertl (toys), Lighting Corp. of America, Rexair (vacuum cleaners), Spartus (clocks), Universal Gym Equipment, and Valley Recreation Products (pinball machines and pool tables). The company, which was spun off from British conglomerate Hanson PLC in 1995, is selling off many of its poorer-performing assets to focus on its strongest components and pare the debt left over from the spin-off.

USAA

9800 Fredericksburg Rd.
San Antonio, TX 78288
Phone: 210-498-2211
Fax: 210-498-9940

CEO: Robert T. Herres
CFO: Josue Robles Jr.
Ownership: Mutual Company

1995 Sales: $6,611 million
1995 Profits: $730 million
Employees: 15,677

200

USAA provides property/casualty insurance to people in the military and offers its other insurance, annuity, and investment products to soldiers and civilians. The company also issues credit cards, runs a travel agency, and operates a buying service for military members to buy discount merchandise, and it has a majority stake in San Antonio amusement park Fiesta Texas, which it helped develop. In addition to military officers, the company's more than 2.7 million members include Secret Service and FBI agents and other selected government officials and their families. USAA has no field agents, finding its members instead through direct marketing and the military grapevine.

USAIR GROUP, INC.

2345 Crystal Dr.
Arlington, VA 22227
Phone: 703-418-7000
Fax: 703-418-7312

CEO: Stephen M. Wolf
CFO: John W. Harper
Symbol: U
Exchange: NYSE

1995 Sales: $7,474 million
1995 Profits: $119 million
Mkt. Value: $1,109 million
Employees: 42,082

Web site: http://www.usair.com

174

USAir Group is a holding company for USAir, the #5 US airline. Operating more than 400 aircraft, the company has hubs in Baltimore/Washington, DC; Charlotte, North Carolina; Philadelphia; and Pittsburgh, and overseas destinations in countries such as the Bahamas, Canada, France, and Germany. It is about 20%-owned by British Airways, with which it has a code-sharing reservation agreement. USAir Group also owns Allegheny Airlines and other aviation subsidiaries. The company's plans to end years of losses (stemming largely from price wars) included cutting annual costs by over $1 billion, reducing underperforming flights, and seeking a merger.

Union Mutual Life Insurance, now known as **UNUM,** hired a woman, **Lucy Wright,** as its chief actuary in 1866.

— Hoover's Handbook of American Business 1996

HISTORY

USF&G CORPORATION

100 Light St.
Baltimore, MD 21202
Phone: 410-547-3000
Fax: 410-625-5682

CEO: Norman P. Blake Jr.
CFO: Dan L. Hale
Symbol: FG
Exchange: NYSE

1995 Sales: $3,459 million
1995 Profits: $209 million
Mkt. Value: $1,742 million
Employees: 6,187

361

USF&G is a holding company for several firms that provide a variety of insurance products. Its largest subsidiary, United States Fidelity and Guaranty, is one of the largest US property/casualty insurers, handling both commercial and personal property/casualty insurance, reinsurance, and fidelity-surety lines. Fidelity and Guaranty Life Insurance offers life insurance and individual and annuity insurance products. Through its Family and Business Insurance Group, USF&G is working to build its small- and middle-market business and personal lines; it is looking for profits to come particularly from workers' compensation and personal auto insurance.

USG CORPORATION

125 S. Franklin St.
Chicago, IL 60606
Phone: 312-606-4000
Fax: 312-606-4093

CEO: William C. Foote
CFO: Richard H. Fleming
Symbol: USG
Exchange: NYSE

1995 Sales: $2,444 million
1995 Loss: ($32) million
Mkt. Value: $1,180 million
Employees: 12,400

Web site: http://usgcorp.com

USG owns leading makers, marketers, and distributors of wallboard and other building materials. Subsidiary United States Gypsum is the world's leading manufacturer of gypsum wallboard, with about 1/3 of the US market. Its L&W Supply is the leading US distributor of wallboard and related materials. USG Interiors is the top US maker of acoustic ceiling grids and a leading producer of acoustic ceiling panels. USG also owns a Mexican gypsum products maker, Yeso Panamericano, and holds a majority stake in CGC, the largest producer of gypsum wallboard in eastern Canada.

Gary, Indiana, is named for **Elbert Henry Gary**, who was chairman of **US Steel** in 1905, when the company broke ground for a new mill there.

— *People's Chronology*

USX CORPORATION

600 Grant St.
Pittsburgh, PA 15219
Phone: 412-433-1121
Fax: 412-954-2704

CEO: Thomas J. Usher
CFO: Robert M. Hernandez

1995 Sales: $18,214 million
1995 Profits: $214 million
Employees: 42,774

Energy and steel conglomerate USX Corporation is a diversified giant with 3 operating units, each with its own separate class of stock. USX-U.S. Steel is the US's #1 integrated steelmaker. It also produces domestic coal and iron ore and provides engineering, consulting, mineral resource management, and real estate management services. USX-Marathon Group produces, refines, and sells oil and natural gas. It has production operations in 8 countries and operates 4 US-based refineries as well as gas stations in 16 states. USX-Delhi Group purchases, gathers, processes, transports, and markets natural gas. Its gas-gathering activities take place primarily in Texas and Oklahoma.

UTILICORP UNITED INC.

911 Main St.
Kansas City, MO 64105
Phone: 816-421-6600
Fax: 816-467-3663

CEO: Richard C. Green Jr.
CFO: Terry G. Westbrook
Symbol: UCU
Exchange: NYSE

1995 Sales: $2,799 million
1995 Profits: $80 million
Mkt. Value: $1,333 million
Employees: 4,700

Web site: http://www.utilicorp.com

UtiliCorp is a multinational utility holding company, selling electricity and natural gas to about 1.7 million customers in 8 states, Canada, and Australia. Operating subsidiaries include Missouri Public Service, WestPlains Energy, Peoples Natural Gas, Michigan Gas Utilities, West Virginia Power, Northern Minnesota Utilities, and Kansas Public Service.
In addition, the company has stakes in 2 New Zealand electric utilities and has joint ventures with several UK utilities to sell natural gas to wholesale and industrial customers. UtiliCorp has announced plans to merge with utility company Kansas City Power & Light.

VALERO ENERGY CORPORATION

530 McCullough Ave.
San Antonio, TX 78215
Phone: 210-246-2000
Fax: 210-246-2646

CEO: William E. Greehey
CFO: Don M. Heep
Symbol: VLO
Exchange: NYSE

1995 Sales: $3,020 million
1995 Profits: $60 million
Mkt. Value: $1,083 million
Employees: 1,658

Valero Energy is a diversified energy company that produces and transports natural gas and natural gas liquids. The company and its subsidiary, Valero Natural Gas Partners, refines crude oil and high-sulfur atmospheric residual oil into products such as reformulated gasoline at its Texas refinery. Valero also owns an 8,000-mile network of natural gas transmission and gathering lines throughout Texas. It purchases natural gas for resale to distribution companies, electric utilities, other pipelines, and industrial customers (including Conoco) in the US and Mexico, and provides 3rd-party gas transportation services.

VF CORPORATION

1047 N. Park Rd.
Wyomissing, PA 19610
Phone: 610-378-1151
Fax: 610-375-9371

CEO: Mackey J. McDonald
CFO: Gerard G. Johnson
Symbol: VFC
Exchange: NYSE

1995 Sales: $5,062 million
1995 Profits: $157 million
Mkt. Value: $3,594 million
Employees: 64,000

VF is the nation's largest maker of denim jeans, holding about 1/3 of the market. The company gets more than half its revenues from its Jeanswear division, which makes Lee, Rustler, and Wrangler brands. Other apparel brands include Vanity Fair (lingerie and loungewear), Jantzen (sportswear), Red Kap (industrial work clothes), and Healthtex (infants' and children's clothes). VF is concentrating on internal expansion, launching a major push overseas (marketing its Vanity Fair line in Europe) and introducing a new brand of licensed team apparel, Lee Sport, that includes T-shirts and headwear.

VIACOM INC.

1515 Broadway
New York, NY 10036
Phone: 212-258-6000
Fax: 212-258-6354

CEO: Sumner M. Redstone
CFO: George S. Smith Jr.
Symbol: VIA
Exchange: AMEX

1995 Sales: $11,780 million
1995 Profits: $223 million
Mkt. Value: $14,603 million
Employees: 81,700

Web site: http://www.paramount.com

Viacom is one of the world's leading media companies. It owns such cable channels as MTV, Nickelodeon/Nick at Nite, pay movie channels (Showtime), and 50% of the USA Network, Comedy Central, and the All News Channel. It is a major producer of leading TV shows and a syndicator of popular TV programs (the "Star Trek" series, "Cheers"). Viacom owns Paramount Pictures, a major movie producer ("Braveheart"), and is a leading book publisher (Simon & Schuster). Through Blockbuster Music and Blockbuster Video it is the world's top video and music retailer. The entertainment giant also owns a score of radio and TV stations. Media Mogul and company CEO Sumner Redstone owns about 60% of Viacom's common stock.

THE VONS COMPANIES, INC.

618 Michillinda Ave.
Arcadia, CA 91007
Phone: 818-821-7000
Fax: 818-821-7933

CEO: Lawrence A. Del Santo
CFO: Pamela K. Knous
Symbol: VON
Exchange: NYSE

1995 Sales: $5,071 million
1995 Profits: $68 million
Mkt. Value: $1,356 million
Employees: 29,600

One of the largest supermarket chains in Southern California, Vons operates more than 300 stores from the center of the state to the Mexican border and into the Las Vegas area under the names Vons (traditional supermarkets) and Pavilions (upscale supermarkets). More than half of its stores offer separate service departments for floral, bakery, and deli products, and the company operates its own facilities for producing milk, ice cream, and baked goods. The company offers 1,500 private-label store-brand items, which account for about 1/6 of its grocery sales, and continues to boost sales from private-label products.

WABAN INC.

1 Mercer Rd.
Natick, MA 01760
Phone: 508-651-6500
Fax: 508-651-6623

CEO: Herbert J. Zarkin
CFO: Edward J. Weisberger
Symbol: WBN
Exchange: NYSE

1995 Sales: $3,978 million
1995 Profits: $73 million
Mkt. Value: $858 million
Employees: 19,252

Waban operates 2 retail chains: warehouse clubs and home improvement superstores. BJ's Wholesale Club, which consists of more than 60 stores, is the #1 membership warehouse club in the Northeast. The chain, which has more than 3 million members, offers fresh, frozen, and canned food as well as general merchandise, including office equipment, small appliances, apparel, and housewares. Waban's HomeBase home improvement chain operates more than 70 stores in 10 western states (primarily California) and is one of the largest home improvement chains in that region. It sells lumber, tools, paint, and garden supplies.

WACHOVIA CORPORATION

100 N. Main St.
Winston-Salem, NC 27150
Phone: 910-770-5000
Fax: 910-737-7021

CEO: L.M. Baker Jr.
CFO: Robert S. McCoy Jr.
Symbol: WB
Exchange: NYSE

1995 Sales: $3,755 million
1995 Profits: $603 million
Mkt. Value: $7,624 million
Employees: 15,996

Wachovia Corporation is a southeastern interstate bank holding company. Its principal banking subsidiaries, Wachovia Bank of Georgia, Wachovia Bank of North Carolina, and Wachovia Bank of South Carolina, provide a full array of consumer, commercial, corporate, and retail banking sevices. First National Bank of Atlanta offers credit card services for Wachovia's affiliated banks. Wachovia Trust Services provides fiduciary and investment management services. Wachovia Corporation also offers investment, leasing, credit life and accident insurance, corporate financing, local government securities sales and trading, and foreign exchange. It has about 500 offices in Georgia, North Carolina, and South Carolina.

WALGREEN CO.

200 Wilmot Rd.
Deerfield, IL 60015
Phone: 708-940-2500
Fax: 847-940-2804

CEO: Charles R. Walgreen III
CFO: Roger L. Polark
Symbol: WAG
Exchange: NYSE

1995 Sales: $10,395 million
1995 Profits: $321 million
Mkt. Value: $7,969 million
Employees: 68,800

Web site: http://www.walgreens.com

Walgreen is the largest drugstore chain in the US (ranked by sales), with more than 2,000 outlets in the US and Puerto Rico. It offers prescription and over-the-counter drugs as well as general merchandise. As more customers use managed care or drug benefit plans, Walgreen is working to sign up these providers to increase its customer base and sales of its nonprescription items, such as cosmetics, cigarettes, and liquor. It is also remodeling its stores and adding new technology (including Intercom Plus, which allows customers to request refills 24 hours a day via a touch-tone telephone).

WAL-MART STORES, INC.

702 S.W. Eighth St.
Bentonville, AR 72716
Phone: 501-273-4000
Fax: 501-273-8650

CEO: David D. Glass
CFO: John B. Menzer
Symbol: WMT
Exchange: NYSE

1995 Sales: $93,627 million
1995 Profits: $2,740 million
Mkt. Value: $54,495 million
Employees: 675,000

Web site: http://www.wal-mart.com

Wal-Mart is the world's largest retailer, operating about 2,000 Wal-Marts and more than 400 Sam's Clubs in the US. Wal-Mart competes with such discount retail chains as Kmart and Dayton Hudson's Target and traditional full-line department stores, such as Sears and J.C. Penney. As part of its strategy to increase Sam's Clubs sales, Wal-Mart is emphasizing the clubs' role as a commercial supply source rather than a consumer store. The company is consolidating its #1 position by rapidly opening stores in Brazil, Canada, China, Hong Kong, and Mexico.

THE WALT DISNEY COMPANY

500 S. Buena Vista St.
Burbank, CA 91521
Phone: 818-560-1000
Fax: 818-560-1930

CEO: Michael D. Eisner
CFO: Richard Nanula
Symbol: DIS
Exchange: NYSE

1995 Sales: $12,112 million
1995 Profits: $1,380 million
Mkt. Value: $47,107 million
Employees: 71,000

Web site: http://www.disney.com

The Walt Disney Company is one of the largest media conglomerates in the world, vying for the top spot with rival Time Warner (which is buying Turner Broadcasting). Walt Disney has interests in motion pictures ("The Lion King") and television ("Home Improvement"), along with theme parks and music and book publishing. Disney's Capital Cities/ABC division includes the ABC TV network, several TV stations, and shares in 3 cable channels, including ESPN. Led by CEO Michael Eisner, Disney continues to search for new opportunities to build on a brand name recognized around the world.

NUMBERS

What a difference a decade (and execs like **Michael Eisner** and **Jeffrey Katzenberg**) can make. As recently as 1986 **Walt Disney** stock failed to hit the 14-point mark; in 1995 it never fell as low as triple that number, and revenue and earnings (even before the acquisition of Capital Cities/ABC) had grown about fivefold.

— Hoover's Guide to the Top Southern California Companies

WARNER-LAMBERT COMPANY

201 Tabor Rd.
Morris Plains, NJ 07950
Phone: 201-540-2000
Fax: 201-540-3761

CEO: Melvin R. Goodes
CFO: Ernest J. Larini
Symbol: WLA
Exchange: NYSE

1995 Sales: $7,040 million
1995 Profits: $740 million
Mkt. Value: $13,928 million
Employees: 37,000

Web site: http://www.warner-lambert.com

Warner-Lambert manufactures and markets drugs, consumer health care products, and confectionery. The company's pharmaceuticals include analgesics, anesthetics, and hemostatic agents. Its consumer health care products include Zantac 75 over-the-counter ulcer treatment, Neosporin and Polysporin topical antibiotics, Sudafed cold and sinus remedies, Listerine mouthwash, and Actifed antihistamines and allergy products. The company also produces chewing gum and breath mints, including Trident, Dentyne, Chiclets, Clorets, and Certs. About half of Warner-Lambert's sales come from outside the US, and it continues to build its international business, taking major steps to establish a presence in China.

WELLPOINT HEALTH NETWORKS INC.

21555 Oxnard St.
Woodland Hills, CA 91367
Phone: 818-703-4000
Fax: 818-703-3389

CEO: Leonard D. Schaeffer
CFO: Yon Y. Jorden
Symbol: WLP
Exchange: NYSE

1995 Sales: $3,107 million
1995 Profits: $180 million
Mkt. Value: $3,346 million
Employees: 4,000

WellPoint Health Networks is one of the largest US managed health care companies, serving more than 2.6 million medical members and 7 million pharmacy and dental members. WellPoint operates health maintenance organizations (HMOs), preferred provider organizations (PPOs), and specialty managed care networks such as dental and mental health plans through subsidiaries such as CaliforniaCare Health Plans, WellPoint Dental Plan, and WellPoint Pharmacy Plan. It also sells life insurance through subsidiary WellPoint Life Insurance and workers' compensation services through subsidiary UniCARE Financial. The firm's planned marriage with Health Systems International fell apart in late 1995 over issues of control.

WELLS FARGO & COMPANY

420 Montgomery St.
San Francisco, CA 94163
Phone: 415-477-1000
Fax: 415-677-9075

CEO: Paul Hazen
CFO: Rodney L. Jacobs
Symbol: WFC
Exchange: NYSE

1995 Sales: $5,409 million
1995 Profits: $1,032 million
Mkt. Value: $11,343 million
Employees: 19,700

Web site: http://www.wellsfargo.com

245

Wells Fargo is the largest bank in California after its takeover of First Interstate. The company's core business is consumer retail banking, including checking and savings accounts and consumer loans. With its First Interstate acquisition, Wells Fargo now boasts more than $100 billion in assets. Wells Fargo HSBC Trade Bank, a joint venture between Wells Fargo and the Hong Kong & Shanghai Bank, also expands the number of branch services the bank offers. Investors Walter Annenberg and Warren Buffett own substantial interests in the bank.

WESTINGHOUSE ELECTRIC CORPORATION

11 Stanwix St.
Pittsburgh, PA 15222
Phone: 412-244-2000
Fax: 412-642-4874

CEO: Michael H. Jordan
CFO: Fredic G. Reynolds
Symbol: WX
Exchange: NYSE

1995 Sales: $9,605 million
1995 Profits: $15 million
Mkt. Value: $7,890 million
Employees: 77,813

Web site: http://www.westinghouse.com

135

Diversified international giant Westinghouse has broadcasting, power generation, and refrigeration. Its Westinghouse/CBS Group is a leading US television and radio broadcaster, carrying such TV programs as "60 Minutes" and "Late Night with David Letterman." Subsidiary Thermo King is a global leader in transport refrigeration. The power generation unit designs and services nuclear power plants, and provides turbine-generators for power plants worldwide. In a continuing effort to pare down debt, Westinghouse has sold its defense electronics unit to Northrop Grumman and has announced plans to sell its Environmental Services unit.

IDEAS

Phil Weyerhaeuser was a key early supporter of the concept of reforestation in the 1930s, when **Weyerhaeuser Co.** began using the slogan "Timber is a Crop." As an EVP he chose the company's 130,000-acre Clemons tract in Washington State for an experiment that was dedicated in 1941 as the nation's first tree farm.

— *Pioneers of American Business*, compiled by Sterling Slappey

WESTVACO CORPORATION

299 Park Ave.
New York, NY 10171
Phone: 212-688-5000
Fax: 212-318-5050

CEO: John A. Luke Jr.
CFO: James E. Stoveken Jr.
Symbol: W
Exchange: NYSE

1995 Sales: $3,303 million
1995 Profits: $281 million
Mkt. Value: $3,144 million
Employees: 14,300

377

Westvaco is a major producer of paper and paperboard products in the US and Brazil. The company makes bleached paperboard, printing paper, folding cartons, envelopes, linerboard, kraft papers, coated paperboard, and cartons for liquid products. It also manufactures specialty chemicals such as surfactants, printing ink resins, and activated carbon products, and it produces lumber, sells timber from its timberlands, and develops land. The company owns about 1.5 million acres of timberland in the US and Brazil. About 1/5 of its sales are to customers outside the US.

WEYERHAEUSER COMPANY

33663 Weyerhsr. Way S.	CEO: John W. Creighton Jr.	1995 Sales: $11,788 million
Federal Way, WA 98003	CFO: William C. Stivers	1995 Profits: $799 million
Phone: 206-924-2345	Symbol: WY	Mkt. Value: $9,094 million
Fax: 206-924-7407	Exchange: NYSE	Employees: 39,431

Weyerhaeuser is the world's largest private owner of softwood timber, with about 6 million acres of US timberland and cutting rights to about 18 million acres in Canada. The company's forest products include logs, lumber, plywood, linerboard, doors, veneer, paneling, and particleboard. It also produces papermaking chemicals, pulp, newsprint, coated and uncoated papers, shipping containers, and containerboard. In addition, the company develops commercial and residential properties. Almost all of Weyerhaeuser's sales come from US markets, but it is working to increase its overseas operations. It has signed a deal with a South African forest products company to distribute logs internationally.

WHIRLPOOL CORPORATION

2000 N. M-63	CEO: David R. Whitwam	1995 Sales: $8,347 million
Benton Harbor, MI 49022	CFO: John P. Cunningham Jr.	1995 Profits: $209 million
Phone: 616-923-5000	Symbol: WHR	Mkt. Value: $4,320 million
Fax: 616-923-5486	Exchange: NYSE	Employees: 45,435

Web site: http://www.whirlpool.com

Whirlpool, the #1 maker of washers and dryers in the US, is also the world's top producer overall of major home appliances. Refrigerators, air conditioners, dishwashers, dehumidifiers, freezers, microwave ovens, ranges, and trash compactors are among the products the company makes and sells under brand names such as Coolerator, KitchenAid, Roper, Speed Queen, and Whirlpool. It also manufactures the Kenmore line for Sears. Foreign sales account for more than 1/3 of the company's total, and Whirlpool is a leading appliance maker in Europe (after Electrolux and Bosch-Siemens). The company is concentrating on emerging markets in Asia and Latin America.

WHITMAN CORPORATION

3501 Algonquin Rd.	CEO: Bruce S. Chelberg	1995 Sales: $2,947 million
Rolling Meadows, IL 60008	CFO: Thomas L. Bindley	1995 Profits: $134 million
Phone: 847-818-5000	Symbol: WH	Mkt. Value: $2,419 million
Fax: 847-818-5045	Exchange: NYSE	Employees: 16,841

Web site: http://www.whitmancorp.com

Whitman Corporation has a diversified collection of businesses. The company's Pepsi-Cola General Bottlers is the largest independent Pepsi bottler in the US and also distributes noncola products such as A&W Root Beer and Canada Dry ginger ale. Whitman's Midas International is the largest franchised network for servicing mufflers in the world. Hussmann Corp. produces merchandising and refrigeration systems for the commercial food industry, such as bottle coolers, refrigerated display cases, and commercial/industrial refrigeration systems. Whitman is expanding both its bottling operations and Midas International's operations in Europe.

WILLAMETTE INDUSTRIES, INC.

1300 S.W. Fifth Ave.	CEO: Steven R. Rogel	1995 Sales: $3,874 million
Portland, OR 97201	CFO: J. A. Parsons	1995 Profits: $515 million
Phone: 503-227-5581	Symbol: WMTT	Mkt. Value: $3,258 million
Fax: 503-273-5603	Exchange: Nasdaq	Employees: 13,180

A vertically integrated, geographically diverse forest products company, Willamette owns 1.2 million acres of timberland in the Northwest and the South and operates plants in more than 20 states. The company makes bag paper, pulp, business forms, containerboard, corrugated containers, cut sheet paper, fine paper, inks, laminated beams, lumber, medium-density fiberboard, particleboard, paper bags, plywood, and other forest products. The up-and-down market has led the company to seek diversification, especially in the growth area of recycling. Willamette is also expanding its brown-paper product line and is the world's largest producer of glue-laminated wood beams, an alternative building product.

THE WILLIAMS COMPANIES, INC.

1 Williams Center	CEO: Keith E. Bailey	1995 Sales: $2,856 million
Tulsa, OK 74172	CFO: Jack D. McCarthy	1995 Profits: $1,318 million
Phone: 918-588-2000	Symbol: WMB	Mkt. Value: $5,136 million
Fax: 918-588-2296	Exchange: NYSE	Employees: 9,946

Web site: http://www.twc.com/twc

The Williams Companies is engaged in 2 main businesses. It is the #1 transporter of natural gas and also provides telecommunication services. The company's Williams Field Services Group provides natural gas gathering and processing services in New Mexico. Its Williams Pipe Line subsidiary transports petroleum products, liquefied petroleum gas, and crude oil to its truck and rail terminals throughout the Midwest. Subsidiary Williams Telecommunications Systems sells customer-premise telephone and data equipment nationwide. Transco, another subsidiary, owns the Transcontinental Gas Pipe Line Corporation and maintains 10,500 miles of pipeline.

WINN-DIXIE STORES, INC.

5050 Edgewood Court	CEO: A. Dano Davis	1995 Sales: $11,788 million
Jacksonville, FL 32254	CFO: Richard P. McCook	1995 Profits: $232 million
Phone: 904-783-5000	Symbol: WIN	Mkt. Value: $5,324 million
Fax: 904-783-5294	Exchange: NYSE	Employees: 123,000

Winn-Dixie is one of the US's largest food retailers, with more than 1,100 stores in 13 states (primarily in the South) and the Bahamas operating under the names Winn-Dixie, the City Meat Markets, Marketplace, Thriftway, and Buddies. The company also produces a range of private-label products, from pizza to peanut butter and coffee to cheese. Like many of its rivals, Winn-Dixie is moving to ever-larger stores, closing small or unprofitable outlets and replacing them with larger units. The company, which offers shop-at-home services via phone and fax, is also testing selling groceries via online and cable services.

WMX TECHNOLOGIES, INC.

3003 Butterfield Rd.	CEO: Dean L. Buntrock	1995 Sales: $10,979 million
Oak Brook, IL 60521	CFO: James E. Koenig	1995 Profits: $604 million
Phone: 708-572-8800	Symbol: WMX	Mkt. Value: $14,901 million
Fax: 708-572-3094	Exchange: NYSE	Employees: 73,200

Web site: http://www.wmx.com

WMX provides environmental and management services such as waste management and recycling. It is one of the world's largest waste collection and disposal companies, serving about 11 million residential and one million commercial and industrial customers in North America. Subsidiary Chemical Waste Management transports, treats, and disposes of hazardous waste for commercial, industrial, and government customers. It also provides street sweeping and parking lot cleaning services and Port-O-Let portable sanitation services to commercial and special event customers. WMX is boosting its presence in the rapidly growing recycling market through acquisitions.

WOOLWORTH CORPORATION

233 Broadway	CEO: Roger N. Farah	1995 Sales: $8,224 million
New York, NY 10279	CFO: J. H. Cannon	1995 Loss: ($164) million
Phone: 212-553-2000	Symbol: Z	Mkt. Value: $2,112 million
Fax: 212-553-2042	Exchange: NYSE	Employees: 119,000

The last of the five-and-dimes, Woolworth is abandoning its roots as a general merchandiser and is building an eclectic collection of specialty stores, including Foot Locker (athletic footwear), AfterThoughts (boutiques), and Kinney (shoes). Leading the charge into specialty retailing is CEO Roger Farah, a former executive with R.H. Macy, who plans to continue the company's shift to specialty retailing with the addition of costume jewelry and accessories, casual apparel, and home furnishings. He also has sold underperforming specialty chains (such as Kids Mart/Little Folks) and is reducing the number of employees in order to cut costs.

WORLDCOM, INC.

515 E. Amite St.	CEO: Bernard J. Ebbers	1995 Sales: $3,640 million
Jackson, MS 39201	CFO: Scott D. Sullivan	1995 Profits: $235 million
Phone: 601-360-8600	Symbol: WCOM	Mkt. Value: $8,160 million
Fax: 601-974-8350	Exchange: Nasdaq	Employees: 7,500

Web site: http://www.wcom.com

342

WorldCom is a leading US long-distance telecommunications provider. Services include 24-hour long distance, "800" travel service, data services, inbound "800" service, "one plus" dialing, operator services, and private-line networks. The company has acquired or merged with more than 36 competitors, including Metromedia Communications, Advanced Telecommunications, and Resurgens Communication Group, to give it operations in every state and in 220 other countries. WorldCom also owns the Wiltel fiber-optic network, giving it ownership of its own transmission facilities, and IDB Communications, the #1 independent transmitter of sports events in the US.

W. R. GRACE & CO.

1 Town Center Rd.	CEO: Albert J. Costello	1995 Sales: $5,784 million
Boca Raton, FL 33486	CFO: Peter D. Houchin	1995 Loss: ($326) million
Phone: 407-362-2000	Symbol: GRA	Mkt. Value: $7,808 million
Fax: 407-362-2193	Exchange: NYSE	Employees: 21,228

228

W. R. Grace is a leading manufacturer of specialty chemicals (petroleum fluid cracking catalysts, polyolefin catalysts, silica and zeolite absorbents), packaging materials (shrink wrap, foam trays, plastic containers), construction materials (concrete and cement additives, fireproofing and waterproofing systems), and container products (closure sealant systems and specialty polymers). The company has announced plans to sell its water treatment products and its plant biotechnology businesses. It also has agreed to sell a majority interest in National Medical Care, the US's #1 provider of kidney dialysis products and related services, to German dialysis company Fresenius AG.

W.W. GRAINGER, INC.

5500 W. Howard St.	CEO: Richard L. Keyser	1995 Sales: $3,277 million
Skokie, IL 60077	CFO: P. O. Loux	1995 Profits: $187 million
Phone: 847-793-9030	Symbol: GWW	Mkt. Value: $3,496 million
Fax: 847-982-3489	Exchange: NYSE	Employees: 11,800

Web site: http://www.grainger.com

381

W.W. Grainger is a leading nationwide distributor of maintenance, repair, and operating supplies for commercial, contractor, industrial, and institutional clients. The company's merchandise includes Speedaire air compressors, Dem-Kote spray paints and equipment, Dayton electric motors, fans, gear motors, and Demco transmission belts. It also sells heating equipment and controls, hydraulic equipment, janitorial supplies, Teel liquid pumps, office equipment, power and hand tools, and shop tools. Hospitals, restaurants, and other institutional users account for the majority of Grainger's sales. The company sells its products through a national network of more than 300 branches.

XEROX CORPORATION

800 Long Ridge Rd.
Stamford, CT 06904
Phone: 203-968-3000
Fax: 203-968-4559

CEO: Paul A. Allaire
CFO: Barry D. Romeril
Symbol: XRX
Exchange: NYSE

1995 Sales: $18,963 million
1995 Loss: ($472) million
Mkt. Value: $14,358 million
Employees: 85,200

Web site: http://www.xerox.com

Where paper and digital technology meet, Xerox is there. The company, whose name is synonymous with copiers, makes color and noncolor copiers, scanners, printers, and document processing software. Its R&D program is concentrating on 3 developing markets: digital printing, color systems, and network systems. Xerox is forming a production venture in China with Fuji Xerox, allowing it to compete directly with its Japanese rivals already in China. Its new family of networked color laser printers and software products, including DocuWeb and InterDoc, allows documents to be printed via the Internet and the World Wide Web.

YELLOW CORPORATION

10777 Barkley
Overland Park, KS 66211
Phone: 913-967-4300
Fax: 913-967-4384

CEO: George E. Powell III
CFO: H. A. Trucksess III
Symbol: YELL
Exchange: Nasdaq

1995 Sales: $3,057 million
1995 Loss: ($30) million
Mkt. Value: $316 million
Employees: 34,700

Web site: http://www.yellowcorp.com

Yellow Corporation is one of the nation's largest trucking companies, with direct service to more than 35,000 points in all 50 states, plus Canada, Mexico, and Puerto Rico. It also makes shipments to Europe through an alliance with the Royal Frans Maas Group based in the Netherlands. Yellow Freight System, the corporation's largest subsidiary, is the largest provider of less-than-truckload (LTL) transportation in the US. Another subsidiary, Yellow Logistics Services, provides integrated logistic management services and warehousing for a number of industries. The company is cutting costs by closing terminals and using more part-time labor.

YORK INTERNATIONAL CORPORATION

631 S. Richland Ave.
York, PA 17403
Phone: 717-771-7890
Fax: 717-771-7440

CEO: Robert N. Pokelwaldt
CFO: Dean T. DuCray
Symbol: YRK
Exchange: NYSE

1995 Sales: $2,930 million
1995 Loss: ($96) million
Mkt. Value: $2,017 million
Employees: 19,000

Web site: http://www.york.com

York is the 3rd largest US manufacturer of heating, ventilating, air-conditioning, and refrigeration equipment after United Technologies' Carrier and American Standard's Trane. It makes air-cooled chillers, central air-handling units, control devices, variable air-volume units, water-cooled chillers, packaged refrigeration systems, and screw compressors. The firm's brand names include Bristol, Fraser-Johnston, Frick, Homeair, Moncrief, Rite Coil, Seveso, and York. The company, which has manufacturing plants in the US and 11 other countries and sells its products in about 120 countries, continues to work to boost its overseas operations through an aggressive acquisition strategy.

Xerox got a lesson in computer applications from a back-country clothing retailer. While studying L.L. Bean warehouse operations in Maine, a Xerox distribution manager found a computer mapping the floor locations of the items in each individual order, then organizing workers' trips to cut travel time. Xerox adopted the system.

— *Xerox: American Samurai*, by Gary Jacobson and John Hillkirk

The Empire State still boasts the greatest number of FORTUNE 500 headquarters, dominated by banks, brokerage houses, and insurance firms. But New York slipped by two in FORTUNE's latest tally, reducing its total to 63. The problem isn't attitude but acquisitions: Westinghouse bought CBS, and Disney absorbed Capital Cities/ABC. California, meanwhile, gained four companies, to 55. Advanced Micro Devices helped its home state by squeezing in at No. 500. The Northeast in general saw economic power slip away: Massachusetts, Connecticut, New Jersey, and Rhode Island each lost one company.

RANK

		500 REVENUES RANK	REVENUES $ MILLIONS	PROFITS $ MILLIONS
ALABAMA 2 COMPANIES				
1	BRUNO'S	440	2,869.6	33.3
2	SCI SYSTEMS	465	2,673.8	45.2
	TOTAL		5,543.4	78.5
ARIZONA 4 COMPANIES				
1	PHELPS DODGE	303	4,185.4	746.6
2	DIAL	347	3,575.1	(16.6)
3	CIRCLE K	349	3,565.6	18.7
4	MICROAGE	422	2,941.1	0.2
	TOTAL		14,267.2	748.9
ARKANSAS 5 COMPANIES				
1	WAL-MART STORES	4	93,627.0	2,740.0
2	DILLARD DEPARTMENT STORES	214	6,097.1	167.2
3	TYSON FOODS	239	5,511.2	219.2
4	BEVERLY ENTERPRISES	385	3,228.6	(8.1)
5	ALLTEL	396	3,109.7	354.6
	TOTAL		111,573.6	3,472.9
CALIFORNIA 55 COMPANIES				
1	CHEVRON	18	32,094.0	930.0
2	HEWLETT-PACKARD	20	31,519.0	2,433.0
3	BANKAMERICA CORP.	37	20,386.0	2,664.0
4	ATLANTIC RICHFIELD	55	16,739.0	1,376.0
5	SAFEWAY	59	16,397.5	326.3
6	INTEL	61	16,202.0	3,566.0
7	MCKESSON	87	13,325.5	404.5
8	ROCKWELL INTERNATIONAL	90	13,009.0	742.0
9	WALT DISNEY	102	12,112.1	1,380.1
10	APPLE COMPUTER	114	11,062.0	424.0
11	OCCIDENTAL PETROLEUM	121	10,423.0	511.0
12	PACIFIC GAS & ELECTRIC	133	9,621.8	1,338.9
13	FLUOR	140	9,301.4	231.8
14	PACIFIC TELESIS GROUP	144	9,042.0	(2,312.0)
15	BERGEN BRUNSWIG	153	8,447.6	63.9
16	EDISON INTERNATIONAL	155	8,405.0	739.0
17	UNOCAL	172	7,527.0	260.3
18	NORTHROP GRUMMAN	192	6,818.0	252.0
19	LEVI STRAUSS ASSOCIATES	198	6,707.6	734.7
20	TRANSAMERICA	213	6,101.1	470.5
21	SUN MICROSYSTEMS	222	5,901.9	335.8
22	MERISEL	227	5,801.8	(9.2)
23	WELLS FARGO & CO.	245	5,409.0	1,032.0
24	CONSOLIDATED FREIGHTWAYS	251	5,281.1	57.4
25	VONS	263	5,070.7	68.1
26	FIRST INTERSTATE BANCORP	274	4,827.5	885.1
27	SEAGATE TECHNOLOGY	288	4,539.6	260.1
28	H.F. AHMANSON	296	4,397.5	216.2
29	GAP	297	4,395.3	354.0

RANK		500 REVENUES RANK	REVENUES $ MILLIONS	PROFITS $ MILLIONS
30	DOLE FOOD	305	4,152.8	23.3
31	FHP INTERNATIONAL	319	3,909.4	37.3
32	PACIFICARE HEALTH SYSTEMS	334	3,731.0	108.1
33	MATTEL	343	3,638.8	357.8
34	GREAT WESTERN FIN. CORP.	350	3,556.4	261.0
35	FOOD 4 LESS HOLDINGS	354	3,494.0	(216.0)
36	TIMES MIRROR	355	3,491.0	1,226.8
37	COMPUTER SCIENCES	367	3,372.5	110.7
38	QUANTUM	368	3,368.0	81.6
39	LITTON INDUSTRIES	372	3,319.7	135.0
40	TENET HEALTHCARE	373	3,318.0	165.0
41	PACIFIC MUTUAL LIFE INS.	390	3,160.5	85.1
42	SOUTHERN PACIFIC RAIL	391	3,151.3	(3.4)
43	AVERY DENNISON	394	3,113.9	143.7
44	WELLPOINT HEALTH NETWORKS	397	3,107.1	180.0
45	APPLIED MATERIALS	405	3,061.9	454.1
46	ORACLE	417	2,966.9	441.5
47	AMERICAN PRESIDENT	434	2,896.0	30.3
48	FLEETWOOD ENTERPRISES	448	2,855.7	84.6
49	HEALTH SYSTEMS INTL.	458	2,732.1	89.6
50	LONGS DRUG STORES	468	2,644.4	46.2
51	TELEDYNE	478	2,567.8	162.0
52	GOLDEN WEST FIN. CORP.	491	2,470.0	234.5
53	AST RESEARCH	492	2,467.8	(99.3)
54	FOUNDATION HEALTH	494	2,459.9	49.4
55	ADVANCED MICRO DEVICES	500	2,429.7	300.5
	TOTAL		392,301.6	24,224.9

COLORADO 4 COMPANIES

RANK		500 REVENUES RANK	REVENUES $ MILLIONS	PROFITS $ MILLIONS
1	US WEST	106	11,746.0	1,317.0
2	TELE-COMMUNICATIONS	190	6,851.0	(171.0)
3	CYPRUS AMAX MINERALS	387	3,207.0	124.0
4	MANVILLE	457	2,733.8	116.0
	TOTAL		24,537.8	1,386.0

CONNECTICUT 22 COMPANIES

RANK		500 REVENUES RANK	REVENUES $ MILLIONS	PROFITS $ MILLIONS
1	GENERAL ELECTRIC	7	70,028.0	6,573.0
2	UNITED TECHNOLOGIES	30	22,802.0	750.0
3	GTE	38	19,957.0	(2,144.0)
4	XEROX	41	18,963.0	(472.0)
5	AETNA LIFE & CASUALTY	91	12,978.0	251.7
6	ITT HARTFORD GROUP	100	12,150.0	559.0
7	TENNECO	150	8,899.0	735.0
8	TOSCO	176	7,284.1	77.1
9	GENERAL RE	181	7,210.2	824.9
10	CHAMPION INTERNATIONAL	188	6,972.0	771.8
11	AMERICAN BRANDS	221	5,904.9	540.4
12	UNION CARBIDE	223	5,888.0	925.0
13	DUN & BRADSTREET	242	5,415.1	320.8
14	PITNEY BOWES	324	3,861.2	583.1

RANK

		500 REVENUES RANK	REVENUES $ MILLIONS	PROFITS $ MILLIONS
15	NORTHEAST UTILITIES	330	3,749.0	282.4
16	OLIN	392	3,149.5	139.9
17	PRAXAIR	393	3,146.0	262.0
18	PITTSTON	428	2,926.1	98.0
19	CALDOR	455	2,764.5	(4.6)
20	ECHLIN	459	2,717.9	154.4
21	ULTRAMAR	460	2,714.4	69.6
22	STANLEY WORKS	473	2,624.3	59.1
	TOTAL		232,104.2	11,356.6
	DELAWARE 4 COMPANIES			
1	E.I. DU PONT DE NEMOURS	13	37,607.0	3,293.0
2	PHARMACIA & UPJOHN	183	7,094.6	738.7
3	COLUMBIA GAS SYSTEM	470	2,635.2	(360.7)
4	MBNA	479	2,565.4	353.1
	TOTAL		49,902.2	4,024.1
	DISTRICT OF COLUMBIA 5 COMPANIES			
1	FED. NATL. MORTGAGE ASSN.	32	22,246.0	2,372.0
2	MCI COMMUNICATIONS	68	15,265.0	548.0
3	MARRIOTT INTERNATIONAL	147	8,960.7	246.9
4	STUDENT LOAN MKTG. ASSN.	318	3,916.6	496.4
5	GEICO	408	3,054.0	247.6
	TOTAL		53,442.3	3,910.9
	FLORIDA 12 COMPANIES			
1	WINN-DIXIE STORES	103	11,787.8	232.2
2	PUBLIX SUPER MARKETS	136	9,470.7	242.1
3	W.R. GRACE	228	5,784.2	(325.9)
4	FPL GROUP	236	5,592.5	553.3
5	OFFICE DEPOT	249	5,313.2	132.4
6	RYDER SYSTEM	258	5,167.4	147.7
7	ECKERD	268	4,997.1	93.4
8	BARNETT BANKS	339	3,680.0	533.3
9	HARRIS	357	3,480.9	154.5
10	TECH DATA	398	3,086.6	21.5
11	FLORIDA PROGRESS	407	3,055.6	238.9
12	KNIGHT-RIDDER	456	2,751.8	160.1
	TOTAL		64,167.8	2,183.5
	GEORGIA 14 COMPANIES			
1	UNITED PARCEL SERVICE	35	21,045.0	1,043.0
2	COCA-COLA	48	18,018.0	2,986.0
3	BELLSOUTH	49	17,886.0	(1,232.0)
4	HOME DEPOT	66	15,470.4	731.5
5	GEORGIA-PACIFIC	75	14,292.0	1,018.0
6	DELTA AIR LINES	98	12,194.0	408.0
7	SOUTHERN	142	9,180.0	1,103.0
8	AFLAC	182	7,190.6	349.1
9	COCA-COLA ENTERPRISES	196	6,773.0	82.0
10	GENUINE PARTS	252	5,261.9	309.2

RANK		500 REVENUES RANK	REVENUES $ MILLIONS	PROFITS $ MILLIONS
11	SUNTRUST BANKS	332	3,740.3	565.5
12	TURNER BROADCASTING	363	3,437.0	103.0
13	ALUMAX	427	2,926.1	237.4
14	SHAW INDUSTRIES	439	2,869.8	52.3
	TOTAL		140,284.1	7,756.0
	IDAHO 4 COMPANIES			
1	ALBERTSON'S	96	12,585.0	465.0
2	BOISE CASCADE	265	5,057.7	351.9
3	MICRON TECHNOLOGY	419	2,952.7	844.1
4	MORRISON KNUDSEN	484	2,530.9	(484.0)
	TOTAL		23,126.3	1,177.0
	ILLINOIS 40 COMPANIES			
1	STATE FARM GROUP	12	40,809.9	1,271.2
2	SEARS ROEBUCK	15	35,181.0	1,801.0
3	AMOCO	23	27,665.0	1,862.0
4	MOTOROLA	24	27,037.0	1,781.0
5	ALLSTATE	31	22,793.0	1,904.0
6	SARA LEE	50	17,719.0	804.0
7	CATERPILLAR	63	16,072.0	1,136.0
8	UAL	70	14,943.0	349.0
9	AMERITECH	84	13,427.8	2,007.6
10	ARCHER DANIELS MIDLAND	92	12,671.9	795.9
11	WMX TECHNOLOGIES	115	10,979.3	603.9
12	FIRST CHICAGO NBD CORP.	117	10,681.0	1,150.0
13	WALGREEN	122	10,395.1	320.8
14	DEERE	123	10,290.5	706.1
15	ABBOTT LABORATORIES	128	10,012.2	1,688.7
16	MCDONALD'S	131	9,794.5	1,427.3
17	BAXTER INTERNATIONAL	132	9,730.0	649.0
18	STONE CONTAINER	175	7,351.2	255.5
19	UNICOM	189	6,910.0	639.5
20	R.R. DONNELLEY & SONS	201	6,511.8	298.8
21	QUAKER OATS	206	6,365.2	802.0
22	NAVISTAR INTERNATIONAL	208	6,342.0	164.0
23	HOUSEHOLD INTERNATIONAL	260	5,144.4	453.2
24	INLAND STEEL INDUSTRIES	275	4,781.5	146.8
25	AON	286	4,610.7	403.0
26	FMC	287	4,566.6	215.6
27	ILLINOIS TOOL WORKS	306	4,152.2	387.6
28	PREMARK INTERNATIONAL	348	3,573.6	237.6
29	MORTON INTERNATIONAL	370	3,354.9	294.1
30	W.W. GRAINGER	381	3,276.9	186.7
31	SERVICEMASTER	388	3,202.5	105.9
32	BRUNSWICK	401	3,076.5	127.2
33	WHITMAN	420	2,946.5	133.5
34	TRIBUNE	442	2,863.6	278.2
35	DEAN FOODS	472	2,630.2	80.1
36	NEWELL	488	2,498.4	222.5

RANK

		500 REVENUES RANK	REVENUES $ MILLIONS	PROFITS $ MILLIONS
37	USG	496	2,444.0	(32.0)
38	COTTER	497	2,437.0	N.A.
39	ACE HARDWARE	498	2,436.0	N.A.
40	GENERAL INSTRUMENT	499	2,432.0	123.8
	TOTAL		394,109.9	25,781.1
	INDIANA 7 COMPANIES			
1	ELI LILLY	171	7,535.4	2,290.9
2	LINCOLN NATIONAL	199	6,633.3	482.2
3	ASSOCIATED INSURANCE	217	6,037.5	(98.0)
4	CUMMINS ENGINE	253	5,245.0	224.0
5	BINDLEY WESTERN	281	4,672.5	16.4
6	CONSECO	444	2,860.7	220.4
7	BALL	475	2,591.7	(18.6)
	TOTAL		35,576.1	3,117.3
	IOWA 2 COMPANIES			
1	PRINCIPAL MUTUAL LIFE INS.	119	10,561.0	554.0
2	MAYTAG	410	3,039.5	(20.5)
	TOTAL		13,600.5	533.5
	KANSAS 2 COMPANIES			
1	SPRINT	80	13,599.5	395.3
2	YELLOW	406	3,056.6	(30.1)
	TOTAL		16,656.1	365.2
	KENTUCKY 3 COMPANIES			
1	ASHLAND	113	11,251.1	23.9
2	HUMANA	279	4,702.0	190.0
3	PROVIDIAN	366	3,388.0	345.0
	TOTAL		19,341.1	558.9
	LOUISIANA 1 COMPANY			
1	ENTERGY	209	6,274.4	520.0
	TOTAL		6,274.4	520.0
	MAINE 2 COMPANIES			
1	UNUM	308	4,122.9	281.1
2	HANNAFORD BROS.	477	2,568.1	70.2
	TOTAL		6,691.0	351.3
	MARYLAND 5 COMPANIES			
1	LOCKHEED MARTIN	29	22,853.0	682.0
2	BLACK & DECKER	238	5,566.2	224.0
3	GIANT FOOD	336	3,695.6	94.2
4	USF&G	361	3,458.8	209.4
5	BALTIMORE GAS & ELECTRIC	424	2,934.8	338.0
	TOTAL		38,508.4	1,547.6
	MASSACHUSETTS 16 COMPANIES			
1	DIGITAL EQUIPMENT	77	13,813.1	121.8

RANK		500 REVENUES RANK	REVENUES $ MILLIONS	PROFITS $ MILLIONS
2	RAYTHEON	107	11,716.0	792.5
3	LIBERTY MUTUAL INS. GROUP	139	9,308.0	410.0
4	FLEET FINANCIAL GROUP	166	7,919.4	610.0
5	MASS. MUTUAL LIFE INS.	193	6,804.1	229.4
6	GILLETTE	195	6,794.7	823.5
7	JOHN HANCOCK MUT. LIFE INS.	224	5,845.5	340.8
8	BANK OF BOSTON CORP.	243	5,410.6	541.0
9	TJX	294	4,447.5	26.3
10	STOP & SHOP	309	4,116.1	67.9
11	WABAN	316	3,978.4	73.0
12	REEBOK INTERNATIONAL	356	3,481.5	164.8
13	HARCOURT GENERAL	383	3,241.9	165.9
14	ALLMERICA FINANCIAL	384	3,238.9	133.9
15	STAPLES	404	3,068.1	73.7
16	STATE STREET BOSTON CORP.	495	2,445.7	247.1
	TOTAL		95,629.5	4,821.6

MICHIGAN 14 COMPANIES

RANK		500 REVENUES RANK	REVENUES	PROFITS
1	GENERAL MOTORS	1	168,828.6	6,880.7
2	FORD MOTOR	2	137,137.0	4,139.0
3	CHRYSLER	9	53,195.0	2,025.0
4	KMART	16	34,654.0	(571.0)
5	DOW CHEMICAL	36	20,957.0	2,078.0
6	WHIRLPOOL	159	8,347.0	209.0
7	KELLOGG	187	7,003.7	490.3
8	MASCO	276	4,779.0	(441.7)
9	LEAR SEATING	278	4,714.4	91.6
10	CMS ENERGY	321	3,890.0	204.0
11	DTE ENERGY	344	3,635.5	405.9
12	COMERICA	395	3,112.6	413.4
13	KELLY SERVICES	463	2,689.8	69.5
14	SPARTAN STORES	487	2,512.4	N.A.
	TOTAL		455,456.0	15,993.7

MINNESOTA 14 COMPANIES

RANK		500 REVENUES RANK	REVENUES	PROFITS
1	DAYTON HUDSON	28	23,516.0	311.0
2	SUPERVALU	58	16,563.8	43.3
3	MINNESOTA MINING & MFG.	63	16,105.0	976.0
4	NORTHWEST AIRLINES	143	9,084.9	392.0
5	GENERAL MILLS	156	8,393.6	367.4
6	NORWEST CORP.	170	7,582.3	956.0
7	HONEYWELL	197	6,731.3	333.6
8	UNITED HEALTHCARE	232	5,670.0	286.0
9	ST. PAUL COS.	244	5,409.6	521.2
10	BEST BUY	262	5,079.6	57.7
11	FIRST BANK SYSTEM	371	3,328.3	568.1
12	HORMEL FOODS	409	3,046.2	120.4
13	NASH FINCH	437	2,888.8	17.4
14	NORTHERN STATES POWER	476	2,568.6	275.8
	TOTAL		115,968.0	5,225.9

THE FORTUNE 500 RANKED WITHIN STATES

		500 REVENUES RANK	REVENUES $ MILLIONS	PROFITS $ MILLIONS
MISSISSIPPI 1 COMPANY				
1	WORLDCOM	342	3,640.0	234.5
	TOTAL		3,640.0	234.5
MISSOURI 13 COMPANIES				
1	MCDONNELL DOUGLAS	74	14,332.0	(416.0)
2	ANHEUSER-BUSCH	97	12,325.5	642.3
3	MAY DEPARTMENT STORES	99	12,187.0	752.0
4	EMERSON ELECTRIC	127	10,012.9	907.7
5	MONSANTO	146	8,962.0	739.0
6	FARMLAND INDUSTRIES	178	7,256.9	N.A.
7	RALSTON PURINA	180	7,210.3	296.4
8	JEFFERSON SMURFIT	311	4,093.0	243.1
9	TRANS WORLD AIRLINES	374	3,316.8	(227.5)
10	BOATMEN'S BANCSHARES	415	2,996.1	418.8
11	UTILICORP UNITED	452	2,798.5	79.8
12	GRAYBAR ELECTRIC	454	2,774.4	36.7
13	PAYLESS CASHWAYS	464	2,685.7	(128.5)
	TOTAL		90,951.1	3,343.8
NEBRASKA 5 COMPANIES				
1	CONAGRA	26	24,108.9	495.6
2	IBP	94	12,667.6	257.9
3	BERKSHIRE HATHAWAY	293	4,487.7	725.2
4	MUTUAL OF OMAHA INS.	307	4,134.3	70.7
5	PETER KIEWIT SONS'	431	2,902.0	244.0
	TOTAL		48,300.5	1,793.4
NEW HAMPSHIRE 1 COMPANY				
1	TYCO INTERNATIONAL	289	4,534.7	214.0
	TOTAL		4,534.7	214.0
NEW JERSEY 23 COMPANIES				
1	PRUDENTIAL INS. OF AMERICA	11	41,330.0	579.0
2	JOHNSON & JOHNSON	43	18,842.0	2,403.0
3	MERCK	56	16,681.1	3,335.2
4	ALLIEDSIGNAL	73	14,346.0	875.0
5	AMERICAN HOME PRODUCTS	86	13,376.1	1,680.4
6	TOYS "R" US	137	9,426.9	148.1
7	CPC INTERNATIONAL	154	8,431.5	512.1
8	CAMPBELL SOUP	177	7,278.0	698.0
9	WARNER-LAMBERT	186	7,039.8	739.5
10	PUBLIC SVC. ENTER. GROUP	212	6,164.2	662.3
11	CHUBB	215	6,089.2	696.6
12	INGERSOLL-RAND	230	5,729.0	270.3
13	AMERICAN STANDARD	255	5,221.5	111.7
14	SCHERING-PLOUGH	259	5,150.6	886.6
15	UNION CAMP	301	4,211.7	451.1
16	SUPERMARKETS GENL. HLDGS.	304	4,182.1	75.5
17	FIRST DATA	312	4,081.2	(84.2)

RANK		500 REVENUES RANK	REVENUES $ MILLIONS	PROFITS $ MILLIONS
18	GENERAL PUBLIC UTILITIES	325	3,804.7	440.1
19	FOSTER WHEELER	400	3,081.9	28.5
20	U.S. INDUSTRIES	429	2,908.4	(89.3)
21	AUTOMATIC DATA PROC.	436	2,893.7	394.8
22	ENGELHARD	450	2,840.1	137.5
23	BECTON DICKINSON	461	2,712.5	251.7
	TOTAL		195,822.2	15,203.5
NEW YORK 63 COMPANIES				
1	AT&T	5	79,609.0	139.0
2	INTL. BUSINESS MACHINES	6	71,940.0	4,178.0
3	PHILIP MORRIS	10	53,139.0	5,450.0
4	TEXACO	14	36,787.0	607.0
5	CITICORP	19	31,690.0	3,464.0
6	PEPSICO	21	30,421.0	1,606.0
7	METROPOLITAN LIFE INS.	22	27,977.0	(559.4)
8	AMERICAN INTL. GROUP	25	25,874.0	2,510.4
9	MERRILL LYNCH	33	21,513.0	1,114.0
10	INTERNATIONAL PAPER	39	19,797.0	1,153.0
11	LOEWS	39	18,770.0	1,765.7
12	AMERICAN EXPRESS	53	16,942.0	1,564.0
13	TRAVELERS GROUP	57	16,583.0	1,834.0
14	NEW YORK LIFE INSURANCE	62	16,201.7	625.2
15	RJR NABISCO HOLDINGS	65	16,008.0	611.0
16	EASTMAN KODAK	67	15,269.0	1,252.0
17	CHEMICAL BANKING CORP.	71	14,884.0	1,805.0
18	J.P. MORGAN & CO.	76	13,838.0	1,296.0
19	BRISTOL-MYERS SQUIBB	79	13,767.0	1,812.0
20	LEHMAN BROTHERS HOLDINGS	82	13,476.0	242.0
21	NYNEX	85	13,406.9	(1,849.9)
22	VIACOM	105	11,780.2	222.5
23	TEACHERS INS. & ANNUITY	109	11,646.2	752.0
24	MELVILLE	110	11,516.4	(657.1)
25	CHASE MANHATTAN CORP.	112	11,336.0	1,165.0
26	MORGAN STANLEY GROUP	116	10,949.0	720.0
27	PFIZER	126	10,021.4	1,572.9
28	SALOMON	149	8,933.0	457.0
29	ITT INDUSTRIES	151	8,884.0	708.0
30	BANKERS TRUST N.Y. CORP.	152	8,600.0	215.0
31	COLGATE-PALMOLIVE	158	8,358.2	172.0
32	WOOLWORTH	161	8,224.0	(164.0)
33	TIME WARNER	163	8,067.0	(166.0)
34	COLLEGE RET. EQUITIES FUND	164	7,950.6	N.A.
35	DEAN WITTER DISCOVER	165	7,934.4	856.4
36	AMERADA HESS	173	7,524.8	(394.4)
37	CONSOLIDATED EDISON OF N.Y.	204	6,401.5	723.9
38	ITT	207	6,346.0	147.0
39	GUARDIAN LIFE OF AMERICA	211	6,172.3	125.0
40	ARROW ELECTRONICS	220	5,919.4	202.5
41	LORAL	240	5,484.4	288.4

RANK

RANK		500 REVENUES RANK	REVENUES $ MILLIONS	PROFITS $ MILLIONS
42	CORNING	246	5,346.1	(50.8)
43	BANK OF NEW YORK CO.	247	5,327.0	914.0
44	PAINE WEBBER GROUP	248	5,320.1	80.8
45	AVON PRODUCTS	292	4,492.1	256.5
46	AVNET	299	4,300.0	140.3
47	NIAGARA MOHAWK POWER	317	3,917.3	248.0
48	MARSH & MCLENNAN	326	3,770.3	402.9
49	BEAR STEARNS	329	3,753.6	240.6
50	DOVER	331	3,745.9	278.3
51	PENN TRAFFIC	352	3,536.6	(79.6)
52	WESTVACO	377	3,302.7	280.8
53	TURNER CORP.	378	3,281.5	1.3
54	ASARCO	389	3,197.8	169.2
55	LONG ISLAND LIGHTING	402	3,075.1	303.3
56	READER'S DIGEST ASSN.	403	3,068.5	264.0
57	MCGRAW-HILL	423	2,935.3	227.1
58	RELIANCE GROUP HOLDINGS	430	2,906.0	88.1
59	ESTÉE LAUDER	432	2,899.1	121.2
60	REPUBLIC NEW YORK CORP.	445	2,859.6	288.6
61	ALLEGHENY POWER SYSTEM	467	2,647.8	239.7
62	COMPUTER ASSOCIATES INTL.	474	2,623.0	431.9
63	OLSTEN	485	2,518.9	90.5
	TOTAL		818,765.7	42,501.8

NORTH CAROLINA 7 COMPANIES

1	NATIONSBANK CORP.	60	16,298.0	1,950.0
2	FIRST UNION CORP.	118	10,582.9	1,430.2
3	LOWE'S	184	7,075.4	226.0
4	DUKE POWER	280	4,676.7	714.5
5	WACHOVIA CORP.	328	3,755.4	602.5
6	NUCOR	359	3,462.0	274.5
7	CAROLINA POWER & LIGHT	414	3,006.6	372.6
	TOTAL		48,857.0	5,570.3

OHIO 30 COMPANIES

1	PROCTER & GAMBLE	17	33,434.0	2,645.0
2	KROGER	27	23,937.8	302.8
3	FEDERATED DEPT. STORES	69	15,048.5	74.6
4	GOODYEAR TIRE & RUBBER	88	13,165.9	611.0
5	NATIONWIDE INS. ENTERPRISE	108	11,702.4	182.7
6	TRW	125	10,172.4	446.2
7	BANC ONE CORP.	145	8,970.9	1,277.9
8	LIMITED	167	7,881.4	961.5
9	CARDINAL HEALTH	168	7,806.1	85.0
10	DANA	169	7,794.5	288.1
11	EATON	191	6,821.7	398.8
12	KEYCORP	216	6,054.0	825.0
13	AMERICAN ELECTRIC POWER	231	5,670.3	529.9
14	MEAD	256	5,179.4	350.0
15	REVCO D.S.	295	4,431.9	58.3
16	LTV	300	4,283.2	184.8

RANK		500 REVENUES RANK	REVENUES $ MILLIONS	PROFITS $ MILLIONS
17	CHIQUITA BRANDS INTL.	313	4,026.6	9.2
18	OWENS-ILLINOIS	327	3,763.2	169.1
19	AMERICAN FINANCIAL GROUP	345	3,629.6	191.2
20	OWENS-CORNING	346	3,612.0	231.0
21	NATIONAL CITY CORP.	362	3,449.9	465.1
22	SHERWIN-WILLIAMS	382	3,273.8	200.7
23	PARKER HANNIFIN	386	3,214.4	218.2
24	CINERGY	411	3,031.4	347.2
25	PROGRESSIVE	413	3,011.9	250.5
26	MERCANTILE STORES	421	2,944.3	123.2
27	CALIBER SYSTEMS	482	2,547.6	(27.2)
28	OFFICEMAX	483	2,542.5	125.8
29	CENTERIOR ENERGY	486	2,515.5	220.5
30	OHIO EDISON	493	2,465.8	317.2
	TOTAL		216,382.9	12,063.3

OKLAHOMA 5 COMPANIES

RANK		500 REVENUES RANK	REVENUES	PROFITS
1	FLEMING	52	17,501.6	42.0
2	PHILLIPS PETROLEUM	81	13,521.0	469.0
3	MAPCO	375	3,310.0	74.7
4	KERR-MCGEE	426	2,928.0	(31.2)
5	WILLIAMS	447	2,855.7	1,318.2
	TOTAL		40,116.3	1,872.7

OREGON 7 COMPANIES

RANK		500 REVENUES RANK	REVENUES	PROFITS
1	NIKE	277	4,760.8	399.7
2	THRIFTY PAYLESS HOLDINGS	284	4,658.8	(34.7)
3	WILLAMETTE INDUSTRIES	323	3,873.6	514.8
4	FRED MEYER	364	3,428.7	30.3
5	PACIFICORP	365	3,400.9	505.0
6	U.S. BANCORP	433	2,897.3	329.0
7	LOUISIANA-PACIFIC	449	2,843.2	(51.7)
	TOTAL		25,863.3	1,692.4

PENNSYLVANIA 33 COMPANIES

RANK		500 REVENUES RANK	REVENUES	PROFITS
1	CIGNA	42	18,955.0	211.0
2	USX	47	18,214.0	214.0
3	BELL ATLANTIC	83	13,429.5	1,858.3
4	ALCOA	95	12,654.9	790.5
5	ALCO STANDARD	130	9,891.8	202.7
6	WESTINGHOUSE ELECTRIC	134	9,605.0	15.0
7	UNION PACIFIC	148	8,942.0	946.0
8	SUN	157	8,370.0	140.0
9	H.J. HEINZ	162	8,086.8	591.0
10	PPG INDUSTRIES	185	7,057.7	767.6
11	UNISYS	203	6,460.4	(624.6)
12	PNC BANK CORP.	205	6,389.5	408.1
13	ARAMARK	235	5,600.6	93.5
14	AMP	254	5,227.2	427.3
15	VF	264	5,062.3	157.3
16	CROWN CORK & SEAL	266	5,053.8	74.9

RANK

		500 REVENUES RANK	REVENUES $ MILLIONS	PROFITS $ MILLIONS
17	BETHLEHEM STEEL	272	4,867.5	179.6
18	AMERISOURCE HEALTH	282	4,668.9	10.2
19	RITE AID	290	4,533.9	141.3
20	MELLON BANK CORP.	291	4,514.0	691.0
21	PECO ENERGY	302	4,186.2	609.7
22	AIR PRODUCTS & CHEMICALS	320	3,891.0	368.2
23	ROHM & HAAS	322	3,884.0	292.0
24	HERSHEY FOODS	337	3,690.7	281.9
25	CONRAIL	338	3,686.0	264.0
26	U.S. HEALTHCARE	353	3,517.8	380.7
27	INTELLIGENT ELECTRONICS	358	3,474.6	(19.0)
28	COMCAST	369	3,362.9	(43.9)
29	CONSOLIDATED NATURAL GAS	376	3,307.3	21.3
30	YORK INTERNATIONAL	425	2,929.9	(96.1)
31	CORESTATES FINAN. CORP.	441	2,868.0	452.2
32	PP&L RESOURCES	466	2,650.0	350.4
33	ARMSTRONG WORLD IND.	471	2,635.1	123.3
	TOTAL		**211,668.3**	**10,279.4**

RHODE ISLAND 2 COMPANIES

1	TEXTRON	129	9,973.0	479.0
2	HASBRO	446	2,858.2	155.6
	TOTAL		**12,831.2**	**634.6**

SOUTH CAROLINA 2 COMPANIES

1	FLAGSTAR	435	2,893.8	(55.2)
2	SONOCO PRODUCTS	462	2,706.2	164.5
	TOTAL		**5,600.0**	**109.3**

SOUTH DAKOTA 1 COMPANY

1	GATEWAY 2000	340	3,676.3	173.0
	TOTAL		**3,676.3**	**173.0**

TENNESSEE 5 COMPANIES

1	COLUMBIA/HCA HEALTHCARE	51	17,695.0	961.1
2	FEDERAL EXPRESS	138	9,392.1	297.6
3	EASTMAN CHEMICAL	267	5,040.0	559.0
4	SERVICE MERCHANDISE	314	4,018.5	50.3
5	PROVIDENT COS.	481	2,555.3	115.6
	TOTAL		**38,700.9**	**1,983.6**

TEXAS 37 COMPANIES

1	EXXON	3	110,009.0	6,470.0
2	J.C. PENNEY	34	21,419.0	838.0
3	AMR	54	16,910.0	167.0
4	COMPAQ COMPUTER	72	14,755.0	789.0
5	KIMBERLY-CLARK	78	13,788.6	33.2
6	TEXAS INSTRUMENTS	89	13,128.0	1,088.0
7	SBC COMMUNICATIONS	93	12,669.7	(930.0)
8	SYSCO	101	12,118.0	251.8
9	COASTAL	124	10,223.4	270.4

RANK		500 REVENUES RANK	REVENUES $ MILLIONS	PROFITS $ MILLIONS
10	ENRON	141	9,189.0	519.7
11	UNITED SERVICES AUTO. ASSN.	200	6,610.9	730.3
12	AMERICAN GENERAL	202	6,495.0	545.0
13	BURLINGTON NO. SANTA FE	210	6,183.0	92.0
14	HALLIBURTON	218	5,951.3	168.3
15	TANDY	225	5,839.1	212.0
16	CONTINENTAL AIRLINES	226	5,825.0	224.0
17	BROWNING-FERRIS INDUSTRIES	229	5,779.4	384.6
18	TEXAS UTILITIES	233	5,638.7	(138.6)
19	DRESSER INDUSTRIES	234	5,628.7	197.1
20	DELL COMPUTER	250	5,296.0	272.0
21	FOXMEYER HEALTH	257	5,177.1	41.6
22	PANENERGY	269	4,967.5	303.6
23	LYONDELL PETROCHEMICAL	270	4,936.0	389.0
24	COOPER INDUSTRIES	271	4,885.9	94.0
25	HOUSTON INDUSTRIES	298	4,388.4	1,124.0
26	CENTRAL & SOUTH WEST	333	3,735.0	420.8
27	NGC	341	3,665.9	92.7
28	TEMPLE-INLAND	360	3,460.0	281.0
29	CENTEX	380	3,277.5	92.2
30	VALERO ENERGY	412	3,019.8	59.8
31	DIAMOND SHAMROCK	418	2,956.7	47.3
32	SOUTHWEST AIRLINES	438	2,872.8	182.6
33	NORAM ENERGY	443	2,862.1	65.5
34	COMPUSA	451	2,813.1	23.0
35	BAKER HUGHES	469	2,637.5	105.4
36	MAXXAM	480	2,565.2	57.5
37	PENNZOIL	489	2,490.0	(305.1)
	TOTAL		354,167.3	15,258.7
UTAH 2 COMPANIES				
1	AMERICAN STORES	45	18,308.9	316.8
2	SMITH'S FOOD & DRUG CTRS.	399	3,083.7	(40.5)
	TOTAL		21,392.6	276.3
VIRGINIA 13 COMPANIES				
1	MOBIL	8	66,724.0	2,376.0
2	FEDERAL HOME LOAN MTG.	135	9,519.0	1,091.0
3	CSX	120	10,504.0	618.0
4	USAIR GROUP	174	7,474.3	119.3
5	REYNOLDS METALS	179	7,252.0	389.0
6	JAMES RIVER CORP. OF VA.	194	6,799.5	126.4
7	CIRCUIT CITY STORES	237	5,582.9	167.9
8	NORFOLK SOUTHERN	283	4,668.0	712.7
9	DOMINION RESOURCES	285	4,651.7	425.0
10	GANNETT	315	4,006.7	477.3
11	GENERAL DYNAMICS	351	3,544.0	321.0
12	UNIVERSAL	379	3,280.9	25.6
13	OWENS & MINOR	416	2,976.5	(11.3)
	TOTAL		136,983.5	6,837.9

THE FORTUNE 500 RANKED WITHIN STATES

		500 REVENUES RANK	REVENUES $ MILLIONS	PROFITS $ MILLIONS
WASHINGTON 7 COMPANIES				
1	BOEING	40	19,515.0	393.0
2	PRICECOSTCO	46	18,247.3	133.9
3	WEYERHAEUSER	104	11,787.7	798.9
4	MICROSOFT	219	5,937.0	1,453.0
5	PACCAR	273	4,848.2	252.8
6	NORDSTROM	310	4,113.5	165.1
7	SAFECO	335	3,722.7	399.0
	TOTAL		68,171.4	3,595.7
WISCONSIN 6 COMPANIES				
1	NORTHWESTERN MUTUAL LIFE	111	11,483.3	458.5
2	JOHNSON CONTROLS	160	8,330.3	195.8
3	MANPOWER	241	5,484.2	128.0
4	CASE	261	5,105.0	337.0
5	AID ASSN. FOR LUTHERANS	453	2,795.8	114.5
6	ROUNDY'S	490	2,488.2	N.A.
	TOTAL		35,686.8	1,233.8

RANK

		500 REVENUES RANK	$ MILLIONS	REVENUES % CHANGE FROM '94	EMPLOYEES NUMBER	% CHANGE FROM '94
AEROSPACE 8 COMPANIES						
1	LOCKHEED MARTIN	29	22,853	74	160,000	94
2	UNITED TECHNOLOGIES	30	22,802	8	170,600	(1)
3	BOEING	40	19,515	(11)	105,000	(9)
4	ALLIEDSIGNAL	73	14,346	12	88,500	1
5	MCDONNELL DOUGLAS	74	14,332	9	63,612	(3)
6	TEXTRON	129	9,973	3	57,000	8
7	NORTHROP GRUMMAN	192	6,818	2	37,300	(12)
8	GENERAL DYNAMICS	351	3,544	(4)	27,700	14
AIRLINES 8 COMPANIES						
1	AMR	54	16,910	5	110,000	0
2	UAL	70	14,943	7	79,410	2
3	DELTA AIR LINES	98	12,194	(1)	59,717	(16)
4	NORTHWEST AIRLINES	143	9,085	(1)	45,124	2
5	USAIR GROUP	174	7,474	7	42,082	(6)
6	CONTINENTAL AIRLINES	226	5,825	3	32,300	(15)
7	TRANS WORLD AIRLINES	374	3,317	(3)	22,927	4
8	SOUTHWEST AIRLINES	438	2,873	11	19,933	19
APPAREL 2 COMPANIES						
1	LEVI STRAUSS ASSOCIATES	198	6,708	10	37,700	3
2	VF	264	5,062	2	64,000	(6)
BEVERAGES 4 COMPANIES						
1	COCA-COLA	48	18,018	11	31,000	(6)
2	ANHEUSER-BUSCH	97	12,326	2	42,529	—
3	COCA-COLA ENTERPRISES	196	6,773	13	33,000	10
4	WHITMAN	420	2,947	11	16,841	10
BROKERAGE 5 COMPANIES						
1	MERRILL LYNCH	33	21,513	18	46,000	5
2	LEHMAN BROTHERS HLDGS.	82	13,476	47	7,800	(8)
3	SALOMON	149	8,933	42	8,439	(7)
4	PAINE WEBBER GROUP	248	5,320	34	15,900	(4)
5	BEAR STEARNS	329	3,754	9	7,481	2
BUILDING MATERIALS, GLASS 6 COMPANIES						
1	CORNING	246	5,346	11	41,000	(5)
2	OWENS-ILLINOIS	327	3,763	3	30,100	13
3	OWENS-CORNING	346	3,612	8	17,300	2
4	MANVILLE	457	2,734	7	7,500	(46)
5	ARMSTRONG WORLD IND.	471	2,635	(4)	20,500	—
6	USG	496	2,444	7	12,400	1
CHEMICALS 17 COMPANIES						
1	E.I. DU PONT DE NEMOURS	13	37,607	8	105,000	(2)
2	DOW CHEMICAL	36	20,957	5	39,500	(26)
3	OCCIDENTAL PETROLEUM	121	10,423	11	17,280	(12)
4	MONSANTO	146	8,962	8	28,514	(3)
5	PPG INDUSTRIES	185	7,058	11	31,200	1
6	UNION CARBIDE	223	5,888	21	11,521	(4)

THE FORTUNE **500** RANKED BY INDUSTRIES

		500 REVENUES RANK	REVENUES $ MILLIONS	REVENUES % CHANGE FROM '94	EMPLOYEES NUMBER	EMPLOYEES % CHANGE FROM '94
7	W.R. GRACE	228	5,784	13	21,228	(47)
8	EASTMAN CHEMICAL	267	5,040	16	17,709	1
9	LYONDELL PETROCHEMICAL	270	4,936	28	2,732	20
10	FMC	287	4,567	13	22,164	4
11	AIR PRODUCTS & CHEM.	320	3,891	12	14,800	11
12	ROHM & HAAS	322	3,884	10	11,670	(4)
13	MORTON INTERNATIONAL	370	3,355	18	13,800	5
14	SHERWIN-WILLIAMS	382	3,274	6	18,458	3
15	OLIN	392	3,150	18	13,000	2
16	PRAXAIR	393	3,146	16	18,822	6
17	ENGELHARD	450	2,840	19	5,075	(13)
	COMMERCIAL BANKS 31 COMPANIES					
1	CITICORP	19	31,690	0	85,300	3
2	BANKAMERICA CORP.	37	20,386	23	95,288	6
3	NATIONSBANK CORP.	60	16,298	24	58,322	(5)
4	CHEMICAL BANKING CORP.	71	14,884	17	39,078	(7)
5	J.P. MORGAN & CO.	76	13,838	16	15,600	(9)
6	CHASE MANHATTAN CORP.	112	11,336	1	33,365	(9)
7	FIRST CHICAGO NBD CORP.	117	10,681	209	35,328	98
8	FIRST UNION CORP.	118	10,583	69	44,536	40
9	BANC ONE CORP.	145	8,971	14	46,900	(4)
10	BANKERS TRUST N.Y. CORP.	152	8,600	15	14,000	(4)
11	FLEET FINANCIAL GROUP	166	7,919	78	30,800	43
12	NORWEST CORP.	170	7,582	26	45,404	17
13	PNC BANK CORP.	205	6,390	36	26,757	27
14	KEYCORP	216	6,054	13	28,905	(1)
15	BANK OF BOSTON CORP.	243	5,411	19	17,881	(3)
16	WELLS FARGO & CO.	245	5,409	9	19,700	1
17	BANK OF NEW YORK CO.	247	5,327	25	15,850	2
18	FIRST INTERSTATE BANCORP	274	4,828	14	27,200	(1)
19	MELLON BANK CORP.	291	4,514	14	24,300	0
20	WACHOVIA CORP.	328	3,755	26	15,996	3
21	SUNTRUST BANKS	332	3,740	15	19,415	0
22	BARNETT BANKS	339	3,680	19	20,175	7
23	NATIONAL CITY CORP.	362	3,450	19	20,767	2
24	FIRST BANK SYSTEM	371	3,328	40	13,231	10
25	COMERICA	395	3,113	22	13,500	3
26	BOATMEN'S BANCSHARES	415	2,996	31	17,023	20
27	US BANCORP	433	2,897	50	14,081	33
28	CORESTATES FINAN. CORP.	441	2,868	15	13,598	11
29	REPUBLIC NEW YORK CORP.	445	2,860	12	4,900	(11)
30	MBNA	479	2,565	38	11,171	3
31	STATE ST. BOSTON CORP.	495	2,446	30	11,324	2
	COMPUTER AND DATA SERVICES 8 COMPANIES					
1	UNISYS	203	6,460	(13)	37,400	(19)
2	MICROSOFT	219	5,937	28	17,801	17
3	DUN & BRADSTREET	242	5,415	11	49,500	4
4	FIRST DATA	312	4,081	85	36,000	137
5	COMPUTER SCIENCES	367	3,373	31	32,900	15

RANK

RANK		500 REVENUES RANK	REVENUES $ MILLIONS	% CHANGE FROM '94	EMPLOYEES NUMBER	% CHANGE FROM '94
6	ORACLE	417	2,967	48	16,882	40
7	AUTOMATIC DATA PROC.	436	2,894	17	25,000	14
8	COMPUTER ASSOC. INTL.	474	2,623	22	7,550	8

COMPUTERS, OFFICE EQUIPMENT 13 COMPANIES

RANK		500 REVENUES RANK	REVENUES $ MILLIONS	% CHANGE FROM '94	EMPLOYEES NUMBER	% CHANGE FROM '94
1	INTL. BUSINESS MACHINES	6	71,940	12	252,215	4
2	HEWLETT-PACKARD	20	31,519	26	102,300	4
3	COMPAQ COMPUTER	72	14,755	36	20,470	15
4	DIGITAL EQUIPMENT	77	13,813	3	61,700	(21)
5	APPLE COMPUTER	114	11,062	20	15,403	6
6	SUN MICROSYSTEMS	222	5,902	26	14,498	9
7	DELL COMPUTER	250	5,296	52	8,400	31
8	SEAGATE TECHNOLOGY	288	4,540	30	65,000	23
9	PITNEY BOWES	324	3,861	1	27,723	(15)
10	GATEWAY 2000	340	3,676	36	8,708	60
11	QUANTUM	368	3,368	58	7,265	143
12	SCI SYSTEMS	465	2,674	41	13,185	10
13	AST RESEARCH	492	2,468	4	6,595	(5)

DIVERSIFIED FINANCIALS 11 COMPANIES

RANK		500 REVENUES RANK	REVENUES $ MILLIONS	% CHANGE FROM '94	EMPLOYEES NUMBER	% CHANGE FROM '94
1	FED NATL. MORTGAGE ASSN.	32	22,246	20	3,300	(6)
2	AMERICAN EXPRESS	53	16,942	3	70,347	(3)
3	MORGAN STANLEY GROUP	116	10,949	—	9,238	12
4	FED. HOME LOAN MORTGAGE	135	9,519	38	3,319	4
5	COLLEGE RET. EQUITIES FUND	164	7,951	4	4,345	4
6	DEAN WITTER DISCOVER	165	7,934	20	30,779	8
7	AMERICAN GENERAL	202	6,495	34	15,300	13
8	HOUSEHOLD INTERNATIONAL	260	5,144	12	13,066	(16)
9	BERKSHIRE HATHAWAY	292	4,488	17	25,000	14
10	STUDENT LOAN MKTG. ASSN.	317	3,917	28	4,741	(5)
11	MARSH & MCLENNAN	325	3,770	10	27,100	4

ELECTRIC AND GAS UTILITIES 34 COMPANIES

RANK		500 REVENUES RANK	REVENUES $ MILLIONS	% CHANGE FROM '94	EMPLOYEES NUMBER	% CHANGE FROM '94
1	PACIFIC GAS & ELECTRIC	133	9,622	(8)	21,000	(5)
2	SOUTHERN	142	9,180	11	31,882	15
3	EDISON INTERNATIONAL	155	8,405	1	16,434	(1)
4	UNICOM	189	6,910	10	17,100	(7)
5	CON. EDISON OF NEW YORK	204	6,402	3	16,582	(3)
6	ENTERGY	209	6,274	5	13,521	(13)
7	PUBLIC SVC. ENTR. GROUP	212	6,164	4	11,452	(4)
8	AMERICAN ELECTRIC POWER	231	5,670	3	18,502	(6)
9	TEXAS UTILITIES	233	5,639	(0)	11,729	9
10	FPL GROUP	236	5,592	3	11,353	(4)
11	DUKE POWER	280	4,677	4	17,121	0
12	DOMINION RESOURCES	285	4,652	4	10,592	(2)
13	HOUSTON INDUSTRIES	298	4,388	10	8,891	(23)
14	PECO ENERGY	302	4,186	4	7,217	(20)
15	NIAGARA MOHAWK POWER	317	3,917	(6)	8,800	(4)
16	CMS ENERGY	321	3,890	7	10,072	1
17	GENERAL PUBLIC UTILITIES	325	3,805	4	10,310	(2)
18	NORTHEAST UTILITIES	330	3,749	3	8,800	(4)

THE FORTUNE **500** RANKED BY INDUSTRIES

		500 REVENUES RANK	REVENUES $ MILLIONS	REVENUES % CHANGE FROM '94	EMPLOYEES NUMBER	EMPLOYEES % CHANGE FROM '94
19	CENTRAL & SOUTH WEST	333	3,735	3	7,925	(2)
20	DTE ENERGY	344	3,636	3	8,340	(1)
21	PACIFICORP	365	3,401	(3)	12,621	(2)
22	CONSOL. NATURAL GAS	376	3,307	9	6,600	(13)
23	LONG ISLAND LIGHTING	402	3,075	0	5,688	(4)
24	FLORIDA PROGRESS	407	3,056	10	7,174	(3)
25	CINERGY	411	3,031	4	8,600	(3)
26	CAROLINA POWER & LIGHT	414	3,007	5	7,203	(8)
27	BALTIMORE GAS & ELEC.	424	2,935	5	8,156	12
28	UTILICORP UNITED	452	2,799	85	4,700	0
29	PP&L RESOURCES	466	2,650	(3)	6,661	(11)
30	ALLEGHENY POWER SYSTEM	467	2,648	8	5,905	(3)
31	COLUMBIA GAS SYSTEM	470	2,635	(7)	9,981	0
32	NORTHERN STATES POWER	476	2,569	3	7,495	(2)
33	CENTERIOR ENERGY	486	2,516	4	6,532	(3)
34	OHIO EDISON	493	2,466	4	4,812	(7)

ELECTRONICS, ELECTRICAL EQUIPMENT 20 COMPANIES

1	GENERAL ELECTRIC	7	70,028	8	222,000	0
2	MOTOROLA	24	27,037	22	142,000	8
3	INTEL	61	16,202	41	41,600	28
4	TEXAS INSTRUMENTS	89	13,128	27	59,574	6
5	ROCKWELL INTERNATIONAL	90	13,009	16	82,671	15
6	RAYTHEON	107	11,716	17	76,000	26
7	EMERSON ELECTRIC	127	10,013	16	78,900	7
8	WESTINGHOUSE ELECTRIC	134	9,605	4	77,813	(8)
9	WHIRLPOOL	159	8,347	3	45,435	16
10	LORAL	240	5,484	37	28,900	(11)
11	AMP	254	5,227	30	40,800	34
12	COOPER INDUSTRIES	271	4,886	(22)	40,400	(17)
13	HARRIS	357	3,481	3	26,600	(6)
14	LITTON INDUSTRIES	372	3,320	(27)	29,100	0
15	APPLIED MATERIALS	405	3,062	84	10,537	62
16	MAYTAG	410	3,040	(10)	16,595	(16)
17	MICRON TECHNOLOGY	419	2,953	81	8,080	48
18	TELEDYNE	478	2,568	7	18,000	0
19	GENERAL INSTRUMENT	499	2,432	19	12,300	0
20	ADVANCED MICRO DEVICES	500	2,430	14	12,797	7

ENGINEERING, CONSTRUCTION 7 COMPANIES

1	FLUOR	140	9,301	9	41,678	5
2	HALLIBURTON	218	5,951	4	57,300	0
3	TURNER CORP.	378	3,281	24	2,500	4
4	CENTEX	380	3,278	2	6,395	(24)
5	FOSTER WHEELER	400	3,082	36	12,650	8
6	PETER KIEWIT SONS'	431	2,902	(3)	14,300	2
7	MORRISON KNUDSEN	484	2,531	(4)	4,887	(46)

ENTERTAINMENT 4 COMPANIES

1	WALT DISNEY	102	12,112	20	71,000	9
2	VIACOM	105	11,780	54	81,700	17

THE FORTUNE 500 RANKED BY INDUSTRIES

		REVENUES		EMPLOYEES	
	500 REVENUES RANK	$ MILLIONS	% CHANGE FROM '94	NUMBER	% CHANGE FROM '94
3	TIME WARNER	163	8,067	9	35,800	24
4	TURNER BROADCASTING	363	3,437	22	6,000	0

FOOD 19 COMPANIES

1	CONAGRA	26	24,109	3	90,871	4
2	SARA LEE	50	17,719	14	149,100	2
3	RJR NABISCO HOLDINGS	65	16,008	4	76,000	8
4	ARCHER DANIELS MIDLAND	92	12,672	11	14,833	(7)
5	IBP	94	12,668	5	34,000	13
6	CPC INTERNATIONAL	154	8,431	14	52,502	25
7	GENERAL MILLS	156	8,394	(1)	9,900	(92)
8	H.J. HEINZ	162	8,087	15	42,200	18
9	CAMPBELL SOUP	177	7,278	9	43,781	(1)
10	FARMLAND INDUSTRIES	178	7,257	9	12,700	15
11	RALSTON PURINA	180	7,210	(6)	31,837	(41)
12	KELLOGG	187	7,004	7	14,487	(7)
13	QUAKER OATS	206	6,365	7	17,300	(14)
14	TYSON FOODS	239	5,511	8	64,000	15
15	DOLE FOOD	305	4,153	8	43,000	(7)
16	CHIQUITA BRANDS INTL.	313	4,027	2	36,000	(20)
17	HERSHEY FOODS	337	3,691	2	13,300	(5)
18	HORMEL FOODS	409	3,046	(1)	10,600	12
19	DEAN FOODS	472	2,630	8	11,800	(2)

FOOD AND DRUG STORES 23 COMPANIES

1	KROGER	27	23,938	4	200,000	0
2	AMERICAN STORES	45	18,309	(0)	121,000	3
3	SAFEWAY	59	16,398	5	113,000	3
4	ALBERTSON'S	96	12,585	6	80,000	5
5	WINN-DIXIE STORES	103	11,788	6	123,000	10
6	WALGREEN	122	10,395	13	68,800	11
7	PUBLIX SUPER MARKETS	136	9,471	8	95,000	6
8	VONS	263	5,071	1	29,600	6
9	ECKERD	268	4,997	10	46,437	8
10	THRIFTY PAYLESS HOLDINGS	284	4,659	39	31,200	(3)
11	RITE AID	290	4,534	5	36,700	34
12	REVCO D.S.	295	4,432	77	32,000	78
13	SUPERMKTS. GENL. HLDGS.	304	4,182	(7)	30,000	(2)
14	STOP & SHOP	309	4,116	9	37,000	23
15	GIANT FOOD	336	3,696	4	25,000	2
16	CIRCLE K	349	3,566	7	20,500	3
17	PENN TRAFFIC	352	3,537	6	28,000	0
18	FOOD 4 LESS HOLDINGS	354	3,494	—	14,687	0
19	SMITH'S FOOD & DRUG	399	3,084	3	20,277	2
20	BRUNO'S	440	2,870	1	25,600	(6)
21	LONGS DRUG STORES	468	2,644	3	16,000	3
22	HANNAFORD BROS.	477	2,568	12	20,438	24
23	SPARTAN STORES	487	2,512	15	3,200	9

FOOD SERVICES 4 COMPANIES

1	PEPSICO	21	30,421	7	480,000	2

		500 REVENUES RANK	REVENUES		EMPLOYEES	
			$ MILLIONS	% CHANGE FROM '94	NUMBER	% CHANGE FROM '94
2	MCDONALD'S	131	9,795	18	212,000	16
3	ARAMARK	235	5,601	9	140,000	5
4	FLAGSTAR	435	2,894	(18)	88,000	(2)

FOREST AND PAPER PRODUCTS 18 COMPANIES

1	INTERNATIONAL PAPER	39	19,797	32	81,500	16
2	GEORGIA-PACIFIC	75	14,292	12	47,500	1
3	KIMBERLY-CLARK	78	13,789	87	55,341	30
4	WEYERHAEUSER	104	11,788	13	39,431	8
5	STONE CONTAINER	175	7,351	28	25,900	(11)
6	CHAMPION INTERNATIONAL	188	6,972	31	24,100	(2)
7	JAMES RIVER CORP. OF VA.	194	6,800	26	27,250	(19)
8	MEAD	256	5,179	1	15,200	(6)
9	BOISE CASCADE	265	5,058	22	17,820	7
10	UNION CAMP	301	4,212	24	18,258	(3)
11	JEFFERSON SMURFIT	311	4,093	27	16,200	(2)
12	WILLAMETTE INDUSTRIES	323	3,874	29	13,180	8
13	TEMPLE-INLAND	360	3,460	18	15,400	3
14	WESTVACO	377	3,303	26	14,300	1
15	AVERY DENNISON	394	3,114	9	15,500	1
16	FLEETWOOD ENTERPRISES	448	2,856	21	18,000	13
17	LOUISIANA-PACIFIC	449	2,843	(6)	13,000	0
18	SONOCO PRODUCTS	462	2,706	18	19,000	10

GENERAL MERCHANDISERS 13 COMPANIES

1	WAL-MART STORES	4	93,627	12	675,000	13
2	SEARS ROEBUCK	15	35,181	(36)	275,000	(24)
3	KMART	16	34,654	1	250,000	(25)
4	DAYTON HUDSON	28	23,516	10	214,000	10
5	J.C. PENNEY	34	21,419	2	205,000	1
6	FEDERATED DEPT. STORES	69	15,049	81	119,000	7
7	MAY DEPARTMENT STORES	99	12,187	(0)	130,000	9
8	DILLARD DEPT. STORES	214	6,097	6	40,312	7
9	NORDSTROM	310	4,114	6	34,700	(1)
10	FRED MEYER	364	3,429	10	27,000	0
11	HARCOURT GENERAL	383	3,242	(11)	16,935	10
12	MERCANTILE STORES	421	2,944	4	19,500	3
13	CALDOR	455	2,764	4	24,000	0

HEALTH CARE 11 COMPANIES

1	COLUMBIA/HCA HEALTHCARE	51	17,695	59	240,000	53
2	UNITED HEALTHCARE	232	5,670	50	25,000	160
3	HUMANA	279	4,702	29	16,800	39
4	FHP INTERNATIONAL	319	3,909	58	13,000	(7)
5	PACIFICARE HEALTH SYS.	334	3,731	29	4,438	15
6	US HEALTHCARE	353	3,518	18	4,980	17
7	TENET HEALTHCARE	373	3,318	(4)	69,050	78
8	BEVERLY ENTERPRISES	385	3,229	8	83,000	1
9	WELLPOINT HEALTH NETWKS.	397	3,107	11	4,000	5
10	HEALTH SYSTEMS INTL.	458	2,732	18	2,500	0
11	FOUNDATION HEALTH	494	2,460	43	8,896	79

THE FORTUNE 500 RANKED BY INDUSTRIES

		500 REVENUES RANK	REVENUES $ MILLIONS	REVENUES % CHANGE FROM '94	EMPLOYEES NUMBER	EMPLOYEES % CHANGE FROM '94
HOTELS, CASINOS, RESORTS 2 COMPANIES						
1	MARRIOTT INTERNATIONAL	147	8,961	6	179,400	10
2	ITT	207	6,346	—	38,000	—
INDUSTRIAL AND FARM EQUIPMENT 12 COMPANIES						
1	CATERPILLAR	64	16,072	12	54,352	1
2	DEERE	123	10,291	14	33,375	(3)
3	INGERSOLL-RAND	230	5,729	27	41,133	14
4	DRESSER INDUSTRIES	234	5,629	6	31,457	8
5	BLACK & DECKER	238	5,566	6	34,200	(4)
6	CUMMINS ENGINE	253	5,245	11	24,300	(5)
7	AMERICAN STANDARD	255	5,221	17	43,000	13
8	CASE	261	5,105	16	15,700	(7)
9	DOVER	331	3,746	21	25,332	10
10	PARKER HANNIFIN	386	3,214	25	30,590	14
11	YORK INTERNATIONAL	425	2,930	21	19,000	19
12	BAKER HUGHES	469	2,637	5	15,200	3
INSURANCE: LIFE AND HEALTH (MUTUAL) 13 COMPANIES						
1	PRUDENTIAL INS. OF AMER.	11	41,330	10	92,966	(6)
2	METROPOLITAN LIFE INS.	22	27,977	1	40,797	(23)
3	NEW YORK LIFE INSURANCE	62	16,202	13	7,867	(1)
4	NATIONWIDE INS. ENTRPR.	108	11,702	5	27,983	(2)
5	TEACHERS INS. & ANNUITY*	109	11,646	10	4,345	1
6	NORTHWESTERN MUT. LIFE	111	11,483	20	3,344	0
7	PRINCIPAL MUT. LIFE INS.	119	10,561	33	17,392	7
8	MASS. MUTUAL LIFE INS.	193	6,804	29	9,395	6
9	GUARDIAN LIFE INS. OF AM.	211	6,172	4	5,322	(1)
10	JOHN HANCOCK MUT. LIFE	224	5,845	6	7,996	(13)
11	MUTUAL OF OMAHA INS.	307	4,134	4	8,152	(2)
12	PACIFIC MUT. LIFE INS.	390	3,160	13	2,700	6
13	AID ASSN. FOR LUTHERANS*	453	2,796	2	1,580	3
INSURANCE: LIFE AND HEALTH (STOCK) 11 COMPANIES						
1	CIGNA	42	18,955	3	47,000	(3)
2	AETNA LIFE & CASUALTY	91	12,978	(26)	40,212	(2)
3	AFLAC	182	7,191	18	4,070	10
4	LINCOLN NATIONAL	199	6,633	(5)	10,250	14
5	TRANSAMERICA	213	6,101	14	10,400	(4)
6	ASSOCIATED INSURANCE**	217	6,037	72	16,290	27
7	AON	286	4,611	11	27,000	0
8	UNUM	308	4,123	14	6,900	(4)
9	PROVIDIAN	366	3,388	14	9,000	0
10	CONSECO	444	2,861	54	3,219	(9)
11	PROVIDENT COS.	481	2,555	(7)	1,848	(60)
INSURANCE: PROPERTY AND CASUALTY (MUTUAL) 2 COMPANIES						
1	STATE FARM GROUP	12	40,810	5	71,437	5
2	LIBERTY MUTUAL INS. GRP.	139	9,308	4	23,000	5

* NOT A MUTUAL COMPANY, BUT REPORTED FINANCIAL DATA BASED ON STATUATORY ACCOUNTING.
** NOT A STOCK COMPANY, BUT REPORTED FINANCIAL DATA ACCORDING TO GENERALLY ACCEPTED ACCOUNTING PRINCIPLES.

		500 REVENUES RANK	REVENUES $ MILLIONS	REVENUES % CHANGE FROM '94	EMPLOYEES NUMBER	EMPLOYEES % CHANGE FROM '94
INSURANCE: PROPERTY AND CASUALTY (STOCK) 16 COMPANIES						
1	AMERICAN INTL. GROUP	25	25,874	16	32,000	0
2	ALLSTATE	31	22,793	—	44,349	—
3	LOEWS	44	18,770	39	7,500	(73)
4	TRAVELERS GROUP	57	16,583	(10)	48,000	(8)
5	ITT HARTFORD GROUP	100	12,150	9	21,000	0
6	GENERAL RE	181	7,210	88	3,426	4
7	USAA*	200	6,611	7	15,677	(4)
8	CHUBB	215	6,089	7	11,000	5
9	ST. PAUL COS.	244	5,410	15	12,300	(5)
10	SAFECO	335	3,723	5	7,466	(1)
11	AMERICAN FINANCIAL GROUP	345	3,630	105	9,800	128
12	USF&G	361	3,459	7	6,187	(2)
13	ALLMERICA FINANCIAL	384	3,239	(1)	6,800	15
14	GEICO	408	3,054	12	8,278	2
15	PROGRESSIVE	413	3,012	25	7,970	6
16	RELIANCE GROUP HOLDINGS	430	2,906	(5)	8,775	(6)
MAIL, PACKAGE, AND FREIGHT DELIVERY 3 COMPANIES						
1	UNITED PARCEL SERVICE	35	21,045	8	337,000	5
2	FEDERAL EXPRESS	138	9,392	11	94,201	6
3	PITTSTON	428	2,926	10	23,900	34
MARINE SERVICES 1 COMPANY						
1	AMERICAN PRESIDENT	434	2,896	4	5,200	(4)
METAL PRODUCTS 9 COMPANIES						
1	GILLETTE	195	6,795	12	33,500	2
2	CROWN CORK & SEAL	266	5,054	14	20,409	(9)
3	MASCO	276	4,779	7	20,500	(60)
4	TYCO INTERNATIONAL	289	4,535	39	34,000	42
5	ILLINOIS TOOL WORKS	306	4,152	20	21,200	9
6	U.S. INDUSTRIES	429	2,908	—	18,640	0
7	STANLEY WORKS	473	2,624	5	19,784	2
8	BALL	475	2,592	(0)	7,424	(42)
9	NEWELL	488	2,498	20	23,000	15
METALS 9 COMPANIES						
1	ALCOA	95	12,655	22	72,000	17
2	REYNOLDS METALS	179	7,252	21	29,800	1
3	BETHLEHEM STEEL	272	4,868	1	19,500	(2)
4	INLAND STEEL INDUSTRIES	275	4,781	6	15,410	—
5	LTV	300	4,283	(5)	14,400	(13)
6	PHELPS DODGE	303	4,185	27	15,343	(1)
7	NUCOR	359	3,462	16	6,200	5
8	ALUMAX	427	2,926	6	14,196	1
9	MAXXAM	480	2,565	21	12,000	(4)
MINING, CRUDE-OIL PRODUCTION 2 COMPANIES						
1	CYPRUS AMAX MINERALS	387	3,207	15	9,683	2
2	ASARCO	389	3,198	57	12,200	53

* NOT A STOCK COMPANY, BUT REPORTED FINANCIAL DATA ACCORDING TO GENERALLY ACCEPTED ACCOUNTING PRINCIPLES.

RANK

		500 REVENUES RANK	REVENUES $ MILLIONS	REVENUES % CHANGE FROM '94	EMPLOYEES NUMBER	EMPLOYEES % CHANGE FROM '94
MOTOR VEHICLES AND PARTS 13 COMPANIES						
1	GENERAL MOTORS	1	168,829	9	709,000	2
2	FORD MOTOR	2	137,137	7	346,990	3
3	CHRYSLER	9	53,195	2	126,000	4
4	TRW	125	10,172	12	66,500	4
5	TENNECO	150	8,899	(33)	60,000	2
6	ITT INDUSTRIES	151	8,884	(63)	58,000	(47)
7	JOHNSON CONTROLS	160	8,330	21	59,200	8
8	DANA	169	7,795	16	45,900	16
9	EATON	191	6,822	13	52,000	2
10	NAVISTAR INTERNATIONAL	208	6,342	19	16,079	8
11	PACCAR	273	4,848	8	14,200	(3)
12	LEAR SEATING	278	4,714	50	35,600	42
13	ECHLIN	459	2,718	22	23,400	14
PETROLEUM REFINING 20 COMPANIES						
1	EXXON	3	110,009	8	82,000	(5)
2	MOBIL	8	66,724	12	50,400	(14)
3	TEXACO	14	36,787	9	28,247	(6)
4	CHEVRON	18	32,094	3	43,019	(6)
5	AMOCO	23	27,665	3	42,689	(1)
6	USX	47	18,214	8	42,774	(1)
7	ATLANTIC RICHFIELD	55	16,739	7	22,000	(5)
8	PHILLIPS PETROLEUM	81	13,521	9	17,400	(5)
9	ASHLAND	113	11,251	18	32,800	4
10	COASTAL	124	10,223	2	15,500	(5)
11	SUN	157	8,370	7	11,995	(18)
12	UNOCAL	172	7,527	6	12,509	(5)
13	AMERADA HESS	173	7,525	12	9,574	(3)
14	TOSCO	176	7,284	14	3,750	10
15	MAPCO	375	3,310	8	6,204	3
16	VALERO ENERGY	412	3,020	64	1,658	0
17	DIAMOND SHAMROCK	418	2,957	13	11,250	75
18	KERR-MCGEE	426	2,928	(13)	3,976	(28)
19	ULTRAMAR	460	2,714	10	2,800	(7)
20	PENNZOIL	489	2,490	(3)	9,758	(7)
PHARMACEUTICALS 10 COMPANIES						
1	JOHNSON & JOHNSON	43	18,842	20	82,300	1
2	MERCK	56	16,681	11	45,200	(5)
3	BRISTOL-MYERS SQUIBB	79	13,767	15	48,400	1
4	AMERICAN HOME PRODUCTS	86	13,376	49	64,712	(13)
5	PFIZER	126	10,021	21	43,800	7
6	ABBOTT LABORATORIES	128	10,012	9	50,241	2
7	ELI LILLY	171	7,535	8	26,800	(12)
8	PHARMACIA & UPJOHN	183	7,095	99	34,000	101
9	WARNER-LAMBERT	186	7,040	10	37,000	3
10	SCHERING-PLOUGH	259	5,151	11	20,100	(5)
PIPELINES 5 COMPANIES						
1	ENRON	141	9,189	2	6,692	(4)

		500 REVENUES RANK	REVENUES		EMPLOYEES	
			$ MILLIONS	% CHANGE FROM '94	NUMBER	% CHANGE FROM '94
2	PANENERGY	269	4,968	8	5,000	(9)
3	NGC	341	3,666	15	1,100	3
4	NORAM ENERGY	443	2,862	2	6,703	(2)
5	WILLIAMS	447	2,856	7	9,946	21
	PUBLISHING, PRINTING 7 COMPANIES					
1	R.R. DONNELLEY & SONS	201	6,512	33	41,000	5
2	GANNETT	315	4,007	5	35,300	(2)
3	TIMES MIRROR	355	3,491	(9)	21,877	(19)
4	READER'S DIGEST ASSN.	403	3,069	9	6,200	(7)
5	MCGRAW-HILL	423	2,935	6	15,004	(2)
6	TRIBUNE	442	2,864	33	10,500	0
7	KNIGHT-RIDDER	456	2,752	4	21,022	2
	RAILROADS 6 COMPANIES					
1	CSX	120	10,504	9	47,965	3
2	UNION PACIFIC	148	8,942	10	51,200	9
3	BURLINGTON NO. SANTA FE	210	6,183	24	45,655	49
4	NORFOLK SOUTHERN	283	4,668	2	26,944	(1)
5	CONRAIL	338	3,686	(1)	23,510	(5)
6	SOUTHERN PACIFIC RAIL	391	3,151	0	19,049	6
	RUBBER AND PLASTIC PRODUCTS 2 COMPANIES					
1	GOODYEAR TIRE & RUBBER	88	13,166	7	87,390	(3)
2	PREMARK INTERNATIONAL	347	3,574	4	24,300	2
	SAVINGS INSTITUTIONS 3 COMPANIES					
1	H.F. AHMANSON	296	4,398	30	9,344	(5)
2	GREAT WESTERN FIN. CORP.	350	3,556	19	14,393	(8)
3	GOLDEN WEST FIN. CORP.	491	2,470	29	4,165	7
	SCIENTIFIC, PHOTOGRAPHIC, AND CONTROL EQUIPMENT 6 COMPANIES					
1	XEROX	41	18,963	6	85,200	(3)
2	MINNESOTA MINING & MFG.	63	16,105	7	70,687	(17)
3	EASTMAN KODAK	67	15,269	(9)	96,600	0
4	BAXTER INTERNATIONAL	132	9,730	4	35,500	(34)
5	HONEYWELL	197	6,731	11	50,100	(1)
6	BECTON DICKINSON	461	2,713	6	18,100	(3)
	SOAPS, COSMETICS 5 COMPANIES					
1	PROCTER & GAMBLE	17	33,434	10	99,200	3
2	COLGATE-PALMOLIVE	158	8,358	10	37,300	14
3	AVON PRODUCTS	292	4,492	4	31,800	5
4	DIAL	347	3,575	1	31,356	(4)
5	ESTÉE LAUDER	432	2,899	13	9,900	(1)
	SPECIALIST RETAILERS 20 COMPANIES					
1	PRICECOSTCO	46	18,247	11	52,000	11
2	HOME DEPOT	66	15,470	24	80,000	14
3	MELVILLE	110	11,516	2	96,832	(18)
4	TOYS "R" US	137	9,427	8	59,973	3
5	WOOLWORTH	161	8,224	(1)	119,000	0
6	LIMITED	167	7,881	8	104,000	(2)

THE FORTUNE 500 RANKED BY INDUSTRIES

RANK		500 REVENUES RANK	REVENUES $ MILLIONS	REVENUES % CHANGE FROM '94	EMPLOYEES NUMBER	EMPLOYEES % CHANGE FROM '94
7	LOWE'S	184	7,075	16	44,500	18
8	TANDY	225	5,839	18	45,300	(1)
9	CIRCUIT CITY STORES	237	5,583	35	31,413	33
10	OFFICE DEPOT	249	5,313	25	30,000	15
11	BEST BUY	262	5,080	69	25,300	66
12	TJX	294	4,448	16	63,000	66
13	GAP	297	4,395	18	60,000	9
14	SERVICE MERCHANDISE	314	4,019	(1)	26,850	(7)
15	WABAN	316	3,978	9	19,252	6
16	STAPLES	404	3,068	53	10,332	(16)
17	COMPUSA	451	2,813	31	7,963	2
18	PAYLESS CASHWAYS	464	2,686	(2)	18,100	(2)
19	OFFICEMAX	483	2,543	38	20,000	11
20	COTTER	497	2,437	(5)	4,186	5

TELECOMMUNICATIONS 15 COMPANIES

1	AT&T	5	79,609	6	299,300	(2)
2	GTE	38	19,957	0	106,000	(5)
3	BELLSOUTH	49	17,886	6	87,571	(5)
4	MCI COMMUNICATIONS	68	15,265	14	50,367	24
5	SPRINT	80	13,600	7	48,300	(6)
6	BELL ATLANTIC	83	13,430	(3)	61,800	(15)
7	AMERITECH	84	13,428	7	65,345	3
8	NYNEX	85	13,407	1	65,800	1
9	SBC COMMUNICATIONS	93	12,670	9	59,300	1
10	US WEST	106	11,746	2	61,047	(1)
11	PACIFIC TELESIS GROUP	144	9,042	(5)	48,062	(7)
12	TELE-COMMUNICATIONS	190	6,851	39	39,000	22
13	WORLDCOM	342	3,640	64	7,500	0
14	COMCAST	369	3,363	145	12,200	82
15	ALLTEL	396	3,110	5	15,698	(4)

TEMPORARY HELP 3 COMPANIES

1	MANPOWER	241	5,484	28	8,719	18
2	KELLY SERVICES	463	2,690	14	5,600	17
3	OLSTEN	485	2,519	11	8,800	11

TEXTILES 1 COMPANY

1	SHAW INDUSTRIES	439	2,870	3	24,608	0

TOBACCO 3 COMPANIES

1	PHILIP MORRIS	10	53,139	(1)	151,000	(8)
2	AMERICAN BRANDS	221	5,905	(30)	27,700	(20)
3	UNIVERSAL	379	3,281	10	30,000	20

TOYS, SPORTING GOODS 2 COMPANIES

1	MATTEL	343	3,639	14	25,000	14
2	HASBRO	446	2,858	7	13,000	4

TRANSPORTATION EQUIPMENT 1 COMPANY

1	BRUNSWICK	401	3,077	8	20,900	0

RANK

		500 REVENUES RANK	REVENUES $ MILLIONS	% CHANGE FROM '94	EMPLOYEES NUMBER	% CHANGE FROM '94
TRUCK LEASING 1 COMPANY						
1	RYDER SYSTEM	258	5,167	10	44,503	3
TRUCKING 3 COMPANIES						
1	CONSOL. FREIGHTWAYS	251	5,281	13	41,600	3
2	YELLOW	406	3,057	7	34,700	4
3	CALIBER SYSTEMS	482	2,548	(44)	25,700	(49)
WASTE MANAGEMENT 2 COMPANIES						
1	WMX TECHNOLOGIES	115	10,979	9	73,200	(2)
2	BROWNING-FERRIS IND.	229	5,779	34	43,000	16
WHOLESALERS 25 COMPANIES						
1	FLEMING	52	17,502	11	44,000	4
2	SUPERVALU	58	16,564	4	43,500	2
3	MCKESSON	87	13,326	7	12,200	(16)
4	SYSCO	101	12,118	11	28,100	7
5	ALCO STANDARD	130	9,892	24	36,500	19
6	BERGEN BRUNSWIG	153	8,448	13	4,770	12
7	CARDINAL HEALTH	168	7,806	35	4,000	14
8	ARROW ELECTRONICS	220	5,919	27	7,200	12
9	MERISEL	227	5,802	28	3,250	6
10	GENUINE PARTS	252	5,262	8	22,500	6
11	FOXMEYER HEALTH	257	5,177	(4)	2,823	(6)
12	NIKE	277	4,761	26	14,240	50
13	BINDLEY WESTERN	281	4,672	16	894	12
14	AMERISOURCE HEALTH	282	4,669	9	2,600	10
15	AVNET	299	4,300	21	9,000	13
16	REEBOK INTERNATIONAL	356	3,481	6	6,700	3
17	INTELLIGENT ELECTRONICS	358	3,475	11	3,500	201
18	W.W. GRAINGER	381	3,277	8	11,800	4
19	TECH DATA	398	3,087	28	2,625	16
20	OWENS & MINOR	416	2,976	24	3,350	29
21	MICROAGE	422	2,941	32	2,088	21
22	NASH FINCH	437	2,889	2	11,500	(8)
23	GRAYBAR ELECTRIC	454	2,774	17	6,200	11
24	ROUNDY'S	490	2,488	1	4,839	1
25	ACE HARDWARE	498	2,436	5	3,917	7
MISCELLANEOUS 1 COMPANY						
1	SERVICEMASTER	388	3,203	7	34,000	0

TARGET THE COMPANIES IN YOUR AREA WITH HOOVER'S REGIONAL BUSINESS GUIDES

Each Guide Includes

- An overview of the area's economy and major industries, in-depth and capsule profiles of the top companies in each area, and lists of the largest and fastest-growing area companies ranked by sales and by employment.

- In-depth profiles containing operations overviews, company strategies, histories, up to 10 years of key financial and stock data, lists of products, executives' names, headquarters addresses, and phone and fax numbers. The capsule profiles include headquarters addresses, phone and fax numbers, key officers' names, industry designations, stock symbols, sales figures, and employment data.

HOOVER'S GUIDE TO THE TOP CHICAGO COMPANIES

Features 130 in-depth profiles and 615 capsule profiles.

ITEM #HCA96 • Trade paper • $24.95 • ISBN 1-878753-68-1 • 6" x 9" • 408 pp.

HOOVER'S GUIDE TO THE TOP NEW YORK COMPANIES

Features 150 in-depth profiles and 1,350 capsule profiles.

ITEM #HNY96 • Trade paper • $24.95 • ISBN 1-878753-59-2 • 6" x 9" • 656 pp.

HOOVER'S GUIDE TO THE TOP SOUTHERN CALIFORNIA COMPANIES

Features 129 in-depth profiles and 870 capsule profiles.

ITEM #HLA94 • Trade paper • $24.95 • ISBN 1-878753-53-3 • 6" x 9" • 438 pp.

HOOVER'S GUIDE TO THE TOP TEXAS COMPANIES
Second Edition

Features 125 in-depth profiles and 850 capsule profiles.

ITEM #HGTC96 • Trade paper • $24.95 • ISBN 1-878753-93-2 • 6" x 9" • 448 pp.

See our catalog online at www.hoovers.com

For a free catalog or to order call 800-486-8666 or e-mail orders@hoovers.com